113418

D0934475

SAYINGS PARALLELS

PUBLISHED VOLUMES

R. Alan Culpepper, *Anatomy of the Fourth Gospel*
Fred O. Francis and J. Paul Sampley, eds., *Pauline Parallels*
Robert W. Funk, ed., *New Gospel Parallels: Volume One, The Synoptic Gospels*
Robert W. Funk, ed., *New Gospel Parallels: Volume Two, John and the Other Gospels*
John Dominic Crossan, ed., *Sayings Parallels: A Workbook for the Jesus Tradition*

SAYINGS PARALLELS

A Workbook for the Jesus Tradition

designed and edited by

JOHN DOMINIC CROSSAN

Fortress Press
Philadelphia

Library of Congress Cataloging in Publication Data

Crossan, John Dominic.
    Sayings parallels.

    Bibliography: p.
    Includes index.
    1. Jesus Christ—Words—Indexes.   I. Title
    BT306.C765   1986   226'.0663   85–16220
    ISBN 0–8006–2109–3
    ISBN 0–8006–1909–9 (pbk.)

TYPESET ON AN IBYCUS SYSTEM AT POLEBRIDGE PRESS
                                                1–2109 (C)
1814B86   Printed in the United States of America   1–1909 (P)

for Sarah

Contents

Foundations & Facets: New Testament has two major divisions as indicated by the title.

Much of the more creative biblical scholarship on the contemporary scene is devoted to *Facets* of biblical texts: to units of the text smaller than canonical books, or to aspects of the New Testament that ignore the boundaries of books and canon. In one sense, *Facets* refers to any textual unit or group of units that does not coincide with the boundaries of canonical books. In another sense, *Facets* refers to aspects of the biblical materials that are being addressed by newly emerging biblical disciplines: literary criticism and its partner, narratology, and the social sciences in various guises. These two senses of *Facets* produce the second major division of the series with its two subdivisions: Literary Facets and Social Facets.

The creative and innovative impulses in current scholarship are also linked to emerging new methods in biblical criticism or to the reconception of old ones. In addition, the collections of primary comparative material made early in this century cry out to be replaced by new collections, at once more comprehensive and more scientifically structured. These two needs have shaped the first division of the series: *Foundations*. And *Foundations* are of two types: Reference works and Texts for Comparison.

Together, the two divisions of *Foundations & Facets* will form the basis for the next phase of biblical scholarship.

Polebridge Press
Riverbend 1985

Robert W. Funk, editor

Several key ideas for the form and content of this workbook derived from conversations in "The Jesus Seminar," a group of scholars who study and write, meet and discuss the development of the Jesus tradition. I am grateful to them and especially to the Seminar's convener and director, Robert W. Funk.

I am also grateful to two scholars for help with especially difficult materials. Professor Ron Cameron helped me understand the units in the *Apocryphon of James* (CG 1,2), both through his published work and in private correspondence. Professor R. Alan Culpepper is presently working on ways of isolating aphoristic units, for which we do not have parallels elsewhere, within the dialogues and discourses of John. His assistance, from work in progress, has already enriched the Johannine materials in this book. I would hope that it might be able to expand considerably those materials for a second edition.

If a book is worth doing, it's worth doing beautifully. I thank most especially Charlene Matejovsky of Polebridge Press for acting always and successfully on that principle.

DePaul University
December 1985

John Dominic Crossan

Sayings and Parallels

This book is concerned with the words rather than the deeds of Jesus. But even the words are limited to *sayings,* that is, units which could or did exist in the tradition as isolated segments passed on in different contexts. This leaves out, for example, those short, terse commands or comments of Jesus uttered during cures or exorcisms and inextricably linked to some such situation. This is not done because the miracles are of lesser importance but because they demand and deserve an entire comparative study all to themselves.

Sayings Parallels is a workbook for the study of the Jesus tradition. Its existence and structure derives from one basic postulate: *the exact same unit often appears in different sources, genres, and versions within the Jesus tradition.* That is what is meant by parallel sayings. And this phenomenon and its explanation will have implications even for those cases where there are no parallels and the unit appears in only one instance. That basic postulate is taken as a factual statement although, of course, its implication and interpretation, its importance and significance are open to very different visions. But, granted that preliminary postulate, an attempt was made in this book to present the data as neutrally as possible. The work is to facilitate discussion of that factual diversity rather than to promote a set understanding of its presence.

First, the Jesus tradition is conserved both in intracanonical and extracanonical *sources.* The questions begin immediately. Is the duality or mutuality of those twin streams of any importance? What is the relationship between them? Are they dependent on or independent of one another? If there is dependence, which way does it run? Above all, how are the value and validity of those preceding questions to be assessed?

The book presupposes that those questions are worth asking but intends to leave the answers as open as possible. But how can one even present both intracanonical and extracanonical sources in a neutral fashion? To cite them fully requires a somewhat monumental book. To cite them selectively may infer decisions on authenticity and inauthenticity that invalidate any prior neutrality. The solution is to take the full intracanonical repertoire as well as other very early texts and within that declared data base to cite *all* instances involved. Hence the data base given in the next section is the chosen corpus and within it a full inventory will be made. This means that any text cited comes from a work which has been fully and completely inventoried. It also means that other works can be added to the corpus at later dates without having to redo the entire catalogue or renumber the entire inventory.

Second, the same saying of Jesus often appears within the tradition in different *genres,* now as an aphorism within a series of sayings, now as a response in a dialogue, and now again as a climactic conclusion to a story. The questions continue. What does that phenomenon mean for the nature of the Jesus tradition? Have sayings been expanded, developed, and interpreted by being located within dialogues and stories? Are the dialogues and stories historical vignettes digested, abbreviated, and summarized as sayings? What is the relation between history and hermeneutics, between recollection and interpretation in these generic transfers?

Special attention must be paid to the asterisks which point a unit from one genre to another. For example, a unit appearing in the aphorisms section will be set in bold italic. If the same unit appears in the dialogues or stories, there will be no such emphasis. That intends deliberately to raise the question of the relationship between setting and saying for such units. Any decisions established in those cases may also, of course, have ramifications elsewhere. Are there setting-saying combinations that were always such, right from their initial transmission? How would such combinations have worked in the oral period?

Third, there are different *versions* of the same saying present within intracanonical and extracanonical sources, and, if we leave that aside for the moment, within varied intracanonical texts, and even within the same single intracanonical text itself. Again the questions multiply. Did Jesus utter the same saying in quite divergent ways at several times or in several places? Did hearers and transmitters repeat the same saying with unintentional lapses of memory and recall? What part did the minor variations standard in oral tradition play in this process? Is there major and deliberate interpretational and creative activity from both oral tradition and written transmission in such diversity?

We begin with texts which are not units, sections, and fragments, except for the accidental vagaries of manuscript disintegration. They are full-length writings with their own dignity and integrity. If one does not grant some significance to the basic postulate mentioned above, the dismemberment practiced in this book may well seem an ultimate impertinence after about two thousand years of holistic survival. It is only the parallelism of the same unit in divergent sources, genres, and versions that draws forceful attention to the unit itself and thus permits and even provokes one to read horizontally across the corpus and not just vertically down each text in its own entirety. It is to that parallelism's cry for attention that this workbook responds.

It must be admitted and emphasized that certain texts resist quite strenuously and successfully the dismemberment effected in this book. In John, for example, it is very easy to isolate a saying if one already knows it from parallels elsewhere. But when one has no such parallel from elsewhere, John triumphs completely. Verse after verse reads like an isolated saying but there is surely no gain in dismembering John into hundreds of unparalleled sayings nor is there at present any sure way of knowing that they had ever existed as such. This means that much more work must be done on John to appreciate those cases where the dialogues and discourses use traditional Jesus sayings not known to us from elsewhere.

Sayings Parallels, then, sets out the diversity of Jesus' sayings in terms of source, genre, and version by presenting the full catalogue of the phenomenon across the designated corpus.

Sayings and Genres

The sayings of the Jesus tradition are considered within four major genres: parables, aphorisms, dialogues, and stories. Since the same unit can and does move from one genre to another, it is clear that intermediate cases and examples are quite possible and that disagreement on where exactly to locate a given instance may easily occur.

Parables can be understood in a wider or narrower sense. In the wider and Semitic acceptance parables are essentially comparisons or metaphors. Here the range of parable extends from *aphoristic parables,* such as Mark 3:24–25, through *extended parables,* such as Matt 7:24–27, and on to *narrative parables,* such as Luke 15:11–32. In the narrower and Aristotelian acceptance, parables refer only to that last category. They are realistic but metaphorical stories. When those twin understandings are compared, it is the intermediate category of the extended parable that is both most interesting and most difficult. Theoretically, an aphoristic parable could be expanded into a narrative parable, and, vice versa, a narrative parable could be digested into an aphoristic parable. What is here called an extended parable could well be either one going in either direction. One notices, however, that in an extended parable such as Matt 7:24–25 the three-point narrative sequence of building, flooding, standing is already totally implicit in the opening image, "built upon the rock," and would be quite understandable even without those specifications. So also is all of 7:26–27 implicit in "built upon the sand." In general, therefore, both aphoristic parables and extended parables are inventoried here as aphorisms. *Parables* are taken in their narrower sense as narrative parables, that is, metaphorical stories where the narrative sequence is not just the explicit unfolding of what is already totally and obviously implicit in the metaphor itself.

Because the narrative parables are often imbedded in hermeneutical contexts, both text and context are given for that genre. But the parable itself is set in bold italic.

Aphorisms are distinguished from proverbs in that the former emphasizes individual and personal vision while the latter underlines collective and social wisdom. They represent the poles of the prose miniature as continuum, and their creative interplay presupposes that continuum. No attempt has been made here to distinguish generically between aphorism and proverb. The reason is that even if and when Jesus quotes proverbs or spoke proverbially he seemed to do so less to support collective wisdom than to promote his own personal vision. Nevertheless, the inclusion of all non-narrative sayings as aphorisms intends to open rather than close the discussion concerning proverb and aphorism in the teaching of Jesus.

Dialogues are discursive interactions between disciples or others and

Jesus. They may have one or two and sometimes even multiple inter-changes. The usual format is a comment, question, or request to Jesus which begets a response, answer, or reaction from Jesus. In some cases Jesus himself initiates the dialogue. When dialogues are present in the overall structure of narrative gospel, it may be difficult to separate them categor-ically from stories. But their importance for the discourse gospels so dear to Gnostic Christianity warrants their separate consideration even if some cases are not that separable from stories.

Stories about Jesus are narrative sequences with beginning, middle, and end. They are included here when they contain sayings by Jesus. Such sayings often serve as their climax and may well be found elsewhere within dialogues or even as isolated aphoristic sayings. At a minimum, stories have a location or situation in time or place and, at a maximum, the saying they contain has a significant interaction with that location or situation.

A certain fluidity between those four categories is both expected and welcomed. The sayings refuse to obey the categories absolutely for cate-gories are not axiomatic constraints but analytical tools. Intermediate examples and disputed instances are appreciated as the appropriate subjec-tion of exegetical criticism to authorial creativity. As noted earlier, the fifth major category of the Jesus tradition, that of *miracles,* is not indexed in this volume for reasons of practical space and also to allow it fuller separate consideration elsewhere. But here once again there are intermediate in-stances where miracles contain sayings over and above the minimal dia-logue of the cure or exorcism and these are catalogued among the stories. So just as aphorism can merge into dialogue and dialogue into story, so also can story merge into miracle.

Within each of the four generic categories the units are numbered sequen-tially in the order given in the data base. Although it is not possible to have a totally untendentious sequence, that of the data base for this book is pre-sented in a form as neutral as possible with regard to theories of source, dependence, or authenticity. Whenever a saying is found in more than one genre, for example, as an aphorism, and/or dialogue, and/or story, it will be indexed at its appropriate number in each category. Asterisked cross refer-ences intend only to draw attention to that simultaneous presence and not to emphasize any more general connections. But, in a way, those asterisks are at the heart of the workbook. What exactly does the presence of sayings in different genres indicate about the nature of the Jesus tradition itself?

One final word. The four generic categories adopted for this book may be exemplified and somewhat vindicated from a total analysis of the *Gospel of Thomas* discovered in 1945 at Nag Hammadi in Upper Egypt. A full and detailed inventory of this document reveals that it contains (1) fifteen *parables,* in GThom 8:1, 9, 20:2, 21:2, 21:4, 57, 63:1, 64:1, 65:1, 76:1, 96:1, 97, 98, 107, 109; (2) nineteen *dialogues* in GThom 6:1+14, 12, 13, 18, 20, 21:1–2, 22:3–4, 24, 37, 43, 51, 52, 53, 61, 79, 91, 104, 113, 114; (3) five *stories* in GThom 22:1–2, 60, 72, 99, 100; and (4) one hundred and twelve *aphorisms,* which take up all of the text apart from those units just

mentioned.

1. New Testament Writings

1. Matt   Matthew
2. Mark   Mark
3. Luke   Luke
4. John   John
5. Rest of New Testament
   Acts   Acts
   1 Cor   1 Corinthians
   1 Thess   1 Thessalonians
   1 Tim   1 Timothy
   2 Tim   2 Timothy
   Jas   James
   1 Pet   1 Peter
   2 Pet   2 Peter
   1 John   1 John
   Rev   Revelation

2. Fragmentary Manuscripts

6. PEger2   Papyrus Egerton 2
A fragment of an unknown gospel dated to the beginning of II C.E. Contains: healing of a leper, controversy over payment of taxes, miracle of Jesus on the Jordan, plus two segments closely related to the Gospel of John. (Koester 2:181–83)

7. POxy 840   Papyrus Oxyrhynchus 840
POxy 840 is a single leaf of a Greek parchment codex that can be dated to IV C.E. It contains: the conclusion of a discourse between Jesus and his disciples and a controversy story involving Jesus and a Pharisaic chief priest in the temple court. (Cameron: 53)

8. POxy 1224   Oxyrhynchus Papyrus 1224
POxy 1224 is the remains of a papyrus codex containing fragments of an unknown gospel. It can be dated to the beginning of IV C.E.

9. Fayyum Fragment
Fayyum Fragment is a fragment of III C.E. containing an excerpt from an unknown gospel. The text is too fragmentary to warrant definitive conclusions. (Hennecke 1:115–16)

10. GPet   Gospel of Peter
GPet is preserved only as a fragment discovered in upper Egypt in 1886–1887; the language is Greek and the fragment dates to the VIII or IX C.E. However, two   xvii

Greek papyrus fragments from Oxyrhynchus, dating to late II or early III C.E., may also belong to GPet.

GPet contains a passion narrative, an epiphany story, an account of the empty tomb, and the beginning of a resurrection story.

In its original form, GPet may have arisen in the second half of I C.E. (Koester 2:162–63; Cameron: 76–78)

3. Nag Hammadi Codices

11. ApJas   Apocryphon of James

ApJas is a Coptic translation of a Greek original containing a dialogue of Jesus with Peter and James. ApJas was found among the codices of the Nag Hammadi Library in Egypt in 1945.

ApJas lacks a narrative framework; like GThom and Q, it consists entirely of sayings, parables, prophecies, and rules governing the Christian community attributed to Jesus. It is the risen Jesus who speaks. The whole is embedded in a letter purportedly written in Hebrew by James.

ApJas was probably composed during the course of II C.E. (Koester 2:224–25; Cameron: 55–57)

12. GThom   Gospel of Thomas

GThom is a sayings gospel: it consists of wisdom sayings, parables, proverbs, and prophecies attributed to Jesus. It has virtually no narrative content.

GThom is extant in complete form only in a Coptic translation found among the fifty-two tractates that make up the Coptic Gnostic Library discovered at Nag Hammadi, Egypt, in 1945. Three fragments of the original Greek version of GThom were discovered at Oxyrhynchus in Egypt around the turn of the century (POxy 1, 654, 655: see these entries).

GThom is widely regarded as an independent witness to the sayings of Jesus, comparable in form to so-called Q, a sayings collection believed to function as one of two sources utilized by Matthew and Luke in creating their gospels.

GThom can probably be dated to the second half of I C.E. (Koester 2:150–54; Cameron: 23–25)

POxy 1   Oxyrhynchus Papyrus 1

POxy 1 is a fragment from a Greek papyrus codex dated ca. 200 C.E. It is written on both sides (recto and verso) and contains sayings 26, 27, 28, 29, 30 with the end of 77, 31, 32, 33 of the Gospel of Thomas.

POxy 1 is from a different copy of Greek GThom than either POxy 654 or 655.

POxy 654   Oxyrhynchus Papyrus 654

POxy 654 is a fragment of forty-two lines of sayings of Jesus appearing on the back of a survey-list of various pieces of land. The fragment is dated to III C.E. It contains the prologue and the first five sayings of the Gospel of Thomas in Greek.

POxy 654 is from a different copy of Greek GThom than either POxy 1 or 655.

POxy 655   Oxyrhynchus Papyrus 655

POxy 655 is made up of eight small scraps of a papyrus scroll dated not later than 250 C.E. It contains five sayings of Jesus, which correspond to Coptic GThom 36, 37, 38, 39, 40.

POxy 655 is from a different copy of Greek GThom than either POxy 1 or 654.

13. DialSav   Dialogue of the Savior

DialSav is a fragmentary and composite document containing dialogues of Jesus with three of his disciples, Judas, Matthew, and Miriam. It was found at Nag Hammadi, Egypt, in 1945.

The earlier portions of the dialogue may be dated to the second half of I C.E., while the final form of DialSav is probably to be dated to the second half of II C.E.

DialSav is closely related to GThom and the Gospel of John. (Koester 2:154–55; Cameron: 38–39)

4. *Apostolic Fathers*

14. 1 Clem   1 Clement

A letter from Clement of Rome to the church at Corinth, ca. 95 C.E.

15. 2 Clem   2 Clement

A sermon attributed to Clement of Rome, dating ca. 150 C.E.

16. Ign   Epistles of Ignatius

Ignatius, Bishop of Antioch in Syria, wrote several letters while enroute to martyrdom at Rome under Trajan, ca. 110–117 C.E.

    (1) Ign Eph   *To the Ephesians*
    (2) Ign Magn   *To the Magnesians*
    (3) Ign Tral   *To the Trallians*
    (4) Ign Rom   *To the Romans*
    (5) Ign Phld   *To the Philadelphians*
    (6) Ign Smyr   *To the Smyrnaeans*
    (7) Ign Pol   *To Polycarp*

17. Pol Phil   Epistle(s) of Polycarp, *To the Philippians*

Polycarp, Bishop of Smyrna in Asia Minor, was martyred under Marcus Aurelius, ca. 160 C.E. Two separate letters are now combined in one: Pol Phil 13–14 dates from early II C.E. but Pol Phil 1–12 dates from middle II C.E. (Koester 2:306)

18. Did   *Didache*

A compendium of teachings or catechetical work attributed to the twelve apostles; early II C.E.

19. Barn   *Epistle of Barnabas*

Barn allegorizes the Old Testament to interpret the passion of Jesus. It may date from before the end of I C.E. (Koester 2:277)

20. Herm   *Shepherd of Hermes*

Herm details morality required by an apocalyptic call to conversion. It is composed of Visions (Vis), Mandates (Man), and Similitudes (Sim). Date could be from 60–160 C.E., but most likely ca. 100 C.E. (Koester 2:258)

5. Patristic Citations

21. GNaz   Gospel of the Nazoreans

GNaz is an expanded version of the Gospel of Matthew. It is preserved in quotations and allusions in the Church Fathers and in marginal notations found in a number of medieval manuscripts. These marginal notations appear to go back to a single "Zion Gospel" edition composed prior to 500 C.E. GNaz is evidently a translation into Aramaic or Syriac of Greek Matthew, with additions.

GNaz is first quoted by Hegesippus ca. 180 C.E. Its provenance is probably western Syria. (Koester 2:201–2; Cameron: 97–98)

22. GEbi   Gospel of the Ebionites

A Jewish-Christian gospel preserved only in quotations by Ephiphanius (IV C.E.). The original title is unknown. The Ebionites were Greek-speaking Jewish Christians who flourished II–III C.E. Their gospel, erroneously called the Hebrew Gospel by Epiphanius, probably dates to mid-II C.E. (Koester 2:202–3; Cameron: 103–4)

23. GHeb   Gospel of the Hebrews

GHeb contains traditions of Jesus' pre-existence and coming into the world, his baptism and temptation, a few of his sayings, and an account of his resurrected appearance to James, his brother (1 Cor 15:7). The provenance of GHeb is probably Egypt. It was composed sometime between mid-I C.E. and mid-II C.E. GHeb has been lost except for quotations and allusions preserved by the Church Fathers. (Koester 2:223–24; Cameron: 83–85)

24. GEgy   Gospel of the Egyptians

GEgy consists of sayings of Jesus. The few fragments extant are preserved in Greek by Clement of Alexandria (end of II C.E.). The gospel appears to be oriented to sexual asceticism, to judge by the few remaining fragments. GEgy arose in the period 50–150 C.E. (Koester 2:229–30; Cameron: 49–51)

Modern Authors

Cameron   *The Other Gospels: Non-Canonical Gospel Texts*. Edited by Ron Cameron. Philadelphia: Westminster Press, 1982.

Hennecke   Edgar Hennecke, *New Testament Apocrypha*. Edited by Wilhelm Schneemelcher. English translation edited by R. McL. Wilson. Vol. 1: *Gospels and Related Writings*. Philadelphia: The Westminster Press, 1963.

Koester   Helmut Koester, *Introduction to the New Testament*. Vol. 2: *History and Literature of Early Christianity*. Foundations and Facets. Philadelphia: Fortress Press, 1982.

Sigla

{ }   Braces indicate words the editors of a text take to be erroneous or superfluous.

< >   Angular brackets denote an editorial correction of a scribal error or omission.

[ ]   Square brackets indicate a gap in the manuscript. If letters or words appear within brackets, they have been supplied or restored by the editors.

PARABLES

Matt 13:3b–8 (§P1.1)

[1] That same day Jesus went out of the house and sat beside the sea. [2] And great crowds gathered about him, so that he got into a boat and sat there; and the whole crowd stood on the beach. [3] And he told them many things in parables, saying: *"A sower went out to sow. [4] And as he sowed, some seeds fell along the path, and the birds came and devoured them. [5] Other seeds fell on rocky ground, where they had not much soil, and immediately they sprang up, since they had no depth of soil, [6] but when the sun rose they were scorched; and since they had no root they withered away. [7] Other seeds fell upon thorns, and the thorns grew up and choked them. [8] Other seeds fell on good soil and brought forth grain, some a hundredfold, some sixty, some thirty.* [9] He who has ears, let him hear."

[10] Then the disciples came and said to him, "Why do you speak to them in parables?" [11] And he answered them, "To you it has been given to know the secrets of the kingdom of heaven, but to them it has not been given. [12] For to him who has will more be given, and he will have abundance; but from him who has not, even what he has will be taken away. [13] This is why I speak to them in parables, because seeing they do not see, and hearing they do not hear, nor do they understand. [14] With them indeed is fulfilled the prophecy of Isaiah which says:

'You shall indeed hear but never understand,
and you shall indeed see but never perceive.
[15] For this people's heart has grown dull,
and their ears are heavy of hearing,
and their eyes they have closed,
lest they should perceive with their eyes,
and hear with their ears,
and understand with their heart,
and turn for me to heal them.'

[16] But blessed are your eyes, for they see, and your ears, for they hear. [17] Truly, I say to you, many prophets and righteous men longed to see what you see, and did not see it, and to hear what you hear, and did not hear it.

[18] "Hear then the parable of the sower. [19] When any one hears the word of the kingdom and does not understand it, the evil one comes and snatches away what is sown in his heart; this is what was sown along the path. [20] As for what was sown on rocky ground, this is he who hears the word and immediately receives it with joy; [21] yet he has no root in himself, but endures for a while, and when tribulation or persecution arises on account of the word, immediately he falls away. [22] As for what was sown among thorns, this is he who hears the word, but the cares of the world and the delight in riches choke the word, and it proves unfruitful. [23] As for what was sown on good soil, this is he who hears the word and understands it; he indeed bears fruit, and yields, in one case a hundredfold, in another sixty, and in another thirty."

Mark 4:3b–8 (§P1.2)

[1] Again he began to teach beside the sea. And a very large crowd gathered about him, so that he got into a boat and sat in it on the sea; and the whole crowd was beside the sea on the land. [2] And he taught them many things in parables, and in his teaching he said to them: [3] "Listen! *A sower went out to sow. [4] And as he sowed, some seed fell along the path, and the birds came and devoured it. [5] Other seed fell on rocky ground, where it had not much soil, and immediately it sprang up, since it had no depth of soil; [6] and when the sun rose it was scorched, and since it had no root it withered away. [7] Other seed fell among thorns and the thorns grew up and choked it, and it yielded no grain. [8] And other seeds fell into good soil and brought forth grain, growing up and increasing and yielding thirtyfold and sixtyfold and a hundredfold."* [9] And he said, "He who has ears to hear, let him hear."

[10] And when he was alone, those who were about him with the twelve asked him concerning the parables. [11] And he said to them, "To you has been given the secret of the kingdom of God, but for those outside everything is in parables; [12] so that they may indeed see but not perceive, and may

indeed hear but not understand; lest they should turn again, and be forgiven." [13] And he said to them, "Do you not understand this parable? How then will you understand all the parables? [14] The sower sows the word. [15] And these are the ones along the path, where the word is sown; when they hear, Satan immediately comes and takes away the word which is sown in them. [16] And these in like manner are the ones sown upon rocky ground, who, when they hear the word, immediately receive it with joy; [17] and they have no root in themselves, but endure for a while; then, when tribulation or persecution arises on account of the word, immediately they fall away. [18] And others are the ones sown among thorns; they are those who hear the word, [19] but the cares of the world, and the delight in riches, and the desire for other things, enter in and choke the word, and it proves unfruitful. [20] But those that were sown upon the good soil are the ones who hear the word and accept it and bear fruit, thirtyfold and sixtyfold and a hundredfold."

Luke 8:5–8a (§P1.3)

[4] And when a great crowd came together and people from town after town came to him, he said in a parable: [5] *"A sower went out to sow his seed; and as he sowed, some fell along the path, and was trodden under foot, and the birds of the air devoured it. [6] And some fell on the rock; and as it grew up, it withered away, because it had no moisture. [7] And some fell among thorns; and the thorns grew with it and choked it. [8] And some fell into good soil and grew, and yielded a hundredfold."* As he said this, he called out, "He who has ears to hear, let him hear."

[9] And when his disciples asked him what this parable meant, [10] he said, "To you it has been given to know the secrets of the kingdom of God; but for others they are in parables, so that seeing they may not see, and hearing they may not understand. [11] Now the parable is this: The seed is the word of God. [12] The ones along the path are those who have heard; then the devil comes and takes away the word from their hearts, that they may not believe and be saved. [13] And the ones on the rock are those who, when they hear the word, receive it with joy; but these have no root, they believe for a while and in time of temptation fall away. [14] And as for what fell among the thorns, they are those who hear, but as they go on their way they are choked by the cares and riches and pleasures of life, and their fruit does not mature. [15] And as for that in the good soil, they are those who, hearing the word, hold it fast in an honest and good heart, and bring forth fruit with patience."

GThom 9 (§P1.4)

(9) Jesus said, *"Now the sower went out, took a handful (of seeds), and scattered them. Some fell on the road; the birds came and gathered them up. Others fell on rock, did not take root in the soil, and did not produce ears. And others fell on thorns; they choked the seed(s) and worms ate them. And others fell on the good soil and produced good fruit: it bore sixty per measure and a hundred and twenty per measure."*

1 Clem 24:5 (§P1.5)

[1] Let us consider, beloved, how the Master continually proves to us that there will be a future resurrection, of which he has made the first-fruits, by raising the Lord Jesus Christ from the dead. [2] Let us look, beloved, at the resurrection which is taking place at its proper season. [3] Day and night show us a resurrection. The night sleeps, the day arises: the day departs, night comes on. [4] Let us take the crops: how and in what way does the sowing take place? [5] *"The sower went forth"* and cast each of the seeds into the ground, and they fall on to the ground, parched and bare, and suffer decay; then from their decay the greatness of the providence of the Master raises them up, and from one grain more grow and bring forth fruit.

2 THE PLANTED WEEDS

Matt 13:24b (§P2.1)

24 Another parable he put before them, saying, *"The kingdom of heaven may be compared to a man who sowed good seed in his field; 25 but while men were sleeping, his enemy came and sowed weeds among the wheat, and went away. 26 So when the plants came up and bore grain, then the weeds appeared also. 27 And the servants of the householder came and said to him, 'Sir, did you not sow good seed in your field? How then has it weeds?' 28 He said to them, 'An enemy has done this.' The servants said to him, 'Then do you want us to go and gather them?' 29 But he said, 'No, lest in gathering the weeds you root up the wheat along with them. 30 Let both grow together until the harvest; and at harvest time I will tell the reapers, Gather the weeds first and bind them in bundles to be burned, but gather the wheat into my barn.'"*

31 Another parable he put before them, saying, "The kingdom of heaven is like a grain of mustard seed which a man took and sowed in his field; 32 it is the smallest of all seeds, but when it has grown it is the greatest of shrubs and becomes a tree, so that the birds of the air come and make nests in its branches."

33 He told them another parable. "The kingdom of heaven is like leaven which a woman took and hid in three measures of flour, till it was all leavened."

34 All this Jesus said to the crowds in parables; indeed he said nothing to them without a parable. 35 This was to fulfil what was spoken by the prophet:

"I will open my mouth in parables,
I will utter what has been hidden
    since the foundation of the world."

36 Then he left the crowds and went into the house. And his disciples came to him, saying, "Explain to us the parable of the weeds of the field." 37 He answered, "He who sows the good seed is the Son of man; 38 the field is the world, and the good seed means the sons of the kingdom; the weeds are the sons of the evil one, 39 and the enemy who sowed them is the devil; the harvest is the close of the age, and the reapers are angels. 40 Just as the weeds are gathered and burned with fire, so will it be at the close of the age. 41 The Son of man will send his angels, and they will gather out of his kingdom all causes of sin and all evildoers, 42 and throw them into the furnace of fire; there men will weep and gnash their teeth. 43 Then the righteous will shine like the sun in the kingdom of their Father. He who has ears, let him hear."

GThom 57 (§P2.2)

(57) Jesus said, *"The Kingdom of the Father is like a man who had [good] seed. His enemy came by night and sowed weeds among the good seed. The man did not allow them to pull up the weeds; he said to them, 'I am afraid that you will go intending to pull up the weeds and pull up the wheat along with them.' For on the day of the harvest the weeds will be plainly visible, and they will be pulled up and burned."*

3 THE MUSTARD SEED*

Matt 13:31b–32 (§P3.1)

31 Another parable he put before them, saying, *"The kingdom of heaven is like a grain of mustard seed which a man took and sowed in his field; 32 it is the smallest of all seeds, but when it has grown it is the greatest of shrubs and becomes a tree, so that the birds of the air come and make nests in its branches."*

33 He told them another parable. "The kingdom of heaven is like leaven which a woman took and hid in three measures of flour, till it was all leavened."

* See 337: *The Mustard Seed*

Mark 4:30–32 (§P3.2)

26 And he said, "The kingdom of God is as if a man should scatter seed upon the ground, 27 and should sleep and rise night and day, and the seed should sprout and grow, he knows not how. 28 The earth produces of itself, first the blade, then the ear, then the full grain in the ear. 29 But when the grain is ripe, at once he puts in the sickle, because the harvest has come."

30 And he said, "With what can we compare *the kingdom of God,* or what parable shall we use for it? 31 *It is like a grain of mustard seed, which, when sown upon the ground, is the smallest of all the seeds on earth; 32 yet when it is sown it grows up and becomes the greatest of all shrubs, and puts forth large branches, so that the birds of the air can make nests in its shade."*

Luke 13:18–19 (§P3.3)

18 He said therefore, "What is *the kingdom of God* like? And to what shall I compare it? 19 It is like a grain of mustard seed which a man took and sowed in his garden; and it grew and became a tree, and the birds of the air made nests in its branches."*

20 And again he said, "To what shall I compare the kingdom of God? 21 It is like leaven which a woman took and hid in three measures of flour, till it was all leavened."

GThom 20:1–2 (§P3.4)

(20) 1 The disciples said to Jesus, "Tell us what *the Kingdom of Heaven* is like."

2 He said to them, *"It is like a mustard seed, the smallest of all seeds. But when it falls on tilled soil, it produces a great plant and becomes a shelter for birds of the sky."*

4 THE LEAVEN

Matt 13:33b (§P4.1)

[31] Another parable he put before them, saying, "The kingdom of heaven is like a grain of mustard seed which a man took and sowed in his field; [32] it is the smallest of all seeds, but when it has grown it is the greatest of shrubs and becomes a tree, so that the birds of the air come and make nests in its branches."

[33] He told them another parable. *"The kingdom of heaven is like leaven which a woman took and hid in three measures of flour, till it was all leavened."*

Luke 13:20b–21 (§P4.2)

[18] He said therefore, "What is the kingdom of God like? And to what shall I compare it? [19] It is like a grain of mustard seed which a man took and sowed in his garden; and it grew and became a tree, and the birds of the air made nests in its branches."

[20] And again he said, "To what shall I compare *the kingdom of God? [21] It is like leaven which a woman took and hid in three measures of flour, till it was all leavened."*

GThom 96:1 (§P4.3)

(96) [1] Jesus [said], *"The Kingdom of the Father is like a certain woman. She took a little leaven, [concealed] it in some dough, and made it into large loaves. [2] Let him who has ears hear."*

(97) Jesus said, "The Kingdom of the [Father] is like a certain woman who was carrying a jar full of meal. "While she was walking [on] a road, still some distance from home, the handle of the jar broke and the meal emptied out behind her on the road. She did not realize it; she had noticed no accident. When she reached her house, she set the jar down and found it empty."

(98) Jesus said, "The Kindom of the Father is like a certain man who wanted to kill a powerful man. In his own house he drew his sword and stuck it into the wall in order to find out whether his hand could carry through. Then he slew the powerful man."

5 THE TREASURE

Matt 13:44 (§P5.1)

[44] *"The kingdom of heaven is like treasure hidden in a field, which a man found and covered up; then in his joy he goes and sells all that he has and buys that field.*

[45] "Again, the kingdom of heaven is like a merchant in search of fine pearls, [46] who, on finding one pearl of great value, went and sold all that he had and bought it.

[47] "Again, the kingdom of heaven is like a net which was thrown into the sea and gathered fish of every kind; [48] when it was full, men drew it ashore and sat down and sorted the good into vessels but threw away the bad. [49] So it will be at the close of the age. The angels will come out and separate the evil from the righteous, [50] and throw them into the furnace of fire; there men will weep and gnash their teeth."

GThom 109 (§P5.2)

(109) Jesus said, *"The Kingdom is like a man who had a [hidden] treasure in his field without knowing it. And [after] he died, he left it to his son. The son did not know (about the treasure). He inherited the field and sold [it]. And the one who bought it went plowing and found the treasure. He began to lend money at interest to whomever he wished."*

6 THE PEARL

Matt 13:45–46 (§P6.1)

[44] "The kingdom of heaven is like treasure hidden in a field, which a man found and covered up; then in his joy he goes and sells all that he has and buys that field.

[45] *"Again, the kingdom of heaven is like a merchant in search of fine pearls, [46] who, on finding one pearl of great value, went and sold all that he had and bought it.*

[47] "Again, the kingdom of heaven is like a net which was thrown into the sea and gathered fish of every kind; [48] when it was full, men drew it ashore and sat down and sorted the good into vessels but threw away the bad. [49] So it will be at the close of the age. The angels will come out and separate the evil from the righteous, [50] and throw them into the furnace of fire; there men will weep and gnash their teeth."

GThom 76:1 (§P6.2)

(76) [1] Jesus said, *"The Kingdom of the Father is like a merchant who had a consignment of merchandise and who discovered a pearl. That merchant was shrewd. He sold the merchandise and bought the pearl alone for himself. [2] You too, seek his unfailing and enduring treasure where no moth comes near to devour and no worm destroys."*

7 THE FISHNET

Matt 13:47–48 (§P7.1)

[44] "The kingdom of heaven is like treasure hidden in a field, which a man found and covered up; then in his joy he goes and sells all that he has and buys that field.

[45] "Again, the kingdom of heaven is like a merchant in search of fine pearls, [46] who, on finding one pearl of great value, went and sold all that he had and bought it.

[47] *"Again, the kingdom of heaven is like a net which was thrown into the sea and gathered fish of every kind;* [48] *when it was full, men drew it ashore and sat down and sorted the good into vessels but threw away the bad.* [49] So it will be at the close of the age. The angels will come out and separate the evil from the righteous, [50] and throw them into the furnace of fire; there men will weep and gnash their teeth."

GThom 8:1 (§P7.2)

(8) [1] And He said, *"The man is like a wise fisherman who cast his net into the sea and drew it up from the sea full of small fish. Among them the wise fisherman found a fine large fish. He threw all the small fish back into the sea and chose the large fish without difficulty.* [2] Whoever has ears to hear, let him hear."

8 THE LOST SHEEP

Matt 18:12–13 (§P8.1)

[10] "See that you do not despise one of these little ones; for I tell you that in heaven their angels always behold the face of my Father who is in heaven. [12] *What do you think? If a man has a hundred sheep, and one of them has gone astray, does he not leave the ninety-nine on the mountains and go in search of the one that went astray?* [13] *And if he finds it, truly, I say to you, he rejoices over it more than over the ninety-nine that never went astray.* [14] So it is not the will of my Father who is in heaven that one of these little ones should perish."

Luke 15:4–6 (§P8.2)

[1] Now the tax collectors and sinners were all drawing near to hear him. [2] And the Pharisees and the scribes murmured, saying, "This man receives sinners and eats with them."

[3] So he told them this parable: [4] *"What man of you, having a hundred sheep, if he has lost one of them, does not leave the ninety-nine in the wilderness, and go after the one which is lost, until he finds it?* [5] *And when he has found it, he lays it on his shoulders, rejoicing.* [6] *And when he comes home, he calls together his friends and his neighbors, saying to them, 'Rejoice with me, for I have found my sheep which was lost.'* [7] Just so, I tell you, there will be more joy in heaven over one sinner who repents than over ninety-nine righteous persons who need no repentance.

[8] "Or what woman, having ten silver coins, if she loses one coin, does not light a lamp and sweep the house and seek diligently until she finds it? [9] And when she has found it, she calls together her friends and neighbors, saying, 'Rejoice with me, for I have found the coin which I had lost.' [10] Just so, I tell you, there is joy before the angels of God over one sinner who repents."

[11] And he said, "There was a man who had two sons; [12] and the younger of them said to his father, 'Father, give me the share of property that falls to me.' And he divided his living between them. [13] Not many days later, the younger son gathered all he had and took his journey into a far country, and there he squandered his property in loose living. [14] And when he had spent everything, a great famine arose in that country, and he began to be in want. [15] So he went and joined himself to one of the citizens of that country, who sent him into his fields to feed swine. [16] And he would gladly have fed on the pods that the swine ate; and no one gave him anything. [17] But when he came to himself he said, 'How many of my father's hired servants have bread enough and to spare, but I perish here with hunger! [18] I will arise and go to my father, and I will say to him, "Father, I have sinned against heaven and before you; [19] I am no longer worthy to be called your son; treat me as one of your hired servants."' [20] And he arose and came to his father. But while he was yet at a distance, his father saw him and had compassion, and ran and embraced him and kissed him. [21] And the son said to him, 'Father, I have sinned against heaven and before you; I am no longer worthy to be called your son.' [22] But the father said to his servants, 'Bring quickly the best robe, and put it on him; and put a ring on his hand, and shoes on his feet; [23] and bring the fatted calf and kill it, and let us eat and make merry; [24] for this my son was dead, and is alive again; he was lost, and is found.' And they began to make merry.

[25] "Now his elder son was in the field; and as he came and drew near to the house, he heard music and dancing. [26] And he called one of the servants and asked what this meant. [27] And he said to him, 'Your brother has come, and your father has killed the fatted calf, because he has received him safe and sound.' [28] But he was angry and refused to go in. His father came out and entreated him, [29] but he answered his father, 'Lo, these many years I have served you, and I never disobeyed your command; yet you never gave me a kid, that I might make merry with my friends. [30] But when this son of yours came, who has devoured your living with harlots, you killed for him the fatted calf!' [31] And he said to him, 'Son, you are always with me, and all that is mine is yours. [32] It was fitting to make merry and be glad, for this your brother was dead, and is alive; he was lost, and is found.'"

GThom 107 (§P8.3)

(107) Jesus said, *"The Kingdom is like a shepherd who had a hundred sheep. One of them, the largest, went astray. He left the ninety-nine and looked for that one until he found it. When he had gone to such trouble, he said to the sheep, 'I care for you more than the ninety-nine.'"*

9   THE UNMERCIFUL SERVANT

Matt 18:23–34 (§P9)

²¹ Then Peter came up and said to him, "Lord, how often shall my brother sin against me, and I forgive him? As many as seven times?" ²² Jesus said to him, "I do not say to you seven times, but seventy times seven.

²³ *"Therefore the kingdom of heaven may be compared to a king who wished to settle accounts with his servants.* ²⁴ *When he began the reckoning, one was brought to him who owed him ten thousand talents;* ²⁵ *and as he could not pay, his lord ordered him to be sold, with his wife and children and all that he had, and payment to be made.* ²⁶ *So the servant fell on his knees, imploring him, 'Lord, have patience with me, and I will pay you everything.'* ²⁷ *And out of pity for him the lord of that servant released him and forgave him the debt.* ²⁸ *But that same servant, as he went out, came upon one of his fellow servants who owed him a hundred denarii; and seizing him by the throat he said, 'Pay what you owe.'* ²⁹ *So his fellow servant fell down and besought him, 'Have patience with me, and I will pay you.'* ³⁰ *He refused and went and put him in prison till he should pay the debt.* ³¹ *When his fellow servants saw what had taken place, they were greatly distressed, and they went and reported to their lord all that had taken place.* ³² *Then his lord summoned him and said to him, 'You wicked servant! I forgave you all that debt because you besought me;* ³³ *and should not you have had mercy on your fellow servant, as I had mercy on you?'* ³⁴ *And in anger his lord delivered him to the jailers, till he should pay all his debt.* ³⁵ So also my heavenly Father will do to every one of you, if you do not forgive your brother from your heart."

10   THE VINEYARD LABORERS

Matt 20:1–15 (§P10)

¹ *"For the kingdom of heaven is like a householder who went out early in the morning to hire laborers for his vineyard.* ² *After agreeing with the laborers for a denarius a day, he sent them into his vineyard.* ³ *And going out about the third hour he saw others standing idle in the market place;* ⁴ *and to them he said, 'You go into the vineyard too, and whatever is right I will give you.' So they went.* ⁵ *Going out again about the sixth hour and the ninth hour, he did the same.* ⁶ *And about the eleventh hour he went out and found others standing; and he said to them, 'Why do you stand here idle all day?* ⁷ *They said to him, 'Because no one has hired us.' He said to them, 'You go into the vineyard too.'* ⁸ *And when evening came, the owner of the vineyard said to his steward, 'Call the laborers and pay them their wages, beginning with the last, up to the first.'* ⁹ *And when those hired about the eleventh hour came, each of them received a denarius.* ¹⁰ *Now when the first came, they thought they would receive more; but each of them also received a denarius.* ¹¹ *And on receiving it they grumbled at the householder,* ¹² *saying, 'These last worked only one hour, and you have made them equal to us who have borne the burden of the day and the scorching heat.'* ¹³ *But he replied to one of them, 'Friend, I am doing you no wrong; did you not agree with me for a denarius?* ¹⁴ *Take what belongs to you, and go; I choose to give to this last as I give to you.* ¹⁵ *Am I not allowed to do what I choose with what belongs to me? Or do you begrudge my generosity?'* ¹⁶ So the last will be first, and the first last."

Matt 21:33b–43 (§P11.1)

³³ "Hear another parable. *There was a householder who planted a vineyard, and set a hedge around it, and dug a wine press in it, and built a tower, and let it out to tenants, and went into another country.* ³⁴ *When the season of fruit drew near, he sent his servants to the tenants, to get his fruit;* ³⁵ *and the tenants took his servants and beat one, killed another, and stoned another.* ³⁶ *Again he sent other servants, more than the first; and they did the same to them.* ³⁷ *Afterward he sent his son to them, saying 'They will respect my son.'* ³⁸ *But when the tenants saw the son, they said to themselves, 'This is the heir; come, let us kill him and have his inheritance.'* ³⁹ *And they took him and cast him out of the vineyard, and killed him.* ⁴⁰ *When therefore the owner of the vineyard comes, what will he do to those tenants?"* ⁴¹ *They said to him, "He will put those wretches to a miserable death, and let out the vineyard to other tenants who will give him the fruits in their seasons."*

⁴² *Jesus said to them, "Have you never read in the scriptures:*

'The very stone which the builders
      rejected
has become the head of the corner;
this was the Lord's doing,
and it is marvelous in our eyes'?

⁴³ *Therefore I tell you, the kingdom of God will be taken away from you and given to a nation producing the fruits of it."*

⁴⁵ When the chief priests and the Pharisees heard his parables, they perceived that he was speaking about them. ⁴⁶ But when they tried to arrest him, they feared the multitudes, because they held him to be a prophet.

Mark 12:1b–11 (§P11.2)

¹ And he began to speak to them in parables. *"A man planted a vineyard, and set a hedge around it, and dug a pit for the wine press, and built a tower, and let it out to tenants, and went into another country.* ² *When the time came, he sent a servant to the tenants, to get from them some of the fruit of the vineyard.* ³ *And they took him and beat him, and sent him away empty-handed.* ⁴ *Again he sent to them another servant, and they wounded him in the head, and treated him shamefully.* ⁵ *And he sent another, and him they killed; and so with many others, some they beat and some they killed.* ⁶ *He had still one other, a beloved son; finally he sent him to them, saying, 'They will respect my son.'* ⁷ *But those tenants said to one another, 'This is the heir; come, let us kill him, and the inheritance will be ours.'* ⁸ *And they took him and killed him, and cast him out of the vineyard.* ⁹ *What will the owner of the vineyard do? He will come and destroy the tenants, and give the vineyard to others.* ¹⁰ *Have you not read this scripture:*

'The very stone which the builders
      rejected
has become the head of the corner;
¹¹ this was the Lord's doing,
and it is marvelous in our eyes'?"

¹² And they tried to arrest him, but feared the multitude, for they perceived that he had told the parable against them; so they left him and went away.

Luke 20:9b–18 (§P11.3)

⁹ And he began to tell the people this parable: *"A man planted a vineyard, and let it out to tenants, and went into another country for a long while.* ¹⁰ *When the time came, he sent a servant to the tenants, that they should give him some of the fruit of the vineyard; but the tenants beat him, and sent him away empty-handed.* ¹¹ *And he sent another servant; him also they beat and treated shamefully, and sent him away empty-handed.* ¹² *And he sent yet a third; this one they wounded and cast out.* ¹³ *Then the owner of the vineyard said,*

'What shall I do? I will send my beloved son; it may be they will respect him.' ¹⁴ *But when the tenants saw him, they said to themselves, 'This is the heir; let us kill him, that the inheritance may be ours.'* ¹⁵ *And they cast him out of the vineyard and killed him. What then will the owner of the vineyard do to them?* ¹⁶ *He will come and destroy those tenants, and give the vineyard to others."* When they heard this, they said, "God forbid!" ¹⁷ But he looked at them and said, "What then is this that is written:

'The very stone which the builders re-
      jected
has become the head of the corner'?

¹⁸ Every one who falls on that stone will be broken to pieces; but when it falls on any one it will crush him."*

¹⁹ The scribes and the chief priests tried to lay hands on him at that very hour, but they feared the people; for they perceived that he had told this parable against them.

GThom 65–66 (§P11.4)

(65) ¹ He said, *"There was a good man who owned a vineyard. He leased it to tenant farmers so that they might work it and he might collect the produce from them. He sent his servant so that the tenants might give him the produce of the vineyard. They seized his servant and beat him, all but killing him. The servant went back and told his master. The master said, 'Perhaps <they> did not recognize <him>.' He sent another servant. The tenants beat this one as well. Then the owner sent his son and said, 'Perhaps they will show respect to my son.' Because the tenants knew that it was he who was the heir to the vineyard, they seized him and killed him.* ² *Let him who has ears hear."*

(66) Jesus said, *"Show me the stone which the builders have rejected. That one is the cornerstone."*

* See 355: *The Tenants*

12 THE FEAST*

Matt 22:2–13 (§P12.1)
[33] "Hear another parable. There was a householder who planted a vineyard, and set a hedge around it, and dug a wine press in it, and built a tower, and let it out to tenants, and went into another country. [34] But when the Pharisees heard that he had silenced the Sadducees, they came together. [35] And one of them, a lawyer, asked him a question, to test him. [36] "Teacher, which is the great commandment in the law?" [37] And he said to him, "You shall love the Lord your God with all your heart, and with all your soul, and with all your mind. [38] This is the great and first commandment. [39] And a second is like it, You shall love your neighbor as yourself. [40] On these two commandments depend all the law and the prophets."

[41] Now while the Pharisees were gathered together, Jesus asked them a question, [42] saying, "What do you think of the Christ? Whose son is he?" They said to him, "The son of David." [43] He said to them, "How is it then that David, inspired by the Spirit, calls him Lord, saying,

[44] 'The Lord said to my Lord,
Sit at my right hand,
till I put thy enemies under thy feet'?

[45] If David thus calls him Lord, how is he his son?" [46] And no one was able to answer him a word, nor from that day did any one dare to ask him any more questions. 22 [1] And again Jesus spoke to them in parables, saying, [2] *"The kingdom of heaven may be compared to a king who gave a marriage feast for his son, [3] and sent his servants to call those who were invited to the marriage feast; but they would not come. [4] Again he sent other servants, saying, 'Tell those who are invited, Behold, I have made ready my dinner, my oxen and my fat calves are killed, and everything is ready; come to the marriage feast.' [5] But they made light of it and went off, one to his farm, another to his business, [6] while the rest seized his servants, treated them shamefully, and killed them. [7] The king was angry, and he sent his troops and destroyed those murderers and burned their city. [8] Then he said to his servants, 'The wedding is ready, but those invited were not worthy. [9] Go therefore to the thoroughfares, and invite to the marriage feast as many as you find.' [10] And those servants went out into the streets and gathered all whom they found, both bad and good; so the wedding hall was filled with guests.*

[11] *"But when the king came in to look at the guests, he saw there a man who had no wedding garment; [12] and he said to him, 'Friend, how did you get in here without a wedding garment?' And he was speechless. [13] Then the king said to the attendants, 'Bind him hand and foot, and cast him into the outer darkness; there men will weep and gnash their teeth.'* [14] For many are called, but few are chosen."

Luke 14:16b–23 (§P12.2)
[1] One sabbath when he went to dine at the house of a ruler who belonged to the Pharisees, they were watching him. [2] And behold, there was a man before him who had dropsy. [3] And Jesus spoke to the lawyers and Pharisees, saying, "Is it lawful to heal on the sabbath, or not?" [4] But they were silent. Then he took him and healed him, and let him go. [5] And he said to them, "Which of you, having a son or an ox that has fallen into a well, will not immediately pull him out on a sabbath day?" [6] And they could not reply to this.

[7] Now he told a parable to those who were invited, when he marked how they chose the places of honor, saying to them, [8] "When you are invited by any one to a marriage feast, do not sit down in a place of honor, lest a more eminent man than you be invited by him; [9] and he who invited you both will come and say to you, 'Give place to this man,' and then you will begin with shame to take the lowest place. [10] But when you are invited, go and sit in the lowest place, so that when your host comes he may say to you, 'Friend, go up higher'; then you will be honored in the presence of all who sit at table with you. [11] For every one who exalts himself will be humbled, and he who humbles himself will be exalted."

[12] He said also to the man who had invited him, "When you give a dinner or a banquet, do not invite your friends or your brothers or your kinsmen or rich neighbors, lest they also invite you in return, and you be repaid. [13] But when you give a feast, invite the poor, the maimed, the lame, the blind, [14] and you will be blessed, because they cannot repay you. You will be repaid at the resurrection of the just."

[15] When one of those who sat at table with him heard this, he said to him, "Blessed is he who shall eat bread in the kingdom of God!" [16] But he said to him "A man once gave a great banquet, and invited many; [17] and at the time for the banquet he sent his servant to say to those who had been invited, 'Come; for all is now ready.' [18] But they all alike began to make excuses. The first said to him, 'I have bought a field, and I must go out and see it; I pray you, have me excused.' [19] And another said, 'I have bought five yoke of oxen, and I go to examine them; I pray you, have me excused.' [20] And another said, 'I have married a wife, and therefore I cannot come.' [21] So the servant came and reported this to his master. Then the householder in anger said to his servant, 'Go out quickly to the streets and lanes of the city, and bring in the poor and maimed and blind and lame.' [22] And the servant said, 'Sir, what you commanded has been done, and still there is room.' [23] And the master said to the servant, 'Go out to the highways and hedges, and compel people to come in, that my house may be filled. [24] For I tell you, none of those men who were invited shall taste my banquet.'"

GThom 64:1 (§P12.3)
(64) [1] Jesus said, *"A man had received visitors. And when he had prepared the dinner, he sent his servant to invite the guests. He went to the first one and said to him, 'My master invites you.' He said, 'I have claims against some merchants. They are coming to me this evening. I must go and give them my orders. I ask to be excused from the dinner.' He went to another and said to him, 'My master has invited you.' He said to him, 'I have just bought a house and am required for the day. I shall not have any spare time.' He went to another and said to him, 'My master invites you.' He said to him, 'My friend is going to get married, and I am to prepare the banquet. I shall not be able to come. I ask to be excused from the dinner.' He went to another and said to him, 'My master invites you.' He said to him, 'I have just bought a farm, and I am on my way to collect the rent. I shall not be able to come. I ask to be excused.' The servant returned and said to his master, 'Those whom you invited to the dinner have asked to be excused.' The master said to his servant, 'Go outside to the streets and bring back those whom you happen to meet, so that they may dine.' [2] Businessmen and merchants will not enter the Places of My Father."*

* See 356: *The Feast*

9

13 THE GOOD SAMARITAN*

Matt 22:34–40 (§P13.1)

34 But when the Pharisees heard that he had silenced the Sadducees, they came together. 35 And one of them, a lawyer, asked him a question, to test him. 36 "Teacher, which is the great commandment in the law?" 37 And he said to him, "You shall love the Lord your God with all your heart, and with all your soul, and with all your mind. 38 This is the great and first commandment. 39 And a second is like it, You shall love your neighbor as yourself. 40 On these two commandments depend all the law and the prophets."

Mark 12:28–34 (§P13.2)

28 And one of the scribes came up and heard them disputing with one another, and seeing that he answered them well, asked him, "Which commandment is the first of all?" 29 Jesus answered, "The first is, 'Hear, O Israel: The Lord our God, the Lord is one; 30 and you shall love the Lord your God with all your heart, and with all your soul, and with all your mind, and with all your strength.' 31 The second is this, 'You shall love your neighbor as yourself.'

There is no other commandment greater than these." 32 And the scribe said to him, "You are right, Teacher; you have truly said that he is one, and there is no other but he; 33 and to love him with all the heart, and with all the understanding, and with all the strength, and to love one's neighbor as oneself, is much more than all whole burnt offerings and sacrifices." 34 And when Jesus saw that he answered wisely, he said to him, "You are not far from the kingdom of God." And after that no one dared to ask him any question.

Luke 10:30b–35 (§P13.3)

25 And behold, a lawyer stood up to put him to the test, saying, "Teacher, what shall I do to inherit eternal life?" 26 He said to him, "What is written in the law? How do you read?" 27 And he answered, "You shall love the Lord your God with all your heart, and with all your soul, and with all your strength, and with all your mind; and your neighbor as yourself." 28 And he said to him, "You have answered right; do this, and you will live."
29 But he, desiring to justify himself, said to Jesus, "And who is my neighbor?" 30 Jesus replied, *"A man was going down from Jerusalem to Jericho, and he fell among robbers, who stripped him and beat him, and departed, leaving him half dead. 31 Now by chance a priest was going down that road; and when he saw him he passed by on the other side. 32 So likewise a Levite, when he came to the place and saw him, passed by on the other side. 33 But a Samaritan, as he journeyed, came to where he was; and when he saw him, he had compassion, 34 and went to him and bound up his wounds, pouring on oil and wine; then he set him on his own beast and brought him to an inn, and took care of him. 35 And the next day he took out two denarii and gave them to the innkeeper, saying, 'Take care of him; and whatever more you spend, I will repay you when I come back.' 36 Which of these three, do you think, proved neighbor to the man who fell among the robbers?"* 37 He said, "The one who showed mercy on him." And Jesus said to him "Go and do likewise."

* See 358: *The Great Commandment*

14 THE CLOSED DOOR*

Matt 25:1–12 (§P14.1)

1 *"Then the kingdom of heaven shall be compared to ten maidens who took their lamps and went to meet the bridegroom. 2 Five of them were foolish, and five were wise. 3 For when the foolish took their lamps, they took no oil with them; 4 but the wise took flasks of oil with their lamps. 5 As the bridegroom was delayed, they all slumbered and slept. 6 But at midnight there was a cry, 'Behold, the bridegroom! Come out to meet him.' 7 Then all those maidens rose and trimmed their lamps. 8 And the foolish said to the wise, 'Give us some of your oil, for our lamps are going out.' 9 But the wise replied, 'Perhaps there will not be enough for us and for you; go rather to the dealers and buy for yourselves.' 10 And while they went to buy, the* bridegroom came, and those who were ready went in with him to the marriage feast; and the door was shut. 11 Afterward the other maidens came also, saying, 'Lord, lord, open to us.' 12 But he replied, 'Truly, I say to you, I do not know you.' 13 Watch therefore, for you know neither the day nor the hour."

Luke 13:25 (§P14.2)

22 He went on his way through towns and villages, teaching, and journeying toward Jerusalem. 23 And some one said to him, "Lord, will those who are saved be few?" And he said to them, 24 "Strive to enter by the narrow door; for many, I tell you, will seek to enter and will not be able. 25 *When once the householder has risen up and shut the door, you will begin to stand outside and to knock at the door, saying, 'Lord, open to us.' He will answer you, 'I do not know where you come from.'* 26 Then you will begin to say, 'We ate and drank in your presence, and you taught in our streets.' 27 But he will say, 'I tell you, I do not know where you come from; depart from me, all you workers of iniquity!' 28 There you will weep and gnash your teeth, when you see Abraham and Isaac and Jacob and all the prophets in the kingdom of God and you yourselves thrust out. 29 And men will come from east and west, and from north and south, and sit at table in the kingdom of God. 30 And behold, some are last who will be first, and some are first who will be last."

* See 208: *The Closed Door*

15 THE ENTRUSTED MONEY

Matt 25:14–30 (§P15.1)

14 *"For it will be as when a man going on a journey called his servants and entrusted to them his property;* 15 *to one he gave five talents, to another two, to another one, to each according to his ability. Then he went away.* 16 *He who had received the five talents went at once and traded with them; and he made five talents more.* 17 *So also, he who had the two talents made two talents more.* 18 *But he who had received the one talent went and dug in the ground and hid his master's money.* 19 *Now after a long time the master of those servants came and settled accounts with them.* 20 *And he who had received the five talents came forward, bringing five talents more, saying, 'Master, you delivered to me five talents; here I have made five talents more.'* 21 *His master said to him, 'Well done, good and faithful servant; you have been faithful over a little, I will set you over much; enter into the joy of your master.'* 22 *And he also who had the two talents came forward, saying, 'Master, you delivered to me two talents; here I have made two talents more.'* 23 *His master said to him, 'Well done, good and faithful servant; you have been faithful over a little, I will set you over much; enter into the joy of your master.'* 24 *He also who had received the one talent came forward, saying, 'Master, I knew you to be a hard man, reaping where you did not sow, and gathering where you did not winnow;* 25 *so I was afraid, and I went and hid your talent in the ground. Here you have what is yours.'* 26 *But his master answered him, 'You wicked and slothful servant! You knew that I reap where I have not sowed, and gather where I have not winnowed?* 27 *Then you ought to have invested my money with the bankers, and at my coming I should have received what was my own with interest.* 28 *So take the talent from him, and give it to him who has the ten talents.* 29 *For to every one who has will more be given, and he will have abundance; but from him who has not, even what he has will be taken away.* 30 *And cast the worthless servant into the outer darkness; there men will weep and gnash their teeth.'"*

Luke 19:12b–27 (§P15.2)

11 As they heard these things, he proceeded to tell a parable, because he was near to Jerusalem, and because they supposed that the kingdom of God was to appear immediately. 12 He said therefore, *"A nobleman went into a far country to receive a kingdom and then return.* 13 *Calling ten of his servants, he gave them ten pounds, and said to them, 'Trade with these till I come.'* 14 *But his citizens hated him and sent an embassy after him, saying, 'We do not want this man to reign over us.'* 15 *When he returned, having received the kingdom, he commanded these servants, to whom he had given the money, to be called to him, that he might know what they had gained by trading.* 16 *The first came before him, saying, 'Lord, your pound has made ten pounds more.'* 17 *And he said to him, 'Well done, good servant! Because you have been faithful in a very little, you shall have authority over ten cities.'* 18 *And the second came, saying, 'Lord, your pound has made five pounds.'* 19 *And he said to him, 'And you are to be over five cities.'* 20 *Then another came, saying, 'Lord, here is your pound, which I kept laid away in a napkin;* 21 *for I was afraid of you, because you are a severe man; you take up what you did not lay down, and reap what you did not sow.'* 22 *He said to him, 'I will condemn you out of your own mouth, you wicked servant! You knew that I was a severe man, taking up what I did not lay down and reaping what I did not sow?* 23 *Why then did you not put my money into the bank, and at my coming I should have collected it with interest?'* 24 *And he said to those who stood by, 'Take the pound from him, and give it to him who has the ten pounds.'* 25 *(And they said to him, 'Lord, he has ten pounds!')* 26 *'I tell you, that to every one who has will more be given; but from him who has not, even what he has will be taken away.* 27 *But as for these enemies of mine, who did not want me to reign over them, bring them here and slay them before me.'"*

GNaz 18 (§P15.3)

(18) But since the Gospel (written) in Hebrew characters which has come into our hands enters the threat not against the man who had hid (the talent), but against him who had lived dissolutely—*for he (the master) had three servants: one who squandered his master's substance with harlots and flute-girls, one who multiplied the gain, and one who hid the talent; and accordingly one was accepted (with joy), another merely rebuked, and another cast into prison*—I wonder whether in Matthew the threat which is uttered after the word against the man who did nothing may refer not to him, but by epanalepsis to the first who had feasted and drunk with the drunken. (Eusebius, *Theophania* 22 [on Matthew 25:14–15])

Mark 4:26b–29 (§P16.1)

[26] And he said, *"The kingdom of God is as if a man should scatter seed upon the ground,* [27] *and should sleep and rise night and day, and the seed should sprout and grow, he knows not how.* [28] *The earth produces of itself, first the blade, then the ear, then the full grain in the ear.* [29] *But when the grain is ripe, at once he puts in the sickle, because the harvest has come."*

[30] And he said, "With what can we compare the kingdom of God, or what parable shall we use for it? [31] It is like a grain of mustard seed, which, when sown upon the ground, is the smallest of all the seeds on earth; [32] yet when it is sown it grows up and becomes the greatest of all shrubs, and puts forth large branches, so that the birds of the air can make nests in its shade."

GThom 21:4 (§P16.2)

(21) [1] Mary said to Jesus, "Whom are Your disciples like?"

[2] He said, "They are like children who have settled in a field which is not theirs. When the owners of the field come, they will say, 'Let us have back our field.' They (will) undress in their presence in order to let them have back their field and to give it back to them. [3] Therefore I say to you, if the owner of a house knows that the thief is coming, he will begin his vigil before he comes and will not let him dig through into his house of his domain to carry away his goods. You, then, be on your guard against the world. Arm yourselves with great strength lest the robbers find a way to come to you, for the difficulty which you expect will (surely) materialize. [4] *Let there be among you a man of understanding. When the grain ripened, he came quickly with his sickle in his hand and reaped it.* [5] Whoever has ears to hear, let him hear."

Mark 13:34–36 (§P17.1)

[32] "But of that day or that hour no one knows, not even the angels in heaven, nor the Son, but only the Father. [33] Take heed, watch; for you do not know when the time will come. [34] *It is like a man going on a journey, when he leaves home and puts his servants in charge, each with his work, and commands the doorkeeper to be on watch.* [35] *Watch therefore—for you do not know when the master of the house will come, in the evening, or at midnight, or at cockcrow, or in the morning—* [36] *lest he come suddenly and find you asleep.* [37] And what I say to you I say to all: Watch."

Luke 12:35–38 (§P17.2)

[35] *"Let your loins be girded and your lamps burning,* [36] *and be like men who are waiting for their master to come home from the marriage feast, so that they may open to him at once when he comes and knocks.* [37] *Blessed are those servants whom the master finds awake when he comes; truly, I say to you, he will gird himself and have them sit at table, and he will come and serve them.* [38] *If he comes in the second watch, or in the third, and finds them so, blessed are those servants!* [39] But know this, that if the householder had known at what hour the thief was coming, he would not have left his house to be broken into. [40] You also must be ready; for the Son of man is coming at an unexpected hour."

Did 16:1a (§P17.3)

[1] *"Watch" over your life: "let your lamps" be not quenched "and your loins" be not ungirded, but be "ready,"* for ye know not "the hour in which our Lord cometh." [2] But be frequently gathered together seeking the things which are profitable for your souls, for the whole time of your faith shall not profit you except ye be found perfect at the last time.

18 THE RICH FARMER

Luke 12:16b–20 (§P18.1)

[13] One of the multitude said to him, "Teacher, bid my brother divide the inheritance with me." [14] But he said to him, "Man, who made me a judge or divider over you?" [15] And he said to them, "Take heed, and beware of all covetousness; for a man's life does not consist in the abundance of his possessions." [16] And he told them a parable, saying, *"The land of a rich man brought forth plentifully;* [17] *and he thought to himself, 'What shall I do, for I have nowhere to store my crops?'* [18] *And he said, 'I will do this: I will pull down my barns, and build larger ones; and there I will store all my grain and my goods.* [19] *And I will say to my soul, Soul, you have ample goods laid up for many years; take your ease, eat, drink, be merry.'* [20] *But God said to him, 'Fool! This night your soul is required of you; and the things you have prepared, whose will they be?'* [21] So is he who lays up treasure for himself, and is not rich toward God."

GThom 63:1 (§P18.2)

(63) [1] Jesus said, *"There was a rich man who had much money. He said, 'I shall put my money to use so that I may sow, reap, plant, and fill my storehouse with produce, with the result that I shall lack nothing.' Such were his intentions, but that same night he died.* [2] Let him who has ears hear."

(64) [1] Jesus said, "A man had received visitors. And when he had prepared the dinner, he sent his servant to invite the guests. He went to the first one and said to him, 'My master invites you.' He said, 'I have claims against some merchants. They are coming to me this evening. I must go and give them my orders. I ask to be excused from the dinner.' He went to another and said to him, 'My master has invited you.' He said to him, 'I have just bought a house and am required for the day. I shall not have any spare time.' He went to another and said to him, 'My master invites you.' He said to him, 'My friend is going to get married, and I am to prepare the banquet. I shall not be able to come. I ask to be excused from the dinner.' He went to another and said to him, 'My master invites you.' He said to him, 'I have just bought a farm, and I am on my way to collect the rent. I shall not be able to come. I ask to be excused.' The servant returned and said to his master, 'Those whom you invited to the dinner have asked to be excused.' The master said to his servant, 'Go outside to the streets and bring back those whom you happen to meet, so that they may dine.' [2] Businessmen and merchants will not enter the Places of My Father."

(65) [1] He said, "There was a good man who owned a vineyard. He leased it to tenant farmers so that they might work it and he might collect the produce from them. He sent his servant so that the tenants might give him the produce of the vineyard. They seized his servant and beat him, all but killing him. The servant went back and told his master. The master said, 'Perhaps <they> did not recognize <him>.' He sent another servant. The tenants beat this one as well. Then the owner sent his son and said, 'Perhaps they will show respect to my son.' Because the tenants knew that it was he who was the heir to the vineyard, they seized him and killed him. [2] Let him who has ears hear."

19 THE BARREN TREE

Luke 13:6b–9 (§P19)

[1] There were some present at that very time who told him of the Galileans whose blood Pilate had mingled with their sacrifices. [2] And he answered them, "Do you think that these Galileans were worse sinners than all the other Galileans, because they suffered thus? [3] I tell you, No; but unless you repent you will all likewise perish. [4] Or those eighteen upon whom the tower in Siloam fell and killed them, do you think that they were worse offenders than all the others who dwelt in Jerusalem? [5] I tell you, No; but unless you repent you will all likewise perish."

[6] And he told this parable: *"A man had a fig tree planted in his vineyard; and he came seeking fruit on it and found none.* [7] *And he said to the vinedresser, 'Lo, these three years I have come seeking fruit on this fig tree, and I find none. Cut it down; why should it use up the ground?'* [8] *And he answered him, 'Let it alone, sir, this year also, till I dig about it and put on manure.* [9] *And if it bears fruit next year, well and good; but if not, you can cut it down.'"*

20 THE TOWER BUILDER

Luke 14:28–30 (§P20)

²⁵ Now great multitudes accompanied him; and he turned and said to them, ²⁶ "If any one comes to me and does not hate his own father and mother and wife and children and brothers and sisters, yes, and even his own life, he cannot be my disciple. ²⁷ Whoever does not bear his own cross and come after me, cannot be my disciple. ²⁸ *For which of you, desiring to build a tower, does not first sit down and count the cost, whether he has enough to complete it?* ²⁹ *Otherwise, when he has laid a foundation, and is not able to finish, all who see it begin to mock him,* ³⁰ *saying, 'This man began to build, and was not able to finish.'* ³¹ Or what king, going to encounter another king in war, will not sit down first and take counsel whether he is able with ten thousand to meet him who comes against him with twenty thousand? ³² And if not, while the other is yet a great way off, he sends an embassy and asks terms of peace."

21 THE WARRING KING

Luke 14:31–32 (§P21)

²⁵ Now great multitudes accompanied him; and he turned and said to them, ²⁶ "If any one comes to me and does not hate his own father and mother and wife and children and brothers and sisters, yes, and even his own life, he cannot be my disciple. ²⁷ Whoever does not bear his own cross and come after me, cannot be my disciple. ²⁸ For which of you, desiring to build a tower, does not first sit down and count the cost, whether he has enough to complete it? ²⁹ Otherwise, when he has laid a foundation, and is not able to finish, all who see it begin to mock him, ³⁰ saying, 'This man began to build, and was not able to finish.' ³¹ *Or what king, going to encounter another king in war, will not sit down first and take counsel whether he is able with ten thousand to meet him who comes against him with twenty thousand?* ³² *And if not, while the other is yet a great way off, he sends an embassy and asks terms of peace.* ³³ So therefore, whoever of you does not renounce all that he has cannot be my disciple."

Luke 15:8–9 (§P22)

¹ Now the tax collectors and sinners were all drawing near to hear him. ² And the Pharisees and the scribes murmured, saying, "This man receives sinners and eats with them."

³ So he told them this parable: ⁴ "What man of you, having a hundred sheep, if he has lost one of them, does not leave the ninety-nine in the wilderness, and go after the one which is lost, until he finds it? ⁵ And when he has found it, he lays it on his shoulders, rejoicing. ⁶ And when he comes home, he calls together his friends and his neighbors, saying to them, 'Rejoice with me, for I have found my sheep which was lost.' ⁷ Just so, I tell you, there will be more joy in heaven over one sinner who repents than over ninety-nine righteous persons who need no repentance.

⁸ *Or what woman, having ten silver coins, if she loses one coin, does not light a lamp and sweep the house and seek diligently until she finds it? ⁹ And when she has found it, she calls together her friends and neighbors, saying, 'Rejoice with me, for I have found the coin which I had lost.'* ¹⁰ Just so, I tell you, there is joy before the angels of God over one sinner who repents."

¹¹ And he said, "There was a man who had two sons; ¹² and the younger of them said to his father, 'Father, give me the share of property that falls to me.' And he divided his living between them. ¹³ Not many days later, the younger son gathered all he had and took his journey into a far country, and there he squandered his property in loose living. ¹⁴ And when he had spent everything, a great famine arose in that country, and he began to be in want. ¹⁵ So he went and joined himself to one of the citizens of that country, who sent him into his fields to feed swine. ¹⁶ And he would gladly have fed on the pods that the swine ate; and no one gave him anything. ¹⁷ But when he came to himself he said, 'How many of my father's hired servants have bread enough and to spare, but I perish here with hunger! ¹⁸ I will arise and go to my father, and I will say to him, "Father, I have sinned against heaven and before you; ¹⁹ I am no longer worthy to be called your son; treat me as one of your hired servants."' ²⁰ And he arose and came to his father. But while he was yet at a distance, his father saw him and had compassion, and ran and embraced him and kissed him. ²¹ And the son said to him, 'Father, I have sinned against heaven and before you; I am no longer worthy to be called your son.' ²² But the father said to his servants, 'Bring quickly the best robe, and put it on him; and put a ring on his hand, and shoes on his feet; ²³ and bring the fatted calf and kill it, and let us eat and make merry; ²⁴ for this my son was dead, and is alive again; he was lost, and is found.' And they began to make merry.

²⁵ "Now his elder son was in the field; and as he came and drew near to the house, he heard music and dancing. ²⁶ And he called one of the servants and asked what this meant. ²⁷ And he said to him, 'Your brother has come, and your father has killed the fatted calf, because he has received him safe and sound.' ²⁸ But he was angry and refused to go in. His father came out and entreated him, ²⁹ but he answered his father, 'Lo, these many years I have served you, and I never disobeyed your command; yet you never gave me a kid, that I might make merry with my friends. ³⁰ But when this son of yours came, who has devoured your living with harlots, you killed for him the fatted calf!' ³¹ And he said to him, 'Son, you are always with me, and all that is mine is yours. ³² It was fitting to make merry and be glad, for this your brother was dead, and is alive; he was lost, and is found.'"

Luke 15:11b–32 (§P23)

[1] Now the tax collectors and sinners were all drawing near to hear him. [2] And the Pharisees and the scribes murmured, saying, "This man receives sinners and eats with them."

[3] So he told them this parable: [4] "What man of you, having a hundred sheep, if he has lost one of them, does not leave the ninety-nine in the wilderness, and go after the one which is lost, until he finds it? [5] And when he has found it, he lays it on his shoulders, rejoicing. [6] And when he comes home, he calls together his friends and his neighbors, saying to them, 'Rejoice with me, for I have found my sheep which was lost.' [7] Just so, I tell you, there will be more joy in heaven over one sinner who repents than over ninety-nine righteous persons who need no repentance.

[8] "Or what woman, having ten silver coins, if she loses one coin, does not light a lamp and sweep the house and seek diligently until she finds it? [9] And when she has found it, she calls together her friends and neighbors, saying, 'Rejoice with me, for I have found the coin which I had lost.' [10] Just so, I tell you, there is joy before the angels of God over one sinner who repents."

[11] And he said, *"There was a man who had two sons;* [12] *and the younger of them said to his father, 'Father, give me the share of property that falls to me.' And he divided his living between them.* [13] *Not many days later, the younger son gathered all he had and took his journey into a far country, and there he squandered his property in loose living.* [14] *And when he had spent everything, a great famine arose in that country, and he began to be in want.* [15] *So he went and joined himself to one of the citizens of that country, who sent him into his fields to feed swine.* [16] *And he would gladly have fed on the pods that the swine ate; and no one gave him anything.* [17] *But when he came to himself he said, 'How many of my father's hired servants have bread enough and to spare, but I perish here with hunger!* [18] *I will arise and go to my father, and I will say to him, "Father, I have sinned against heaven and before you;* [19] *I am no longer worthy to be called your son; treat me as one of your hired servants."'* [20] *And he arose and came to his father. But while he was yet at a distance, his father saw him and had compassion, and ran and embraced him and kissed him.* [21] *And the son said to him, 'Father, I have sinned against heaven and before you; I am no longer worthy to be called your son.'* [22] *But the father said to his servants, 'Bring quickly the best robe, and put it on him; and put a ring on his hand, and shoes on his feet;* [23] *and bring the fatted calf and kill it, and let us eat and make merry;* [24] *for this my son was dead, and is alive again; he was lost, and is found.' And they began to make merry.*

[25] *"Now his elder son was in the field; and as he came and drew near to the house, he heard music and dancing.* [26] *And he called one of the servants and asked what this meant.* [27] *And he said to him, 'Your brother has come, and your father has killed the fatted calf, because he has received him safe and sound.'* [28] *But he was angry and refused to go in. His father came out and entreated him,* [29] *but he answered his father, 'Lo, these many years I have served you, and I never disobeyed your command; yet you never gave me a kid, that I might make merry with my friends.* [30] *But when this son of yours came, who has devoured your living with harlots, you killed for him the fatted calf!'* [31] *And he said to him, 'Son, you are always with me, and all that is mine is yours.* [32] *It was fitting to make merry and be glad, for this your brother* was dead, and is alive; he was lost, and is found.'"

Luke 16:1-7 (§P24)

[1] *He also said to the disciples, "There was a rich man who had a steward, and charges were brought to him that this man was wasting his goods.* [2] *And he called him and said to him, 'What is this that I hear about you? Turn in the account of your stewardship, for you can no longer be steward.'* [3] *And the steward said to himself, 'What shall I do, since my master is taking the stewardship away from me? I am not strong enough to dig, and I am ashamed to beg.* [4] *I have decided what to do, so that people may receive me into their houses when I am put out of the stewardship.'* [5] *So, summoning his master's debtors one by one, he said to the first, 'How much do you owe my master?'* [6] *He said, 'A hundred measures of oil.' And he said to him, 'Take your bill, and sit down quickly and write fifty.'* [7] *Then he said to another, 'And how much do you owe?' He said, 'A hundred measures of wheat.' He said to him, 'Take your bill, and write eighty.'* [8] The master commended the dishonest steward for his shrewdness; for the sons of this world are more shrewd in dealing with their own generation than the sons of light. [9] And I tell you, make friends for yourselves by means of unrighteous mammon, so that when it fails they may receive you into the eternal habitations.

[10] "He who is faithful in a very little is faithful also in much; and he who is dishonest in a very little is dishonest also in much. [11] If then you have not been faithful in the unrighteous mammon, who will entrust to you the true riches? [12] And if you have not been faithful in that which is another's, who will give you that which is your own? [13] No servant can serve two masters; for either he will hate the one and love the other, or he will be devoted to the one and despise the other. You cannot serve God and mammon."

[14] The Pharisees, who were lovers of money, heard all this, and they scoffed at him. [15] But he said to them, "You are those who justify yourselves before men, but God knows your hearts; for what is exalted among men is an abomination in the sight of God.

[16] "The law and the prophets were until John; since then the good news of the kingdom of God is preached, and every one enters it violently. [17] But it is easier for heaven and earth to pass away, than for one dot of the law to become void.

[18] "Every one who divorces his wife and marries another commits adultery, and he who marries a woman divorced from her husband commits adultery.

[19] "There was a rich man, who was clothed in purple and fine linen and who feasted sumptuously every day. [20] And at his gate lay a poor man named Lazarus, full of sores, [21] who desired to be fed with what fell from the rich man's table; moreover the dogs came and licked his sores. [22] The poor man died and was carried by the angels to Abraham's bosom. The rich man also died and was buried; [23] and in Hades, being in torment, he lifted up his eyes, and saw Abraham far off and Lazarus in his bosom. [24] And he called out, 'Father Abraham, have mercy upon me, and send Lazarus to dip the end of his finger in water and cool my tongue; for I am in anguish in this flame.' [25] But Abraham said, 'Son, remember that you in your lifetime received your good things, and Lazarus in like manner evil things; but now he is comforted here, and you are in anguish. [26] And besides all this, between us and you a great chasm has been fixed, in order that those who would pass from here to you may not be able, and none may cross from there to us.' [27] And he said, 'Then I beg you, father, to send him to my father's house, [28] for I have five brothers, so that he may warn them, lest they also come into this place of torment.' [29] But Abraham said, 'They have Moses and the prophets; let them hear them.' [30] And he said, 'No, father Abraham; but if some one goes to them from the dead, they will repent.' [31] He said to him, 'If they do not hear Moses and the prophets, neither will they be convinced if some one should rise from the dead.'"

Luke 16:19–31 (§P25)

[1] He also said to the disciples, "There was a rich man who had a steward, and charges were brought to him that this man was wasting his goods. [2] And he called him and said to him, 'What is this that I hear about you? Turn in the account of your stewardship, for you can no longer be steward.' [3] And the steward said to himself, 'What shall I do, since my master is taking the stewardship away from me? I am not strong enough to dig, and I am ashamed to beg. [4] I have decided what to do, so that people may receive me into their houses when I am put out of the stewardship.' [5] So, summoning his master's debtors one by one, he said to the first, 'How much do you owe my master?' [6] He said, 'A hundred measures of oil.' And he said to him, 'Take your bill, and sit down quickly and write fifty.' [7] Then he said to another, 'And how much do you owe?' He said, 'A hundred measures of wheat.' He said to him, 'Take your bill, and write eighty.' [8] The master commended the dishonest steward for his shrewdness; for the sons of this world are more shrewd in dealing with their own generation than the sons of light. [9] And I tell you, make friends for yourselves by means of unrighteous mammon, so that when it fails they may receive you into the eternal habitations.

[10] "He who is faithful in a very little is faithful also in much; and he who is dishonest in a very little is dishonest also in much. [11] If then you have not been faithful in the unrighteous mammon, who will entrust to you the true riches? [12] And if you have not been faithful in that which is another's, who will give you that which is your own? [13] No servant can serve two masters; for either he will hate the one and love the other, or he will be devoted to the one and despise the other. You cannot serve God and mammon."

[14] The Pharisees, who were lovers of money, heard all this, and they scoffed at him. [15] But he said to them, "You are those who justify yourselves before men, but God knows your hearts; for what is exalted among men is an abomination in the sight of God.

[16] "The law and the prophets were until John; since then the good news of the kingdom of God is preached, and every one enters it violently. [17] But it is easier for heaven and earth to pass away, than for one dot of the law to become void.

[18] "Every one who divorces his wife and marries another commits adultery, and he who marries a woman divorced from her husband commits adultery.

[19] *"There was a rich man, who was clothed in purple and fine linen and who feasted sumptuously every day. [20] And at his gate lay a poor man named Lazarus, full of sores, [21] who desired to be fed with what fell from the rich man's table; moreover the dogs came and licked his sores. [22] The poor man died and was carried by the angels to Abraham's bosom. The rich man also died and was buried; [23] and in Hades, being in torment, he lifted up his eyes, and saw Abraham far off and Lazarus in his bosom. [24] And he called out, 'Father Abraham, have mercy upon me, and send Lazarus to dip the end of his finger in water and cool my tongue; for I am in anguish in this flame.' [25] But Abraham said, 'Son, remember that you in your lifetime received your good things, and Lazarus in like manner evil things; but now he is comforted here, and you are in anguish. [26] And besides all this, between us and you a great chasm has been fixed, in order that those who would pass from here to you may not be able, and none may cross from there to us.' [27] And he said, 'Then I beg you, father, to send him to my father's house, [28] for I have five brothers, so that he may warn them, lest they also come into this place of torment.' [29] But Abraham said, 'They have Moses and the prophets; let them hear them.' [30] And he said, 'No, father Abraham; but if some one goes to them from the dead, they will repent.' [31] He said to him, 'If they do not hear Moses and the prophets, neither will they be convinced if some one should rise from the dead.'"*

26   THE UNJUST JUDGE

Luke 18:2–5 (§P26)

[1] And he told them a parable, to the effect that they ought always to pray and not lose heart. [2] He said, *"In a certain city there was a judge who neither feared God nor regarded man; [3] and there was a widow in that city who kept coming to him and saying, 'Vindicate me against my adversary.' [4] For a while he refused; but afterward he said to himself, 'Though I neither fear God nor regard man, [5] yet because this widow bothers me, I will vindicate her, or she will wear me out by her continual coming.'"* [6] And the Lord said, "Hear what the unrighteous judge says. [7] And will not God vindicate his elect, who cry to him day and night? Will he delay long over them? [8] I tell you, he will vindicte them speedily. Nevertheless, when the Son of man comes, will he find faith on earth?"

27 PHARISEE AND PUBLICAN

Luke 18:10–13 (§P27)

⁹ He also told this parable to some who trusted in themselves that they were righteous and despised others: ¹⁰ *"Two men went up into the temple to pray, one a Pharisee and the other a tax collector.* ¹¹ *The Pharisee stood and prayed thus with himself, 'God, I thank thee that I am not like other men, extortioners, unjust, adulterers, or even like this tax collector.* ¹² *I fast twice a week, I give tithes of all that I get.'* ¹³ *But the tax collector, standing far off, would not even lift up his eyes to heaven, but beat his breast, saying, 'God, be merciful to me a sinner!'* ¹⁴ I tell you, this man went down to his house justified rather than the other; for every one who exalts himself will be humbled, but he who humbles himself will be exalted."

28 THE PALM SHOOT

ApJas 6:8b (§P28)

⁵ "I first spoke with you in parables, and you did not understand. Now, in turn, I speak with you openly, and you do not perceive. But it is you who were to me a parable in parables and what is apparent in what are open.

⁶ "Be zealous to be saved without being urged. Rather, be ready on your (pl.) own and, if possible, go before me. For thus the Father will love you.

⁷ "Become haters of hypocrisy and evil thought. For it is thought which gives birth to hypocrisy, but hypocrisy is far from the truth.

⁸ "Let not *the Kingdom of Heaven* wither away. For it *is like a date-palm <shoot> whose fruits dropped down around it. It put forth buds and, when they blossomed, they, (i.e., the fruits) caused the productivity (of the date-palm) to dry up.* Thus it is also with the fruit which came from the single root: when it (i.e., the fruit) was <picked>, fruits were collected by many. It was really good. Is it (not) possible now to produce the plants anew for you (sing.), (and) to find it (i.e., the Kingdom)?

⁹ "<Since> I have been glorified in this manner before this time, why do you (pl.) restrain me when I am eager to go? For after my [suffering] you have constrained me to remain with you eighteen more days (or: <months>) for the sake of the parables. ¹⁰ It sufficed for some persons <to> pay attention to the teaching and to understand 'The Shepherds' and 'The Seed' and 'The Building' and 'The Lamps of the Virgins' and 'The Wage of the Workers' and 'The Double Drachma' and 'The Woman.'"

29 GRAIN OF WHEAT

ApJas 6:11b (§P29)

¹¹ "Become zealous about the Word. For the Word's first characteristic is faith; the second is love; the third is works. Now from these comes life. *For the Word is like a grain of wheat. When someone sowed it, he believed in it; and when it sprouted, he loved it, because he looked (forward to) many grains in the place of one; and when he worked (it), he was saved, because he prepared it for food. Again he left (some grains) to sow.* Thus it is also possible for you (pl.) to receive for yourselves the Kingdom of Heaven: unless you receive it through knowledge, you will not be able to find it."

30 EAR OF GRAIN

ApJas 8:2b (§P30)

¹ When we heard these things, we became distressed. ² Now when he saw that we were distressed, he said: "This is why I say this to you (pl.), that you may know yourselves. *For the Kingdom of Heaven is like an ear of grain which sprouted in a field. And when it ripened, it scattered its fruit and, in turn, filled the field with ears of grain for another year.* You also: be zealous to reap for yourselves an ear of life, in order that you may be filled with the Kingdom."

31 CHILDREN IN FIELD★

GThom 21:1–2 (§P31)

(21) [1] Mary said to Jesus, "Whom are Your *disciples* like?"

[2] He said, "They *are like children who have settled in a field which is not theirs. When the owners of the field come, they will say, 'Let us have back our field.' They (will) undress in their presence in order to let them have back their field and to give it back to them.* [3] Therefore I say to you, if the owner of a house knows that the thief is coming, he will begin his vigil before he comes and will not let him dig through into his house of his domain to carry away his goods. You, then, be on your guard against the world. Arm yourselves with great strength lest the robbers find a way to come to you, for the difficulty which you expect will (surely) materialize. [4] Let there be among you a man of understanding. When the grain ripened, he came quickly with his sickle in his hand and reaped it. [5] Whoever has ears to hear, let him hear."

★ See 376: *Children in Field*

32 THE EMPTY JAR

GThom 97 (§P32)

(96) [1] Jesus [said], "The Kingdom of the Father is like a certain woman. She took a little leaven, [concealed] it in some dough, and made it into large loaves. [2] Let him who has ears hear."

(97) Jesus said, *"The Kingdom of the [Father] is like a certain woman who was carrying a jar full of meal. While she was walking [on] a road, still some distance from home, the handle of the jar broke and the meal emptied out behind her on the road. She did not realize it; she had noticed no accident. When she reached her house, she set the jar down and found it empty."*

(98) Jesus said, "The Kingdom of the Father is like a certain man who wanted to kill a powerful man. In his own house he drew his sword and stuck it into the wall in order to find out whether his hand could carry through. Then he slew the powerful man."

33 THE ASSASSIN

GThom 98 (§P33)

(96) [1] Jesus [said], "The Kingdom of the Father is like a certain woman. She took a little leaven, [concealed] it in some dough, and made it into large loaves. [2] Let him who has ears hear."

(97) Jesus said, "The Kingdom of the [Father] is like a certain woman who was carrying a jar full of meal. While she was walking [on] a road, still some distance from home, the handle of the jar broke and the meal emptied out behind her on the road. She did not realize it; she had noticed no accident. When she reached her house, she set the jar down and found it empty."

(98) Jesus said, *"The Kingdom of the Father is like a certain man who wanted to kill a powerful man. In his own house he drew his sword and stuck it into the wall in order to find out whether his hand could carry through. Then he slew the powerful man."*

IESUS

APHORISMS

34 KINGDOM AND REPENTANCE*

Matt 3:2 (§A1.1)

[1] In those days came John the Baptist, preaching in the wilderness of Judea, [2] *"Repent, for the kingdom of heaven is at hand."* [3] For this is he who was spoken of by the prophet Isaiah when he said,

"The voice of one crying in the wilderness:
Prepare the way of the Lord,
make his paths straight."

[4] Now John wore a garment of camel's hair, and a leather girdle around his waist; and his food was locusts and wild honey. [5] Then went out to him Jerusalem and all Judea and all the region about the Jordan, [6] and they were baptized by him in the river Jordan, confessing their sins.

Matt 4:17b (§A1.2)

[12] Now when he heard that John had been arrested, he withdrew into Galilee; [13] and leaving Nazareth he went and dwelt in Capernaum by the sea, in the territory of Zebulun and Naphtali, [14] that what was spoken by the prophet Isaiah might be fulfilled:

[15] "The land of Zebulun and the land of Naphtali,
toward the sea, across the Jordan,
Galilee of the Gentiles—
[16] the people who sat in darkness
have seen a great light,
and for those who sat in the region and shadow of death
light has dawned."

[17] From that time Jesus began to preach, saying, *"Repent, for the kingdom of heaven is at hand."*

Mark 1:15 (§A1.3)

[14] Now after John was arrested Jesus came into Galilee, preaching the gospel of God, [15] and saying, *"The time is fulfilled, and the kingdom of God is at hand; repent, and believe in the gospel."*

* See 406: *Kingdom and Repentance*

35 TREE CUT DOWN*

Matt 3:10b (§A2.1)

[7] But when he saw many of the Pharisees and Sadducees coming for baptism, he said to them, "You brood of vipers! Who warned you to flee from the wrath to come? [8] Bear fruit that befits repentance, [9] and do not presume to say to yourselves, 'We have Abraham as our father'; for I tell you, God is able from these stones to raise up children to Abraham. [10] Even now the axe is laid to the root of the trees; *every tree therefore that does not bear good fruit is cut down and thrown into the fire."*

Matt 7:19 (§A2.2)

[15] "Beware of false prophets, who come to you in sheep's clothing but inwardly are ravenous wolves. [16] You will know them by their fruits. Are grapes gathered from thorns, or figs from thistles? [17] So, every sound tree bears good fruit, but the bad tree bears evil fruit. [18] A sound tree cannot bear evil fruit, nor can a bad tree bear good fruit. [19] *Every tree that does not bear good fruit is cut down and thrown into the fire.* [20] Thus you will know them by their fruits."

* See 407: *Tree Cut Down*

Luke 3:9b (§A2.3)

[7] He said therefore to the multitudes that came out to be baptized by him, "You brood of vipers! Who warned you to flee from the wrath to come? [8] Bear fruits that befit repentance, and do not begin to say to yourselves, 'We have Abraham as our father'; for I tell you, God is able from these stones to raise up children to Abraham. [9] Even now the axe is laid to the root of the trees; *every tree therefore that does not bear good fruit is cut down and thrown into the fire."*

36 BLESSED THE POOR

Matt 5:3 (§A3.1)

[1] Seeing the crowds, he went up on the mountain, and when he sat down his disciples came to him. [2] And he opened his mouth and taught them, saying:
[3] *"Blessed are the poor in spirit, for theirs is the kingdom of heaven."*

Luke 6:20b (§A3.2)

[20] And he lifted up his eyes on his disciples, and said: *"Blessed are you poor, for yours is the kingdom of God."*

GThom 54 (§A3.3)

(54) Jesus said, *"Blessed are the poor, for yours is the Kingdom of Heaven."*

Pol Phil 2:3b (§A3.4)

[2] Now "he who raised him" from the dead "will also raise us up" if we do his will, and walk in his commandments and love the things which he loved, refraining from all unrighteousness, covetousness, love of money, evil speaking, false witness, "rendering not evil for evil, or railing for railing," or blow for blow, or curse for curse, [3] but remembering what the Lord taught when he said, "Judge not that ye be not judged, forgive and it shall be forgiven unto you, be merciful that ye may obtain mercy, with what measure ye mete, it shall be measured to you again," and, *"Blessed are the poor,* and they who are persecuted for righteousness' sake, *for theirs is the Kingdom of God."*

37 BLESSED THE SAD

Matt 5:4 (§A4.1)
4 *"Blessed are those who mourn, for they shall be comforted."*

Luke 6:21b (§A4.2)
21 ... *"Blessed are you that weep now, for you shall laugh."*

John 16:20, 22 (§A4.3)
20 "Truly, truly, I say to you, *you will weep and lament,* but the world will rejoice; *you will be sorrowful, but your sorrow will turn into joy.* 21 When a woman is in travail she has sorrow, because her hour has come; but when she is delivered of the child, she no longer remembers the anguish, for joy that a child is born into the world. 22 *So you have sorrow now, but I will see you again and your hearts will rejoice, and no one will take your joy from you."*

DialSav 13–14 (§A4.4)
(13) [Mary] said, "Lord, behold! Whence [...]... *the body [while I] weep,* and whence while I [...]?"

(14) The Lord said, "[...] *weep on account of its works [...] remain and the mind laughs [...]...[...] [...]... spirit.* If one does not [...] darkness, he will be able to see [...]. So I tell you [...] light is the darkness [...]... stand in [...] not see the light [...] the lie [...]... they brought them from [...]...[...].... You will give [...]... and [... exist] forever. [...]... [...]... [...] ever. Then [all] the powers which are above as well as those [below] will [...] you. In that place [there will] be weeping and [gnashing] of teeth over the end of [all] these things."

38 BLESSED THE MEEK

Matt 5:5 (§A5.1)
5 *"Blessed are the meek, for they shall inherit the earth."*

Did 3:7 (§A5.2)
6 My child, be not a grumbler, for this leads to blasphemy, nor stubborn, nor a thinker of evil, for from all these are blasphemies engendered. 7 but *be thou "meek, for the meek shall inherit the earth;"* 8 be thou longsuffering, and merciful and guileless, and quiet, and good, and ever fearing the words which thou hast heard.

39 BLESSED THE HUNGRY

Matt 5:6 (§A6.1)
6 *"Blessed are those who hunger and thirst for righteousness, for they shall be satisfied."*

Luke 6:21a (§A6.2)
21 *"Blessed are you that hunger now, for you shall be satisfied."*

GThom 69:2 (§A6.3)
(69) 1 Jesus said, "Blessed are they who have been persecuted within themselves. It is they who have truly come to know the Father. 2 *Blessed are the hungry, for the belly of him who desires will be filled."*

40 BLESSED THE MERCIFUL

Matt 5:7 (§A7)
[7] *"Blessed are the merciful, for they shall obtain mercy."*

41 BLESSED THE PURE

Matt 5:8 (§A8)
[8] *"Blessed are the pure in heart, for they shall see God."*

42 BLESSED THE PEACEMAKERS

Matt 5:9 (§A9)
[9] *"Blessed are the peacemakers, for they shall be called sons of God."*

43 BLESSED THE PERSECUTED

Matt 5:10 (§A10.1)
[10] *"Blessed are those who are persecuted for righteousness' sake, for theirs is the kingdom of heaven."*

Matt 5:11–12 (§A10.2)
[11] *"Blessed are you when men revile you and persecute you and utter all kinds of evil against you falsely on my account.* [12] *Rejoice and be glad, for your reward is great in heaven, for so men persecuted the prophets who were before you."*

Luke 6:22–23 (§A10.3)
[22] *"Blessed are you when men hate you, and when they exclude you and revile you, and cast out your name as evil, on account of the Son of man!* [23] *Rejoice in that day, and leap for joy, for behold, your reward is great in heaven; for so their fathers did to the prophets."*

1 Pet 3:14a (§A10.4)
[13] Now who is there to harm you if you are zealous for what is right? [14] *But even if you do suffer for righteousness' sake, you will be blessed.* Have no fear of them, nor be troubled, [15] but in your hearts reverence Christ as Lord. Always be prepared to make a defense to any one who calls you to account for the hope that is in you, yet do it with gentleness and reverence; [16] and keep your conscience clear, so that, when you are abused, those who revile your good behavior in Christ may be put to shame. [17] For it is better to suffer for doing right, if that should be God's will, than for doing wrong.

1 Pet 4:14 (§A10.5)
[12] Beloved, do not be surprised at the fiery ordeal which comes upon you to prove you, as though something strange were happening to you. [13] But rejoice in so far as you share Christ's sufferings, that you may also rejoice and be glad when his glory is revealed. [14] *If you are reproached for the name of Christ, you are blessed, because the spirit of glory and of God rests upon you.* [15] But let none of you suffer as a murderer, or a thief, or a wrongdoer, or a mischiefmaker; [16] yet if one suffers as a Christian, let him not be ashamed, but under that name let him glorify God.

GThom 68 (§A10.6)
(68) Jesus said, *"Blessed are you when you are hated and persecuted. Wherever you have been persecuted they will find no Place."*

GThom 69:1 (§A10.7)
(69) [1] Jesus said, *"Blessed are they who have been persecuted within themselves. It is they who have truly come to know the Father.* [2] Blessed are the hungry, for the belly of him who desires will be filled."

Pol Phil 2:3c (§A10.8)
[2] Now "he who raised him" from the dead "will also raise us up" if we do his will, and walk in his commandments and love the things which he loved, refraining from all unrighteousness, covetousness, love of money, evil speaking, false witness, "rendering not evil for evil, or railing for railing," or blow for blow, or curse for curse, [3] but remembering what the Lord taught when he said, "Judge not that ye be not judged, forgive and it shall be forgiven unto you, be merciful that ye may obtain mercy, with what measure ye mete, it shall be measured to you again," and, *"Blessed are* the poor, and *they who are persecuted for righteousness' sake, for theirs is the Kingdom of God."*

44 SALTING THE SALT

Matt 5:13 (§A11.1)
[13] *"You are the salt of the earth; but if salt has lost its taste, how shall its saltness be restored? It is no longer good for anything except to be thrown out and trodden under foot by men."*

Mark 9:50a (§A11.2)
[49] "For every one will be salted with fire. [50] *Salt is good; but if the salt has lost its saltness, how will you season it?* Have salt in yourselves, and be at peace with one another."

Luke 14:34–35a (§A11.3)
[34] *"Salt is good; but if salt has lost its taste, how shall its saltness be restored?* [35] *It is fit neither for the land nor for the dunghill; men throw it away."*

Matt 5:14a (§A12.1)

[14] *"You are the light of the world.* A city set on a hill cannot be hid."

John 8:12 (§A12.2)

[12] Again Jesus spoke to them, saying, *"I am the light of the world; he who follows me will not walk in darkness, but will have the light of life."* [13] The Pharisees then said to him, "You are bearing witness to yourself; your testimony is not true." [14] Jesus answered, "Even if I do bear witness to myself, my testimony is true, for I know whence I have come and whither I am going, but you do not know whence I come or whither I am going. [15] You judge according to the flesh, I judge no one. [16] Yet even if I do judge, my judgment is true, for it is not I alone that judge, but I and he who sent me."

John 9:4–5 (§A12.3)

[1] As he passed by, he saw a man blind from his birth. [2] And his disciples asked him, "Rabbi, who sinned, this man or his parents, that he was born blind?" [3] Jesus answered, "It was not that this man sinned, or his parents, but that the works of God might be made manifest in him. [4] *We must work the works of him who sent me, while it is day; night comes, when no one can work.* [5] *As long as I am in the world, I am the light of the world."* [6] As he said this, he spat on the ground and made clay of the spittle and anointed the man's eyes with the clay, [7] saying to him, "Go, wash in the pool of Siloam" (which means Sent). So he went and washed and came back seeing.

John 11:9–10 (§A12.4)

[5] Now Jesus loved Martha and her sister and Lazarus. [6] So when he heard that he was ill, he stayed two days longer in the place where he was. [7] Then after this he said to the disciples, "Let us go into Judea again." [8] The disciples said to him, "Rabbi, the Jews were but now seeking to stone you, and are you going there again?" [9] Jesus answered, *"Are there not twelve hours in the day? If any one walks in the day, he does not stumble, because he sees the light of this world.* [10] *But if any one walks in the night, he stumbles, because the light is not in him."* [11] Thus he spoke, and then he said to them, "Our friend Lazarus has fallen asleep, but I go to awake him out of sleep." [12] The disciples said to him, "Lord, if he has fallen asleep, he will recover." [13] Now Jesus had spoken of his death, but they thought that he meant taking rest in sleep. [14] Then Jesus told them plainly, "Lazarus is dead; [15] and for your sake I am glad that I was not there, so that you may believe. But let us go to him." [16] Thomas, called the Twin, said to his fellow disciples, "Let us also go, that we may die with him."

John 12:35–36 (§A12.5)

[27] "Now is my soul troubled. And what shall I say? 'Father, save me from this hour'? No, for this purpose I have come to this hour. [28] Father, glorify thy name." Then a voice came from heaven, "I have glorified it, and I will glorify it again." [29] The crowd standing by heard it and said that it had thundered. Others said, "An angel has spoken to him." [30] Jesus answered, "This voice has come for your sake, not for mine. [31] Now is the judgment of this world, now shall the ruler of this world be cast out; [32] and I, when I am lifted up from the earth, will draw all men to myself." [33] He said this to show by what death he was to die. [34] The crowd answered him, "We have heard from the law that the Christ remains for ever. How can you say that the Son of man must be lifted up? Who is this Son of man?" [35] Jesus said to them, *"The light is with you for a little longer. Walk while you have the light, lest the darkness overtake you; he who walks in the darkness does not know where he goes. [36] While you have the light, believe in the light, that you may become sons of light."*

When Jesus had said this, he departed and hid himself from them.

POxy655 24 (§A12.6)

(24) [3] *[. . . There is light within a man] of light, [and he (or: it) lights up the whole] world. [If he (or: it) does not shine, he (or: it)] is [darkness].*

GThom 24:3 (§A12.7)

(24) [1] His disciples said to Him, "Show us the place where You are, since it is necessary for us to seek it."

[2] He said to them, "Whoever has ears, let him hear. [3] *There is light within a man of light, and he (or: it) lights up the whole world. If he (or: it) does not shine, he (or: it) is darkness."*

DialSav 14b (§A12.8)

(14) The Lord said, "[. . .] weep on account of its works [. . .] remain and the mind laughs [. . .]. . .[. . .] [. . .]. . . spirit. *If one does not [. . .] darkness, he will be able to see [. . .]. So I tell you [. . .] light is the darkness [. . .]. . . stand in [. . .] not see the light [. . .] the lie [. . .]. . . they brought them from [. . .]. . .[. . .]. . . .* You will give [. . .]. . . and [. . . exist] forever. [. . .]. . . [. . .]. . . [. . .] ever. Then [all] the powers which are above as well as those [below] will [. . .] you. In that place [there will] be weeping and [gnashing] of teeth over the end of [all] these things."

DialSav 34b (§A12.9)

(34) He [said] to them, "That which supports [the earth] is that which supports the heaven. When a Word comes forth from the Greatness, it will come on what supports the heaven and the earth. For the earth does not move. Were it to move, it would fall, though in order that the First Word might not fail. For it was that which established the cosmos and inhabited it and inhaled fragrance from it. For, . . .[. . .]. . . which do not move I [. . .]. . . you, all the sons of [men. For] you are from [that] place. [In] the hearts of those who speak out of [joy] and truth you exist. Even if it comes forth in [the body] of the Father among men and is not received, still it [does] return to its place. Whoever [does not] know [the work] of perfection [knows] nothing. *If one does not stand in the darkness, he will not be able to see the light."*

* See 325 & 414: *The World's Light*

---

46 THE MOUNTAIN CITY

Matt 5:14b (§A13.1)

[14] "You are the light of the world. *A city set on a hill cannot be hid."*

POxy1 32 (§A13.2)

(32) Jesus said, *"A city built on a high mountain and fortified cannot fall, nor can it be hidden."*

GThom 32 (§A13.3)

(32) Jesus said, *"A city being built on a high mountain and fortified cannot fall, nor can it be hidden."*

47 LAMP AND BUSHEL

Matt 5:15 (§A14.1)
15 *"Nor do men light a lamp and put it under a bushel, but on a stand, and it gives light to all in the house."*

Mark 4:21 (§A14.2)
21 And he said to them, *"Is a lamp brought in to be put under a bushel, or under a bed, and not on a stand?* 22 For there is nothing hid, except to be made manifest; nor is anything secret, except to come to light."

Luke 8:16 (§A14.3)
16 *"No one after lighting a lamp covers it with a vessel, or puts it under a bed, but puts it on a stand, that those who enter may see the light.* 17 For nothing is hid that shall not be made manifest, nor anything secret that shall not be known and come to light."

Luke 11:33 (§A14.4)
33 *"No one after lighting a lamp puts it in a cellar or under a bushel, but on a stand, that those who enter may see the light.* 34 Your eye is the lamp of your body; when your eye is sound, your whole body is full of light; but when it is not sound, your body is full of darkness. 35 Therefore be careful lest the light in you be darkness. 36 If then your whole body is full of light, having no part dark, it will be wholly bright, as when a lamp with its rays gives you light."

GThom 33:2 (§A14.5)
(33) [1] Jesus said, "Preach from your housetops that which you will hear in your ear {(and) in the other ear}. [2] *For no one lights a lamp and puts it under a bushel, nor does he put it in a hidden place, but rather he sets it on a lampstand so that everyone who enters and leaves will see its light."*

48 YOUR GOOD WORKS

Matt 5:16 (§A15)
16 *"Let your light so shine before men, that they may see your good works and give glory to your Father who is in heaven."*

49 NOT TO ABOLISH

Matt 5:17 (§A16)
17 *"Think not that I have come to abolish the law and the prophets; I have come not to abolish them but to fulfil them."*

50 NOT ONE IOTA

Matt 5:18 (§A17.1)
18 *"For truly, I say to you, till heaven and earth pass away, not an iota, not a dot, will pass from the law until all is accomplished."*

Luke 16:17 (§A17.2)
16 "The law and the prophets were until John; since then the good news of the kingdom of God is preached, and every one enters it violently. 17 *But it is easier for heaven and earth to pass away, than for one dot of the law to become void."*

51 THE LEAST COMMANDMENT

Matt 5:19 (§A18)
[19] *"Whoever then relaxes one of the least of these commandments and teaches men so, shall be called least in the kingdom of heaven; but he who does them and teaches them shall be called great in the kingdom of heaven."*

52 GREATER RIGHTEOUSNESS

Matt 5:20 (§A19)
[20] *"For I tell you, unless your righteousness exceeds that of the scribes and Pharisees, you will never enter the kingdom of heaven."*

53 AGAINST ANGER

Matt 5:21–22 (§A20.1)
[21] *"You have heard that it was said to the men of old, 'You shall not kill; and whoever kills shall be liable to judgment.'* [22] *But I say to you that every one who is angry with his brother shall be liable to judgment; whoever insults his brother shall be liable to the council, and whoever says, 'You fool!' shall be liable to the hell of fire."*

GNaz 4 (§A20.2)
(4) The phrase *"without a cause"* is lacking in some witnesses and in the Jewish Gospel. (Variant to Matthew 5:22 in the "Zion Gospel" Edition)

54 PRAYER AND FORGIVENESS

Matt 5:23–24 (§A21.1)
[23] *"So if you are offering your gift at the altar, and there remember that your brother has something against you,* [24] *leave your gift there before the altar and go; first be reconciled to your brother, and then come and offer your gift."*

Did 14:2 (§A21.2)
[1] On the Lord's Day of the Lord come together, break bread and hold Eucharist, after confessing your transgressions that your offering may be pure; [2] *but let none who has a quarrel with his fellow join in your meeting until they be reconciled, that your sacrifice be not defiled.* [3] For this is that which was spoken by the Lord, "In every place and time offer me a pure sacrifice, for I am a great king," saith the Lord, "and my name is wonderful among the heathen."

55   BEFORE THE JUDGMENT

Matt 5:25–26 (§A22.1)
[25] *"Make friends quickly with your accuser, while you are going with him to court, lest your accuser hand you over to the judge, and the judge to the guard, and you be put in prison;* [26] *truly, I say to you, you will never get out till you have paid the last penny."*

Luke 12:58–59 (§A22.2)
[57] "And why do you not judge for yourselves what is right? [58] *As you go with your accuser before the magistrate, make an effort to settle with him on the way, lest he drag you to the judge, and the judge hand you over to the officer, and the officer put you in prison.* [59] *I tell you, you will never get out till you have paid the very last copper."*

Did 1:5b (§A22.3)
[5]Give to everyone that asks thee, and do not refuse, for the Father's will is that we give to all from the gifts we have received. Blessed is he that gives according to the mandate; for he is innocent. Woe to him who receives; for if any man receive alms under pressure of need he is innocent; but he who receives it without need shall be tried as to why he took and for what, *and being in prison he shall be examined as to his deeds, and "he shall not come out thence until he pay the last farthing."*

56   AGAINST LUST

Matt 5:28b (§A23.1)
[27] "You have heard that it was said, 'You shall not commit adultery.' [28] But I say to you that *every one who looks at a woman lustfully has already committed adultery with her in his heart."*

Did 1:4a (§A23.2)
[4]*"Abstain from carnal"* and bodily *"lusts."* "If any man smite thee on the right cheek, turn to him the other cheek also," and thou wilt be perfect. "If any man impress thee to go with him one mile, go with him two. If any man take thy coat, give him thy shirt also, If any man will take from thee what is thine, refuse it not—not even if thou canst."

57   HAND, FOOT, EYE

Matt 5:29–30 (§A24.1)
[29]*"If your right eye causes you to sin, pluck it out and throw it away; it is better that you lose one of your members than that your whole body be thrown into hell.* [30] *And if your right hand causes you to sin, cut it off and throw it away; it is better that you lose one of your members than that your whole body go into hell."*

Matt 18:8–9 (§A24.2)
[8] *"And if your hand or your foot causes you to sin, cut it off and throw it away; it is better for you to enter life maimed or lame than with two hands or two feet to be thrown into the eternal fire.* [9] *And if your eye causes you to sin, pluck it out and throw it away; it is better for you to enter life with one eye than with two eyes to be thrown into the hell of fire."*

Mark 9:43,45,47 (§A24.3)
[43] *"And if your hand causes you to sin, cut it off; it is better for you to enter life maimed than with two hands to go to hell, to the unquenchable fire.* [45] *And if your foot causes you to sin, cut it off; it is better for you to enter life lame than with two feet to be thrown into hell.* [47] *And if your eye causes you to sin, pluck it out; it is better for you to enter the kingdom of God with one eye than with two eyes to be thrown into hell,* [48] where their worm does not die, and the fire is not quenched."

58 AGAINST DIVORCE*

Matt 5:32b (§A25.1)

[31] "It was also said, 'Whoever divorces his wife, let him give her a certificate of divorce.' [32] But I say to you that *every one who divorces his wife, except on the ground of unchastity, makes her an adulteress; and whoever marries a divorced woman commits adultery.*"

Matt 19:9b (§A25.2)

[3] And Pharisees came up to him and tested him by asking, "Is it lawful to divorce one's wife for any cause?" [4] He answered, "Have you not read that he who made them from the beginning made them male and female, [5] and said, 'For this reason a man shall leave his father and mother and be joined to his wife, and the two shall become one flesh'? [6] So they are no longer two but one flesh. What therefore God has joined together, let not man put asunder." [7] They said to him, "Why then did Moses command one to give a certificate of divorce, and to put her away?" [8] He said to them, "For your hardness of heart Moses allowed you to divorce your wives, but from the beginning it was not so. [9] And I say to you: *whoever divorces his wife, except for unchastity, and marries another, commits adultery.*"

[10] The disciples said to him, "If such is the case of a man with his wife, it is not expedient to marry." [11] But he said to them, "Not all men can receive this saying, but only those to whom it is given. [12] For there are eunuchs who have been so from birth, and there are eunuchs who have been made eunuchs by men, and there are eunuchs who have made themselves eunuchs for the sake of the kingdom of heaven. He who is able to receive this, let him receive it."

Mark 10:11b–12 (§A25.3)

[2] And Pharisees came up and in order to test him asked, "Is it lawful for a man to divorce his wife?" [3] He answered them, "What did Moses command you?" [4] They said, "Moses allowed a man to write a certificate of divorce, and to put her away." [5] But Jesus said to them, "For your hardness of heart he wrote you this commandment. [6] But from the beginning of creation, 'God made them male and female.' [7] 'For this reason a man shall leave his father and mother and be joined to his wife, [8] and the two shall become one flesh.' So they are no longer two but one flesh. [9] What therefore God has joined together, let not man put asunder."

[10] And in the house the disciples asked him again about this matter. [11] And he said to them, "*Whoever divorces his wife and marries another, commits adultery against her;* [12] *and if she divorces her husband and marries another, she commits adultery.*"

Luke 16:18 (§A25.4)

[14] The Pharisees, who were lovers of money, heard all this, and they scoffed at him. [15] But he said to them, "You are those who justify yourselves before men, but God knows your hearts; for what is exalted among men is an abomination in the sight of God.

[16] "The law and the prophets were until John; since then the good news of the kingdom of God is preached, and every one enters it violently. [17] But it is easier for heaven and earth to pass away, than for one dot of the law to become void.

[18] "*Every one who divorces his wife and marries another commits adultery, and he who marries a woman divorced from her husband commits adultery.*"

1 Cor 7:10–11 (§A25.5)

[1] Now concerning the matters about which you wrote. It is well for a man not to touch a woman. [2] But because of the temptation to immorality, each man should have his own wife and each woman her own husband. [3] The husband should give to his wife her conjugal rights, and likewise the wife to her husband. [4] For the wife does not rule over her own body, but the husband does; likewise the husband does not rule over his own body, but the wife does. [5] Do not refuse one another except perhaps by agreement for a season, that you may devote yourselves to prayer; but then come together again, lest Satan tempt you through lack of self-control. [6] I say this by way of concession, not of command. [7] I wish that all were as I myself am. But each has his own special gift from God, one of one kind and one of another.

[8] To the unmarried and the widows I say that it is well for them to remain single as I do. [9] But if they cannot exercise self-control, they should marry. For it is better to marry than to be aflame with passion.

[10] To the married I give charge, not I but the Lord, that *the wife should not separate from her husband* [11] (but if she does, let her remain single or else be reconciled to her husband)—*and that the husband should not divorce his wife.*

Herm Man 4.1:6b,10 (§A25.6)

[4] I said to him, "Sir, allow me to ask you a few questions." "Say on," said he. "Sir," said I, "if a man have a wife faithful in the Lord, and he finds her out in some adultery, does the husband sin if he lives with her?" [5] "So long as he is ignorant," said he, "he does not sin, but if the husband knows her sin, and the wife does not repent, but remains in her fornication, and the husband go on living with her, he becomes a partaker of her sin, and shares in her adultery." [6] "What then," said I, "sir, shall the husband do if the wife remain in this disposition?" "Let him put her away," he said, "and let the husband remain by himself. But '*if he put his wife away and marry another he also commits adultery himself.*'" [7] "If then," said I, "Sir, after the wife be put away she repent, and wish to return to her own husband, shall she not be received?" [8] "Yes," said he; "if the husband do not receive her he sins and covers himself with a great sin; but it is necessary to receive the sinner who repents, but not often, for the servants of God have but one repentance. Therefore, for the sake of repentance the husband ought not to marry. This is the course of action for wife and husband. [9] Not only," said he, "is it adultery if a man defile his flesh, but whosoever acts as do the heathen is also guilty of adultery, so that if anyone continue in such practices, and repent not, depart from him and do not live with him, otherwise you are also a sharer in his sin. [10] *For this reason it was enjoined on you to live by yourselves, whether husband or wife,* for in such cases repentance is possible. [11] I, therefore," said he, "am not giving an opportunity to laxity that this business be thus concluded, but in order that he who has sinned sin no more, and for his former sin there is one who can give healing, for he it is who has the power over all."

* See 326: Against Divorce

59   AGAINST OATHS

Matt 5:34b–37 (§A26.1)

³³ "Again you have heard that it was said to the men of old, 'You shall not swear falsely, but shall perform to the Lord what you have sworn.' ³⁴ But I say to you, *Do not swear at all, either by heaven, for it is the throne of God,* ³⁵ *or by the earth, for it is his footstool, or by Jerusalem, for it is the city of the great King.* ³⁶ *And do not swear by your head, for you cannot make one hair white or black.* ³⁷ *Let what you say be simply 'Yes' or 'No'; anything more than this comes from evil."*

Matt 23:22 (§A26.2)

¹⁶ "Woe to you, blind guides, who say, 'If any one swears by the temple, it is nothing; but if any one swears by the gold of the temple, he is bound by his oath.' ¹⁷ You blind fools! For which is greater, the gold or the temple that has made the gold sacred? ¹⁸ And you say, 'If any one swears by the altar, it is nothing; but if any one swears by the gift that is on the altar, he is bound by his oath.' ¹⁹ You blind men! For which is greater, the gift or the altar that makes the gift sacred? ²⁰ So he who swears by the altar, swears by it and by everything on it; ²¹ and he who swears by the temple, swears by it and by him who dwells in it; ²² and *he who swears by heaven, swears by the throne of God and by him who sits upon it."*

Jas 5:12 (§A26.3)

¹² *But above all, my brethren, do not swear, either by heaven or by earth or with any other oath, but let your yes be yes and your no be no, that you may not fall under condemnation.*

60   THE OTHER CHEEK

Matt 5:39b–41 (§A27.1)

³⁸ "You have heard that it was said, 'An eye for an eye and a tooth for a tooth.' ³⁹ But I say to you, do not resist one who is evil. But *if any one strikes you on the right cheek, turn to him the other also;* ⁴⁰ *and if any one would sue you and take your coat, let him have your cloak as well;* ⁴¹ *and if any one forces you to go one mile, go with him two miles.* ⁴² Give to him who begs from you, and do not refuse him who would borrow from you."

Luke 6:29 (§A27.2)

²⁷ "But I say to you that hear, Love your enemies, do good to those who hate you, ²⁸ bless those who curse you, pray for those who abuse you. ²⁹ *To him who strikes you on the cheek, offer the other also; and from him who takes away your coat do not withhold even your shirt.* ³⁰ Give to every one who begs from you; and of him who takes away your goods do not ask them again. ³¹ And as you wish that men would do to you, do so to them. ³² "If you love those who love you, what credit is that to you? For even sinners love those who love them. ³³ And if you do good to those who do good to you, what credit is that to you? For even sinners do the same. ³⁴ And if you lend to those from whom you hope to receive, what credit is that to you? Even sinners lend to sinners, to receive as much again. ³⁵ But love your enemies, and do good, and lend, expecting nothing in return; and your reward will be great, and you will be sons of the Most High; for he is kind to the ungrateful and the selfish. ³⁶ Be merciful, even as your Father is merciful."

Did 1:4b (§A27.3)

¹ There are two Ways, one of Life and one of Death, and there is a great difference between the two Ways.

² The Way of Life is this: "First, thou shalt love the God who made thee, secondly, thy neighbour as thyself; and whatsoever thou wouldst not have done to thyself, do not thou to another."

³ Now, the teaching of these words is this: "Bless those that curse you, and pray for your enemies, and fast for those that persecute you. For what credit is it to you if you love those that love you? Do not even the heathen do the same?" But, for your part, "love those that hate you," and you will have no enemy. ⁴ "Abstain from carnal" and bodily "lusts." *"If any man smite thee on the right cheek, turn to him the other cheek also," and thou wilt be perfect. "If any man impress thee to go with him one mile, go with him two. If any man take thy coat, give him thy shirt also.* If any man will take from thee what is thine, refuse it not"—not even if thou canst. ⁵ Give to everyone that asks thee, and do not refuse, for the Father's will is that we give to all from the gifts we have received. Blessed is he that gives according to the mandate; for he is innocent. Woe to him who receives; for if any man receive alms under pressure of need he is innocent; but he who receives it without need shall be tried as to why he took and for what, and being in prison he shall be examined as to his deeds, and "he shall not come out thence until he pay the last farthing."

61   GIVE WITHOUT RETURN

Matt 5:42 (§A28.1)

[38] "You have heard that it was said, 'An eye for an eye and a tooth for a tooth.' [39] But I say to you, do not resist one who is evil. But if any one strikes you on the right cheek, turn to him the other also; [40] and if any one would sue you and take your coat, let him have your cloak as well; [41] and if any one forces you to go one mile, go with him two miles. [42] *Give to him who begs from you, and do not refuse him who would borrow from you.*"

Luke 6:30 (§A28.2)

[27] "But I say to you that hear, Love your enemies, do good to those who hate you, [28] bless those who curse you, pray for those who abuse you. [29] To him who strikes you on the cheek, offer the other also; and from him who takes away your coat do not withhold even your shirt. [30] *Give to every one who begs from you; and of him who takes away your goods do not ask them again.* [31] And as you wish that men would do to you, do so to them. [32] If you love those who love you, what credit is that to you? For even sinners love those who love them. [33] And if you do good to those who do good to you, what credit is that to you? For even sinners do the same. [34] And if you lend to those from whom you hope to receive, what credit is that to you? Even sinners lend to sinners, to receive as much again. [35] But love your enemies, and do good, and lend, expecting nothing in return; and your reward will be great, and you will be sons of the Most High; for he is kind to the ungrateful and the selfish. [36] Be merciful, even as your Father is merciful."

GThom 95 (§A28.3)

(95) [Jesus said], *"If you have money, do not lend it at interest, but give [it] to one from whom you will not get it back."*

Did 1:4b–5a (§A28.4)

[1] There are two Ways, one of Life and one of Death, and there is a great difference between the two Ways.

[2] The Way of Life is this: "First, thou shalt love the God who made thee, secondly, thy neighbour as thyself; and whatsoever thou wouldst not have done to thyself, do not thou to another."

[3] Now, the teaching of these words is this: "Bless those that curse you, and pray for your enemies, and fast for those that persecute you. For what credit is it to you if you love those that love you? Do not even the heathen do the same?" But, for your part, "love those that hate you," and you will have no enemy. [4] "Abstain from carnal" and bodily "lusts." "If any man smite thee on the right cheek, turn to him the other cheek also," and thou wilt be perfect. "If any man impress thee to go with him one mile, go with him two. If any man take thy coat, give him thy shirt also, *If any man will take from thee what is thine, refuse it not"*—not even *if thou canst.* [5] *Give to everyone that asks thee, and do not refuse,* for the Father's will is that we give to all from the gifts we have received. Blessed is he that gives according to the mandate; for he is innocent. Woe to him who receives; for if any man receive alms under pressure of need he is innocent; but he who receives it without need shall be tried as to why he took and for what, and being in prison he shall be examined as to his deeds, and "he shall not come out thence until he pay the last farthing."

62   LOVE YOUR ENEMIES

Matt 5:44b–45 (§A29.1)

[43] "You have heard that it was said, 'You shall love your neighbor and hate your enemy.' [44] But I say to you, *Love your enemies and pray for those who persecute you,* [45] *so that you may be sons of your Father who is in heaven; for he makes his sun rise on the evil and on the good, and sends rain on the just and on the unjust.*"

Luke 6:27b–28,35ac (§A29.2)

[27] "But I say to you that hear, *Love your enemies, do good to those who hate you,* [28] *bless those who curse* you, pray for those who abuse you.

[35] But *love your enemies*, and *do good,* and lend, expecting nothing in return; and your reward will be great, *and you will be sons of the Most High; for he is kind to the ungrateful and the selfish."*

POxy1224 2 (§A29.3)

(2) *And pray for your enemies.* For he who is not [against you] is for you. [He who today] is far-off—tomorrow will be [near to you]. . . .

Pol Phil 12:3 (§A29.4)

[3] "Pray for all the saints. *Pray* also for the Emperors," and for potentates, and princes, and *for "those who persecute you and hate you,"* and for "the enemies of the Cross" that "your fruit may be manifest among all men, that you may be perfected" in him.

Did 1:3ac (§A29.5)

[1] There are two Ways, one of Life and one of Death, and there is a great difference between the two Ways.

[2] The Way of Life is this: "First, thou shalt love the God who made thee, secondly, thy neighbour as thyself; and whatsoever thou wouldst not have done to thyself, do not thou to another."

[3] Now, the teaching of these words is this: *"Bless those that curse you, and pray for your enemies, and fast for those that persecute you.* For what credit is it to you if you love those that love you? Do not even the heathen do the same?" *But, for your part, "love those that hate you,"* and you will have no enemy.

63 BETTER THAN SINNERS

Matt 5:45–47 (§A30.1)

⁴³ "You have heard that it was said, 'You shall love your neighbor and hate your enemy.' ⁴⁴ But I say to you, Love your enemies and pray for those who persecute you, ⁴⁵ *so that you may be sons of your Father who is in heaven; for he makes his sun rise on the evil and on the good, and sends rain on the just and on the unjust. ⁴⁶ For if you love those who love you, what reward have you? Do not even the tax collectors do the same? ⁴⁷ And if you salute only your brethren, what more are you doing than others? Do not even the Gentiles do the same?"*

Luke 6:32–35 (§A30.2)

³² *"If you love those who love you, what credit is that to you? For even sinners love those who love them. ³³ And if you do good to those who do good to you, what credit is that to you? For even sinners do the same. ³⁴ And if you lend to those from whom you hope to receive, what credit is that to you? Even sinners lend to sinners, to receive as much again. ³⁵ But love your enemies, and do good, and lend, expecting nothing in return; and your reward will be great, and you will be sons of the Most High; for he is kind to the ungrateful and the selfish."*

2 Clem 13:4a (§A30.3)

²For the Lord says, "Every way is my name blasphemed among all the heathen," and again, "Woe unto him on whose account my name is blasphemed." Wherein is it blasphemed? ³In that you do not do what I desire. For when the heathen hear from our mouth the oracles of God, they wonder at their beauty and greatness; afterwards, when they find out that our deeds are unworthy of the words which we speak, they turn from their wonder to blasphemy, saying that it is a myth and delusion. ⁴For when they hear from us that God says: *"It is no credit to you, if ye love them that love you, but it is a credit to you, if ye love your enemies, and those that hate you"*;—when they hear this they wonder at this extraordinary goodness; but when they see that we not only do not love those that hate us, but not even those who love us, they laugh us to scorn, and the name is blasphemed.

Ign Pol 2:1a (§A30.4)

¹*If you love good disciples, it is no credit to you*; rather bring to subjection by your gentleness the more troublesome. Not all wounds are healed by the same plaster. Relieve convulsions by fomentations.

Did 1:3b (§A30.5)

¹There are two Ways, one of Life and one of Death, and there is a great difference between the two Ways.

²The Way of Life is this: "First, thou shalt love the God who made thee, secondly, thy neighbour as thyself; and whatsoever thou wouldst not have done to thyself, do not thou to another."

³Now, the teaching of these words is this: "Bless those that curse you, and pray for your enemies, and fast for those that persecute you. *For what credit is it to you if you love those that love you? Do not even the heathen do the same?"* But, for your part, "love those that hate you," and you will have no enemy.

64 AS YOUR FATHER

Matt 5:48 (§A31.1)

⁴⁸ *"You, therefore, must be perfect, as your heavenly Father is perfect."*

Luke 6:36 (§A31.2)

³⁶ *"Be merciful, even as your Father is merciful."*

65 PIETY BEFORE MEN

Matt 6:1 (§A32)

¹ *"Beware of practicing your piety before men in order to be seen by them; for then you will have no reward from your Father who is in heaven."*

66 ON ALMSGIVING

Matt 6:2–4 (§A33)
[2] *"Thus, when you give alms, sound no trumpet before you, as the hypocrites do in the synagogues and in the streets, that they may be praised by men. Truly, I say to you, they have received their reward.* [3] *But when you give alms, do not let your left hand know what your right hand is doing,* [4] *so that your alms may be in secret; and your Father who sees in secret will reward you."*

67 ON SECRECY

Matt 6:3b (§A34.1)
[3] "But when you give alms, *do not let your left hand know what your right hand is doing."*

GThom 62:2 (§A34.2)
(62) [1] Jesus said, "It is to those [who are worthy of My] mysteries that I tell My mysteries. [2] *Do not let your left hand know what your right hand is doing."*

68 ON PRAYER

Matt 6:5 (§A35.1)
[5] *"And when you pray, you must not be like the hypocrites; for they love to stand and pray in the synagogues and at the street corners, that they may be seen by men. Truly, I say to you, they have received their reward.* [6] But when you pray, go into your room and shut the door and pray to your Father who is in secret; and your Father who sees in secret will reward you.
[9] Pray then like this:
Our Father who art in heaven,
Hallowed be thy name.
[10] Thy kingdom come,
Thy will be done,
On earth as it is in heaven.
[11] Give us this day our daily bread;
[12] And forgive us our debts,
As we also have forgiven our debtors;
[13] And lead us not into temptation,
But deliver us from evil.
[14] For if you forgive men their trespasses, your heavenly Father also will forgive you; [15] but if you do not forgive men their trespasses, neither will your Father forgive your trespasses."

Did 8:2a (§A35.2)
[2] *And do not pray as the hypocrites,* but as the Lord commanded in his Gospel, pray thus: "Our Father, who are in Heaven, hallowed by thy Name, thy Kingdon come, thy will be done, as in Heaven so also upon earth; give us to-day our daily bread, and forgive us our debt as we forgive our debtors, and lead us not into trial, but deliver us from the Evil One, for thine is the power and the glory for ever." [3] Pray thus three times a day.

69 GENTILES AND PRAYER

Matt 6:7–8 (§A36)
[7] *"And in praying do not heap up empty phrases as the Gentiles do; for they think that they will be heard for their many words.* [8] *Do not be like them, for your Father knows what you need before you ask him."*

70 THE LORD'S PRAYER★

Matt 6:9b–13 (§A37.1)
[9] "Pray then like this:
"Our Father who art in heaven,
Hallowed be thy name.
[10] *Thy kingdom come,*
Thy will be done,
    On earth as it is in heaven.
[11] *Give us this day our daily bread;*
[12] *And forgive us our debts,*
    As we also have forgiven our debtors;
[13] *And lead us not into temptation,*
    But deliver us from evil."

Luke 11:2b–4 (§A37.2)
[1] He was praying in a certain place, and when he ceased, one of his disciples said to him, "Lord teach us to pray, as John taught his disciples." [2] And he said to them, "When you pray, say:
"Father, hallowed be thy name. Thy kingdom come. [3] *Give us each day our daily bread;* [4] *and forgive us our sins, for we ourselves forgive every one who is indebted to us; and lead us not into temptation."*

Did 8:2b–3 (§A37.3)
[2] And do not pray as the hypocrites, but as the Lord commanded in his Gospel, pray thus: *"Our Father, who are in Heaven, hallowed by thy Name, thy Kingdom come, thy will be done, as in Heaven so also upon earth; give us to-day our daily bread, and forgive us our debt as we forgive our debtors, and lead us not into trial, but deliver us from the Evil One, for thine is the power and the glory for ever."* [3] Pray thus three times a day.

GNaz 5 (§A37.4)
(5) In the so-called Gospel according to the Hebrews instead of "essential to existence" I found *"mahar,"* which means "of tomorrow," so that the sense is:
Our bread of tomorrow—that is, of the future—give us this day. (Jerome, *Commentary on Matthew* 1 [on Matthew 6:11])

★ See 415: *The Lord's Prayer*

71 TEMPTATION AND PERSECUTION★

Matt 6:13 (§A38.1)
[13] *"And lead us not into temptation,*
But deliver us from evil."

Luke 11:4b (§A38.2)
[4] *"and forgive us our sins, for we ourselves forgive every one who is indebted to us; and lead us not into temptation."*

ApJas 4:1b (§A38.3)
[1] And I answered and said to him: "Lord, we can obey you if you wish. For we have forsaken our fathers and our mothers and our villages and have followed you. *Grant us, [therefore], not to be tempted by the wicked devil."*
[2] The Lord answered and said: "What is your (pl.) merit when you do the will of the Father as if it had not been given to you by him as a gift, while you are tempted by Satan? [3] But if you are oppressed by Satan and are persecuted and you do his (i.e., the Father's) will, I [say] that he will love you and will make you equal with me and will consider that you have become [beloved] through his providence according to your free choice. [4] Will you not cease, then, being lovers of the flesh and being afraid of sufferings? [5] Or do you not know that you have not yet been mistreated and have not yet been accused unjustly, nor have you yet been shut up in prison, nor have you yet been condemned lawlessly, nor have you yet been crucified <without> reason, nor have you yet been buried <shamefully>, as (was) I myself, by the evil one? [6] Do you dare to spare the flesh, you for whom the spirit is an encircling wall? [7] If you contemplate the world, how long it is <before> you and also how long it is after you, you will find that your life is one single day and your sufferings, one single hour. [8] For the good (pl.) will not enter the world."

Did 8:2 (§A38.4)
[2] And do not pray as the hypocrites, but as the Lord commanded in his Gospel, pray thus: "Our Father, who are in Heaven, hallowed by thy Name, thy Kingdon come, thy will be done, as in Heaven so also upon earth; give us to-day our daily bread, and forgive us our debt as we forgive our debtors, and *lead us not into trial, but deliver us from the Evil One,* for thine is the power and the glory for ever."

★ See 327: *Temptation and Persecution*

72 FORGIVENESS FOR FORGIVENESS

Matt 6:14–15 (§A39.1)
[14] *"For if you forgive men their trespasses, your heavenly Father also will forgive you;* [15] *but if you do not forgive men their trespasses, neither will your Father forgive your trespasses."*

Mark 11:25 (§A39.2)
[20] As they passed by in the morning, they saw the fig tree withered away to its roots. [21] And Peter remembered and said to him, "Master, look! The fig tree which you cursed has withered." [22] And Jesus answered them, "Have faith in God. [23] Truly, I say to you, whoever says to this mountain, 'Be taken up and cast into the sea,' and does not doubt in his heart, but believes that what he says will come to pass, it will be done for him. [24] Therefore I tell you, whatever you ask in prayer, believe that you have received it, and it will be yours. [25] *And whenever you stand praying, forgive, if you have anything against any one; so that your Father also who is in heaven may forgive you your trespasses."*

Luke 6:37c (§A39.3)
[37] "Judge not, and you will not be judged; condemn not, and you will not be condemned; *forgive, and you will be forgiven;* [38] give, and it will be given to you; good measure, pressed down, shaken together, running over, will be put into your lap. For the measure you give will be the measure you get back."

1 Clem 13:2b (§A39.4)
[1] Let us, therefore, be humble-minded, brethren, putting aside all arrogance and conceit and foolishness and wrath, and let us do that which is written (for the Holy Spirit says, "Let not the wise man boast himself in his wisdom, nor the strong man in his strength, nor the rich man in his riches, but he that boasteth let him boast in the Lord, to seek him out and to do judgment and righteousness"), especially remembering the words of the Lord Jesus which he spoke when he was teaching gentleness and longsuffering. [2] For he spoke thus: "Be merciful, that ye may obtain mercy. *Forgive, that ye may be forgiven.* As ye do, so shall it be done unto you. As ye give, so shall it be given unto you. As ye judge, so shall ye be judged. As ye are kind, so shall kindness be shewn you. With what measure ye mete, it shall be measured to you."

Pol Phil 2:3c (§A39.5)
[2] Now "he who raised him" from the dead "will also raise us up" if we do his will, and walk in his commandments and love the things which he loved, refraining from all unrighteousness, covetousness, love of money, evil speaking, false witness, "rendering not evil for evil, or railing for railing," or blow for blow, or curse for curse, [3] but remembering what the Lord taught when he said, "Judge not that ye be not judged, *forgive and it shall be forgiven unto you,* be merciful that ye may obtain mercy, with what measure ye mete, it shall be measured to you again," and, "Blessed are the poor, and they who are persecuted for righteousness' sake, for theirs is the Kingdom of God."

Pol Phil 6:2a (§A39.6)
[2] *If then we pray the Lord to forgive us, we also ought to forgive,* for we stand before the eyes of the Lord and of God, and "we must all appear before the judgment seat of Christ, and each must give an account of himself."

73 ON FASTING

Matt 6:16–18 (§A40.1)
[16] *"And when you fast, do not look dismal, like the hypocrites, for they disfigure their faces that their fasting may be seen by men. Truly, I say to you, they have received their reward.* [17] *But when you fast, anoint your head and wash your face,* [18] *that your fasting may not be seen by men but by your Father who is in secret; and your Father who sees in secret will reward you."*

Did 8:1 (§A40.2)
[1] *Let not your fasts be with the hypocrites, for they fast on Mondays and Thursdays, but do you fast on Wednesdays, and Fridays.*

74   TREASURE IN HEAVEN

Matt 6:19–20 (§A41.1)
[19] *"Do not lay up for yourselves treasures on earth, where moth and rust consume and where thieves break in and steal,* [20] *but lay up for yourselves treasures in heaven, where neither moth nor rust consumes and where thieves do not break in and steal."*

Luke 12:33 (§A41.2)
[33] *"Sell your possessions, and give alms; provide yourselves with purses that do not grow old, with a treasure in the heavens that does not fail, where no thief approaches and no moth destroys."*

GThom 76:2 (§A41.3)
(76) [1] Jesus said, "The Kingdom of the Father is like a merchant who had a consignment of merchandise and who discovered a pearl. That merchant was shrewd. He sold the merchandise and bought the pearl alone for himself. [2] *You too, seek his unfailing and enduring treasure where no moth comes near to devour and no worm destroys."*

75   HEART AND TREASURE

Matt 6:21 (§A42.1)
[21] *"For where your treasure is, there will your heart be also."*

Luke 12:34 (§A42.2)
[34] *"For where your treasure is, there will your heart be also."*

76   THE BODY'S LIGHT★

Matt 6:22–23 (§A43.1)
[22] *"The eye is the lamp of the body. So, if your eye is sound, your whole body will be full of light;* [23] *but if your eye is not sound, your whole body will be full of darkness. If then the light in you is darkness, how great is the darkness!"*

★ See 381: *Jesus and Salome*

Luke 11:34–36 (§A43.2)
[34] *"Your eye is the lamp of your body; when your eye is sound, your whole body is full of light; but when it is not sound, your body is full of darkness.* [35] *Therefore be careful lest the light in you be darkness.* [36] *If then your whole body is full of light, having no part dark, it will be wholly bright, as when a lamp with its rays gives you light."*

DialSav 8 (§A43.3)
(8) The Savior [said], *"The lamp [of the body] is the mind. As long as [the things inside] you are set in order, that is, [...]..., your bodies are [luminous]. As long as your hearts are [dark], the luminosity you anticipate [...] I have...[...]...I will go...[...]...my word...[...] I send...[...]."*

77 SERVING TWO MASTERS

Matt 6:24 (§A44.1)

[24] "No one can serve two masters; for either he will hate the one and love the other, or he will be devoted to one and despise the other. You cannot serve God and mammon."

Luke 16:13 (§A44.2)

[13] "No servant can serve two masters; for either he will hate the one and love the other, or he will be devoted to the one and despise the other. You cannot serve God and mammon."

GThom 47:2 (§A44.3)

(47) [1] Jesus said, "It is impossible for a man to mount two horses or to stretch two bows. [2] And it is impossible for a servant to serve two masters; otherwise, he will honor the one and treat the other contemptuously. [3] No man drinks old wine and immediately desires to drink new wine. [4] And new wine is not put into old wineskins, lest they burst; nor is old wine put into a new wineskin, lest it spoil it. An old patch is not sewn onto a new garment, because a tear would result."

2 Clem 6:1,6 (§A44.4)

[1] And the Lord says:—"No servant can serve two masters." If we desire to serve both God and Mammon it is unprofitable to us, [2] "For what is the advantage if a man gain the whole world but lose his soul?" [3] Now the world that is, and the world to come are two enemies. [4] This world speaks of adultery, and corruption, and love of money, and deceit, but that world bids these things farewell. [5] We cannot then be the friends of both; but we must bid farewell to this world, to consort with that which is to come. [6] We reckon that it is better to hate the things which are here, for they are little, and short-lived, and corruptible, but to love the things which are there, the good things which are incorruptible.

78 AGAINST ANXIETIES

Matt 6:25–33 (§A45.1)

[25] "Therefore I tell you, do not be anxious about your life, what you shall eat or what you shall drink, nor about your body, what you shall put on. Is not life more than food, and the body more than clothing? [26] Look at the birds of the air: they neither sow nor reap nor gather into barns, and yet your heavenly Father feeds them. Are you not of more value than they? [27] And which of you by being anxious can add one cubit to his span of life? [28] And why are you anxious about clothing? Consider the lilies of the field, how they grow; they neither toil nor spin; [29] yet I tell you, even Solomon in all his glory was not arrayed like one of these. [30] But if God so clothes the grass of the field, which today is alive and tomorrow is thrown into the oven, will he not much more clothe you, O men of little faith? [31] Therefore do not be anxious, saying, 'What shall we eat?' or 'What shall we drink?' or 'What shall we wear?' [32] For the Gentiles seek all these things; and your heavenly Father knows that you need them all. [33] But seek first his kingdom and his righteousness, and all these things shall be yours as well."

Luke 12:22–31 (§A45.2)

[22] And he said to his disciples, "Therefore I tell you, do not be anxious about your life, what you shall eat, nor about your body, what you shall put on. [23] For life is more than food, and the body more than clothing. [24] Consider the ravens: they neither sow nor reap, they have neither storehouse nor barn, and yet God feeds them. Of how much more value are you than the birds! [25] And which of you by being anxious can add a cubit to his span of life? [26] If then you are not able to do as small a thing as that, why are you anxious about the rest? [27] Consider the lilies, how they grow; they neither toil nor spin; yet I tell you, even Solomon in all his glory was not arrayed like one of these. [28] But if God so clothes the grass which is alive in the field today and tomorrow is thrown into the oven, how much more will he clothe you, O men of little faith! [29] And do not seek what you are to eat and what you are to drink, nor be of anxious mind. [30] For all the nations of the world seek these things; and your Father knows that you need them. [31] Instead, seek his kingdom, and these things shall be yours as well."

POxy655 36 (§A45.3)

(36) [Jesus said, "Do not be concerned] from morning [until evening and] from evening [until] morning, neither [about] your [food] and what [you will] eat, [nor] about [your clothing] and what you [will] wear. [You are far] better than the [lilies] which [neither] card nor [spin]. As for you, when you have no garment, what [will you put on]? Who might add to your stature? He it is who will give you your cloak."

GThom 36 (§A45.4)

(36) Jesus said, "Do not be concerned from morning until evening and from evening until morning about what you will wear."

79 TOMORROW'S ANXIETY

Matt 6:34a (§A46)
[34] *"Therefore do not be anxious about tomorrow, for tomorrow will be anxious for itself.* Let the day's own trouble be sufficient for the day."

80 THE DAY'S EVIL

Matt 6:34b (§A47.1)
[34] "Therefore do not be anxious about tomorrow, for tomorrow will be anxious for itself. *Let the day's own trouble be sufficient for the day."*

DialSav 53a (§A47.2)
(53) Mary said, "Thus with respect to 'the wickedness of each day,' and 'the laborer is worthy of his food,' and 'the disciple resembles his teacher.'" She uttered this as a woman who had understood completely.

81 JUDGMENT FOR JUDGMENT

Matt 7:1–2a (§A48.1)
[1] *"Judge not, that you be not judged.* [2] *For with the judgment you pronounce you will be judged,* and the measure you give will be the measure you get."

Luke 6:37a (§A48.2)
[37] *"Judge not, and you will not be judged;* condemn not, and you will not be condemned; forgive, and you will be forgiven; [38] give, and it will be given to you; good measure, pressed down, shaken together, running over, will be put into your lap. For the measure you give will be the measure you get back."

1 Clem 13:2e (§A48.3)
[2] For he spoke thus: "Be merciful, that ye may obtain mercy. Forgive, that ye may be forgiven. As ye do, so shall it be done unto you. As ye give, so shall it be given unto you. *As ye judge, so shall ye be judged.* As ye are kind, so shall kindness be shewn you. With what measure ye mete, it shall be measured to you."

Pol Phil 2:3b (§A48.4)
[2] Now "he who raised him" from the dead "will also raise us up" if we do his will, and walk in his commandments and love the things which he loved, refraining from all unrighteousness, covetousness, love of money, evil speaking, false witness, "rendering not evil for evil, or railing for railing," or blow for blow, or curse for curse, [3] but remembering what the Lord taught when he said, *"Judge not that ye be not judged,* forgive and it shall be forgiven unto you, be merciful that ye may obtain mercy, with what measure ye mete, it shall be measured to you again," and, "Blessed are the poor, and they who are persecuted for righteousness' sake, for theirs is the Kingdom of God."

82 MEASURE FOR MEASURE

Matt 7:2b (§A49.1)
[1] "Judge not, that you be not judged. [2] For with the judgment you pronounce you will be judged, and *the measure you give will be the measure you get."*

Mark 4:24b (§A49.2)
[24] And he said to them, "Take heed what you hear; *the measure you give will be the measure you get, and still more will be given you.* [25] For to him who has will more be given; and from him who has not, even what he has will be taken away."

Luke 6:38c (§A49.3)
[37] "Judge not, and you will not be judged; condemn not, and you will not be condemned; forgive, and you will be forgiven; [38] give, and it will be given to you; good measure, pressed down, shaken together, running over, will be put into your lap. *For the measure you give will be the measure you get back."*

1 Clem 13:2g (§A49.4)
[1] Let us, therefore, be humble-minded, brethren, putting aside all arrogance and conceit and foolishness and wrath, and let us do that which is written (for the Holy Spirit says, "Let not the wise man boast himself in his wisdom, nor the strong man in his strength, nor the rich man in his riches, but he that boasteth let him boast in the Lord, to seek him out and to do judgment and righteousness"), especially remembering the words of the Lord Jesus which he spoke when he was teaching gentleness and longsuffering. [2] For he spoke thus: "Be merciful, that ye may obtain mercy. Forgive, that ye may be forgiven. As ye do, so shall it be done unto you. As ye give, so shall it be given unto you. As ye judge, so shall ye be judged. As ye are kind, so shall kindness be shewn you. *With what measure ye mete, it shall be measured to you."*

Pol Phil 2:3e (§A49.5)
[2] Now "he who raised him" from the dead "will also raise us up" if we do his will, and walk in his commandments and love the things which he loved, refraining from all unrighteousness, covetousness, love of money, evil speaking, false witness, "rendering not evil for evil, or railing for railing," or blow for blow, or curse for curse, [3] but remembering what the Lord taught when he said, "Judge not that ye be not judged, forgive and it shall be forgiven unto you, be merciful that ye may obtain mercy, *with what measure ye mete, it shall be measured to you again,"* and, "Blessed are the poor, and they who are persecuted for righteousness' sake, for theirs is the Kingdom of God."

83 SPECK AND LOG

Matt 7:3–5 (§A50.1)
[3] *"Why do you see the speck that is in your brother's eye, but do not notice the log that is in your own eye? [4] Or how can you say to your brother, 'Let me take the speck out of your eye,' when there is the log in your own eye? [5] You hypocrite, first take the log out of your own eye, and then you will see clearly to take the speck out of your brother's eye."*

Luke 6:41–42 (§A50.2)
[41] *"Why do you see the speck that is in your brother's eye, but do not notice the log that is in your own eye? [42] Or how can you say to your brother, 'Brother, let me take out the speck that is in your eye,' when you yourself do not see the log that is in your own eye? You hypocrite, first take the log out of your own eye, and then you will see clearly to take out the speck that is in your brother's eye."*

POxy1 26 (§A50.3)
(26) *[. . .] and then you (sg.) will see clearly to cast the mote from your (sg.) brother's eye.*

GThom 26 (§A50.4)
(26) Jesus said, *"You see the mote in your brother's eye, but you do not see the beam in your own eye. When you cast the beam out of your own eye, then you will see clearly to cast the mote from your brother's eye."*

84 DOGS AND SWINE

Matt 7:6 (§A51.1)
[6] *"Do not give dogs what is holy; and do not throw your pearls before swine, lest they trample them under foot and turn to attack you."*

GThom 93 (§A51.2)
(93) <Jesus said,> *"Do not give what is holy to dogs, lest they throw them on the dung-heap. Do not throw the pearls to swine, lest they grind it [to bits]."*

Did 9:5b (§A51.3)
[5] But let none eat or drink of your Eucharist except those who have been baptised in the Lord's Name. For concerning this also did the Lord say, *"Give not that which is holy to the dogs."*

The first page of the *Gospel of Thomas* from
the Nag Hammadi Codices. Photograph
courtesy of the Institute for Antiquity and
Christianity, Claremont, California.

Matt 7:7–8 (§A52.1)

[7] *"Ask, and it will be given you; seek, and you will find; knock, and it will be opened to you. [8] For every one who asks receives, and he who seeks finds, and to him who knocks it will be opened."*

Matt 21:22 (§A52.2)

[20] When the disciples saw it they marveled, saying, "How did the fig tree wither at once?" [21] And Jesus answered them, "Truly, I say to you, if you have faith and never doubt, you will not only do what has been done to the fig tree, but even if you say to this mountain, 'Be taken up and cast into the sea,' it will be done. [22] *And whatever you ask in prayer, you will receive, if you have faith."*

Mark 11:24 (§A52.3)

[20] As they passed by in the morning, they saw the fig tree withered away to its roots. [21] And Peter remembered and said to him, "Master, look! The fig tree which you cursed has withered." [22] And Jesus answered them, "Have faith in God. [23] Truly, I say to you, whoever says to this mountain, 'Be taken up and cast into the sea,' and does not doubt in his heart, but believes that what he says will come to pass, it will be done for him. [24] *Therefore I tell you, whatever you ask in prayer, believe that you have received it, and it will be yours.* [25] And whenever you stand praying, forgive, if you have anything against any one; so that your Father also who is in heaven may forgive you your trespasses."

Luke 11:9–10 (§A52.4)

[9] "And I tell you, *Ask, and it will be given you; seek, and you will find; knock, and it will be opened to you. [10] For every one who asks receives, and he who seeks finds, and to him who knocks it will be opened."*

* See 328: *Ask, Seek, Knock*

John 14:13 (§A52.5)

[12] "Truly, truly, I say to you, he who believes in me will also do the works that I do; and greater works than these will he do, because I go to the Father. [13] *Whatever you ask in my name, I will do it, that the Father may be glorified in the Son; [14] if you ask anything in my name, I will do it."*

John 15:7 (§A52.6)

[1] "I am the true vine, and my Father is the vinedresser. [2] Every branch of mine that bears no fruit, he takes away, and every branch that does bear fruit he prunes, that it may bear more fruit. [3] You are already made clean by the word which I have spoken to you. [4] Abide in me, and I in you. As the branch cannot bear fruit by itself, unless it abides in the vine, neither can you, unless you abide in me. [5] I am the vine, you are the branches. He who abides in me, and I in him, he it is that bears much fruit, for apart from me you can do nothing. [6] If a man does not abide in me, he is cast forth as a branch and withers; and the branches are gathered, thrown into the fire and burned. [7] *If you abide in me, and my words abide in you, ask whatever you will, and it shall be done for you."*

John 15:16b (§A52.7)

[12] "This is my commandment, that you love one another as I have loved you. [13] Greater love has no man than this, that a man lay down his life for his friends. [14] You are my friends if you do what I command you. [15] No longer do I call you servants, for the servant does not know what his master is doing; but I have called you friends, for all that I have heard from my Father I have made known to you. [16] You did not choose me, but I chose you and appointed you that you should go and bear fruit and that your fruit should abide; so that *whatever you ask the Father in my name, he may give it to you.* [17] This I command you, to love one another."

John 16:23-24,26a (§A52.8)

[20]"Truly, truly, I say to you, you will weep and lament, but the world will rejoice; you will be sorrowful, but your sorrow will turn into joy. [21] When a woman is in travail she has sorrow, because her hour has come; but when she is delivered of the child, she no longer remembers the anguish, for joy that a child is born into the world. [22] So you have sorrow now, but I will see you again and your hearts will rejoice, and no one will take your joy from you. [23] *In that day you will ask nothing of me. Truly, truly, I say to you, if you ask anything of the Father, he will give it to you in my name.* [24] *Hitherto you have asked nothing in my name; ask, and you will receive, that your joy may be full.*

[25] "I have said this to you in figures; the hour is coming when I shall no longer speak to you in figures but tell you plainly of the Father. [26] *In that day you will ask in my name;* and I do not say to you that I shall pray the Father for you; [27] for the Father himself loves you, because you have loved me and have believed that I came from the Father. [28] I came from the Father and have come into the world; again, I am leaving the world and going to the Father."

POxy654 2 (§A52.9)

(2) [Jesus said], *"Let him who seeks continue [seeking until] he finds. When he finds, [he will be amazed. And] when he becomes [amazed], he will rule. And [once he has ruled], he will [attain rest]."*

GThom 2 (§A52.10)

(2) Jesus said, *"Let him who seeks continue seeking until he finds. When he finds, he will become troubled. When he becomes troubled, he will be astonished, and he will rule over the All."*

GThom 92:1 (§A52.11)

(92) [1] Jesus said, *"Seek and you will find.* [2] Yet, what you asked Me about in former times and which I did not tell you then, now I do desire to tell, but you do not inquire after it."

GThom 94 (§A52.12)

(94) Jesus [said], *"He who seeks will find, and [he who knocks] will be let in."*

DialSav 9-10 (§A52.13)

(9) *His [disciples said, "Lord], who is it who seeks, and [. . .] reveals?"*

(10) *[The Lord said . . .], "He who seeks [. . .] reveals . . .[. . .]."*

(11) [Matthew said, "Lord, when] I [. . .] and [when] I speak, who is it who . . .[. . .] . . . who listens?"

(12) [The Lord] said, "it is the one who speaks who also [listens], and it is the one who can see who also reveals."

DialSav 20c (§A52.14)

(19) And Matthew [asked him] [. . .]. . . took . . . [. . .]. . . it is he who . . . [. . .]."

(20) The Lord [said], "[. . . stronger] than . . . [. . .]. . . you . . . [. . .]. . .[. . .]. . . to follow [you] and all the works [. . .] your hearts. For just as your hearts [. . .], so [. . .] the means to overcome the powers [above] as well as those below [. . .]. I say to you, let him [who possesses] power renounce [it and repent]. *And [let] him who [. . .] seek and find and [rejoice]."*

GHeb 4a (§A52.15)

(4a) As also it stands written in the Gospel of the Hebrews:

He that marvels shall reign, and he that has reigned shall rest. (Clement, *Stromateis* 2.9.45.5)

GHeb 4b (§A52.16)

(4b) To those words (from Plato, *Timaeus* 90) this is equivalent:

He that seeks will not rest until he finds; and he that has found shall marvel; and he that has marvelled shall reign; and he that has reigned shall rest. (Clement, *Stromateis* 5.14.96.3)

86 GOOD GIFTS

Matt 7:9–11 (§A53.1)
[9] *"Or what man of you, if his son asks him for bread, will give him a stone?* [10] *Or if he asks for a fish, will give him a serpent?* [11] *If you then, who are evil, know how to give good gifts to your children, how much more will your Father who is in heaven give good things to those who ask him!"*

Luke 11:11–13 (§A53.2)
[11] *"What father among you, if his son asks for a fish, will instead of a fish give him a serpent;* [12] *or if he asks for an egg, will give him a scorpion?* [13] *If you then, who are evil, know how to give good gifts to your children, how much more will the heavenly Father give the Holy Spirit to those who ask him!"*

87 THE GOLDEN RULE

Matt 7:12 (§A54.1)
[12] *"So whatever you wish that men would do to you, do so to them;* for this is the law and the prophets."

Luke 6:31 (§A54.2)
[31] *"And as you wish that men would do to you, do so to them."*

Acts 15:20, 29 (§A54.3)*
[13] After they finished speaking, James replied, "Brethren, listen to me. [14] Simeon has related how God first visited the Gentiles, to take out of them a people for his name. [15] And with this the words of the prophets agree, as it is written,
[16] 'After this I will return,
and I will rebuild the dwelling of David,
    which has fallen;
I will rebuild its ruins,
and I will set it up,
[17] that the rest of men may seek the Lord,
and all the Gentiles who are called by my
    name,
[18] says the Lord, who has made these
    things known from of old.'
[19] Therefore my judgment is that we should not trouble those of the Gentiles who turn to God, [20] but should write to them to abstain from the pollutions of idols and from unchastity and from what is strangled and from blood.* [21] For from early generations Moses has had in every city those who preach him, for he is read every sabbath in the synagogues."

[22] Then it seemed good to the apostles and the elders, with the whole church, to choose men from among them and send them to Antioch with Paul and Barnabas. They sent Judas called Barsabbas, and Silas, leading men among the brethren, [23] with the following letter: "The brethren, both the apostles and the elders, to the brethren who are of the Gentiles in Antioch and Syria, and Cilicia, greeting. [24] Since we have heard that some persons from us have troubled you with words, unsettling your minds, although we gave them no instructions, [25] it has seemed good to us, having come to one accord, to choose men and send them to you with our beloved Barnabas and Paul, [26] men who have risked their lives for the sake of our Lord Jesus Christ. [27] We have therefore sent Judas and Silas, who themselves will tell you the same things by word of mouth. [28] For it has seemed good to the Holy Spirit and to us to lay upon you no greater burden than these necessary things: [29] that you abstain from what has been sacrificed to idols and from blood and from what is strangled and from unchastity.* If you keep yourselves from these, you will do well. Farewell."

*The Western text omits "what is strangled" and adds *"and whatsoever you do not wish done to yourselves, do not do to others"* as the conclusion of 15:20 and 15:29a.

POxy654 6:2b (§A54.4)
(6) [1] [His disciples] questioned him [and said], "How [shall we] fast? [How shall we pray]? How [shall we give alms]? What [diet] shall [we] observe?"
[2] Jesus said, "[Do not tell lies, [3] and] *do not do what you [hate,* for all things are plain in the sight] of truth. [4] [For nothing] hidden [will not become manifest]."

GThom 6:2b (§A54.5)
(6) [1] His disciples questioned Him and said to Him, "Do You want us to fast? How shall we pray? Shall we give alms? What diet shall we observe?"
[2] Jesus said, "Do not tell lies, [3] and *do not do what you hate,* for all things are plain in the sight of Heaven. [4] For nothing hidden will not become manifest, and nothing covered will remain without being uncovered."

Did 1:2b (§A54.6)
[1] There are two Ways, one of Life and one of Death, and there is a great difference between the two Ways.
[2] The Way of Life is this: "First, thou shalt love the God who made thee, secondly, thy neighbour as thyself; and *whatsoever thou wouldst not have done to thyself, do not thou to another."*

88 THE NARROW DOOR*

Matt 7:13-14 (§A55.1)
[13] *"Enter by the narrow gate; for the gate is wide and the way is easy, that leads to destruction, and those who enter by it are many.* [14] *For the gate is narrow and the way is hard, that leads to life, and those who find it are few."*

* See 416: *The Narrow Door*

Luke 13:24 (§A55.2)
[22] He went on his way through towns and villages, teaching, and journeying toward Jerusalem. [23] And some one said to him, "Lord, will those who are saved be few?" And he said to them, [24] *"Strive to enter by the narrow door; for many, I tell you, will seek to enter and will not be able."*

89 IN SHEEP'S CLOTHING

Matt 7:15 (§A56)
[15] *"Beware of false prophets, who come to you in sheep's clothing but inwardly are ravenous wolves."*

90 TREES AND HEARTS

Matt 7:16-20 (§A57.1)
[16] *"You will know them by their fruits. Are grapes gathered from thorns, or figs from thistles?* [17] *So, every sound tree bears good fruit, but the bad tree bears evil fruit.* [18] *A sound tree cannot bear evil fruit, nor can a bad tree bear good fruit.* [19] *Every tree that does not bear good fruit is cut down and thrown into the fire.* [20] *Thus you will know them by their fruits."*

Matt 12:31-35 (§A57.2)
[31] "Therefore I tell you, every sin and blasphemy will be forgiven men, but the blasphemy against the Spirit will not be forgiven. [32] And whoever says a word against the Son of man will be forgiven, but whoever speaks against the Holy Spirit will not be forgiven, either in this age or in the age to come. [33] *Either make the tree good, and its fruit good; or make the tree bad, and its fruit bad; for the tree is known by its fruit.* [34] *You brood of vipers! how can you speak good, when you are evil? For out of the abundance of the heart the mouth speaks.* [35] *The good man out of his good treasure brings forth good, and the evil man out of his evil treasure brings forth evil."*

Luke 6:43-45 (§A57.3)
[43] *"For no good tree bears bad fruit, nor again does a bad tree bear good fruit;* [44] *for each tree is known by its own fruit. For figs are not gathered from thorns, nor are grapes picked from a bramble bush.* [45] *The good man out of the good treasure of his heart produces good, and the evil man out of his evil treasure produces evil; for out of the abundance of the heart his mouth speaks."*

GThom 45 (§A57.4)
(45) [1] Jesus said, *"Grapes are not harvested from thorns, nor are figs gathered from thistles, for they do not produce fruit.* [2] *A good man brings forth good from his storehouse; an evil man brings forth evil things from his evil storehouse, which is in his heart, and says evil things.* [3] *For out of the abundance of the heart he brings forth evil things."*

Ign Eph 14:2b (§A57.5)
[2] No man who professes faith sins, nor does he hate who has obtained love. *"The tree is known by its fruits"*: so they who profess to be of Christ shall be seen by their deeds. For the "deed" is not in present profession, but is shown by the power of faith, if a man continue to the end.

INVOCATION WITHOUT OBEDIENCE*

Matt 7:21 (§A58.1)

²¹ *"Not every one who says to me, 'Lord, Lord,' shall enter the kingdom of heaven, but he who does the will of my Father who is in heaven."*

Luke 6:46 (§A58.2)

⁴⁶ *"Why do you call me 'Lord, Lord,' and not do what I tell you?"*

PEger2 3 (§A58.3)

(3) . . . [ca]me to him to put him to the pro[of] and to tempt him, whilst [they said]: "Master Jesus, we know that thou art come [from God], for what thou doest bears a tes-t[imony] (to thee which goes) beyond (that) of all the prophets. [Wherefore tell] us: is it admissible [to p]ay to the kings the (charges) appertaining to their rule? [Should we] pay [th]em or not?" But Jesus saw through their [in]tention, became [angry] and said to them: *"Why call ye me*

with yo[ur mou]th Master and yet [do] not what I say? Well has Is[aiah] prophesied [concerning y]ou saying: This [people honours] me with the[ir li]ps but their heart is far from me; [their worship is] vain. [They teach] precepts [of men]." (Fragment 2, recto [lines 43–59])

2 Clem 3:4a (§A58.4)

¹Seeing, then, that he has shewn such mercy towards us, first that we who are living do not sacrifice to the dead gods, and do not worship them, but through him know the father of truth, what is the true knowledge concerning him except that we should not deny him through whom we knew him? ²And he himself also says, "Whosoever confessed me before men, I will confess him before my Father"; ³this then is our reward, if we confess him through whom we were saved. ⁴But how do we confess him? *By doing what he says,*

and not disregarding his commandments, and honouring him not only with our lips, but "with all our heart and all our mind." ⁵And he says also in Isaiah, "This people honoureth me with their lips, but their heart is far from me."

2 Clem 4:2 (§A58.5)

¹Le us, then, not merely call him Lord, for this will not save us. ²For he says, *"Not everyone that saith to me Lord, Lord, shall be saved, but he that doeth righteousness."* ³So then, brethren, let us confess him in our deeds, by loving one another, by not committing adultery, nor speaking one against another, nor being jealous, but by being self-controlled, merciful, good; and we ought to sympathise with each other, and not to be lovers of money. By these deeds we confess him, and not by the opposite kind.

* See 417: *Invocation Without Obedience*

DEPART FROM ME

Matt 7:22–23 (§A59.1)

²² *"On that day many will say to me, 'Lord, Lord, did we not prophesy in your name, and cast out demons in your name, and do many mighty works in your name?' ²³ And then will I declare to them, 'I never knew you; depart from me, you evildoers.'"*

Luke 13:26–27 (§A59.2)

²⁶ *"Then you will begin to say, 'We ate and drank in your presence, and you taught in our streets.' ²⁷ But he will say, 'I tell you, I do not know where you come from; depart from me, all you workers of iniquity!'"*

2 Clem 4:5b (§A59.3)

⁴And we must not fear men rather than God. ⁵*For this reason, if you do these things, the Lord said, "If ye be gathered together with me in my bosom, and do not my commandments, I will cast you out, and will say to you, Depart from me, I know not whence ye are, ye workers of iniquity."*

GNaz 6 (§A59.4)

(6) The Jewish Gospel reads here as follows:

If ye be in my bosom and do not the will of my Father in heaven, I will cast you out of my bosom. (Variant to Matthew 7:5—or better to Matthew 7:21–23—in the "Zion Gospel" Edition)

93 ROCK OR SAND

Matt 7:24–27 (§A60.1)

²⁴"*Every one then who hears these words of mine and does them will be like a wise man who built his house upon the rock;* ²⁵*and the rain fell, and the floods came, and the winds blew and beat upon that house, but it did not fall, because it had been founded on the rock.* ²⁶*And every one who hears these words of mine and does not do them will be like a foolish man who built his house upon the sand;* ²⁷*and the rain fell, and the floods came, and the wind blew and beat against that house, and it fell; and great was the fall of it.*"

Luke 6:47–49 (§A60.2)

⁴⁷"*Every one who comes to me and hears my words and does them, I will show you what he is like:* ⁴⁸*he is like a man building a house, who dug deep, and laid the foundation upon rock; and when a flood arose, the stream broke against that house, and could not shake it, because it had been well built.* ⁴⁹*But he who hears and does not do them is like a man who built a house on the ground without a foundation; against which the stream broke, and immediately it fell, and the ruin of that house was great.*"

94 PATRIARCHS AND GENTILES*

Matt 8:11–12 (§A61.1)

⁵As he entered Capernaum, a centurion came forward to him, beseeching him ⁶and saying, "Lord, my servant is lying paralyzed at home, in terrible distress." ⁷And he said to him, "I will come and heal him." ⁸But the centurion answered him, "Lord, I am not worthy to have you come under my roof; but only say the word, and my servant will be healed. ⁹For I am a man under authority, with soldiers under me; and I say to one, 'Go,' and he goes, and to another, 'Come,' and he comes, and to my slave, 'Do this,' and he does it." ¹⁰When Jesus heard him, he marveled, and said to those who followed him, "Truly, I say to you, not even in Israel have I found such faith. ¹¹*I tell you, many will come from east and west and sit at table with Abraham, Isaac, and Jacob in the kingdom of heaven,* ¹²*while the sons of the kingdom will be thrown into the outer darkness; there men will weep and gnash their teeth.*" ¹³And to the centurion Jesus said, "Go; be it done for you as you have believed." And the servant was healed at that very moment.

Luke 13:28–29 (§A61.2)

²²He went on his way through towns and villages, teaching, and journeying toward Jerusalem. ²³And some one said to him, "Lord, will those who are saved be few?" And he said to them, ²⁴"Strive to enter by the narrow door; for many, I tell you, will seek to enter and will not be able. ²⁵When once the householder has risen up and shut the door, you will begin to stand outside and to knock at the door, saying, 'Lord, open to us.' He will answer you, 'I do not know where you come from.' ²⁶Then you will begin to say, 'We ate and drank in your presence, and you taught in our streets.' ²⁷But he will say, 'I tell you, I do not know where you come from; depart from me, all you workers of iniquity!' ²⁸*There you will weep and gnash your teeth, when you see Abraham and Isaac and Jacob and all the prophets in the kingdom of God and you yourselves thrust out.* ²⁹*And men will come from east and west, and from north and south, and sit at table in the kingdom of God.*"

2 Esdr 1:33–39a (§A61.3)

²⁸"Thus says the Lord Almighty: Have I not entreated you as a father entreats his sons or a mother her daughters or a nurse her children, ²⁹that you should be my people and I should be your God, and that you should be my sons and I should be your father? ³⁰I gathered you as a hen gathers her brood under her wings. But now, what shall I do to you? I will cast you out from my presence. ³¹When you offer oblations to me, I will turn my face from you; for I have rejected your feast days, and new moons, and curcuscisions of the flesh. ³²I sent to you my servants the prophets, but you have taken and slain them and torn their bodies in pieces; their blood I will require of you, says the Lord.

³³"*Thus says the Lord Almighty: Your house is desolate; I will drive you out as the wind drives straw;* ³⁴*and your sons will have no children, because with you they have neglected my commandment and have done what is evil in my sight.* ³⁵*I will give your houses to a people that will come, who without having heard me will believe. Those to whom I have shown no signs will do what I have commanded.* ³⁶*They have seen no prophets, yet will recall their former state.* ³⁷*I call to witness the gratitude of the people that is to come, whose children rejoice with gladness; though they do not see me with bodily eyes, yet with the spirit they will believe the things I have said.*

³⁸"*And now, father, look with pride and see the people coming from the east;* ³⁹*to them I will give as leaders Abraham, Isaac, and Jacob* and Hose'a and Amos and Micah and Jo'el and Obadi'ah and Jonah ⁴⁰and Nahum and Habak'kuk, Zephani'ah, Haggai, Zechariah and Mal'achi, who is also called the Messenger of the Lord."

* See 419: *Patriarchs and Gentiles*

Matt 8:12b (§A62.1)

[5] As he entered Capernaum, a centurion came forward to him, beseeching him [6] and saying, "Lord, my servant is lying paralyzed at home, in terrible distress." [7] And he said to him, "I will come and heal him." [8] But the centurion answered him, "Lord, I am not worthy to have you come under my roof; but only say the word, and my servant will be healed. [9] For I am a man under authority, with soldiers under me; and I say to one, 'Go,' and he goes, and to another, 'Come,' and he comes, and to my slave, 'Do this,' and he does it." [10] When Jesus heard him, he marveled, and said to those who followed him, "Truly, I say to you, not even in Israel have I found such faith. [11] I tell you, many will come from east and west and sit at table with Abraham, Isaac, and Jacob in the kingdom of heaven, [12] while the sons of the kingdom will be thrown into the outer darkness; *there men will weep and gnash their teeth.*" [13] And to the centurion Jesus said, "Go; be it done for you as you have believed." And the servant was healed at that very moment.

Matt 13:42b (§A62.2)

[36] Then he left the crowds and went into the house. And his disciples came to him, saying, "Explain to us the parable of the weeds of the field." [37] He answered, "He who sows the good seed is the Son of man; [38] the field is the world, and the good seed means the sons of the kingdom; the weeds are the sons of the evil one, [39] and the enemy who sowed them is the devil; the harvest is the close of the age, and the reapers are angels. [40] Just as the weeds are gathered and burned with fire, so will it be at the close of the age. [41] The Son of man will send his angels, and they will gather out of his kingdom all causes of sin and all evildoers, [42] and throw them into the furnace of fire; *there men will weep and gnash their teeth.* [43] Then the righteous will shine like the sun in the kingdom of their Father. He who has ears, let him hear."

Matt 13:50b (§A62.3)

[47] "Again, the kingdom of heaven is like a net which was thrown into the sea and gathered fish of every kind; [48] when it was full, men drew it ashore and sat down and sorted the good into vessels but threw away the bad. [49] So it will be at the close of the age. The angels will come out and separate the evil from the righteous, [50] and throw them into the furnace of fire; *there men will weep and gnash their teeth.*"

Matt 22:13b (§A62.4)

[1] And again Jesus spoke to them in parables, saying, [2] "The kingdom of heaven may be compared to a king who gave a marriage feast for his son, [3] and sent his servants to call those who were invited to the marriage feast; but they would not come. [4] Again he sent other servants, saying, 'Tell those who are invited, Behold, I have made ready my dinner, my oxen and my fat calves are killed, and everything is ready; come to the marriage feast.' [5] But they made light of it and went off, one to his farm, another to his business, [6] while the rest seized his servants, treated them shamefully, and killed them. [7] The king was angry, and he sent his troops and destroyed those murderers and burned their city. [8] Then he said to his servants, 'The wedding is ready, but those invited were not worthy. [9] Go therefore to the thoroughfares, and invite to the marriage feast as many as you find.' [10] And those servants went out into the streets and gathered all whom they found, both bad and good; so the wedding hall was filled with guests.

[11] "But when the king came in to look at the guests, he saw there a man who had no wedding garment; [12] and he said to him, 'Friend, how did you get in here without a wedding garment?' And he was speechless. [13] Then the king said to the attendants, 'Bind him hand and foot, and cast him into the outer darkness; *there men will weep and gnash their teeth.*' [14] For many are called, but few are chosen."

Matt 24:51b (§A62.5)

[45] "Who then is the faithful and wise servant, whom his master has set over his household, to give them their food at the proper time? [46] Blessed is that servant whom his master when he comes will find so doing. [47] Truly, I say to you, he will set him over all his possessions. [48] But if that wicked servant says to himself, 'My master is delayed,' [49] and begins to beat his fellow servants, and eats and drinks with the drunken, [50] the master of that servant will come on a day when he does not expect him and at an hour he does not know, [51] and will punish him, and put him with the hypocrites; *there men will weep and gnash their teeth.*"

Matt 25:30b (§A62.6)

14 "For it will be as when a man going on a journey called his servants and entrusted to them his property; 15 to one he gave five talents, to another two, to another one, to each according to his ability. Then he went away. 16 He who had received the five talents went at once and traded with them; and he made five talents more. 17 So also, he who had the two talents made two talents more. 18 But he who had received the one talent went and dug in the ground and hid his master's money. 19 Now after a long time the master of those servants came and settled accounts with them. 20 And he who had received the five talents came forward, bringing five talents more, saying, 'Master, you delivered to me five talents; here I have made five talents more.' 21 His master said to him, 'Well done, good and faithful servant; you have been faithful over a little, I will set you over much; enter into the joy of your master.' 22 And he also who had the two talents came forward, saying, 'Master, you delivered to me two talents; here I have made two talents more.' 23 His master said to him, 'Well done, good and faithful servant; you have been faithful over a little, I will set you over much; enter into the joy of your master.' 24 He also who had received the one talent came forward, saying, 'Master, I knew you to be a hard man, reaping where you did not sow, and gathering where you did not winnow; 25 so I was afraid, and I went and hid your talent in the ground. Here you have what is yours.' 26 But his master answered him, 'You wicked and slothful servant! You knew that I reap where I have not sowed, and gather where I have not winnowed? 27 Then you ought to have invested my money with the bankers, and at my coming I should have received what was my own with interest. 28 So take the talent from him, and give it to him who has the ten talents. 29 For to every one who has will more be given, and he will have abundance; but from him who has not, even what he has will be taken away. 30 And cast the worthless servant into the outer darkness; *there men will weep and gnash their teeth.'"*

Luke 13:28a (§A62.7)

22 He went on his way through towns and villages, teaching, and journeying toward Jerusalem. 23 And some one said to him, "Lord, will those who are saved be few?" And he said to them, 24 "Strive to enter by the narrow door; for many, I tell you, will seek to enter and will not be able. 25 When once the householder has risen up and shut the door, you will begin to stand outside and to knock at the door, saying, 'Lord, open to us.' He will answer you, 'I do not know where you come from.' 26 Then you will begin to say, 'We ate and drank in your presence, and you taught in our streets.' 27 But he will say, 'I tell you, I do not know where you come from; depart from me, all you workers of iniquity!' 28 *There you will weep and gnash your teeth,* when you see Abraham and Isaac and Jacob and all the prophets in the kingdom of God and you yourselves thrust out. 29 And men will come from east and west, and from north and south, and sit at table in the kingdom of God. 30 And behold, some are last who will be first, and some are first who will be last."

DialSav 14e (§A62.8)

(13) [Mary] said, "Lord, behold! Whence [. . .]. . . the body [while I] weep, and whence while I [. . .]?"

(14) The Lord said, "[. . .] weep on account of its works [. . .] remain and the mind laughs [. . .]. . .[. . .] [. . .]. . . spirit. If one does not [. . .] darkness, he will be able to see [. . .]. So I tell you [. . .] light is the darkness [. . .]. . . stand in [. . .] not see the light [. . .] the lie [. . .]. . . they brought them from [. . .]. . .[. . .]. . . . You will give [. . .]. . . and [. . . exist] forever. [. . .]. . . [. . .]. . . [. . .] ever. Then [all] the powers which are above as well as those [below] will [. . .] you. *In that place [there will] be weeping and [gnashing] of teeth over the end of [all] these things.*"

★ See 329: *Gnashing of Teeth*

96 FOXES HAVE HOLES*

Matt 8:20 (§A63.1)
[18] Now when Jesus saw great crowds around him, he gave orders to go over to the other side. [19] And a scribe came up and said to him, "Teacher, I will follow you wherever you go." [20] And Jesus said to him, *"Foxes have holes, and birds of the air have nests; but the Son of man has nowhere to lay his head."*

Luke 9:58 (§A63.2)
[57] As they were going along the road, a man said to him, "I will follow you wherever you go." [58] And Jesus said to him, *"Foxes have holes, and birds of the air have nests; but the Son of man has nowhere to lay his head."*

GThom 86 (§A63.3)
(86) Jesus said, *"[The foxes have their holes] and the birds have [their] nests, but the Son of Man has no place to lay his head and rest."*

* See 420: *Foxes Have Holes*

---

97 RIGHTEOUS AND SINNERS*

Matt 9:13b (§A64.1)
[9] As Jesus passed on from there, he saw a man called Matthew sitting at the tax office; and he said to him, "Follow me." And he rose and followed him.
[10] And as he sat at table in the house, behold, many tax collectors and sinners came and sat down with Jesus and his disciples. [11] And when the Pharisees saw this, they said to his disciples, "Why does your teacher eat with tax collectors and sinners?" [12] But when he heard it, he said, "Those who are well have no need of a physician, but those who are sick. [13] Go and learn what this means, 'I desire mercy, and not sacrifice.' *For I came not to call the righteous, but sinners."*

Mark 2:17b (§A64.2)
[13] He went out again beside the sea; and all the crowd gathered about him, and he taught them. [14] And as he passed on, he saw Levi the son of Alphaeus sitting at the tax office, and he said to him, "Follow me." And he rose and followed him.
[15] And as he sat at table in his house, many tax collectors and sinners were sitting with Jesus and his disciples; for there were many who followed him. [16] And the scribes of the Pharisees, when they saw that he was eating with sinners and tax collectors, said to his disciples, "Why does he eat with tax collectors and sinners?" [17] And when Jesus heard it, he said to them, "Those who are well have no need of a physician, but those who are sick; *I came not to call the righteous, but sinners."*

Luke 5:32 (§A64.3)
[27] After this he went out, and saw a tax collector, named Levi, sitting at the tax office; and he said to him, "Follow me." [28] And he left everything, and rose and followed him.
[29] And Levi made him a great feast in his house; and there was a large company of tax collectors and others sitting at table with them. [30] And the Pharisees and their scribes murmured against his disciples, saying, "Why do you eat and drink with tax collectors and sinners?" [31] And Jesus answered them, "Those who are well have no need of a physician, but those who are sick; [32] *I have not come to call the righteous, but sinners to repentance."*

Luke 19:10 (§A64.4)
[1] He entered Jericho and was passing through. [2] And there was a man named Zacchaeus; he was a chief tax collector, and rich. [3] And he sought to see who Jesus was, but could not, on account of the crowd, because he was small of stature. [4] So he ran on ahead and climbed up into a sycamore tree to see him, for he was to pass that way. [5] And when Jesus came to the place, he looked up and said to him, "Zacchaeus, make haste and come down; for I must stay at your house today." [6] So he made haste and came down, and received him joyfully. [7] And when they saw it they all murmured, "He has gone in to be the guest of a man who is a sinner." [8] And Zacchaeus stood and said to the Lord, "Behold, Lord, the half of my goods I give to the poor; and if I have defrauded any one of anything, I restore it fourfold." [9] And Jesus said to him, "Today salvation has come to this house, since he also is a son of Abraham. [10] *For the Son of man came to seek and to save the lost."*

1 Tim 1:15b (§A64.5)
[12] I thank him who has given me strength for this, Christ Jesus our Lord, because he judged me faithful by appointing me to his service, [13] though I formerly blasphemed and persecuted and insulted him; but I received mercy because I had acted ignorantly in unbelief, [14] and the grace of our Lord overflowed for me with the faith and love that are in Christ Jesus. [15] The saying is sure and worthy of full acceptance, that *Christ Jesus came into the world to save sinners.* And I am the foremost of sinners; [16] but I received mercy for this reason, that in me, as the foremost, Jesus Christ might display his perfect patience for an example to those who were to believe in him for eternal life. [17] To the King of ages, immortal, invisible, the only God, be honor and glory for ever and ever. Amen.

POxy1224 1 (§A64.6)
(1) . . . And the scribes and [Pharisees] and priests, when they sa[w] him, were angry [that with sin] ners in the midst he [reclined] at table. But Jesus heard [it and said:] The he[althy need not the physician.] . . .

2 Clem 2:4b (§A64.7)
[4] And another Scripture also says, *"I came not to call righteous, but sinners";* [5] He means that those who are perishing msut be saved, [6] for it is great and wonderful to give strength, not to the things which are standing, but to those which are falling. [7] So Christ also willed to save the perishing, and he saved many, coming and calling us who were already perishing.

Barn 5:9b (§A64.8)
[8] Furthermore, while teaching Israel and doing such great signs and wonders he preached to them and loved them greatly; [9] but when he chose out his own Apostles who were to preach his Gospel, he chose those who were iniquitous above all sin to show that *"he came not to call the righteous but sinners,"*—then he manifested himself as God's Son.

* See 423: *Righteous and Sinners*

Matt 9:16–17 (§A65.1)

[14] Then the disciples of John came to him, saying, "Why do we and the Pharisees fast, but your disciples do not fast?" [15] And Jesus said to them, "Can the wedding guests mourn as long as the bridegroom is with them? The days will come, when the bridegroom is taken away from them, and then they will fast. [16] *And no one puts a piece of unshrunk cloth on an old garment, for the patch tears away from the garment, and a worse tear is made.* [17] *Neither is new wine put into old wineskins; if it is, the skins burst, and the wine is spilled, and the skins are destroyed; but new wine is put into fresh wineskins, and so both are preserved.*"

Mark 2:21–22 (§A65.2)

[18] Now John's disciples and the Pharisees were fasting; and people came and said to him, "Why do John's disciples and the disciples of the Pharisees fast, but your disciples do not fast?" [19] And Jesus said to them, "Can the wedding guests fast while the bridegroom is with them? As long as they have the bridegroom with them, they cannot fast. [20] The days will come, when the bridegroom is taken away from them, and then they will fast in that day. [21] *No one sews a piece of unshrunk cloth on an old garment; if he does, the patch tears away from it, the new from the old, and a worse tear is made.* [22] *And no one puts new wine into old wineskins; if he does, the wine will burst the skins, and the wine is lost, and so are the skins; but new wine is for fresh skins.*"

Luke 5:36b–38 (§A65.3)

[33] And they said to him, "The disciples of John fast often and offer prayers, and so do the disciples of the Pharisees, but yours eat and drink." [34] And Jesus said to them, "Can you make wedding guests fast while the bridegroom is with them? [35] The days will come, when the bridegroom is taken away from them, and then they will fast in those days." [36] He told them a parable also: *"No one tears a piece from a new garment and puts it upon an old garment; if he does, he will tear the new, and the piece from the new will not match the old.* [37] *And no one puts new wine into old wineskins; if he does, the new wine will burst the skins and it will be spilled, and the skins will be destroyed.* [38] *But new wine must be put into fresh wineskins.* [39] And no one after drinking old wine desires new; for he says, 'The old is good.'"

GThom 47:4 (§A65.4)

(47) [1] Jesus said, "It is impossible for a man to mount two horses or to stretch two bows. [2] And it is impossible for a servant to serve two masters; otherwise, he will honor the one and treat the other contemptuously. [3] No man drinks old wine and immediately desires to drink new wine. [4] *And new wine is not put into old wineskins, lest they burst; nor is old wine put into a new wineskin, lest it spoil it. An old patch is not sewn onto a new garment, because a tear would result.*"

Matt 9:37b–38 (§A66.1)

[35] And Jesus went about all the cities and villages, teaching in their synagogues and preaching the gospel of the kingdom, and healing every disease and every infirmity. [36] When he saw the crowds, he had compassion for them, because they were harassed and helpless, like sheep without a shepherd. [37] Then he said to his disciples, *"The harvest is plentiful, but the laborers are few;* [38] *pray therefore the Lord of the harvest to send out laborers into his harvest."*

Luke 10:2 (§A66.2)

[1] After this the Lord appointed seventy others, and sent them on ahead of him, two by two, into every town and place where he himself was about to come. [2] And he said to them, *"The harvest is plentiful, but the laborers are few; pray therefore the Lord of the harvest to send out laborers into his harvest."*

* See 425: *Harvest is Great*

John 4:35b, 38 (§A66.3)

[35] "Do you not say, 'There are yet four months, then comes the harvest'? *I tell you, lift up your eyes, and see how the fields are already white for harvest.* [36] He who reaps receives wages, and gathers fruit for eternal life, so that sower and reaper may rejoice together. [37] For here the saying holds true, 'One sows and another reaps.' [38] *I sent you to reap that for which you did not labor; others have labored, and you have entered into their labor."*

GThom 73 (§A66.4)

(73) Jesus said, *"The harvest is great but the laborers are few. Beseech the Lord, therefore, to send out laborers to the harvest."*

100 ISRAEL'S LOST SHEEP*

Matt 10:5b–6 (§A67.1)

[1] And he called to him his twelve disciples and gave them authority over unclean spirits, to cast them out, and to heal every disease and every infirmity. [2] The names of the twelve apostles are these: first, Simon, who is called Peter, and Andrew his brother; James the son of Zebedee, and John his brother; [3] Philip and Bartholomew; Thomas and Matthew the tax collector; James the son of Alphaeus, and Thaddaeus; [4] Simon the Cananaean, and Judas Iscariot, who betrayed him.

[5] These twelve Jesus sent out, charging them, *"Go nowhere among the Gentiles, and enter no town of the Samaritans, [6] but go rather to the lost sheep of the house of Israel."*

* See 426: *Israel's Lost Sheep*

Matt 15:24 (§A67.2)

[21] And Jesus went away from there and withdrew to the district of Tyre and Sidon. [22] And behold, a Canaanite woman from that region came out and cried, "Have mercy on me, O Lord, Son of David; my daughter is severely possessed by a demon." [23] But he did not answer her a word. And his disciples came and begged him, saying, "Send her away, for she is crying after us." [24] He answered, *"I was sent only to the lost sheep of the house of Israel."* [25] But she came and knelt before him, saying, "Lord, help me." [26] And he answered, "It is not fair to take the children's bread and throw it to the dogs." [27] She said, "Yes, Lord, yet even the dogs eat the crumbs that fall from their master's table." [28] Then Jesus answered her, "O woman, great is your faith! Be it done for you as you desire." And her daughter was healed instantly.

101 MISSION BY DISCIPLES*

Matt 10:7–8a (§A68.1)

[7] *"And preach as you go, saying, 'The kingdom of heaven is at hand.' [8] Heal the sick, raise the dead, cleanse lepers, cast out demons.* You received without paying, give without pay."

Mark 6:12–13 (§A68.2)

[12] So they went out and preached that men should repent. [13] And they cast out many demons, and anointed with oil many that were sick and healed them.

Luke 9:6 (§A68.3)

[6] And they departed and went through the villages, preaching the gospel and healing everywhere.

* See 427: *Mission By Disciples*

102 GIVE WITHOUT PAY

Matt 10:8b (§A69)

[7] "And preach as you go, saying, 'The kingdom of heaven is at hand.' [8] Heal the sick, raise the dead, cleanse lepers, cast out demons. *You received without paying, give without pay."*

103 ON THE ROAD

Matt 10:10a (§A70.1)
[9] *"Take no gold, nor silver, nor copper in your belts,* [10] *no bag for your journey, nor two tunics, nor sandals, nor a staff."*

Mark 6:8–9 (§A70.2)
[8] He charged them *to take nothing for their journey except a staff; no bread, no bag, no money in their belts;* [9] *but to wear sandals and not put on two tunics.*

Luke 9:3 (§A70.3)
[3] And he said to them, *"Take nothing for your journey, no staff, nor bag, nor bread, nor money; and do not have two tunics."*

Luke 10:4 (§A70.4)
[4] *"Carry no purse, no bag, no sandals; and salute no one on the road."*

104 THE LABORER'S PAY

Matt 10:10b (§A71.1)
[10] "no bag for your journey, nor two tunics, nor sandals, nor a staff; *for the laborer deserves his food."*

Luke 10:7b (§A71.2)
[7] "And remain in the same house, eating and drinking what they provide, *for the laborer deserves his wages;* do not go from house to house."

1 Cor 9:14 (§A71.3)
[14] In the same way, the Lord commanded that those who proclaim the gospel should get their living by the gospel.

1 Tim 5:18b (§A71.4)
[18] for the scripture says, "You shall not muzzle an ox when it is treading out the grain," and, *"The laborer deserves his wages."*

DialSav 53b (§A71.5)
(53) Mary said, "Thus with respect to 'the wickedness of each day,' and *'the laborer is worthy of his food,'* and 'the disciple resembles his teacher.'" She uttered this as a woman who had understood completely.

Did 13:1–2 (§A71.6)
[1] But every true prophet who wishes to settle among you is *"worthy of his food."* [2] Likewise a true teacher *is himself worthy, like the workman, of his food.*

105 IN THE HOUSE

Matt 10:10b–13 (§A72.1)
[10] "no bag for your journey, nor two tunics, nor sandals, nor a staff; *for the laborer deserves his food.* [11] *And whatever town or village you enter, find out who is worthy in it, and stay with him until you depart.* [12] *As you enter the house, salute it.* [13] *And if the house is worthy, let your peace come upon it; but if it is not worthy, let your peace return to you."*

Mark 6:10 (§A72.2)
[10] And he said to them, *"Where you enter a house, stay there until you leave the place."*

Luke 9:4 (§A72.3)
[4] *"And whatever house you enter, stay there, and from there depart."*

Luke 10:5–7 (§A72.4)
[5] *"Whatever house you enter, first say, 'Peace be to this house!'* [6] *And if a son of peace is there, your peace shall rest upon him; but if not, it shall return to you.* [7] *And remain in the same house, eating and drinking what they provide, for the laborer deserves his wages; do not go from house to house."*

106 AT THE TOWN*

Matt 10:14–15 (§A73.1)
[14] *"And if any one will not receive you or listen to your words, shake off the dust from your feet as you leave that house or town.* [15] *Truly, I say to you, it shall be more tolerable on the day of judgment for the land of Sodom and Gomorrah than for that town."*

Mark 6:11 (§A73.2)
[11] *"And if any place will not receive you and they refuse to hear you, when you leave, shake off the dust that is on your feet for a testimony against them."*

Luke 9:5 (§A73.3)
[5] *"And wherever they do not receive you, when you leave that town shake off the dust from your feet as a testimony against them."*

Luke 10:8–12 (§A73.4)
[8] *"Whenever you enter a town and they receive you, eat what is set before you;* [9] *heal the sick in it and say to them, 'The kingdom of God has come near to you.'* [10] *But whenever you enter a town and they do not receive you, go into its streets and say,* [11] *'Even the dust of your town that clings to our feet, we wipe off against you; nevertheless know this, that the kingdom of God has come near.'* [12] *I tell you, it shall be more tolerable on that day for Sodom than for that town."*

1 Cor 10:27 (§A73.5)
[27] If one of the unbelievers invites you to dinner and you are disposed to go, eat whatever is set before you without raising any question on the ground of conscience.

* See 332: *At the Town*

GThom 14:2 (§A73.6)
(6) [1] His disciples questioned Him and said to Him, "Do You want us to fast? How shall we pray? Shall we give alms? What diet shall we observe?"
[2] Jesus said, "Do not tell lies, [3] and do not do what you hate, for all things are plain in the sight of Heaven. [4] For nothing hidden will not become manifest, and nothing covered will remain without being uncovered."
(14) [1] Jesus said to them, "If you fast, you will give rise to sin for yourselves; and if you pray, you will be condemned; and if you give alms, you will do harm to your spirits. [2] *When you go into any land and walk about in the districts, if they receive you, eat what they will set before you, and heal the sick among them.* [3] For what goes into your mouth will not defile you, but that which issues from your mouth—it is that which will defile you."

107 LAMBS AMONG WOLVES

Matt 10:16a (§A74.1)
[16] *"Behold, I send you out as sheep in the midst of wolves;* so be wise as serpents and innocent as doves."

Luke 10:3 (§A74.2)
[3] "Go your way; *behold, I send you out as lambs in the midst of wolves."*

2 Clem 5:2 (§A74.3)
[1] Wherefore, brethren, let us forsake our sojourning in this world, and do the will of him who called us, and let us not fear to go forth from this world, [2] for the Lord said, *"Ye shall be as lambs in the midst of wolves,"* [3] and Peter answered and said to him, "If then the wolves tear the lambs?"

[4] Jesus said to Peter, "Let the lambs have no fear of the wolves after their death; and do ye have no fear of those that slay you, and can do nothing more to you, but fear him who after your death hath power over body and soul, to cast them into the flames of hell."

108 SERPENTS AND DOVES

Matt 10:16b (§A75.1)
[16] "Behold, I send you out as sheep in the midst of wolves; *so be wise as serpents and innocent as doves."*

POxy655 39:2 (§A75.2)
(39) [1] [Jesus said, "The pharisees and the scribes have taken the keys] of [knowledge (gnosis) and] hidden [them. They themselves have not] entered, [nor have they allowed to enter those who were about to] come in. [2] *[You], however, [be as wise as serpents and as]* innocent *[as doves]."*

GThom 39:2 (§A75.3)
(39) [1] Jesus said, "The Pharisees and the scribes have taken the keys of Knowledge and hidden them. They themselves have not entered, nor have they allowed to enter those who wish to. [2] *You, however, be as wise as serpents and as innocent as doves."*

Ign Pol 2:2a (§A75.4)
[2] *"Be prudent as the serpent"* in all things *"and pure as the dove"* for ever. For this reason you consist of flesh and spirit, that you may deal tenderly with the things which appear visibly; but pray that the invisible things may be revealed to you, that you may lack nothing and abound in every gift.

GNaz 7 (§A75.5)
(7) The Jewish Gospel: *(wise) more than serpents.* (Variant to Matthew 10:16 in the "Zion Gospel" Edition)

109   PERSECUTION AND TESTIMONY

Matt 10:17–18 (§A76.1)
17 *"Beware of men; for they will deliver you up to councils, and flog you in their synagogues,* 18 *and you will be dragged before governors and kings for my sake, to bear testimony before them and the Gentiles."*

Mark 13:9 (§A76.2)
9 *"But take heed to yourselves; for they will deliver you up to councils; and you will be beaten in synagogues; and you will stand before governors and kings for my sake, to bear testimony before them."*

Luke 21:12–13 (§A76.3)
12 *"But before all this they will lay their hands on you and persecute you, delivering you up to the synagogues and prisons, and you will be brought before kings and governors for my name's sake.* 13 *This will be a time for you to bear testimony."*

110   SPIRIT UNDER TRIAL

Matt 10:19–20 (§A77.1)
19 *"When they deliver you up, do not be anxious how you are to speak or what you are to say; for what you are to say will be given to you in that hour;* 20 *for it is not you who speak, but the Spirit of your Father speaking through you."*

Mark 13:11 (§A77.2)
11 *"And when they bring you to trial and deliver you up, do not be anxious beforehand what you are to say; but say whatever is given you in that hour, for it is not you who speak, but the Holy Spirit."*

Luke 12:11–12 (§A77.3)
11 *"And when they bring you before the synagogues and the rulers and the authorities, do not be anxious how or what you are to answer or what you are to say;* 12 *for the Holy Spirit will teach you in that very hour what you ought to say."*

Luke 21:14–15 (§A77.4)
14 *"Settle it therefore in your minds, not to meditate beforehand how to answer;* 15 *for I will give you a mouth and wisdom, which none of your adversaries will be able to withstand or contradict."*

John 14:25–26 (§A77.5)
25 "These things I have spoken to you, while I am still with you. 26 But the Counselor, the *Holy Spirit*, whom the *Father* will send in my name, he will *teach* you all things, and bring to your remembrance all that I have said to you."

111   HATRED AND PATIENCE

Matt 10:21–22 (§A78.1)
71 *"Brother will deliver up brother to death, and the father his child, and children will rise against parents and have them put to death;* 22 *and you will be hated by all for my name's sake. But he who endures to the end will be saved."*

Matt 24:9–13 (§A78.2)
9 *"Then they will deliver you up to tribulation, and put you to death; and you will be hated by all nations for my name's sake.* 10 *And then many will fall away, and betray one another, and hate one another.* 11 *And many false prophets will arise and lead many astray.* 12 *And because wickedness is multiplied, most men's love will grow cold.* 13 *But he who endures to the end will be saved."*

Mark 13:12–13 (§A78.3)
12 *"And brother will deliver up brother to death, and the father his child, and children will rise against parents and have them put to death;* 13 *and you will be hated by all for my name's sake. But he who endures to the end will be saved."*

Luke 21:16–19 (§A78.4)
16 *"You will be delivered up even by parents and brothers and kinsmen and friends, and some of you they will put to death;* 17 *you will be hated by all for my name's sake.* 18 *But not a hair of your head will perish.* 19 *By your endurance you will gain your lives."*

Did 16:4–5 (§A78.5)
4 for as lawlessness increaseth they shall *hate one another* and persecute *and betray*, and then shall appear the deceiver of the world as a Son of God, and shall do signs and wonders and the earth shall be given over into his hands and he shall commit iniquities which have never been since the world began. 5 Then shall the creation of mankind come to the fiery trial and *"many shall be offended"* and be lost, *but "they who endure"* in their faith *"shall be saved"* by the curse itself.

112 CITIES OF ISRAEL

Matt 10:23 (§A79)
23 *"When they persecute you in one town, flee to the next; for truly, I say to you, you will not have gone through all the towns of Israel, before the Son of man comes."*

113 DISCIPLE AND SERVANT

Matt 10:24–25a (§A80.1)
24 *"A disciple is not above his teacher, nor a servant above his master;* 25 *it is enough for the disciple to be like his teacher, and the servant like his master.* If they have called the master of the house Beelzebul, how much more will they malign those of his household."

Luke 6:40 (§A80.2)
40 *"A disciple is not above his teacher, but every one when he is fully taught will be like his teacher."*

John 13:16 (§A80.3)
12 When he had washed their feet, and taken his garments, and resumed his place, he said to them, "Do you know what I have done to you? 13 You call me Teacher and Lord; and you are right, for so I am. 14 If I then, your Lord and Teacher, have washed your feet, you also ought to wash one another's feet. 15 For I have given you an example, that you also should do as I have done to you. 16 *Truly, truly, I say to you, a servant is not greater than his master; nor is he who is sent greater than he who sent him."*

John 15:20a (§A80.4)
20 "Remember the word that I said to you, *'A servant is not greater than his master.'* If they persecuted me, they will persecute you; if they kept my word, they will keep yours also. 21 But all this they will do to you on my account, because they do not know him who sent me."

DialSav 53c (§A80.5)
(53) Mary said, "Thus with respect to 'the wickedness of each day,' and 'the laborer is worthy of his food,' and *'the disciple resembles his teacher.'"* She uttered this as a woman who had understood completely.

114 MASTER AND HOUSEHOLD

Matt 10:25b (§A81)
25 "it is enough for the disciple to be like his teacher, and the servant like his master. *If they have called the master of the house Beelzebul, how much more will they malign those of his household."*

115 HIDDEN MADE MANIFEST

Matt 10:26b (§A82.1)
26 "So have no fear of them; *for nothing is covered that will not be revealed, or hidden that will not be known."*

Mark 4:22 (§A82.2)
21 And he said to them, "Is a lamp brought in to be put under a bushel, or under a bed, and not on a stand? 22 *For there is nothing hid, except to be made manifest; nor is anything secret, except to come to light."*

Luke 8:17 (§A82.3)
16 "No one after lighting a lamp covers it with a vessel, or puts it under a bed, but puts it on a stand, that those who enter may see the light. 17 *For nothing is hid that shall not be made manifest, nor anything secret that shall not be known and come to light."*

Luke 12:2 (§A82.4)
2 *"Nothing is covered up that will not be revealed, or hidden that will not be known.* 3 Therefore whatever you have said in the dark shall be heard in the light, and what you have whispered in private rooms shall be proclaimed upon the housetops."

POxy654 5:2 (§A82.5)
(5) 1 Jesus said, "[Recognize what is in] your (sg.) sight, and [that which is hidden] from you (sg.) will become plain [to you (sg.). 2 For there is nothing] hidden which [will] not [become] manifest, 3 nor buried that [will not be raised]."

GThom 5:2 (§A82.6)
(5) 1 Jesus said, "Recognize what is in your sight, and that which is hidden from you will become plain to you. 2 *For there is nothing hidden which will not become manifest."*

POxy654 6:4 (§A82.7)
(6) 1 [His disciples] questioned him [and said], "How [shall we] fast? [How shall we pray]? How [shall we give alms]? What [diet] shall [we] observe?"
2 Jesus said, "[Do not tell lies, 3 and] do not do what you [hate, for all things are plain in the sight] of truth. 4 *[For nothing] hidden [will not become manifest]."*

GThom 6:4 (§A82.8)
(6) 1 His disciples questioned Him and said to Him, "Do You want us to fast? How shall we pray? Shall we give alms? What diet shall we observe?"
2 Jesus said, "Do not tell lies, 3 and do not do what you hate, for all things are plain in the sight of Heaven. 4 *For nothing hidden will not become manifest, and nothing covered will remain without being uncovered."*

116 OPEN PROCLAMATION

Matt 10:27 (§A83.1)
27 *"What I tell you in the dark, utter in the light; and what you hear whispered, proclaim upon the housetops."*

Luke 12:3 (§A83.2)
2 "Nothing is covered up that will not be revealed, or hidden that will not be known. 3 *Therefore whatever you have said in the dark shall be heard in the light, and what you have whispered in private rooms shall be proclaimed upon the housetops."*

GThom 33:1 (§A83.3)
(33) 1 Jesus said, *"Preach from your housetops that which you will hear in your ear [(and) in the other ear].* 2 For no one lights a lamp and puts it under a bushel, nor does he put it in a hidden place, but rather he sets it on a lampstand so that everyone who enters and leaves will see its light."

117 WHOM TO FEAR*

Matt 10:28 (§A84.1)
28 *"And do not fear those who kill the body but cannot kill the soul; rather fear him who can destroy both soul and body in hell."*

Luke 12:4–5 (§A84.2)
4 *"I tell you, my friends, do not fear those who kill the body, and after that have no more that they can do.* 5 *But I will warn you whom to fear: fear him who, after he has killed, has power to cast into hell; yes, I tell you, fear him!"*

* See 333: *Whom to Fear*

2 Clem 5:4b (§A84.3)
1 Wherefore, brethren, let us forsake our sojourning in this world, and do the will of him who called us, and let us not fear to go forth from this world, 2 for the Lord said, "Ye shall be as lambs in the midst of wolves," 3 and Peter answered and said to him, "If then the wolves tear the lambs?" 4 Jesus said to Peter, "Let the lambs have no fear of the wolves after their death; *and do ye have no fear of those that slay you, and can do nothing more to you, but fear him who after your death hath power over body and soul, to cast them into the flames of hell."*

118 GOD AND SPARROWS

Matt 10:29–31 (§A85.1)
[29] *"Are not two sparrows sold for a penny? And not one of them will fall to the ground without your Father's will.* [30] *But even the hairs of your head are all numbered.* [31] *Fear not, therefore; you are of more value than many sparrows."*

Luke 12:6–7 (§A85.2)
[6] *"Are not five sparrows sold for two pennies? And not one of them is forgotten before God.* [7] *Why, even the hairs of your head are all numbered. Fear not; you are of more value than many sparrows."*

119 BEFORE THE ANGELS

Matt 10:32–33 (§A86.1)
[32] *"So every one who acknowledges me before men, I also will acknowledge before my Father who is in heaven;* [33] *but whoever denies me before men, I also will deny before my Father who is in heaven."*

Matt 16:27 (§A86.2)
[27] *"For the Son of man is to come with his angels in the glory of his Father, and then he will repay every man for what he has done."*

Mark 8:38 (§A86.3)
[38] *"For whoever is ashamed of me and of my words in this adulterous and sinful generation, of him will the Son of man also be ashamed, when he comes in the glory of his Father with the holy angels."*

Luke 9:26 (§A86.4)
[26] *"For whoever is ashamed of me and of my words, of him will the Son of man be ashamed when he comes in his glory and the glory of the Father and of the holy angels."*

Luke 12:8–9 (§A86.5)
[8] *"And I tell you, every one who acknowledges me before men, the Son of man also will acknowledge before the angels of God;* [9] *but he who denies me before men will be denied before the angels of God."*

2 Tim 2:12b (§A86.6)
[10] Therefore I endure everything for the sake of the elect, that they also may obtain salvation in Christ Jesus with its eternal glory. [11] The saying is sure:
If we have died with him, we shall also
    live with him;
[12] if we endure, we shall also reign with
    him;
if we deny him, he also will deny us;
[13] if we are faithless, he remains
    faithful—
for he cannot deny himself.

Rev 3:5b (§A86.7)
[5] *"He who conquers shall be clad thus in white garments, and I will not blot his name out of the book of life; I will confess his name before my Father and before his angels.* [6] He who has an ear, let him hear what the Spirit says to the churches.'"

2 Clem 3:2 (§A86.8)
[1] Seeing, then, that he has shewn such mercy towards us, first that we who are living do not sacrifice to the dead gods, and do not worship them, but through him know the father of truth, what is the true knowledge concerning him except that we should not deny him through whom we knew him? [2] And he himself also says, *"Whosoever confessed me before men, I will confess him before my Father";* [3] this then is our reward, if we confess him through whom we were saved. [4] But how do we confess him? By doing what he says, and not disregarding his commandments, and honouring him not only with our lips, but "with all our heart and all our mind." [5] And he says also in Isaiah, "This people honoureth me with their lips, but their heart is far from me."

120 PEACE OR SWORD

Matt 10:34–36 (§A87.1)
[34] *"Do not think that I have come to bring peace on earth; I have not come to bring peace, but a sword.* [35] *For I have come to set a man against his father, and a daughter against her mother, and a daughter-in-law against her mother-in-law;* [36] *and a man's foes will be those of his own household."*

Luke 12:51–53 (§A87.2)
[51] *"Do you think that I have come to give peace on earth? No, I tell you, but rather division;* [52] *for henceforth in one house there will be five divided, three against two and two against three;* [53] *they will be divided, father against son and son against father, mother against daughter and daughter against her mother, mother-in-law against her daughter-in-law and daughter-in-law against her mother-in-law."*

GThom 16 (§A87.3)
(16) Jesus said, *"Men think, perhaps, that it is peace which I have come to cast upon the world. They do not know that it is dissension which I have come to cast upon the earth: fire, sword, and war. For there will be five in a house: three will be against two, and two against three, the father against the son, and the son against the father. And they will stand solitary."*

121 HATING ONE'S FAMILY*

Matt 10:37 (§A88.1)
[37] *"He who loves father or mother more than me is not worthy of me; and he who loves son or daughter more than me is not worthy of me."*

Luke 14:26 (§A88.2)
[25] Now great multitudes accompanied him; and he turned and said to them, [26] *"If any one comes to me and does not hate his own father and mother and wife and chil-*

dren and brothers and sisters, yes, and even his own life, he cannot be my disciple."

GThom 55:1–2a (§A88.3)
(55) [1] Jesus said, *"Whoever does not hate his father and his mother cannot become a disciple to Me.* [2] *And whoever does not hate his brothers and sisters* and take up his cross in My way will not be worthy of Me."

GThom 101 (§A88.4)
(101) <Jesus said,> *"Whoever does not hate his father and his mother as I do cannot become a disciple to Me. And whoever does [not] love his father and his mother as I do cannot become a [disciple] to Me. For My mother [gave me falsehood], but [My] true [Mother] gave me life."*

* See 428: *Hating One's Family*

122 CARRYING ONE'S CROSS*

Matt 10:38 (§A89.1)
[38] *"and he who does not take his cross and follow me is not worthy of me."*

Matt 16:24b (§A89.2)
[24] Then Jesus told his disciples, *"If any man would come after me, let him deny himself and take up his cross and follow me."*

* See 429: *Carrying One's Cross*

Mark 8:34b (§A89.3)
[34] And he called to him the multitude with his disciples, and said to them, *"If any man would come after me, let him deny himself and take up his cross and follow me."*

Luke 9:23b (§A89.4)
[23] And he said to all, *"If any man would come after me, let him deny himself and take up his cross daily and follow me."*

Luke 14:27 (§A89.5)
[27] *"Whoever does not bear his own cross and come after me, cannot be my disciple."*

GThom 55:2 (§A89.6)
(55) [1] Jesus said, "Whoever does not hate his father and his mother cannot become a disciple to Me. [2] And *whoever does not* hate his brothers and sisters and *take up his cross in My way will not be worthy of Me."*

123 SAVING ONE'S LIFE

Matt 10:39 (§A90.1)
[39] *"He who finds his life will lose it, and he who loses his life for my sake will find it."*

Matt 16:25 (§A90.2)
[25] *"For whoever would save his life will lose it, and whoever loses his life for my sake will find it."*

Mark 8:35 (§A90.3)
[35] *"For whoever would save his life will lose it; and whoever loses his life for my sake and the gospel's will save it."*

Luke 9:24 (§A90.4)
[24] *"For whoever would save his life will lose it; and whoever loses his life for my sake, he will save it."*

Luke 17:33 (§A90.5)
[28] "Likewise as it was in the days of Lot— they ate, they drank, they bought, they sold, they planted, they built, [29] but on the day when Lot went out from Sodom fire and sulphur rained from heaven and destroyed them all— [30] so will it be on the day when the Son of man is revealed. [31] On that day, let him who is on the housetop, with his goods in the house, not come down to take them away; and likewise let him who is in the field not turn back. [32] Remember Lot's wife. [33] *Whoever seeks to gain his life will lose it, but whoever loses his life will preserve it."*

John 12:25 (§A90.6)
[20] Now among those who went up to worship at the feast were some Greeks. [21] So these came to Philip, who was from Bethsaida in Galilee, and said to him, "Sir, we wish to see Jesus." [22] Philip went and told Andrew; Andrew went with Philip and they told Jesus. [23] And Jesus answered them, "The hour has come for the Son of man to be glorified. [24] Truly, truly I say to you, unless a grain of wheat falls into the earth and dies, it remains alone; but if it dies, it bears much fruit. [25] *He who loves his life loses it, and he who hates his life in this world will keep it for eternal life.* [26] If any one serves me, he must follow me; and where I am, there shall my servant be also; if any one serves me, the Father will honor him."

124 RECEIVING THE SENDER*

Matt 10:40 (§A91.1)
[40] *"He who receives you receives me, and he who receives me receives him who sent me."*

Matt 18:5 (§A91.2)
[1] At that time the disciples came to Jesus, saying, "Who is the greatest in the kingdom of heaven?" [2] And calling to him a child, he put him in the midst of them, [3] and said, "Truly, I say to you, unless you turn and become like children, you will never enter the kingdom of heaven. [4] Whoever humbles himself like this child, he is the greatest in the kingdom of heaven.
[5] *"Whoever receives one such child in my name receives me."*

Mark 9:37 (§A91.3)
[33] And they came to Capernaum; and when he was in the house he asked them, "What were you discussing on the way?" [34] But they were silent; for on the way they had discussed with one another who was the greatest. [35] And he sat down and called the twelve; and he said to them, "If any one would be first, he must be last of all and servant of all." [36] And he took a child, and put him in the midst of them; and taking him in his arms, he said to them, [37] *"Whoever receives one such child in my name receives me; and whoever receives me, receives not me but him who sent me."*

Luke 9:48a (§A91.4)
[46] And an argument arose among them as to which of them was the greatest. [47] But when Jesus perceived the thought of their hearts, he took a child and put him by his side, [48] and said to them, *"Whoever receives this child in my name receives me, and whoever receives me receives him who sent me;* for he who is least among you all is the one who is great."

Luke 10:16 (§A91.5)
[16] *"He who hears you hears me, and he who rejects you rejects me, and he who rejects me rejects him who sent me."*

John 5:23b (§A91.6)
[19] Jesus said to them, "Truly, truly, I say to you, the Son can do nothing of his own accord, but only what he sees the Father doing; for whatever he does, that the Son does likewise. [20] For the Father loves the Son, and shows him all that he himself is doing; and greater works than these will he show him, that you may marvel. [21] For as the Father raises the dead and gives them life, so also the Son gives life to whom he will. [22] The Father judges no one, but has given all judgment to the Son, [23] that all may honor the Son, even as they honor the Father. *He who does not honor the Son does not honor the Father who sent him.* [24] Truly, truly, I say to you, he who hears my word and believes him who sent me, has eternal life; he does not come into judgment, but has passed from death to life."

John 12:44b (§A91.7)
[44] And Jesus cried out and said, *"He who believes in me, believes not in me but in him who sent me. [45] And he who sees me sees him who sent me."*

John 13:20 (§A91.8)
[20] *"Truly, truly, I say to you, he who receives any one whom I send receives me; and he who receives me receives him who sent me."*

Ign Eph 6:1 (§A91.9)
[1] And the more anyone sees that the bishop is silent, the more let him fear him. *For every one whom the master of the house sends to do his business ought we to receive as him who sent him.* Therefore it is clear that we must regard the bishop as the Lord himself.

Did 11:4 (§A91.10)
[3] And concerning the Apostles and Prophets, act thus according to the ordinance of the Gospel. [4] *Let every Apostle who comes to you be received as the Lord.*

* See 430: *Receiving the Sender*

125 RECEPTION AND REWARD

Matt 10:41 (§A92)
[41] *"He who receives a prophet because he is a prophet shall receive a prophet's reward, and he who receives a righteous man because he is a righteous man shall receive a righteous man's reward."*

126 CUP OF WATER

Matt 10:42 (§A93.1)
[42] *"And whoever gives to one of these little ones even a cup of cold water because he is a disciple, truly, I say to you, he shall not lose his reward."*

Mark 9:41 (§A93.2)
[38] John said to him, "Teacher, we saw a man casting out demons in your name, and we forbade him, because he was not following us." [39] But Jesus said, "Do not forbid him; for no one who does a mighty work in my name will be able soon after to speak evil of me. [40] For he that is not against us is for us. [41] *For truly, I say to you, whoever gives you a cup of water to drink because you bear the name of Christ, will by no means lose his reward."*

127   INTO THE DESERT*

Matt 11:7b–10 (§A94.1)

⁷ As they went away, Jesus began to speak to the crowds concerning John: *"What did you go out into the wilderness to behold? A reed shaken by the wind?* ⁸ *Why then did you go out? To see a man clothed in soft raiment? Behold, those who wear soft raiment are in kings' houses.* ⁹ *Why then did you go out? To see a prophet? Yes, I tell you, and more than a prophet.* ¹⁰ *This is he of whom it is written,*

'Behold, I send my messenger before thy face,
    who shall prepare thy way before thee.'"

* See 432: *Into the Desert*

Mark 1:1–5 (§A94.2)

¹ The beginning of the Gospel of Jesus Christ, the Son of God. ² *As it is written in Isaiah the prophet,*

"Behold, I send my messenger before thy face,
    who shall prepare thy way;
³ *the voice of one crying in the wilderness:*

Prepare the way of the Lord,
    make his paths straight—"

⁴ John the baptizer appeared in the wilderness, preaching a baptism of repentance for the forgiveness of sins. ⁵ And there went out to him all the country of Judea, and all the people of Jerusalem; and they were baptized by him in the river Jordan, confessing their sins.

Luke 7:24b–27 (§A94.3)

²⁴ When the messengers of John had gone, he began to speak to the crowds concerning John: *"What did you go out into the wilderness to behold? A reed shaken by the wind?* ²⁵ *What then did you go out to see? A man clothed in soft clothing? Behold, those who are gorgeously appareled and live in luxury are in kings' courts.* ²⁶ *What then did you go out to see? A prophet? Yes, I tell you, and more than a prophet.* ²⁷ *This is he of whom it is written,*

'Behold, I send my messenger before thy face,
    who shall prepare thy way before thee.'"

GThom 78 (§A94.4)

(78) Jesus said, *"Why have you come out into the desert? To see a reed shaken by the wind? And to see a man clothed in fine garments like your kings and your great men? Upon them are the fine [garments], and they are unable to discern the truth."*

128   GREATER THAN JOHN

Matt 11:11 (§A95.1)

¹¹ *"Truly, I say to you, among those born of women there has risen no one greater than John the Baptist; yet he who is least in the kingdom of heaven is greater than he."*

Luke 7:28 (§A95.2)

²⁸ *"I tell you, among those born of women none is greater than John; yet he who is least in the kingdom of God is greater than he."*

GThom 46 (§A95.3)

(46) Jesus said, *"Among those born of women, from Adam until John the Baptist, there is no one so superior to John the Baptist that his eyes should not be lowered (before him). Yet I have said, whichever one of you comes to be a child will be acquainted with the Kingdom and will become superior to John."*

129   KINGDOM AND VIOLENCE

Matt 11:12–13 (§A96.1)

¹² *"From the days of John the Baptist until now the kingdom of heaven has suffered violence, and men of violence take it by force.* ¹³ *For all the prophets and the law prophesied until John;* ¹⁴ and if you are willing to accept it, he is Elijah who is to come."*

Luke 16:16 (§A96.2)

¹⁶ *"The law and the prophets were until John; since then the good news of the kingdom of God is preached, and every one enters it violently."*

GNaz 8 (§A96.3)

(8) The Jewish Gospel has: *(the kingdom of heaven) is plundered.* (Variant to Matthew 11:12 in the "Zion Gospel" Edition)

Matt 11:15 (§A97.1)

[12] "From the days of John the Baptist until now the kingdom of heaven has suffered violence, and men of violence take it by force. [13] For all the prophets and the law prophesied until John; [14] and if you are willing to accept it, he is Elijah who is to come. [15] *He who has ears to hear, let him hear.*"

Matt 13:9 (§A97.2)

[1] That same day Jesus went out of the house and sat beside the sea. [2] And great crowds gathered about him, so that he got into a boat and sat there; and the whole crowd stood on the beach. [3] And he told them many things in parables, saying: "A sower went out to sow. [4] And as he sowed, some seeds fell along the path, and the birds came and devoured them. [5] Other seeds fell on rocky ground, where they had not much soil, and immediately they sprang up, since they had no depth of soil, [6] but when the sun rose they were scorched; and since they had no root they withered away. [7] Other seeds fell upon thorns, and the thorns grew up and choked them. [8] Other seeds fell on good soil and brought forth grain, some a hundredfold, some sixty, some thirty. [9] *He who has ears, let him hear.*"

Matt 13:43b (§A97.3)

[36] Then he left the crowds and went into the house. And his disciples came to him, saying, "Explain to us the parable of the weeds of the field." [37] He answered, "He who sows the good seed is the Son of man; [38] the field is the world, and the good seed means the sons of the kingdom; the weeds are the sons of the evil one, [39] and the enemy who sowed them is the devil; the harvest is the close of the age, and the reapers are angels. [40] Just as the weeds are gathered and burned with fire, so will it be at the close of the age. [41] The Son of man will send his angels, and they will gather out of his kingdom all causes of sin and all evildoers, [42] and throw them into the furnace of fire; there men will weep and gnash their teeth. [43] Then the righteous will shine like the sun in the kingdom of their Father. *He who has ears, let him hear.*"

Mark 4:9 (§A97.4)

[1] Again he began to teach beside the sea. And a very large crowd gathered about him, so that he got into a boat and sat in it on the sea; and the whole crowd was beside the sea on the land. [2] And he taught them many things in parables, and in his teaching he said to them: [3] "Listen! A sower went out to sow. [4] And as he sowed, some seed fell along the path, and the birds came and devoured it. [5] Other seed fell on rocky ground, where it had not much soil, and immediately it sprang up, since it had no depth of soil; [6] and when the sun rose it was scorched, and since it had no root it withered away. [7] Other seed fell among thorns and the thorns grew up and choked it, and it yielded no grain. [8] And other seeds fell into good soil and brought forth grain, growing up and increasing and yielding thirtyfold and sixtyfold and a hundredfold." [9] And he said, *"He who has ears to hear, let him hear."*

Mark 4:23 (§A97.5)

[21] And he said to them, "Is a lamp brought in to be put under a bushel, or under a bed, and not on a stand? [22] For there is nothing hid, except to be made manifest; nor is anything secret, except to come to light. [23] *If any man has ears to hear, let him hear."* [24] And he said to them, "Take heed what you hear; the measure you give will be the measure you get, and still more will be given you. [25] For to him who has will more be given; and from him who has not, even what he has will be taken away."

Luke 8:8b (§A97.6)

[4] And when a great crowd came together and people from town after town came to him, he said in a parable: [5] "A sower went out to sow his seed; and as he sowed, some fell along the path, and was trodden under foot, and the birds of the air devoured it. [6] And some fell on the rock; and as it grew up, it withered away, because it had no moisture. [7] And some fell among thorns; and the thorns grew with it and choked it. [8] And some fell into good soil and grew, and yielded a hundredfold." As he said this, he called out, *"He who has ears to hear, let him hear."*

Luke 14:35b (§A97.7)

[34] "Salt is good; but if salt has lost its taste, how shall its saltness be restored? [35] It is fit neither for the land nor for the dunghill; men throw it away. *He who has ears to hear, let him hear."*

Rev 2:7a (§A97.8)

[1] "To the angel of the church in Ephesus write: 'The words of him who holds the seven stars in his right hand, who walks among the seven golden lampstands.

[2] "'I know your works, your toil and your patient endurance, and how you cannot bear evil men but have tested those who call themselves apostles but are not, and found them to be false; [3] I know you are enduring patiently and bearing up for my name's sake, and you have not grown weary. [4] But I have this against you, that you have abandoned the love you had at first. [5] Remember and do the works you did at first. If not, I will come to you and remove your lampstand from its place, unless you repent. [6] Yet this you have, you hate the works of the Nicolaitans, which I also hate. [7] *He who has an ear, let him hear what the Spirit says to the churches.* To him who conquers I will grant to eat of the tree of life, which is in the paradise of God.'"

Rev 2:11a (§A97.9)

[8] "And to the angel of the church in Smyrna write: 'The words of the first and the last, who died and came to life.

[9] "'I know your tribulation and your poverty (but you are rich) and the slander of those who say that they are Jews and are not, but are a synagogue of Satan. [10] Do not fear what you are about to suffer. Behold, the devil is about to throw some of you into prison, that you may be tested, and for ten days you will have tribulation. Be faithful unto death, and I will give you the crown of life. [11] *He who has an ear, let him hear what the Spirit says to the churches.* He who conquers shall not be hurt by the second death.'"

Rev 2:17a (§A97.10)

[12] "And to the angel of the church in Pergamum write: 'The words of him who has the sharp two-edged sword.

[13] "'I know where you dwell, where Satan's throne is; you hold fast my name and you did not deny my faith even in the days of Antipas my witness, my faithful one, who was killed among you, where Satan dwells. [14] But I have a few things against you: you have some there who hold the teaching of Balaam, who taught Balak to put a stumbling block before the sons of Israel, that they might eat food sacrificed to idols and practice immorality. [15] So you also have some who hold the teaching of the Nicolaitans. [16] Repent then. If not, I will come to you soon and war against them with the sword of my mouth. [17] *He who has an ear, let him hear what the Spirit says to the churches.* To him who conquers I will give some of the hidden manna, and I will give him a white stone, with a new name written on the stone which no one knows except him who receives it.'"

Rev 3:6 (§A97.11)

[1] "And to the angel of the church in Sardis write: 'The words of him who has the seven spirits of God and the seven stars.

"'I know your works; you have the name of being alive, and you are dead. [2]Awake, and strengthen what remains and is on the point of death, for I have not found your works perfect in the sight of my God. [3]Remember then what you received and heard; keep that, and repent. If you will not awake, I will come like a thief, and you will not know at what hour I will come upon you. [4]Yet you have still a few names in Sardis, people who have not soiled their garments; and they shall walk with me in white, for they are worthy. [5]He who conquers shall be clad thus in white garments, and I will not blot his name out of the book of life; I will confess his name before my Father and before his angels. [6]*He who has an ear, let him hear what the Spirit says to the churches.*'"

Rev 3:13 (§A97.12)

[7]"And to the angel of the church in Philadelphia write: 'The words of the holy one, the true one, who has the key of David, who opens and no one shall shut, who shuts and no one opens.

[8]"'I know your works. Behold, I have set before you an open door, which no one is able to shut; I know that you have but little power, and yet you have kept my word and have not denied my name. [9]Behold, I will make those of the synagogue of Satan who say that they are Jews and are not, but lie—behold, I will make them come and bow down before your feet, and learn that I have loved you. [10]Because you have kept my word of patient endurance, I will keep you from the hour of trial, which is coming on the whole world, to try those who dwell upon the earth. [11]I am coming soon; hold fast what you have, so that no one may seize your crown. [12]He who conquers, I will make him a pillar in the temple of my God; never shall he go out of it, and I will write on him the name of my God, and the name of the city of my God, the new Jerusalem which comes down from my God out of heaven, and my own new name. [13]*He who has an ear, let him hear what the Spirit says to the churches.*'"

Rev 3:22 (§A97.13)

[14]"And to the angel of the church in Laodicea write: 'The words of the Amen, the faithful and true witness, the beginning of God's creation.

[15]"'I know your works: you are neither cold nor hot. Would that you were cold or hot! [16]So, because you are lukewarm, and neither cold nor hot, I will spew you out of my mouth. [17]For you say, I am rich, I have prospered, and I need nothing; not know-ing that you are wretched, pitiable, poor, blind, and naked. [18]Therefore I counsel you to buy from me gold refined by fire, that you may be rich, and white garments to clothe you and to keep the shame of your nakedness from being seen, and salve to anoint your eyes, that you may see. [19]Those whom I love, I reprove and chasten; so be zealous and repent. [20]Behold, I stand at the door and knock; if any one hears my voice and opens the door, I will come in to him and eat with him, and he with me. [21]He who conquers, I will grant him to sit with me on my throne, as I myself conquered and sat down with my Father on his throne. [22]*He who has an ear, let him hear what the Spirit says to the churches.*'"

Rev 13:9a (§A97.14)

[5]And the beast was given a mouth utter-ing haughty and blasphemous words, and it was allowed to exercise authority for forty-two months; [6]it opened its mouth to utter blasphemies against God, blaspheming his name and his dwelling, that is, those who dwell in heaven. [7]Also it was allowed to make war on the saints and to conquer them. And authority was given it over every tribe and people and tongue and nation, [8]and all who dwell on earth will worship it, every one whose name has not been written before the foundation of the world in the book of life of the Lamb that was slain. [9]*If any one has an ear, let him hear:*

If any one is to be taken captive,
   to captivity he goes;
if any one slays with the sword,
   with the sword must he be slain.
Here is a call for the endurance and faith of the saints.

GThom 8:2 (§A97.15)

(8) [1]And He said, "The man is like a wise fisherman who cast his net into the sea and drew it up from the sea full of small fish. Among them the wise fisherman found a fine large fish. He threw all the small fish back into the sea and chose the large fish without difficulty. [2]*Whoever has ears to hear, let him hear.*"

GThom 21:5 (§A97.16)

(21) [1]Mary said to Jesus, "Whom are Your disciples like?"

[2]He said, "They are like children who have settled in a field which is not theirs. When the owners of the field come, they will say, 'Let us have back our field.' They (will) undress in their presence in order to let them have back their field and to give it back to them. [3]Therefore I say to you, if the owner of a house knows that the thief is coming, he will begin his vigil before he comes and will not let him dig through into his house of his domain to carry away his goods. You, then, be on your guard against the world. Arm yourselves with great strength lest the robbers find a way to come to you, for the difficulty which you expect will (surely) materialize. [4]Let there be among you a man of understanding. When the grain ripened, he came quickly with his sickle in his hand and reaped it. [5]*Whoever has ears to hear, let him hear.*"

GThom 24:2 (§A97.17)

(24) [1]His disciples said to Him, "Show us the place where You are, since it is neces-sary for us to seek it."

[2]He said to them, *"Whoever has ears, let him hear.* [3]There is light within a man of light, and he (or: it) lights up the whole world. If he (or: it) does not shine, he (or: it) is darkness."

GThom 63:2 (§A97.18)

(63) [1]Jesus said, "There was a rich man who had much money. He said, 'I shall put my money to use so that I may sow, reap, plant, and fill my storehouse with produce, with the result that I shall lack nothing.' Such were his intentions, but that same night he died. [2]*Let him who has ears hear.*"

GThom 65:2 (§A97.19)

(65) [1]He said, "There was a good man who owned a vineyard. He leased it to tenant farmers so that they might work it and he might collect the produce from them. He sent his servant so that the ten-ants might give him the produce of the vineyard. They seized his servant and beat him, all but killing him. The servant went back and told his master. The master said, 'Perhaps <they> did not recognize <him>.' He sent another servant. The ten-ants beat this one as well. Then the owner sent his son and said, 'Perhaps they will show respect to my son.' Because the ten-ants knew that it was he who was the heir to the vineyard, they seized him and killed him. [2]*Let him who has ears hear.*"

GThom 96:2 (§A97.20)

(96) [1]Jesus [said], "The Kingdom of the Father is like a certain woman. She took a little leaven, [concealed] it in some dough, and made it into large loaves. [2]*Let him who has ears hear.*"

131 WISDOM JUSTIFIED

Matt 11:16–19 (§A98.1)

¹⁶ *"But to what shall I compare this generation? It is like children sitting in the market places and calling to their playmates,*

¹⁷ *'We piped to you, and you did not dance;*
we wailed, and you did not mourn.'

¹⁸ *For John came neither eating nor drinking, and they say, 'He has a demon';* ¹⁹ *the Son of man came eating and drinking, and they say, 'Behold, a glutton and a drunkard, a friend of tax collectors and sinners!' Yet wisdom is justified by her deeds."*

Luke 7:31–35 (§A98.2)

³¹ *"To what then shall I compare the men of this generation, and what are they like?* ³² *They are like children sitting in the market place and calling to one another,*

'We piped to you, and you did not dance;
we wailed, and you did not weep.'

³³ *For John the Baptist has come eating no bread and drinking no wine; and you say, 'He has a demon.'* ³⁴ *The Son of man has come eating and drinking; and you say, 'Behold, a glutton and a drunkard, a friend of tax collectors and sinners!'* ³⁵ *Yet wisdom is justified by all her children."*

132 CITIES OF WOE

Matt 11:21–24 (§A99.1)

²⁰ Then he began to upbraid the cities where most of his mighty works had been done, because they did not repent. ²¹ *"Woe to you, Chorazin! woe to you, Bethsaida! for if the mighty works done in you had been done in Tyre and Sidon, they would have repented long ago in sackcloth and ashes.* ²² *But I tell you, it shall be more tolerable on the day of judgment for Tyre and Sidon than for you.* ²³ *And you, Capernaum, will you be exalted to heaven? You shall be brought down to Hades. For if the mighty works done in you had been done in Sodom, it would have remained until this day.* ²⁴ *But I tell you that it shall be more tolerable on the day of judgment for the land of Sodom than for you."*

Luke 10:13–15 (§A99.2)

¹³ *"Woe to you, Chorazin! woe to you, Bethsaida! for if the mighty works done in you had been done in Tyre and Sidon, they would have repented long ago, sitting in sackcloth and ashes.* ¹⁴ *But it shall be more tolerable in the judgment for Tyre and Sidon than for you.* ¹⁵ *And you, Capernaum, will you be exalted to heaven? You shall be brought down to Hades."*

133 FATHER AND SON*

Matt 11:25–27 (§A100.1)
²⁵ At that time Jesus declared, *"I thank thee, Father, Lord of heaven and earth, that thou hast hidden these things from the wise and understanding and revealed them to babes;* ²⁶ *yea, Father, for such was thy gracious will.* ²⁷ *All things have been delivered to me by my Father; and no one knows the Son except the Father, and no one knows the Father except the Son and any one to whom the Son chooses to reveal him."*

Luke 10:21–22 (§A100.2)
²¹ In that same hour he rejoiced in the Holy Spirit and said, *"I thank thee, Father, Lord of heaven and earth, that thou hast hidden these things from the wise and understanding and revealed them to babes; yea, Father, for such was thy gracious will.* ²² *All things have been delivered to me by my Father; and no one knows who the Son is except the Father, or who the Father is except the Son and any one to whom the Son chooses to reveal him."*

* See 381: *Jesus and Salome*

John 3:35 (§A100.3)
³¹ He who comes from above is above all; he who is of the earth belongs to the earth, and of the earth he speaks; he who comes from heaven is above all. ³² He bears witness to what he has seen and heard, yet no one receives his testimony; ³³ he who receives his testimony sets his seal to this, that God is true. ³⁴ For he whom God has sent utters the words of God, for it is not by measure that he gives the Spirit; ³⁵ *the Father loves the Son, and has given all things into his hand.* ³⁶ He who believes in the Son has eternal life; he who does not obey the Son shall not see life, but the wrath of God rests upon him.

John 13:3a (§A100.4)
¹ Now before the feast of the Passover, when Jesus knew that his hour had come to depart out of this world to the Father, having loved his own who were in the world, he loved them to the end. ² And during supper, when the devil had already put it into the heart of Judas Iscariot, Simon's son, to betray him, ³ *Jesus, knowing that the Father had given all things into his hands,* and that he had come from God and was going to God, ⁴ rose from supper, laid aside his garments, and girded himself with a towel.

GThom 61:4 (§A100.5)
(61) ¹ Jesus said, "Two will rest on a bed: the one will die, the other will live."
² Salome said, "Who are You, man, that You, as though from the One, (or: as <whose son>, that You) have come up on my couch and eaten from my table?"
³ Jesus said to her, "I am He who exists from the Undivided. ⁴ *I was given some of the things of My father."*
⁵ <Salome said,> "I am Your disciple."
⁶ <Jesus said to her,> "Therefore I say, if he is <undivided>, he will be filled with light, but if he is divided, he will be filled with darkness."

GNaz 9 (§A100.6)
(9) The Jewish Gospel: *I thank thee.* (Variant to Matthew 11:25 in the "Zion Gospel" Edition)

134 YOKE AND BURDEN*

Matt 11:28–30 (§A101.1)
²⁸ *"Come to me, all who labor and are heavy laden, and I will give you rest.* ²⁹ *Take my yoke upon you, and learn from me; for I am gentle and lowly in heart, and you will find rest for your souls.* ³⁰ *For my yoke is easy, and my burden is light."*

GThom 90 (§A101.2)
(90) Jesus said, *"Come unto Me, for My yoke is easy and My lordship is mild, and you will find repose for yourselves."*

* See 334: *Yoke and Burden*

DialSav 65–68 (§A101.3)
(65) Matthew said, "[Why] do we not rest [at once]?"
(66) The Lord said, *"When you lay down these burdens!"*
(67) Matthew said, "How does the small join itself to the big?"
(68) The Lord said, *"When you abandon the works which will not be able to follow you, then you will rest."*

135 LORD OF SABBATH

Matt 12:8 (§A102.1)

¹ At that time Jesus went through the grainfields on the sabbath; his disciples were hungry, and they began to pluck heads of grain and to eat. ² But when the Pharisees saw it, they said to him, "Look, your disciples are doing what is not lawful to do on the sabbath." ³ He said to them, "Have you not read what David did, when he was hungry, and those who were with him: ⁴ how he entered the house of God and ate the bread of the Presence, which it was not lawful for him to eat nor for those who were with him, but only for the priests? ⁵ Or have you not read in the law how on the sabbath the priests in the temple profane the sabbath, and are guiltless? ⁶ I tell you, something greater than the temple is here. ⁷ And if you had known what this means, 'I desire mercy, and not sacrifice,' you would not have condemned the guiltless. ⁸ *For the Son of man is lord of the sabbath."*

Mark 2:27–28 (§A102.2)

²³ One sabbath he was going through the grainfields; and as they made their way his disciples began to pluck heads of grain. ²⁴ And the Pharisees said to him, "Look, why are they doing what is not lawful on the sabbath?" ²⁵ And he said to them, "Have you never read what David did, when he was in need and was hungry, he and those who were with him: ²⁶ how he entered the house of God, when Abiathar was high priest, and ate the bread of the Presence, which it is not lawful for any but the priests to eat, and also gave it to those who were with him?" ²⁷ And he said to them, *"The sabbath was made for man, not man for the sabbath; ²⁸ so the Son of man is lord even of the sabbath."*

Luke 6:5 (§A102.3)

¹ On a sabbath, while he was going through the grainfields, his disciples plucked and ate some heads of grain, rubbing them in their hands. ² But some of the Pharisees said, "Why are you doing what is not lawful to do on the sabbath?" ³ And Jesus answered, "Have you not read what David did when he was hungry, he and those who were with him: ⁴ how he entered the house of God, and took and ate the bread of the Presence, which it is not lawful for any but the priests to eat, and also gave it to those with him?" ⁵ And he said to them, *"The Son of man is lord of the sabbath."*

136 BY WHOSE POWER

Matt 12:27–28 (§A103.1)

²² Then a blind and dumb demoniac was brought to him, and he healed him, so that the dumb man spoke and saw. ²³ And all the people were amazed, and said, "Can this be the Son of David?" ²⁴ But when the Pharisees heard it they said, "It is only by Beelzebul, the prince of demons, that this man casts out demons." ²⁵ Knowing their thoughts, he said to them, "Every kingdom divided against itself is laid waste, and no city or house divided against itself will stand; ²⁶ and if Satan casts out Satan, he is divided against himself; how then will his kingdom stand? ²⁷ *And if I cast out demons by Beelzebul, by whom do your sons cast them out? Therefore they shall be your judges. ²⁸ But if it is by the Spirit of God that I cast out demons, then the kingdom of God has come upon you."*

Luke 11:19–20 (§A103.2)

¹⁴ Now he was casting out a demon that was dumb; when the demon had gone out, the dumb man spoke, and the people marveled. ¹⁵ But some of them said, "He casts out demons by Beelzebul, the prince of demons"; ¹⁶ while others, to test him, sought from him a sign from heaven. ¹⁷ But he, knowing their thoughts, said to them, "Every kingdom divided against itself is laid waste, and a divided household falls. ¹⁸ And if Satan also is divided against himself, how will his kingdom stand? For you say that I cast out demons by Beelzebul. ¹⁹ *And if I cast out demons by Beelzebul, by whom do your sons cast them out? Therefore they shall be your judges. ²⁰ But if it is by the finger of God that I cast out demons, then the kingdom of God has come upon you."*

Matt 12:29 (§A104.1)

²² Then a blind and dumb demoniac was brought to him, and he healed him, so that the dumb man spoke and saw. ²³ And all the people were amazed, and said, "Can this be the Son of David?" ²⁴ But when the Pharisees heard it they said, "It is only by Beelzebul, the prince of demons, that this man casts out demons." ²⁵ Knowing their thoughts, he said to them, "Every kingdom divided against itself is laid waste, and no city or house divided against itself will stand; ²⁶ and if Satan casts out Satan, he is divided against himself; how then will his kingdom stand? ²⁷ And if I cast out demons by Beelzebul, by whom do your sons cast them out? Therefore they shall be your judges. ²⁸ But if it is by the Spirit of God that I cast out demons, then the kingdom of God has come upon you. ²⁹ *Or how can one enter a strong man's house and plunder his goods, unless he first binds the strong man? Then indeed he may plunder his house.*"

Mark 3:27 (§A104.2)

²² And the scribes who came down from Jerusalem said, "He is possessed by Beelzebul, and by the prince of demons he casts out the demons." ²³ And he called them to him, and said to them in parables, "How can Satan cast out Satan? ²⁴ If a kingdom is divided against itself, that kingdom cannot stand. ²⁵ And if a house is divided against itself, that house will not be able to stand. ²⁶ And if Satan has risen up against himself and is divided, he cannot stand, but is coming to an end. ²⁷ *But no one can enter a strong man's house and plunder his goods, unless he first binds the strong man; then indeed he may plunder his house.*"

Luke 11:21–22 (§A104.3)

¹⁴ Now he was casting out a demon that was dumb; when the demon had gone out, the dumb man spoke, and the people marveled. ¹⁵ But some of them said, "He casts out demons by Beelzebul, the prince of demons"; ¹⁶ while others, to test him, sought from him a sign from heaven. ¹⁷ But

he, knowing their thoughts, said to them, "Every kingdom divided against itself is laid waste, and a divided household falls. ¹⁸ And if Satan also is divided against himself, how will his kingdom stand? For you say that I cast out demons by Beelzebul. ¹⁹ And if I cast out demons by Beelzebul, by whom do your sons cast them out? Therefore they shall be your judges. ²⁰ But if it is by the finger of God that I cast out demons, then the kingdom of God has come upon you. ²¹ *When a strong man, fully armed, guards his own palace, his goods are in peace;* ²² *but when one stronger than he assails him and overcomes him, he takes away his armor in which he trusted, and divides his spoil.*"

GThom 35 (§A104.4)

(35) Jesus said, "*It is not possible for anyone to enter the house of a strong man and take it by force unless he binds his hands; then he will (be able to) ransack his house.*"

Matt 12:30 (§A105.1)

²⁹ "Or how can one enter a strong man's house and plunder his goods, unless he first binds the strong man? Then indeed he may plunder his house. ³⁰ *He who is not with me is against me, and he who does not gather with me scatters.*"

Mark 9:40 (§A105.2)

³⁸ John said to him, "Teacher, we saw a man casting out demons in your name, and we forbade him, because he was not following us." ³⁹ But Jesus said, "Do not forbid him; for no one who does a mighty work in my name will be able soon after to speak evil of me. ⁴⁰ *For he that is not against us is for us.* ⁴¹ For truly, I say to you, whoever gives you a cup of water to drink because you bear the name of Christ, will by no means lose his reward."

Luke 9:50b (§A105.3)

⁴⁹ John answered, "Master, we saw a man casting out demons in your name, and we forbade him, because he does not follow with us." ⁵⁰ But Jesus said to him, "Do not forbid him; *for he that is not against you is for you.*"

Luke 11:23 (§A105.4)

²¹ "When a strong man, fully armed, guards his own palace, his goods are in peace; ²² but when one stronger than he assails him and overcomes him, he takes away his armor in which he trusted, and divides his spoil. ²³ *He who is not with me is against me, and he who does not gather with me scatters.*"

POxy1224 2 (§A105.5)

(2) And pray for your enemies. *For he who is not [against you] is for you.* [He who today] is far-off—tomorrow will be [near to you]. . . .

ALL SINS FORGIVEN

Matt 12:31–32 (§A106.1)
[31] *"Therefore I tell you, every sin and blasphemy will be forgiven men, but the blasphemy against the Spirit will not be forgiven.* [32] *And whoever says a word against the Son of man will be forgiven, but whoever speaks against the Holy Spirit will not be forgiven, either in this age or in the age to come."*

Mark 3:28–29 (§A106.2)
[28] *"Truly, I say to you, all sins will be forgiven the sons of men, and whatever blasphemies they utter;* [29] *but whoever blasphemes against the Holy Spirit never has forgiveness, but is guilty of an eternal sin"*— [30] for they had said, "He has an unclean spirit."

Luke 12:10 (§A106.3)
[10] *"And every one who speaks a word against the Son of man will be forgiven; but he who blasphemes against the Holy Spirit will not be forgiven."*

GThom 44 (§A106.4)
(44) Jesus said, *"Whoever blasphemes against the Father will be forgiven, and whoever blasphemes against the Son will be forgiven, but whoever blasphemes against the Holy Spirit will not be forgiven either on earth or in heaven."*

Did 11:7b (§A106.5)
[7] Do not test or examine any prophet who is speaking in a spirit, *"for every sin shall be forgiven, but this sin shall not be forgiven."* [8] not everyone who speaks in a spirit is a prophet, except he have the behaviour of the Lord. From his behaviour, then, the false prophet and the true prophet shall be known. [9] And no prophet who orders a meal in a spirit shall eat of it: otherwise he is a false prophet. [10] And every prophet who teaches the truth, if he do not what he teaches, is a false prophet. [11] But no prophet who has been tried and is genuine, though he enact a worldly mystery of the Church, if he teach not others to do what he does himself, shall be judged by you: for he has his judgment with God, for so also did the prophets of old. [12] But whosoever shall say in a spirit 'Give me money, or something else.' you shall not listen to him; but if he tell you to give on behalf of others in want, let none judge him.

BY YOUR WORDS

Matt 12:36–37 (§A107.1)
[36] *"I tell you, on the day of judgment men will render account for every careless word they utter;* [37] *for by your words you will be justified, and by your words you will be condemned."*

JUDGMENT BY PAGANS

Matt 12:41–42 (§A108.1)
[41] *"The men of Nineveh will arise at the judgment with this generation and condemn it; for they repented at the preaching of Jonah, and behold, something greater than Jonah is here.* [42] *The queen of the South will arise at the judgment with this generation and condemn it; for she came from the ends of the earth to hear the wisdom of Solomon, and behold, something greater than Solomon is here."*

Luke 11:31–32 (§A108.2)
[31] *"The queen of the South will arise at the judgment with the men of this generation and condemn them; for she came from the ends of the earth to hear the wisdom of Solomon, and behold, something greater than Solomon is here.* [32] *The men of Nineveh will arise at the judgment with this generation and condemn it; for they repented at the preaching of Jonah, and behold, something greater than Jonah is here."*

142 THE RETURNING DEMON

Matt 12:43–45 (§A109.1)
43 "When the unclean spirit has gone out of a man, he passes through waterless places seeking rest, but he finds none. 44 Then he says, 'I will return to my house from which I came.' And when he comes he finds it empty, swept, and put in order. 45 Then he goes and brings with him seven other spirits more evil than himself, and they enter and dwell there; and the last state of that man becomes worse than the first. So shall it be also with this evil generation."

Luke 11:24–26 (§A109.2)
24 "When the unclean spirit has gone out of a man, he passes through waterless places seeking rest; and finding none he says, 'I will return to my house from which I came.' 25 And when he comes he finds it swept and put in order. 26 Then he goes and brings seven other spirits more evil than himself, and they enter and dwell there; and the last state of that man becomes worse than the first."

143 KNOWING THE MYSTERY⋆

Matt 13:11 (§A110.1)
10 Then the disciples came and said to him, "Why do you speak to them in parables?" 11 And he answered them, *"To you it has been given to know the secrets of the kingdom of heaven, but to them it has not been given.* 12 For to him who has will more be given, and he will have abundance; but from him who has not, even what he has will be taken away."

Mark 4:11 (§A110.2)
10 And when he was alone, those who were about him with the twelve asked him concerning the parables. 11 And he said to them, *"To you has been given the secret of the kingdom of God, but for those outside everything is in parables;* 12 so that they may indeed see but not perceive, and may indeed hear but not understand; lest they should turn again, and be forgiven."

⋆ See 336: *Knowing the Mystery*

Luke 8:10a (§A110.3)
9 And when his disciples asked him what this parable meant, 10 he said, *"To you it has been given to know the secrets of the kingdom of God; but for others they are in parables,* so that seeing they may not see, and hearing they may not understand."

GThom 62:1 (§A110.4)
(62) 1 Jesus said, *"It is to those [who are worthy of My] mysteries that I tell My mysteries.* 2 Do not let your left hand know what your right hand is doing."

Matt 13:12 (§A111.1)

¹⁰Then the disciples came and said to him, "Why do you speak to them in parables?" ¹¹And he answered them, "To you it has been given to know the secrets of the kingdom of heaven, but to them it has not been given. ¹²*For to him who has will more be given, and he will have abundance; but from him who has not, even what he has will be taken away."*

Matt 25:29 (§A111.2)

¹⁴"For it will be as when a man going on a journey called his servants and entrusted to them his property; ¹⁵to one he gave five talents, to another two, to another one, to each according to his ability. Then he went away. ¹⁶He who had received the five talents went at once and traded with them; and he made five talents more. ¹⁷So also, he who had the two talents made two talents more. ¹⁸But he who had received the one talent went and dug in the ground and hid his master's money. ¹⁹Now after a long time the master of those servants came and settled accounts with them. ²⁰And he who had received the five talents came forward, bringing five talents more, saying, 'Master, you delivered to me five talents; here I have made five talents more.' ²¹His master said to him, 'Well done, good and faithful servant; you have been faithful over a little, I will set you over much; enter into the joy of your master.' ²²And he also who had the two talents came forward, saying, 'Master, you delivered to me two talents; here I have made two talents more.' ²³His master said to him, 'Well done, good and faithful servant; you have been faithful over a little, I will set you over much; enter into the joy of your master.' ²⁴He also who had received the one talent came forward, saying, 'Master, I knew you to be a hard man, reaping where you did not sow, and gathering where you did not winnow; ²⁵so I was afraid, and I went and hid your talent in the ground. Here you have what is yours.' ²⁶But his master answered him, 'You wicked and slothful servant! You knew that I reap where I have not sowed, and gather where I have not winnowed? ²⁷Then you ought to have invested my money with the bankers, and at my coming I should have received what was my own with interest. ²⁸So take the talent from him, and give it to him who has the ten talents. ²⁹*For to every one who has will more be given, and he will have abundance; but from him who has not, even what he has will be taken away.* ³⁰And cast the worthless servant into the outer darkness; there men will weep and gnash their teeth.'"

Mark 4:25 (§A111.3)

²⁴And he said to them, "Take heed what you hear; the measure you give will be the measure you get, and still more will be given you. ²⁵*For to him who has will more be given; and from him who has not, even what he has will be taken away."*

Luke 8:18b (§A111.4)

¹⁶"No one after lighting a lamp covers it with a vessel, or puts it under a bed, but puts it on a stand, that those who enter may see the light. ¹⁷For nothing is hid that shall not be made manifest, nor anything secret that shall not be known and come to light. ¹⁸Take heed then how you hear; *for to him who has will more be given, and from him who has not, even what he thinks that he has will be taken away."*

Luke 19:26 (§A111.5)

¹¹As they heard these things, he proceeded to tell a parable, because he was near to Jerusalem, and because they supposed that the kingdom of God was to appear immediately. ¹²He said therefore, "A nobleman went into a far country to receive a kingdom and then return. ¹³Calling ten of his servants, he gave them ten pounds, and said to them, 'Trade with these till I come.' ¹⁴But his citizens hated him and sent an embassy after him, saying, 'We do not want this man to reign over us.' ¹⁵When he returned, having received the kingdom, he commanded these servants, to whom he had given the money, to be called to him, that he might know what they had gained by trading. ¹⁶The first came before him, saying, 'Lord, your pound has made ten pounds more.' ¹⁷And he said to him, 'Well done, good servant! Because you have been faithful in a very little, you shall have authority over ten cities.' ¹⁸And the second came, saying, 'Lord, your pound has made five pounds.' ¹⁹And he said to him, 'And you are to be over five cities.' ²⁰Then another came, saying, 'Lord, here is your pound, which I kept laid away in a napkin; ²¹for I was afraid of you, because you are a severe man; you take up what you did not lay down, and reap what you did not sow.' ²²He said to him, 'I will condemn you out of your own mouth, you wicked servant! You knew that I was a severe man, taking up what I did not lay down and reaping what I did not sow? ²³Why then did you not put my money into the bank, and at my coming I should have collected it with interest?' ²⁴And he said to those who stood by, 'Take the pound from him, and give it to him who has the ten pounds.' ²⁵(And they said to him, 'Lord, he has ten pounds!') ²⁶*I tell you, that to every one who has will more be given; but from him who has not, even what he has will be taken away.* ²⁷But as for these enemies of mine, who did not want me to reign over them, bring them here and slay them before me.'"

GThom 41 (§A111.6)

(41) Jesus said, *"Whoever has something in his hand will receive more, and whoever has nothing will be deprived of even the little he has."*

145 BLESSED THE EYES

Matt 13:16–17 (§A112.1)

[10] Then the disciples came and said to him, "Why do you speak to them in parables?" [11] And he answered them, "To you it has been given to know the secrets of the kingdom of heaven, but to them it has not been given. [12] For to him who has will more be given, and he will have abundance; but from him who has not, even what he has will be taken away. [13] This is why I speak to them in parables, because seeing they do not see, and hearing they do not hear, nor do they understand. [14] With them indeed is fulfilled the prophecy of Isaiah which says:

'You shall indeed hear but never understand,

and you shall indeed see but never perceive.

[15] For this people's heart has grown dull,
and their ears are heavy of hearing,
and their eyes they have closed,
lest they should perceive with their eyes,
and hear with their ears,
and understand with their heart,
and turn for me to heal them.'

[16] *But blessed are your eyes, for they see, and your ears, for they hear.* [17] *Truly, I say to you, many prophets and righteous men longed to see what you see, and did not see it, and to hear what you hear, and did not hear it."*

Luke 10:23b–24 (§A112.2)

[21] In that same hour he rejoiced in the Holy Spirit and said, "I thank thee, Father, Lord of heaven and earth, that thou hast hidden these things from the wise and understanding and revealed them to babes; yea, Father, for such was thy gracious will. [22] All things have been delivered to me by my Father; and no one knows who the Son is except the Father, or who the Father is except the Son and any one to whom the Son chooses to reveal him."

[23] Then turning to the disciples he said privately, *"Blessed are the eyes which see what you see!* [24] *For I tell you that many prophets and kings desired to see what you see, and did not see it, and to hear what you hear, and did not hear it."*

146 PROPHET'S OWN COUNTRY*

Matt 13:57b (§A113.1)

[53] And when Jesus had finished these parables, he went away from there, [54] and coming to his own country he taught them in their synagogue, so that they were astonished, and said, "Where did this man get this wisdom and these mighty works? [55] Is not this the carpenter's son? Is not his mother called Mary? And are not his brothers James and Joseph and Simon and Judas? [56] And are not all his sisters with us? Where then did this man get all this?" [57] And they took offense at him. But Jesus said to them, *"A prophet is not without honor except in his own country and in his own house."* [58] And he did not do many mighty works there, because of their unbelief.

Mark 6:4b (§A113.2)

[1] He went away from there and came to his own country; and his disciples followed him. [2] And on the sabbath he began to teach in the synagogue; and many who heard him were astonished, saying, "Where did this man get all this? What is the wisdom given to him? What mighty works are wrought by his hands! [3] Is not this the carpenter, the son of Mary and brother of James and Joses and Judas and Simon, and are not his sisters here with us?" And they took offense at him. [4] And Jesus said to them, *"A prophet is not without honor, except in his own country, and among his own kin, and in his own house."* [5] And he could do no mighty work there, except that he laid his hands upon a few sick people and healed them. [6] And he marveled because of their unbelief. And he went about among the villages teaching.

Luke 4:23–24 (§A113.3)

[16] And he came to Nazareth, where he had been brought up; and he went to the synagogue, as his custom was, on the sabbath day. And he stood up to read; [17] and there was given to him the book of the prophet Isaiah. He opened the book and found the place where it was written,

[18] "The Spirit of the Lord is upon me,
because he has anointed me to preach
good news to the poor.

He has sent me to proclaim release to the captives

and recovering of sight to the blind,
to set at liberty those who are oppressed,

[19] to proclaim the acceptable year of the Lord."

[20] And he closed the book, and gave it back to the attendant, and sat down; and the eyes of all in the synagogue were fixed on him. [21] And he began to say to them, "Today this scripture has been fulfilled in your hearing." [22] And all spoke well of him, and wondered at the gracious words which proceeded out of his mouth; and they said, "Is not this Joseph's son?" [23] And he said to them, "Doubtless you will quote to me this proverb, *'Physician, heal yourself;* what we have heard you did at Capernaum, do here also in your own country.'" [24] And he said, *"Truly, I say to you, no prophet is acceptable in his own country.* [25] But in truth, I tell you, there were many widows in Israel in the days of Elijah, when the heaven was shut up three years and six months, when there came a great famine over all the land; [26] and Elijah was sent to none of them but only to Zarephath, in the land of Sidon, to a woman who was a widow. [27] And there were many lepers in Israel in the time of the prophet Elisha; and none of them was cleansed, but only Naaman the Syrian." [28] When they heard this, all in the synagogue were filled with wrath. [29] And they rose up and put him out of the city, and led him to the brow of the hill on which their city was built, that they might throw him down headlong. [30] But passing through the midst of them he went away.

John 4:44b (§A113.4)

[43] After the two days he departed to Galilee. [44] For Jesus himself testified that *a prophet has no honor in his own country.* [45] So when he came to Galilee, the Galileans welcomed him, having seen all that he had done in Jerusalem at the feast, for they too had gone to the feast.

POxy1 31 (§A113.5)

(31) Jesus said, *"No prophet is accepted in his own country; no physician heals those who know him."*

GThom 31 (§A113.6)

(31) Jesus said, *"No prophet is accepted in his own village; no physician heals those who know him."*

* See 214: *Physician, Heal Yourself*
* See 436: *Prophet's Own Country*

147 WHAT GOES IN*

Matt 15:11 (§A114.1)

[10] And he called the people to him and said to them, "Hear and understand: [11] *not what goes into the mouth defiles a man, but what comes out of the mouth, this defiles a man.*"

Mark 7:15 (§A114.2)

[14] And he called the people to him again, and said to them, "Hear me, all of you, and understand: [15] *there is nothing outside a man which by going into him can defile him; but the things which come out of a man are what defile him.*"

Acts 10:14b (§A114.3)

[9] The next day, as they were on their journey and coming near the city, Peter went up on the housetop to pray, about the sixth hour. [10] And he became hungry and desired something to eat; but while they were preparing it, he fell into a trance [11] and saw the heaven opened, and something descending, like a great sheet, let down by four corners upon the earth. [12] In it were all kinds of animals and reptiles and birds of the air. [13] And there came a voice to him, "Rise, Peter; kill and eat." [14] But Peter said,

"No, Lord; *for I have never eaten anything that is common or unclean.*" [15] And the voice came to him again a second time, "What God has cleansed, you must not call common." [16] This happened three times, and the thing was taken up at once to heaven.

Acts 11:8b (§A114.4)

[1] Now the apostles and the brethren who were in Judea heard that the Gentiles also had received the word of God. [2] So when Peter went up to Jerusalem, the circumcision party criticized him, [3] saying, "Why did you go to uncircumcised men and eat with them?" [4] But Peter began and explained to them in order: [5] "I was in the city of Joppa praying; and in a trance I saw a vision, something descending, like a great sheet, let down from heaven by four corners; and it came down to me. [6] Looking at it closely I observed animals and beasts of prey and reptiles and birds of the air. [7] And I heard a voice saying to me, 'Rise, Peter; kill and eat.' [8] But I said, 'No, Lord; *for nothing common or unclean has ever entered my mouth.*' [9] But the voice answered a second time from heaven, 'What God has cleansed

you must not call common.' [10] This happened three times, and all was drawn up again into heaven."

GThom 14:3 (§A114.5)

(6) [1] His disciples questioned Him and said to Him, "Do You want us to fast? How shall we pray? Shall we give alms? What diet shall we observe?"

[2] Jesus said, "Do not tell lies, [3] and do not do what you hate, for all things are plain in the sight of Heaven. [4] For nothing hidden will not become manifest, and nothing covered will remain without being uncovered."

(14) [1] Jesus said to them, "If you fast, you will give rise to sin for yourselves; and if you pray, you will be condemned; and if you give alms, you will do harm to your spirits. [2] When you go into any land and walk about in the districts, if they receive you, eat what they will set before you, and heal the sick among them. [3] *For what goes into your mouth will not defile you, but that which issues from your mouth—it is that which will defile you.*"

* See 339 & 438: *What Goes In*

---

148 PLANT ROOTED UP*

Matt 15:13 (§A115.1)

[12] Then the disciples came and said to him, "Do you know that the Pharisees were offended when they heard this saying?" [13] He answered, *"Every plant which my heavenly Father has not planted will be rooted up."*

GThom 40 (§A115.2)

(40) Jesus said, *"A grapevine has been planted outside of the Father, but being unsound, it will be pulled up by its roots and destroyed."*

Ign Tral 11:1b (§A115.3)

[1] Fly from these wicked offshoots, which bear deadly fruit, which if a man eat he presently dies. *For these are not the planting of the Father.* [2] For if they were they would appear as branches of the Cross (and their fruit would be incorruptible) by which through his Passion he calls you who are his members. The head therefore cannot be borne without limbs, since God promises union, that is himself.

* See 340: *Plant Rooted Up*

Ign Phld 3:1b (§A115.4)

[1] Abstain from evil growths, which Jesus Christ does not tend, because *they are not the planting of the Father.* Not that I have found division among you but 'filtering.'

Matt 15:14a (§A116.1)

¹⁰ And he called the people to him and said to them, "Hear and understand: ¹¹ not what goes into the mouth defiles a man, but what comes out of the mouth, this defiles a man." ¹² Then the disciples came and said to him, "Do you know that the Pharisees were offended when they heard this saying?" ¹³ He answered, "Every plant which my heavenly Father has not planted will be rooted up. ¹⁴ *Let them alone; they are blind guides.* And if a blind man leads a blind man, both will fall into a pit."

Matt 23:16a, 17a, 19a, 24a, 26a (§A116.2)

¹⁶ *"Woe to you, blind guides,* who say, 'If any one swears by the temple, it is nothing; but if any one swears by the gold of the temple, he is bound by his oath.' ¹⁷ *You blind fools!* For which is greater, the gold or the temple that has made the gold sacred? ¹⁸ And you say, 'If any one swears by the altar, it is nothing; but if any one swears by the gift that is on the altar, he is bound by his oath.' ¹⁹ *You blind men!* For which is greater, the gift or the altar that makes the gift sacred? ²⁰ So he who swears by the altar, swears by it and by everything on it; ²¹ and he who swears by the temple, swears by it and by him who dwells in it; ²² and he who swears by heaven, swears by the throne of God and by him who sits upon it.

²³ "Woe to you, scribes and Pharisees, hypocrites! for you tithe mint and dill and cummin, and have neglected the weightier matters of the law, justice and mercy and faith; these you ought to have done, without neglecting the others. ²⁴ *You blind guides,* straining out a gnat and swallowing a camel!

²⁵ "Woe to you, scribes and Pharisees, hypocrites! for you cleanse the outside of the cup and of the plate, but inside they are full of extortion and rapacity. ²⁶ *You blind Pharisee!* first cleanse the inside of the cup and of the plate, that the outside also may be clean."

John 9:41b (§A116.3)

³⁹ Jesus said, "For judgment I came into this world, that those who do not see may see, and that those who see may become blind." ⁴⁰ Some of the Pharisees near him heard this, and they said to him, "Are we also blind?" ⁴¹ Jesus said to them, *"If you were blind, you would have no guilt; but now that you say, 'We see,' your guilt remains."*

POxy840 (§A116.4)

(1) First before he does wrong (?) he thinks out everything that is crafty. But be ye on your guard that the same thing may not happen to you as does to them. For not only among the living do evil doers among men receive retribution, but they must also suffer punishment and great torment.

(2) And he took them (the disciples) with him into the place of purification itself and walked about in the Temple court. And a Pharisaic chief priest, Levi (?) by name, fell in with them and s[aid] to the Savior: Who gave thee leave to [trea]d this place of purification and to look upon [the]se holy utensils without having bathed thyself and even without thy disciples having [wa]shed their f[eet]? On the contrary, being defi[led], thou hast trodden the Temple court, this clean p[lace], although no [one who] has [not] first bathed himself or [chang]ed his clot[hes] may tread it and [venture] to vi[ew these] holy utensils! Forthwith [the Savior] s[tood] still with h[is] disciples and [answered]: How stands it (then) with thee, thou art forsooth (also) here in the Temple court. Art thou then clean? He said to him: I am clean. For I have bathed myself in the pool of David and have gone down by the one stair and come up by the other and have put on white and clean clothes, and (only) then have I come hither and have viewed these holy utensils. Then said the Savior to him: *Woe unto you blind that see not!* Thou hast bathed thyself in water that is poured out, in which dogs and swine lie night and day and thou hast washed thyself and hast chafed thine outer skin, which prostitutes also and flute-girls anoint, bathe, chafe and rouge, in order to arouse desire in men, but within they are full of scorpions and of [bad]ness [of every kind]. But I and [my disciples], of whom thou sayest that we have not im[mersed] ourselves, [have been im]mersed in the liv[ing . . .] water which comes down from [. . . B]ut woe unto them that . . .

* See 341: *Pharisees as Blind*

Matt 15:14b (§A117.1)

¹⁴ "Let them alone; they are blind guides. And *if a blind man leads a blind man, both will fall into a pit."*

Luke 6:39b (§A117.2)

³⁹ He also told them a parable: *"Can a blind man lead a blind man? Will they not both fall into a pit?"*

GThom 34 (§A117.3)

(34) Jesus said, *"If a blind man leads a blind man, they will both fall into a pit."*

151

KNOWING THE TIMES*

Matt 16:2–3 (§A118.1)

[1] And the Pharisees and Sadducees came, and to test him they asked him to show them a sign from heaven. [2] He answered them, *"When it is evening, you say, 'It will be fair weather; for the sky is red.' [3] And in the morning, 'It will be stormy today, for the sky is red and threatening.' You know how to interpret the appearance of the sky, but you cannot interpret the signs of the times.* [4] An evil and adulterous generation seeks for a sign, but no sign shall be given to it except the sign of Jonah." So he left them and departed.

Luke 12:54–56 (§A118.2)

[54] He also said to the multitudes, *"When you see a cloud rising in the west, you say at once, 'A shower is coming'; and so it happens.* [55] *And when you see the south wind blowing, you say, 'There will be scorching heat'; and it happens.* [56] *You hypocrites! You know how to interpret the appearance of the earth and sky; but why do you not know how to interpret the present time?"*

* See 342: *Knowing the Times*

GThom 91:2 (§A118.3)

(91) [1] They said to Him, "Tell us who You are so that we may believe in You."

[2] He said to them, *"You read the face of the sky and of the earth, but you have not recognized the one who (or: that which) is before you, and you do not know how to read this moment."*

GNaz 13 (§A118.4)

(13) What is marked with an asterisk (i.e., Matthew 16:2–3) is not found in other manuscripts, also it is not found in the Jewish Gospel. (Variant to Matthew 16:2–3 in the "Zion Gospel" Edition)

152

LEAVEN OF PHARISEES*

Matt 16:6,11b (§A119.1)

[5] When the disciples reached the other side, they had forgotten to bring any bread. [6] Jesus said to them, *"Take heed and beware of the leaven of the Pharisees and Sadducees."* [7] And they discussed it among themselves, saying, "We brought no bread." [8] But Jesus, aware of this, said, "O men of little faith, why do you discuss among yourselves the fact that you have no bread? [9] Do you not yet perceive? Do you not remember the five loaves of the five thousand, and how many baskets you gathered? [10] Or the seven loaves of the four thousand, and how many baskets you gathered? [11] How is it that you fail to perceive that I did not speak about bread? *Beware of the leaven of the Pharisees and Sadducees."* [12] Then they understood that he did not tell them to beware of the leaven of bread, but of the teaching of the Pharisees and Sadducees.

Mark 8:15b (§A119.2)

[14] Now they had forgotten to bring bread; and they had only one loaf with them in the boat. [15] And he cautioned them, saying, *"Take heed, beware of the leaven of the Pharisees and the leaven of Herod."* [16] And they discussed it with one another, saying, "We have no bread." [17] And being aware of it, Jesus said to them, "Why do you discuss the fact that you have no bread? Do you not yet perceive or understand? Are your hearts hardened? [18] Having eyes do you not see, and having ears do you not hear? And do you not remember? [19] When I broke the five loaves for the five thousand, how many baskets full of broken pieces did you take up?" They said to him, "Twelve." [20] "And the seven for the four thousand, how many baskets full of broken pieces did you take up?" And they said to him, "Seven." [21] And he said to them, "Do you not yet understand?"

Luke 12:1b (§A119.3)

[1] In the meantime, when so many thousands of the multitude had gathered together that they trod upon one another, he began to say to his disciples first, *"Beware of the leaven of the Pharisees, which is hypocrisy."*

* See 441: *Leaven of Pharisees*

Matt 16:19b (§A120.1)

¹³ Now when Jesus came into the district of Caesarea Philippi, he asked his disciples, "Who do men say that the Son of man is?" ¹⁴ And they said, "Some say John the Baptist, others say Elijah, and others Jeremiah or one of the prophets." ¹⁵ He said to them, "But who do you say that I am?" ¹⁶ Simon Peter replied, "You are the Christ, the Son of the living God." ¹⁷ And Jesus answered him, "Blessed are you, Simon Bar-Jona! For flesh and blood has not revealed this to you, but my Father who is in heaven. ¹⁸ And I tell you, you are Peter, and on this rock I will build my church, and the powers of death shall not prevail against it. ¹⁹ I will give you the keys of the kingdom of heaven, and *whatever you bind on earth shall be bound in heaven, and whatever you loose on earth shall be loosed in heaven."* ²⁰ Then he strictly charged the disciples to tell no one that he was the Christ.

Matt 18:18 (§A120.2)

¹⁵ "If your brother sins against you, go and tell him his fault, between you and him alone. If he listens to you, you have gained your brother. ¹⁶ But if he does not listen, take one or two others along with you, that every word may be confirmed by the evidence of two or three witnesses. ¹⁷ If he refuses to listen to them, tell it to the church; and if he refuses to listen even to the church, let him be to you as a Gentile and a tax collector. ¹⁸ *Truly, I say to you, whatever you bind on earth shall be bound in heaven, and whatever you loose on earth shall be loosed in heaven."*

John 20:23 (§A120.3)

¹⁹ On the evening of that day, the first day of the week, the doors being shut where the disciples were, for fear of the Jews, Jesus came and stood among them and said to them, "Peace be with you." ²⁰ When he had said this, he showed them his hands and his side. Then the disciples were glad when they saw the Lord. ²¹ Jesus said to them again, "Peace be with you. As the Father has sent me, even so I send you." ²² And when he had said this, he breathed on them, and said to them, "Receive the Holy Spirit. ²³ *If you forgive the sins of any, they are forgiven; if you retain the sins of any, they are retained."*

*See 443: *Binding and Loosing*

Matt 16:21 (§A121.1)

²¹ From that time Jesus began to show his disciples that he must go to Jerusalem and suffer many things from the elders and chief priests and scribes, and be killed, and on the third day be raised. ²² And Peter took him and began to rebuke him, saying, "God forbid, Lord! This shall never happen to you." ²³ But he turned and said to Peter, "Get behind me, Satan! You are a hindrance to me; for you are not on the side of God, but of men."

Matt 17:22b–23a (§A121.2)

²² As they were gathering in Galilee, Jesus said to them, *"The Son of man is to be delivered into the hands of men,* ²³ *and they will kill him, and he will be raised on the third day."* And they were greatly distressed.

Matt 20:18–19 (§A121.3)

¹⁷ And as Jesus was going up to Jerusalem, he took the twelve disciples aside, and on the way he said to them, ¹⁸ *"Behold, we are going up to Jerusalem; and the Son of man will be delivered to the chief priests and scribes, and they will condemn him to death,* ¹⁹ *and deliver him to the Gentiles to be mocked and scourged and crucified, and he will be raised on the third day."*

Matt 26:2b (§A121.4)

² "You know that after two days the Passover is coming, and the *Son of man will be delivered up to be crucified."*

Mark 8:31 (§A121.5)

³¹ And he began to teach them that the Son of man must suffer many things, and be rejected by the elders and the chief priests and the scribes, and be killed, and after three days rise again. ³² And he said this plainly. And Peter took him, and began to rebuke him. ³³ But turning and seeing his disciples, he rebuked Peter, and said, "Get behind me, Satan! For you are not on the side of God, but of men."

Mark 9:31b (§A121.6)

³⁰ They went on from there and passed through Galilee. And he would not have any one know it; ³¹ for he was teaching his disciples, saying to them, *"The Son of man will be delivered into the hands of men, and they will kill him; and when he is killed, after three days he will rise."* ³² But they did not understand the saying, and they were afraid to ask him.

Mark 10:33–34 (§A121.7)

³² And they were on the road, going up to Jerusalem, and Jesus was walking ahead of them; and they were amazed, and those who followed were afraid. And taking the twelve again, he began to tell them what was to happen to him, ³³ saying, *"Behold, we are going up to Jerusalem; and the Son of man will be delivered to the chief priests and the scribes, and they will condemn him to death, and deliver him to the Gentiles;* ³⁴ *and they will mock him, and spit upon him, and scourge him, and kill him; and after three days he will rise."*

Luke 9:22 (§A121.8)

²⁰ And he said to them, "But who do you say that I am?" And Peter answered, "The Christ of God." ²¹ But he charged and commanded them to tell this to no one ²² saying, *"The Son of man must suffer many things, and be rejected by the elders and chief priests and scribes, and be killed, and on the third day be raised."*

Luke 9:44 (§A121.9)

⁴³ And all were astonished at the majesty of God. But while they were all marveling at everything he did, he said to his disciples, ⁴⁴ *"Let these words sink into your ears; for the Son of man is to be delivered into the hands of men."* ⁴⁵ But they did not understand this saying, and it was concealed from them, that they should not perceive it; and they were afraid to ask him about this saying.

Luke 18:31b–33 (§A121.10)

³¹ And taking the twelve, he said to them, *"Behold, we are going up to Jerusalem, and everything that is written of the Son of man by the prophets will be accomplished.* ³² *For he will be delivered to the Gentiles, and will be mocked and shamefully treated and spit upon;* ³³ *they will scourge him and kill him, and on the third day he will rise."* ³⁴ But they understood none of these things; this saying was hid from them, and they did not grasp what was said.

Luke 17:25 (§A121.11)

²² And he said to the disciples, "The days are coming when you will desire to see one of the days of the Son of man, and you will not see it. ²³ And they will say to you, 'Lo, there!' or 'Lo, here!' Do not go, do not follow them. ²⁴ For as lightning flashes and lights up the sky from one side to the other, so will the Son of man be in his day. ²⁵ But first *he must suffer many things and be rejected by this generation."*

* See 444: *Passion-Resurrection Prophecy*

155   WHAT PROFIT?

Matt 16:26a (§A122.1)

²⁶ *"For what will it profit a man, if he gains the whole world and forfeits his life?"*

Mark 8:36 (§A122.2)

³⁶ *"For what does it profit a man, to gain the whole world and forfeit his life?"*

Luke 9:25 (§A122.3)

²⁵ *"For what does it profit a man if he gains the whole world and loses or forfeits himself?"*

2 Clem 6:2 (§A122.4)

¹ And the Lord says:—"No servant can serve two masters." If we desire to serve both God and Mammon it is unprofitable to us, ² *"For what is the advantage if a man gain the whole world but lose his soul?"* ³ Now the world that is, and the world to come are two enemies. ⁴ This world speaks of adultery, and corruption, and love of money, and deceit, but that world bids these things farewell. ⁵ We cannot then be the friends of both; but we must bid farewell to this world, to consort with that which is to come. ⁶ We reckon that it is better to hate the things which are here, for they are little, and short-lived, and corruptible, but to love the things which are there, the good things which are incorruptible.

156   LIFE'S PRICE

Matt 16:26b (§A123.1)
[26] *". . . Or what shall a man give in return for his life?"*

Mark 8:37 (§A123.2)
[37] *"For what can a man give in return for his life?"*

157   SOME STANDING HERE

Matt 16:28 (§A124.1)
[28] *"Truly, I say to you, there are some standing here who will not taste death before they see the Son of man coming in his kingdom."*

Mark 9:1 (§A124.2)
[1] And he said to them, *"Truly, I say to you, there are some standing here who will not taste death before they see that the kingdom of God has come with power."*

Luke 9:27 (§A124.3)
[27] *"But I tell you truly, there are some standing here who will not taste death before they see the kingdom of God."*

158   KINGDOM AND CHILDREN*

Matt 18:3 (§A125.1)
[1] At that time the disciples came to Jesus, saying, "Who is the greatest in the kingdom of heaven?" [2] And calling to him a child, he put him in the midst of them, [3] and said, *"Truly, I say to you, unless you turn and become like children, you will never enter the kingdom of heaven."*

Matt 19:14 (§A125.2)
[13] Then children were brought to him that he might lay his hands on them and pray. The disciples rebuked the people; [14] but Jesus said, *"Let the children come to me, and do not hinder them; for to such belongs the kingdom of heaven."* [15] And he laid his hands on them and went away.

Mark 10:14b (§A125.3)
[13] And they were bringing children to him, that he might touch them; [13] and the disciples rebuked them. [14] But when Jesus saw it he was indignant, and said to them, *"Let the children come to me, do not hinder them; for to such belongs the kingdom of God.* [15] Truly, I say to you, whoever does not receive the kingdom of God like a child shall not enter it."* [16] And he took them in his arms and blessed them, laying his hands upon them.

Luke 18:16b (§A125.4)
[15] Now they were bringing even infants to him that he might touch them; and when the disciples saw it, they rebuked them. [16] But Jesus called them to him, saying, *"Let the children come to me, and do not hinder them; for to such belongs the king-dom of God.* [17] *Truly, I say to you, whoever does not receive the kingdom of God like a child shall not enter it."*

John 3:3, 5 (§A125.5)
[1] Now there was a man of the Pharisees, named Nicodemus, a ruler of the Jews. [2] This man came to Jesus by night and said to him, "Rabbi, we know that you are a teacher come from God; for no one can do these signs that you do, unless God is with him." [3] Jesus answered him, *"Truly, truly, I say to you, unless one is born anew, he cannot see the kingdom of God."* [4] Nicodemus said to him, "How can a man be born when he is old? Can he enter a second time into his mother's womb and be born?" [5] Jesus answered, *"Truly, truly, I say to you, unless one is born of water and the Spirit, he cannot enter the kingdom of God.* [6] That which is born of the flesh is flesh, and that which is born of the Spirit is spirit. [7] Do not marvel that I said to you, 'You must be born anew.'* [8] The wind blows where it wills, and you hear the sound of it, but you do not know whence it comes or whither it goes; so it is with every one who is born of the Spirit."* [9] Nicodemus said to him, "How can this be?" [10] Jesus answered him, "Are you a teacher of Israel, and yet you do not understand this?"

GThom 22 (§A125.6)
(22) [1] Jesus saw infants being suckled. [2] He said to His disciples, *"These infants being suckled are like those who enter the Kingdom."* [3] They said to Him, *"Shall we then, as children, enter the Kingdom?"* [4] Jesus said to them, "When you make the two one, and when you make the inside like the outside and the outside like the inside, and the above like the below, and when you make the male and the female one and the same, so that the male not be male nor the female female; and when you fashion eyes in place of an eye, and a hand in place of a hand, and a foot in place of a foot, and a likeness in place of a likeness; *then will you enter [the Kingdom]."*

2 Clem 12:1–6 (§125.7)
[1] Let us then wait for the kingdom of God, from hour to hour, in love and right-eousness, seeing that we know not the day of the appearing of God. [2] For when the Lord himself was asked by someone when his kingdom would come, he said: "When the two shall be one, and the outside as the inside, and the male with the female neither male nor female." [3] Now "the two are one" when we speak with one another in truth, and there is but one soul in two bodies without dissimulation. [4] And by "the outside as the inside" he means this, that the inside is the soul, and the outside is the body. Therefore, just as your body is visible, so let your soul be apparent in your good works. [5] And by "the male with the female neither male nor female" he means this, that when a brother sees a sister he should have no thought of her as female, nor she of him as male. [6] When you do this, he says, the kingdom of my Father will come.

* See 446: *Kingdom and Children*

159 THE HUMBLE CHILD

Matt 18:4 (§A126)
⁴*"Whoever humbles himself like this child, he is the greatest in the kingdom of heaven."*

160 MILLSTONE AND SEA

Matt 18:6 (§A127.1)
⁶*"but whoever causes one of these little ones who believe in me to sin, it would be better for him to have a great millstone fastened round his neck and to be drowned in the depth of the sea."*

Mark 9:42 (§A127.2)
⁴²*"Whoever causes one of these little ones who believe in me to sin, it would be better for him if a great millstone were hung round his neck and he were thrown into the sea."*

Luke 17:2 (§A127.3)
²*"It would be better for him if a millstone were hung round his neck and he were cast into the sea, than that he should cause one of these little ones to sin."*

1 Clem 46:8b (§A127.4)
⁷Why do we divide and tear asunder the members of Christ, and raise up strife against our own body, and reach such a pitch of madness as to forget that we are members one of another? Remember the words of the Lord Jesus; ⁸for he said, "Woe unto that man: it were good for him if he had not been born, than that he should offend one of my elect; *it were better for him that a millstone be hung on him, and he be cast into the sea, than that he should turn aside one of my elect."* ⁹Your schism has turned aside many, has cast many into discouragement, many to doubt, all of us to grief; and your sedition continues.

161 WOE FOR TEMPTATION

Matt 18:7 (§A128.1)
⁷*"Woe to the world for temptations to sin! For it is necessary that temptations come, but woe to the man by whom the temptation comes!"*

Luke 17:1 (§A128.2)
¹And he said to his disciples, *"Temptations to sin are sure to come; but woe to him by whom they come!"*

162 DESPISING LITTLE ONES

Matt 18:10 (§A129)
[10] *"See that you do not despise one of these little ones; for I tell you that in heaven their angels always behold the face of my Father who is in heaven.* [12] What do you think? If a man has a hundred sheep, and one of them has gone astray, does he not leave the ninety-nine on the mountains and go in search of the one that went astray? [13] And if he finds it, truly, I say to you, he rejoices over it more than over the ninety-nine that never went astray. [14] So it is not the will of my Father who is in heaven that one of these little ones should perish."

163 REPROVING AND FORGIVING

Matt 18:15 (§A130.1)
[15] *"If your brother sins against you, go and tell him his fault, between you and him alone. If he listens to you, you have gained your brother."*

Luke 17:3b (§A130.2)
[1] And he said to his disciples, "Temptations to sin are sure to come; but woe to him by whom they come! [2] It would be better for him if a millstone were hung round his neck and he were cast into the sea, than that he should cause one of these little ones to sin. [3] Take heed to yourselves; *if your brother sins, rebuke him, and if he repents, forgive him."*

164 CHURCH EXCOMMUNICATION

Matt 18:16–17 (§A131)
[16] *"But if he does not listen, take one or two others along with you, that every word may be confirmed by the evidence of two or three witnesses. [17] If he refuses to listen to them, tell it to the church; and if he refuses to listen even to the church, let him be to you as a Gentile and a tax collector."*

165 POWER OF PRAYER

Matt 18:19 (§A132.1)
[19] *"Again I say to you, if two of you agree on earth about anything they ask, it will be done for them by my Father in heaven."*

Ign Eph 5:2b (§A132.2)
[2] Let no man be deceived: unless a man be within the sanctuary he lacks the bread of God, *for if the prayer of one or two has such might,* how much more has that of the bishop and of the whole Church?

166 TWO OR THREE

Matt 18:20 (§A133.1)
20 *"For where two or three are gathered in my name, there am I in the midst of them."*

POxy1 30 (§A133.2)
(30) [Jesus said], *"Where there are [three], they are without God, and where there is but [a single one], I say that I am with [him].* (77) 2 Lift up the stone, and you will find me there. Split the piece of wood, and I am there."

GThom 30 (§A133.3)
(30) Jesus said, *"Where there are three gods, they are gods. Where there are two or one, I am with him."*

GEgy e (§A133.4)
(e) For they declare that the Lord meant to say: with the greater number there is *the Creator, God, the primal cause of existence, but with the one, the elect one, there is the Redeemer, the Son of another, to wit the good God.* (Clement, *Stromateis* 3.68)

167 UNLIMITED FORGIVENESS★

Matt 18:22 (§A134.1)
15 "If your brother sins against you, go and tell him his fault, between you and him alone. If he listens to you, you have gained your brother. . . ."
21 Then Peter came up and said to him, "Lord, how often shall my brother sin against me, and I forgive him? As many as seven times?" 22 Jesus said to him, *"I do not say to you seven times, but seventy times seven."*

★ See 346: *Unlimited Forgiveness*

Luke 17:4 (§A134.2)
3 *"Take heed to yourselves; if your brother sins, rebuke him, and if he repents, forgive him;* 4 *and if he sins against you seven times in the day, and turns to you seven times, and says, 'I repent,' you must forgive him."*

GNaz 15a (§A134.3)
(15a) He (Jesus) said: *If thy brother has sinned with a word and has made thee reparation, receive him seven times in a day.* Simon his disciple said to him: Seven times in a day? The Lord answered and said to him: *Yea, I say unto thee, until seventy times seven times.* For in the prophets also after they were anointed with the Holy Spirit, the word of sin (sinful discourse?) was found. (Jerome, *Adversus Pelagianos* 3.2)

GNaz 15b (§A134.4)
(15b) The Jewish Gospel has after *"seventy times seven times"*: For in the prophets also, after they were anointed with the Holy Spirit, the word of sin (sinful discourse?) was found. (Variant to Matthew 18:22 in the "Zion Gospel" Edition)

168 ABLE TO RECEIVE

Matt 19:12b (§A135.1)
12 "For there are eunuchs who have been so from birth, and there are eunuchs who have been made eunuchs by men, and there are eunuchs who have made themselves eunuchs for the sake of the kingdom of heaven. *He who is able to receive this, let him receive it."*

Ign Smyr 6:1b (§A135.2)
1 Let no one be deceived; even things in heaven and the glory of the angels, and the rulers visible and invisible, even for them there is a judgment if they do not believe on the blood of Christ. *"He that receiveth let him receive."* Let not office exalt anyone, for faith and love is everything, and nothing has been preferred to them.

169 ON TWELVE THRONES*

Matt 19:28 (§A136.1)
[23] And Jesus said to his disciples, "Truly, I say to you, it will be hard for a rich man to enter the kingdom of heaven. [24] Again I tell you, it is easier for a camel to go through the eye of a needle than for a rich man to enter the kingdom of God." [25] When the disciples heard this they were greatly astonished, saying, "Who then can be saved?" [26] But Jesus looked at them and said to them, "With men this is impossible, but with God all things are possible." [27] Then Peter said in reply, "Lo, we have left everything and followed you. What then shall we have?" [28] Jesus said to them, *"Truly, I say to you, in the new world, when the Son of man shall sit on his glorious throne, you who have followed me will also sit on twelve thrones, judging the twelve tribes of Israel."*

Luke 22:28–30 (§A136.2)
[24] A dispute also arose among them, which of them was to be regarded as the greatest. [25] And he said to them, "The kings of the Gentiles exercise lordship over them; and those in authority over them are called benefactors. [26] But not so with you; rather let the greatest among you become as the youngest, and the leader as one who serves. [27] For which is the greater, one who sits at table, or one who serves? Is it not the one who sits at table? But I am among you as one who serves. [28] *"You are those who have continued with me in my trials;* [29] *and I assign to you, as my Father assigned to me, a kingdom,* [30] *that you may eat and drink at my table in my kingdom, and sit on thrones judging the twelve tribes of Israel."*

* See 351: *On Twelve Thrones*

170 FIRST AND LAST

Matt 19:30 (§A137.1)
[27] Then Peter said in reply, "Lo, we have left everything and followed you. What then shall we have?" [28] Jesus said to them, "Truly, I say to you, in the new world, when the Son of man shall sit on his glorious throne, you who have followed me will also sit on twelve thrones, judging the twelve tribes of Israel. [29] And every one who has left houses or brothers or sisters or father or mother or children or lands, for my name's sake, will receive a hundredfold, and inherit eternal life. [30] *But many that are first will be last, and the last first."*

Matt 20:16 (§A137.2)
[1] "For the kingdom of heaven is like a householder who went out early in the morning to hire laborers for his vineyard. [2] After agreeing with the laborers for a denarius a day, he sent them into his vineyard. [3] And going out about the third hour he saw others standing idle in the market place; [4] and to them he said, 'You go into the vineyard too, and whatever is right I will give you.' So they went. [5] Going out again about the sixth hour and the ninth hour, he did the same. [6] And about the eleventh hour he went out and found others standing; and he said to them, 'Why do you stand here idle all day?' [7] They said to him, 'Because no one has hired us.' He said to them, 'You go into the vineyard too.' [8] And when evening came, the owner of the vineyard said to his steward, 'Call the laborers and pay them their wages, beginning with the last, up to the first.' [9] And when those hired about the eleventh hour came, each of them received a denarius. [10] Now when the first came, they thought they would receive more; but each of them also received a denarius. [11] And on receiving it they grumbled at the householder, [12] saying, 'These last worked only one hour, and you have made them equal to us who have borne the burden of the day and the scorching heat.' [13] But he replied to one of them, 'Friend, I am doing you no wrong; did you not agree with me for a denarius? [14] Take what belongs to you, and go; I choose to give to this last as I give to you. [15] Am I not allowed to do what I choose with what belongs to me? Or do you begrudge my generosity?' [16] *So the last will be first, and the first last."*

Mark 10:31 (§A137.3)
[28] Peter began to say to him, "Lo, we have left everything and followed you." [29] Jesus said, "Truly, I say to you, there is no one who has left house or brothers or sisters or mother or father or children or lands, for my sake and for the gospel, [30] who will not receive a hundredfold now in this time, houses and brothers and sisters and mothers and children and lands, with persecutions, and in the age to come eternal life. [31] *But many that are first will be last, and the last first."*

Luke 13:30 (§A137.4)
[29] "And men will come from east and west, and from north and south, and sit at table in the kingdom of God. [30] And behold, *some are last who will be first, and some are first who will be last."*

POxy654 4:2a (§A137.5)
(4) [1] [Jesus said], "The [man old in days] will not hesitate to ask [a small child seven days old] about the place [of life, and] he will [live]. [2] *For many who are [first] will become [last, and] the last will be first,* and [they will become one and the same]."

GThom 4:2a (§A137.6)
(4) [1] Jesus said, "The man old in days will not hesitate to ask a small child seven days old about the place of life, and he will live. [2] *For many who are first will become last,* and they will become one and the same."

Barn 6:13a (§A137.7)
[12] For it is concerning us that the scripture says that he says to the Son, "Let us make man after our image and likeness, and let them rule the beasts of the earth, and the birds of heaven, and the fishes of the sea." And the Lord said, when he saw our fair creation, "Increase and multiply and fill the earth"; these things were spoken to the Son. [13] Again I will show you how he speaks to us. In the last days he made a second creation; and the Lord says, *"See, I make the last things as the first."* To this then the Prophet referred when he proclaimed, "Enter into a land flowing with milk and honey, and rule over it."

Matt 20:22b (§A138.1)

[20] Then the mother of the sons of Zebedee came up to him, with her sons, and kneeling before him she asked him for something. [21] And he said to her, "What do you want?" She said to him, "Command that these two sons of mine may sit, one at your right hand and one at your left, in your kingdom." [22] But Jesus answered, "You do not know what you are asking. Are you able to drink the cup that I am to drink?" They said to him, "We are able." [23] He said to them, "You will drink my cup, but to sit at my right hand and at my left is not mine to grant, but it is for those for whom it has been prepared by my Father."

Mark 10:38b (§A138.2)

[35] And James and John, the sons of Zebedee, came forward to him, and said to him, "Teacher, we want you to do for us whatever we ask of you." [36] And he said to them, "What do you want me to do for you?" [37] And they said to him, "Grant us to sit, one at your right hand and one at your left, in your glory." [38] But Jesus said to them, "You do not know what you are asking. Are you able to drink the cup that I drink, *or to be baptized with the baptism with which I am baptized?*" [39] And they said to him, "We are able." And Jesus said to them, "The cup that I drink you will drink; and with the baptism with which I am baptized, you will be baptized; [40] but to sit at my right hand or at my left is not mine to grant, but it is for those for whom it has been prepared."

Luke 12:50 (§A138.3)

[49] "I came to cast fire upon the earth; and would that it were already kindled! [50] *I have a baptism to be baptized with; and how I am constrained until it is accomplished!* [51] Do you think that I have come to give peace on earth? No, I tell you, but rather division; [52] for henceforth in one house there will be five divided, three against two and two against three; [53] they will be divided, father against son and son against father, mother against daughter and daughter against her mother, mother-in-law against her daughter-in-law and daughter-in-law against her mother-in-law."

* See 353: *Request for Precedence*

Matt 20:25b–28 (§A139.1)

²⁰ Then the mother of the sons of Zebedee came up to him, with her sons, and kneeling before him she asked him for something. ²¹ And he said to her, "What do you want?" She said to him, "Command that these two sons of mine may sit, one at your right hand and one at your left, in your kingdom." ²² But Jesus answered, "You do not know what you are asking. Are you able to drink the cup that I am to drink?" They said to him, "We are able." ²³ He said to them, "You will drink my cup, but to sit at my right hand and at my left is not mine to grant, but it is for those for whom it has been prepared by my Father." ²⁴ And when the ten heard it, they were indignant at the two brothers. ²⁵ But Jesus called them to him and said, *"You know that the rulers of the Gentiles lord it over them, and their great men exercise authority over them.* ²⁶ *It shall not be so among you; but whoever would be great among you must be your servant,* ²⁷ *and whoever would be first among you must be your slave;* ²⁸ *even as the Son of man came not to be served but to serve, and to give his life as a ransom for many."*

Matt 23:11 (§A139.2)

⁸ "But you are not to be called rabbi, for you have one teacher, and you are all brethren. ⁹ And call no man your father on earth, for you have one Father, who is in heaven. ¹⁰ Neither be called masters, for you have one master, the Christ. ¹¹ *He who is greatest among you shall be your servant."*

Mark 9:35b (§A139.3)

³³ And they came to Capernaum; and when he was in the house he asked them, "What were you discussing on the way?" ³⁴ But they were silent; for on the way they had discussed with one another who was the greatest. ³⁵ And he sat down and called the twelve; and he said to them, *"If any one would be first, he must be last of all and servant of all."* ³⁶ And he took a child, and put him in the midst of them; and taking him in his arms, he said to them, ³⁷ "Whoever receives one such child in my name receives me; and whoever receives me, receives not me but him who sent me."

★ See 447: *Leader as Servant*

Mark 10:42b–45 (§A139.4)

³⁵ And James and John, the sons of Zebedee, came forward to him, and said to him, "Teacher, we want you to do for us whatever we ask of you." ³⁶ And he said to them, "What do you want me to do for you?" ³⁷ And they said to him, "Grant us to sit, one at your right hand and one at your left, in your glory." ³⁸ But Jesus said to them, "You do not know what you are asking. Are you able to drink the cup that I drink, or to be baptized with the baptism with which I am baptized?" ³⁹ And they said to him, "We are able." And Jesus said to them, "The cup that I drink you will drink; and with the baptism with which I am baptized, you will be baptized; ⁴⁰ but to sit at my right hand or at my left is not mine to grant, but it is for those for whom it has been prepared." ⁴¹ And when the ten heard it, they began to be indignant at James and John. ⁴² And Jesus called them to him and said to them, *"You know that those who are supposed to rule over the Gentiles lord it over them, and their great men exercise authority over them.* ⁴³ *But it shall not be so among you; but whoever would be great among you must be your servant,* ⁴⁴ *and whoever would be first among you must be slave of all.* ⁴⁵ *For the Son of man also came not to be served but to serve, and to give his life as a ransom for many."*

Luke 9:48b (§A139.5)

⁴⁶ And an argument arose among them as to which of them was the greatest. ⁴⁷ But when Jesus perceived the thought of their hearts, he took a child and put him by his side, ⁴⁸ and said to them, "Whoever receives this child in my name receives me, and whoever receives me receives him who sent me; *for he who is least among you all is the one who is great."*

Luke 22:25–27 (§A139.6)

²⁴ A dispute also arose among them, which of them was to be regarded as the greatest. ²⁵ And he said to them, *"The kings of the Gentiles exercise lordship over them; and those in authority over them are called benefactors.* ²⁶ *But not so with you; rather let the greatest among you become as the youngest, and the leader as one who serves.* ²⁷ *For which is the greater, one who sits at table, or one who serves? Is it not the one who sits at table? But I am among you as one who serves."*

John 13:14 (§A139.7)

¹ Now before the feast of the Passover, when Jesus knew that his hour had come to depart out of this world to the Father, having loved his own who were in the world, he loved them to the end. ² And during supper, when the devil had already put it into the heart of Judas Iscariot, Simon's son, to betray him, ³ Jesus, knowing that the Father had given all things into his hands, and that he had come from God and was going to God, ⁴ rose from supper, laid aside his garments, and girded himself with a towel. ⁵ Then he poured water into a basin, and began to wash the disciples' feet and to wipe them with the towel with which he was girded. ⁶ He came to Simon Peter; and Peter said to him, "Lord, do you wash my feet?" ⁷ Jesus answered him, "What I am doing you do not know now, but afterward you will understand." ⁸ Peter said to him, "You shall never wash my feet." Jesus answered him, "If I do not wash you, you have no part in me." ⁹ Simon Peter said to him, "Lord, not my feet only but also my hands and my head!" ¹⁰ Jesus said to him, "He who has bathed does not need to wash, except for his feet, but he is clean all over; and you are clean, but not every one of you." ¹¹ For he knew who was to betray him; that was why he said, "You are not all clean."

¹² When he had washed their feet, and taken his garments, and resumed his place, he said to them, "Do you know what I have done to you? ¹³ You call me Teacher and Lord; and you are right, for so I am. ¹⁴ *If I then, your Lord and Teacher, have washed your feet, you also ought to wash one another's feet.* ¹⁵ For I have given you an example, that you also should do as I have done to you. ¹⁶ Truly, truly, I say to you, a servant is not greater than his master; nor is he who is sent greater than he who sent him. ¹⁷ If you know these things, blessed are you if you do them. ¹⁸ I am not speaking of you all; I know whom I have chosen; it is that the scripture may be fulfilled, 'He who ate my bread has lifted his heel against me.' ¹⁹ I tell you this now, before it takes place, that when it does take place you may believe that I am he. ²⁰ Truly, truly, I say to you, he who receives any one whom I send receives me; and he who receives me receives him who sent me."

Matt 21:42 (§A140.1)

[33] "Hear another parable. There was a householder who planted a vineyard, and set a hedge around it, and dug a wine press in it, and built a tower, and let it out to tenants, and went into another country. [34] When the season of fruit drew near, he sent his servants to the tenants, to get his fruit; [35] and the tenants took his servants and beat one, killed another, and stoned another. [36] Again he sent other servants, more than the first; and they did the same to them. [37] Afterward he sent his son to them, saying 'They will respect my son.' [38] But when the tenants saw the son, they said to themselves, 'This is the heir; come, let us kill him and have his inheritance.' [39] And they took him and cast him out of the vineyard, and killed him. [40] When therefore the owner of the vineyard comes, what will he do to those tenants?" [41] They said to him, "He will put those wretches to a miserable death, and let out the vineyard to other tenants who will give him the fruits in their seasons."

[42] Jesus said to them, *"Have you never read in the scriptures:*

> *'The very stone which the builders rejected*
> *has become the head of the corner;*
> *this was the Lord's doing,*
> *and it is marvelous in our eyes'?*

[43] Therefore I tell you, the kingdom of God will be taken away from you and given to a nation producing the fruits of it."

[45] When the chief priests and the Pharisees heard his parables, they perceived that he was speaking about them. [46] But when they tried to arrest him, they feared the multitudes, because they held him to be a prophet.

Mark 12:10 (§A140.2)

[1] And he began to speak to them in parables. "A man planted a vineyard, and set a hedge around it, and dug a pit for the wine press, and built a tower, and let it out to tenants, and went into another country. [2] When the time came, he sent a servant to the tenants, to get from them some of the fruit of the vineyard. [3] And they took him and beat him, and sent him away empty-handed. [4] Again he sent to them another servant, and they wounded him in the head, and treated him shamefully. [5] And he sent another, and him they killed; and so with many others, some they beat and some they killed. [6] He had still one other, a beloved son; finally he sent him to them, saying, 'They will respect my son.' [7] But those tenants said to one another, 'This is the heir; come, let us kill him, and the inheritance will be ours.' [8] And they took him and killed him, and cast him out of the vineyard. [9] What will the owner of the vineyard do? He will come and destroy the tenants, and give the vineyard to others. [10] *Have you not read this scripture:*

> *'The very stone which the builders rejected*
> *has become the head of the corner;*
> [11] *this was the Lord's doing,*
> *and it is marvelous in our eyes'?"*

[12] And they tried to arrest him, but feared the multitude, for they perceived that he had told the parable against them; so they left him and went away.

Luke 20:17 (§A140.3)

[9] And he began to tell the people this parable: "A man planted a vineyard, and let it out to tenants, and went into another country for a long while. [10] When the time came, he sent a servant to the tenants, that they should give him some of the fruit of the vineyard; but the tenants beat him, and sent him away empty-handed. [11] And he sent another servant; him also they beat and treated shamefully, and sent him away empty-handed. [12] And he sent yet a third; this one they wounded and cast out. [13] Then the owner of the vineyard said, 'What shall I do? I will send my beloved son; it may be they will respect him.' [14] But when the tenants saw him, they said to themselves, 'This is the heir; let us kill him, that the inheritance may be ours.' [15] And they cast him out of the vineyard and killed him. What then will the owner of the vineyard do to them? [16] He will come and destroy those tenants, and give the vineyard to others." When they heard this, they said, "God forbid!" [17] But he looked at them and said, *"What then is this that is written:*

> *'The very stone which the builders rejected*
> *has become the head of the corner'?*

[18] Every one who falls on that stone will be broken to pieces; but when it falls on any one it will crush him."

[19] The scribes and the chief priests tried to lay hands on him at that very hour, but they feared the people; for they perceived that he had told this parable against them.

GThom 66 (§A140.4)

(65) [1] He said, "There was a good man who owned a vineyard. He leased it to tenant farmers so that they might work it and he might collect the produce from them. He sent his servant so that the tenants might give him the produce of the vineyard. They seized his servant and beat him, all but killing him. The servant went back and told his master. The master said, 'Perhaps <they> did not recognize <him>.' He sent another servant. The tenants beat this one as well. Then the owner sent his son and said, 'Perhaps they will show respect to my son.' Because the tenants knew that it was he who was the heir to the vineyard, they seized him and killed him. [2] Let him who has ears hear."

(66) Jesus said, *"Show me the stone which the builders have rejected. That one is the cornerstone."*

Barn 6:4a (§A140.5)

[4] And again the Prophet says, *"The stone which the builders rejected, this is become the head of the corner,"* and again he says, "This is the great and wonderful day which the Lord made."

174 CALLED AND CHOSEN

Matt 22:14 (§A141.1)
[14] "For many are called, but few are chosen."

Barn 4:14b (§A141.2)
[12]The Lord will "judge" the world" without respect of persons." Each will receive according to his deeds. If he be good his righteousness will lead him, if he be evil the reward of iniquity is before him. [13]Let us never rest as though we were 'called' and slumber in our sins, lest the wicked ruler gain power over us and thrust us out from the Kingdom of the Lord. [14]And consider this also, my brethren, when you see that after such great signs and wonders were wrought in Israel they were even then finally abandoned;—*let us take heed lest as it was written we be found "many called but few chosen."*

175 SON OF DAVID*

Matt 22:43–45 (§A142.1)
[41]Now while the Pharisees were gathered together, Jesus asked them a question, [42]saying, "What do you think of the Christ? Whose son is he?" They said to him, "The son of David." [43]He said to them, *"How is it then that David, inspired by the Spirit, calls him Lord, saying,*
[44]*'The Lord said to my Lord,*
Sit at my right hand,
till I put thy enemies under thy feet'?
[45]*If David thus calls him Lord, how is he his son?"* [46]And no one was able to answer him a word, nor from that day did any one dare to ask him any more questions.

* See 359: *Son of David*

Mark 12:35b–37a (§A142.2)
[35]And as Jesus taught in the temple, he said, *"How can the scribes say that the Christ is the son of David?* [36]*David himself, inspired by the Holy Spirit, declared,*
'The Lord said to my Lord,
Sit at my right hand,
till I put thy enemies under thy feet.'
[37]*David himself calls him Lord; so how is he his son?"* And the great throng heard him gladly.

Luke 20:41–44 (§A142.3)
[41]But he said to them, *"How can they say that the Christ is David's son?* [42]*For David himself says in the Book of Psalms,*
'The Lord said to my Lord,
Sit at my right hand,
[43]*till I make thy enemies a stool for thy feet.'*
[44]*David thus calls him Lord; so how is he his son?"*

Barn 12:10b,11b (§A142.4)
[10]See again Jesus, not as son of man, but as Son of God, but manifested in a type in the flesh. *Since therefore they are going to say that the Christ is David's son, David himself prophesies, fearing and understanding the error of the sinners, "The Lord said to my Lord sit thou on my right hand until I make they enemies thy footstool."* [11]And again Isaiah speaks thus, "The Lord said to Christ my Lord, whose right hand I held, that the nations should obey before him, and I will shatter the strength of Kings." *See how "David calls him Lord" and does not say Son.*

176 ON MOSES' SEAT

Matt 23:2–3 (§A143)
[1]Then said Jesus to the crowds and to his disciples, [2]*"The scribes and the Pharisees sit on Moses' seat;* [3]*so practice and observe whatever they tell you, but not what they do; for they preach, but do not practice."*

177 HELPING WITH BURDENS*

Matt 23:4 (§A144.1)
⁴ *"They bind heavy burdens, hard to bear, and lay them on men's shoulders; but they themselves will not move them with their finger."*

* See 360: *Helping with Burdens*

Luke 11:46b (§A144.2)
⁴⁵ One of the lawyers answered him, "Teacher, in saying this you reproach us also." ⁴⁶ And he said, "Woe to you lawyers also! for *you load men with burdens hard to bear, and you yourselves do not touch the burdens with one of your fingers."*

178 HONORS AND SALUTATIONS

Matt 23:5–7 (§A45.1)
⁵ *"They do all their deeds to be seen by men; for they make their phylacteries broad and their fringes long, ⁶ and they love the place of honor at feasts and the best seats in the synagogues, ⁷ and salutations in the market places, and being called rabbi by men."*

Mark 12:38–39 (§A145.2)
³⁸ And in his teaching he said, *"Beware of the scribes, who like to go about in long robes, and to have salutations in the market places ³⁹ and the best seats in the synagogues and the places of honor at feasts, . . ."*

Luke 11:43 (§A145.3)
⁴³ *"Woe to you Pharisees! for you love the best seat in the synagogues and salutations in the market places."*

Luke 20:46 (§A145.4)
⁴⁵ And in the hearing of all the people he said to his disciples, ⁴⁶ *"Beware of the scribes, who like to go about in long robes, and love salutations in the market places and the best seats in the synagogues and the places of honor at feasts,* ⁴⁷ who devour widows' houses and for a pretense make long prayers. They will receive the greater condemnation."

179 ON TITLES

Matt 23:8–10 (§A146)
⁸ *"But you are not to be called rabbi, for you have one teacher, and you are all brethren. ⁹ And call no man your father on earth, for you have one Father, who is in heaven. ¹⁰ Neither be called masters, for you have one master, the Christ."*

180 EXALTATION AND HUMILIATION

Matt 23:12 (§A147.1)
⁸ "But you are not to be called rabbi, for you have one teacher, and you are all brethren. ⁹ And call no man your father on earth, for you have one Father, who is in heaven. ¹⁰ Neither be called masters, for you have one master, the Christ. ¹¹ He who is greatest among you shall be your servant; ¹² *whoever exalts himself will be humbled, and whoever humbles himself will be exalted.*"

Luke 14:11 (§A147.2)
⁷ Now he told a parable to those who were invited, when he marked how they chose the places of honor, saying to them, ⁸ "When you are invited by any one to a marriage feast, do not sit down in a place of honor, lest a more eminent man than you be invited by him; ⁹ and he who invited you both will come and say to you, 'Give place to this man,' and then you will begin with shame to take the lowest place. ¹⁰ But when you are invited, go and sit in the lowest place, so that when your host comes he may say to you, 'Friend, go up higher'; then you will be honored in the presence of all who sit at table with you. ¹¹ *For every one who exalts himself will be humbled, and he who humbles himself will be exalted.*"

Luke 18:14b (§A147.3)
⁹ He also told this parable to some who trusted in themselves that they were righteous and despised others: ¹⁰ "Two men went up into the temple to pray, one a Pharisee and the other a tax collector. ¹¹ The Pharisee stood and prayed thus with himself, 'God, I thank thee that I am not like other men, extortioners, unjust, adulterers, or even like this tax collector. ¹² I fast twice a week, I give tithes of all that I get.' ¹³ But the tax collector, standing far off, would not even lift up his eyes to heaven, but beat his breast, saying, 'God, be merciful to me a sinner!' ¹⁴ I tell you, this man went down to his house justified rather than the other; *for every one who exalts himself will be humbled, but he who humbles himself will be exalted.*"

181 ON HINDERING OTHERS

Matt 23:13 (§A148.1)
¹³ "*But woe to you, scribes and Pharisees, hypocrites! because you shut the kingdom of heaven against men; for you neither enter yourselves, nor allow those who would enter to go in.*"

Luke 11:52 (§A148.2)
⁵² "*Woe to you lawyers! for you have taken away the key of knowledge; you did not enter yourselves, and you hindered those who were entering.*"

POxy655 39:1 (§A148.3)
(39) ¹ [Jesus said, "*The pharisees and the scribes have taken the keys] of [knowledge (gnosis) and] hidden [them. They themselves have not] entered, [nor have they allowed to enter those who were about to] come in.* ² [You], however, [be as wise as serpents and as] innocent [as doves]."

GThom 39:1 (§A148.4)
(39) ¹ Jesus said, "*The Pharisees and the scribes have taken the keys of Knowledge and hidden them. They themselves have not entered, nor have they allowed to enter those who wish to.* ² You, however, be as wise as serpents and as innocent as doves.*"

GThom 102 (§A148.5)
(102) Jesus said, "*Woe to the Pharisees, for they are like a dog sleeping in the manger of oxen, for neither does he eat nor does he let the oxen eat.*"

182 WIDOWS' HOUSES

Matt 23:14b (§A149.1)
[¹⁴ "Woe to you, scribes and Pharisees, hypocrites? *for you devour widows' houses and for a pretense you make long prayer; therefore you will receive the greater condemnation.*"]

Mark 12:40 (§A149.2)
³⁸ And in his teaching he said, "Beware of the scribes, who like to go about in long robes, and to have salutations in the market places ³⁹ and the best seats in the synagogues and the places of honor at feasts, ⁴⁰ *who devour widows' houses and for a pretense make long prayers. They will receive the greater condemnation.*"

Luke 20:47 (§A149.3)
⁴⁵ And in the hearing of all the people he said to his disciples, ⁴⁶ "Beware of the scribes, who like to go about in long robes, and love salutations in the market places and the best seats in the synagogues and the places of honor at feasts, ⁴⁷ *who devour widows' houses and for a pretense make long prayers. They will receive the greater condemnation.*"

183 FOR A PROSELYTE

Matt 23:15 (§A150)
[15] *"Woe to you, scribes and Pharisees, hypocrites! for you traverse sea and land to make a single proselyte, and when he becomes a proselyte, you make him twice as much a child of hell as yourselves."*

184 AGAINST CASUISTRY

Matt 23:16–21 (§A151)
[16] *"Woe to you, blind guides, who say, 'If any one swears by the temple, it is nothing; but if any one swears by the gold of the temple, he is bound by his oath.'* [17] *You blind fools! For which is greater, the gold or the temple that has made the gold sacred?* [18] *And you say, 'If any one swears by the altar, it is nothing; but if any one swears by the gift that is on the altar, he is bound by his oath.'* [19] *You blind men! For which is greater, the gift or the altar that makes the gift sacred?* [20] *So he who swears by the altar, swears by it and by everything on it;* [21] *and he who swears by the temple, swears by it and by him who dwells in it;* [22] *and he who swears by heaven, swears by the throne of God and by him who sits upon it."*

185 TITHING AND JUSTICE

Matt 23:23 (§A152.1)
[23] *"Woe to you, scribes and Pharisees, hypocrites! for you tithe mint and dill and cummin, and have neglected the weightier matters of the law, justice and mercy and faith; these you ought to have done, without neglecting the others."*

Luke 11:42 (§A152.2)
[42] *"But woe to you Pharisees! for you tithe mint and rue and every herb, and neglect justice and the love of God; these you ought to have done, without neglecting the others."*

186 GNAT AND CAMEL

Matt 23:24 (§A153)
[24] *"You blind guides, straining out a gnat and swallowing a camel!"*

187 INSIDE AND OUTSIDE*

Matt 23:25–26 (§A154.1)
[25] *"Woe to you, scribes and Pharisees, hypocrites! for you cleanse the outside of the cup and of the plate, but inside they are full of extortion and rapacity.* [26] *You blind Pharisee! first cleanse the inside of the cup and of the plate, that the outside also may be clean."*

* See 455: *Inside and Outside*

Luke 11:39–41 (§A154.2)
[37] While he was speaking, a Pharisee asked him to dine with him; so he went in and sat at table. [38] The Pharisee was astonished to see that he did not first wash before dinner. [39] And the Lord said to him, *"Now you Pharisees cleanse the outside of the cup and of the dish, but inside you are full of extortion and wickedness.* [40] *You fools! Did not he who made the outside make the inside also?* [41] *But give for alms those things which are within; and behold, everything is clean for you."*

GThom 89 (§A154.3)
(89) Jesus said, *"Why do you wash the outside of the cup? Do you not realize that he who made the inside is the same one who made the outside?"*

188 LIKE GRAVES

Matt 23:27–28 (§A155.1)
[27] *"Woe to you, scribes and Pharisees, hypocrites! for you are like whitewashed tombs, which outwardly appear beautiful, but within they are full of dead men's bones and all uncleanness.* [28] *So you also outwardly appear righteous to men, but within you are full of hypocrisy and iniquity."*

Luke 11:44 (§A155.2)
[44] *"Woe to you! for you are like graves which are not seen, and men walk over them without knowing it."*

189 THE PROPHETS' TOMBS

Matt 23:29–33 (§A156.1)
[29] *"Woe to you, scribes and Pharisees, hypocrites! for you build the tombs of the prophets and adorn the monuments of the righteous,* [30] *saying, 'If we had lived in the days of our fathers, we would not have taken part with them in shedding the blood of the prophets.'* [31] *Thus you witness against yourselves, that you are sons of those who murdered the prophets.* [32] *Fill up, then, the measure of your fathers.* [33] *You serpents, you brood of vipers, how are you to escape being sentenced to hell?"*

Luke 11:47–48 (§A156.2)
[47] *"Woe to you! for you build the tombs of the prophets whom your fathers killed.* [48] *So you are witnesses and consent to the deeds of your fathers; for they killed them, and you build their tombs."*

190 WISDOM'S ENVOY

Matt 23:34–36 (§A157.1)

[34] *"Therefore I send you prophets and wise men and scribes, some of whom you will kill and crucify, and some you will scourge in your synagogues and persecute from town to town,* [35] *that upon you may come all the righteous blood shed on earth, from the blood of innocent Abel to the blood of Zechariah the son of Barachiah, whom you murdered between the sanctuary and the altar.* [36] *Truly, I say to you, all this will come upon this generation."*

Luke 11:49–51 (§A157.2)

[49] *"Therefore also the Wisdom of God said, 'I will send them prophets and apostles, some of whom they will kill and persecute,'* [50] *that the blood of all the prophets, shed from the foundation of the world, may be required of this generation,* [51] *from the blood of Abel to the blood of Zechariah, who perished between the altar and the sanctuary. Yes, I tell you, it shall be required of this generation."*

2 Esdr 1:32 (§A157.3)

[32] *"I sent to you my servants the prophets, but you have taken and slain them and torn their bodies in pieces; their blood I will require of you, says the Lord."*

GNaz 17 (§A157.4)

(17) In the Gospel which the Nazarenes use, instead of "son of Barachias" we have found written "son of Joiada." (Jerome, *Commentary on Matthew* [on Matthew 23:35])

191 JERUSALEM INDICTED

Matt 23:37–39 (§A158.1)

[37] *"O Jerusalem, Jerusalem, killing the prophets and stoning those who are sent to you! How often would I have gathered your children together as a hen gathers her brood under her wings, and you would not!* [38] *Behold, your house is forsaken and desolate.* [39] *For I tell you, you will not see me again, until you say, 'Blessed is he who comes in the name of the Lord.'"*

Luke 13:34–35 (§A158.2)

[34] *"O Jerusalem, Jerusalem, killing the prophets and stoning those who are sent to you! How often would I have gathered your children together as a hen gathers her brood under her wings, and you would not!* [35] *Behold, your house is forsaken. And I* tell you, you will not see me until you say, 'Blessed is he who comes in the name of the Lord!'"*

2 Esdr 1:30a,32a,33a (§A158.3)

[25] "Because you have forsaken me, I also will forsake you. When you beg mercy of me, I will show you no mercy. [26] When you call upon me, I will not listen to you; for you have defiled your hands with blood, and your feet are swift to commit murder. [27] It is not as though you had forsaken me; you have forsaken yourselves, says the Lord.

[28] "Thus says the Lord Almighty: Have I not entreated you as a father entreats his sons or a mother her daughters or a nurse her children, [29] that you should be my people and I should be your God, and that you should be my sons and I should be your father? [30] *I gathered you as a hen gathers her brood under her wings.* But now, what shall I do to you? I will cast you out from my presence. [31] When you offer oblations to me, I will turn my face from you; for I have rejected your feast days, and new moons, and curcumcisions of the flesh. [32] *I sent to you my servants the prophets, but you have taken and slain them and torn their bodies in pieces;* their blood I will require of you, says the Lord.

[33] "Thus says the Lord Almighty: *Your house is desolate;* I will drive you out as the wind drives straw; [34] and your sons will have no children, because with you they have neglected my commandment and have done what is evil in my sight."

192   TEMPLE'S ACTUAL DESTRUCTION*

Matt 24:2 (§A159.1)
[1] Jesus left the temple and was going away, when his disciples came to point out to him the buildings of the temple. [2] But he answered them, *"You see all these, do you not? Truly, I say to you, there will not be left here one stone upon another, that will not be thrown down."*

Mark 13:2 (§A159.2)
[1] And as he came out of the temple, one of his disciples said to him, "Look, Teacher, what wonderful stones and what wonderful buildings!" [2] And Jesus said to him, *"Do you see these great buildings? There will not be left here one stone upon another, that will not be thrown down."*

Luke 21:6 (§A159.3)
[5] And as some spoke of the temple, how it was adorned with noble stones and offerings, he said, [6] *"As for these things which you see, the days will come when there shall not be left here one stone upon another that will not be thrown down."*

* See 456: *Temple's Actual Destruction*
* See 457: *Jerusalem Destroyed*

Luke 19:44b (§A159.4)
[41] And when he drew near and saw the city he wept over it, [42] saying, "Would that even today you knew the things that make for peace! But now they are hid from your eyes. [43] For the days shall come upon you, when your enemies will cast up a bank about you and surround you, and hem you in on every side, [44] and dash you to the ground, you and your children within you, and *they will not leave one stone upon another in you*; because you did not know the time of your visitation."

193   DECEPTION AND STRIFE*

Matt 24:4–8 (§A160.1)
[3] As he sat on the Mount of Olives, the disciples came to him privately, saying, "Tell us, when will this be, and what will be the sign of your coming and of the close of the age?" [4] And Jesus answered them, *"Take heed that no one leads you astray.* [5] *For many will come in my name, saying, 'I am the Christ,' and they will lead many astray.* [6] *And you will hear of wars and rumors of wars; see that you are not alarmed; for this must take place, but the end is not yet.* [7] *For nation will rise against nation, and kingdom against kingdom, and there will be famines and earthquakes in various places:* [8] *all this is but the beginning of the birth-pangs."*

* See 458: *Deception and Strife*

Mark 13:5–8 (§A160.2)
[3] And as he sat on the Mount of Olives opposite the temple, Peter and James and John and Andrew asked him privately, [4] "Tell us, when will this be, and what will be the sign when these things are all to be accomplished?" [5] And Jesus began to say to them, *"Take heed that no one leads you astray.* [6] *Many will come in my name, saying, 'I am he!' and they will lead many astray.* [7] *And when you hear of wars and rumors of wars, do not be alarmed; this must take place, but the end is not yet.* [8] *For nation will rise against nation, and kingdom against kingdom; there will be earthquakes in various places, there will be famines; this is but the beginning of the birth-pangs."*

Luke 21:8–11 (§A160.3)
[7] And they asked him, "Teacher, when will this be, and what will be the sign when this is about to take place?" [8] And he said, *"Take heed that you are not led astray; for many will come in my name, saying, 'I am he!' and, 'The time is at hand!' Do not go after them.* [9] *And when you hear of wars and tumults, do not be terrified; for this must first take place, but the end will not be at once."* [10] Then he said to them, *"Nation will rise against nation, and kingdom against kingdom;* [11] *there will be great earthquakes, and in various places famines and pestilences; and there will be terrors and great signs from heaven."*

Did 16:3a (§A160.4)
[3] *for in the last days the false prophets and the corrupters shall be multiplied,* and the sheep shall be turned into wolves, and love shall change to hate; . . .

194   GOSPEL AND ESCHATON

Matt 24:14 (§A161.1)
[14] *"And this gospel of the kingdom will be preached throughout the whole world, as a testimony to all nations; and then the end will come."*

Mark 13:10 (§A161.2)
[10] *"And the gospel must first be preached to all nations."*

Matt 24:15–22 (§A162.1)

[15] "So when you see the desolating sacrilege spoken of by the prophet Daniel, standing in the holy place (let the reader understand), [16] then let those who are in Judea flee to the mountains; [17] let him who is on the housetop not go down to take what is in his house; [18] and let him who is in the field not turn back to take his mantle. [19] And alas for those who are with child and for those who give suck in those days! [20] Pray that your flight may not be in winter or on a sabbath. [21] For then there will be a great tribulation, such as has not been from the beginning of the world until now, no, and never will be. [22] And if those days had not been shortened, no human being would be saved; but for the sake of the elect those days will be shortened."

Mark 13:14–20 (§A162.2)

[14] "But when you see the desolating sacrilege set up where it ought not to be (let the reader understand), then let those who are in Judea flee to the mountains; [15] let him who is on the housetop not go down, nor enter his house, to take anything away; [16] and let him who is in the field not turn back to take his mantle. [17] And alas for those who are with child and for those who give suck in those days! [18] Pray that it may not happen in winter. [19] For in those days there will be such tribulation as has not been from the beginning of the creation which God created until now, and never will be. [20] And if the Lord had not shortened the days, no human being would be saved; but for the sake of the elect, whom he chose, he shortened the days."

Luke 17:31–32 (§A162.3)

[31] "On that day, let him who is on the housetop, with his goods in the house, not come down to take them away; and likewise let him who is in the field not turn back. [32] Remember Lot's wife."

Luke 21:20–24 (§A162.4)

[20] "But when you see Jerusalem surrounded by armies, then know that its desolation has come near. [21] Then let those who are in Judea flee to the mountains, and let those who are inside the city depart, and let not those who are out in the country enter it; [22] for these are days of vengeance, to fulfil all that is written. [23] Alas for those who are with child and for those who give suck in those days! For great distress shall be upon the earth and wrath upon this people; [24] they will fall by the edge of the sword, and be led captive among all nations; and Jerusalem will be trodden down by the Gentiles, until the times of the Gentiles are fulfilled."

196   WHEN AND WHERE*

Matt 24:11–12 (§A163.1)

[11] "And many false prophets will arise and lead many astray. [12] And because wickedness is multiplied, most men's love will grow cold."

Matt 24:23–26 (§A163.2)

[23] "Then if any one says to you, 'Lo, here is the Christ!' or 'There he is!' do not believe it. [24] For false Christs and false prophets will arise and show great signs and wonders, so as to lead astray, if possible, even the elect. [25] Lo, I have told you beforehand. [26] So, if they say to you, 'Lo, he is in the wilderness,' do not go out; if they say, 'Lo, he is in the inner rooms' do not believe it."

Mark 13:21–22 (§A163.3)

[21] "And then if any one says to you, 'Look, here is the Christ!' or 'Look, there he is!' do not believe it. [22] False Christs and false prophets will arise and show signs and wonders, to lead astray, if possible, the elect. [23] But take heed; I have told you all things beforehand."

Luke 17:20b,23 (§A163.4)

[20] Being asked by the Pharisees when the kingdom of God was coming, he answered them, "The kingdom of God is not coming with signs to be observed; [21] nor will they say, 'Lo, here it is!' or 'There!' for behold, the kingdom of God is in the midst of you."

[22] And he said to the disciples, "The days are coming when you will desire to see one of the days of the Son of man, and you will not see it. [23] And they will say to you, 'Lo, there!' or 'Lo, here!' Do not go, do not follow them."

POxy654 3:1 (§A163.5)

(3) [1] Jesus said, "[If] those who lead you [say to you, 'See,] the kingdom is in the sky,' then the birds of the sky [will precede you. If they say that] it is under the earth, then the fish of the sea [will enter it, preceding] you. And, the [kingdom of God] is inside of you, [and it is outside of you]. [2] Whoever knows [himself] will discover this. [And when you] come to know yourselves, [you will realize that] you are [sons] of the [living] father. [But if you] [not] know yourselves, [you dwell] in [poverty] and it is you who are that poverty."

GThom 3:1 (§A163.6)

(3) [1] Jesus said, "If those who lead you say to you, 'See, the Kingdom is in the sky,' then the birds of the sky will precede you. If they say to you, 'It is in the sea,' then the fish will precede you. Rather, the Kingdom is inside of you, and it is outside of you. [2] When you come to know yourselves, then you will become known, and you will realize that it is you who are the sons of the living Father. But if you will not know yourselves, you dwell in poverty and it is you who are that poverty."

GThom 51:2 (§A163.7)

(51) [1] His disciples said to Him, "When will the repose of the dead come about, and when will the new world come?"

[2] He said to them, "What you look forward to has already come, but you do not recognize it."

GThom 113:2 (§A163.8)

(113) [1] His disciples said to Him, "When will the Kingdom come?"

[2] <Jesus said,> "It will not come by waiting for it. It will not be a matter of saying 'Here it is' or 'There it is.' Rather, the Kingdom of the Father is spread out upon the earth, and men do not see it."

DialSav 16b (§A163.9)

(16) The Lord said, "There was darkness and water and spirit upon [water]. And I say [to you, . . .] what you seek and inquire after, [behold it is] within you . . . [. . .] . . . the power and the [mystery . . .] spirit, for from . . . [. . .] wickedness [. . .] come . . . [. . .] mind . . . [. . .] behold . . . [. . .] . . . [. . .]."

* See 361: When and Where

197 AS WITH LIGHTNING

Matt 24:27 (§A164.1)
[27] *"For as the lightning comes from the east and shines as far as the west, so will be the coming of the Son of man."*

Luke 17:24 (§A164.2)
[24] *"For as lightning flashes and lights up the sky from one side to the other, so will the Son of man be in his day."*

198 CORPSE AND VULTURES*

Matt 24:28 (§A165.1)
[28] *"Wherever the body is, there the eagles will be gathered together."*

* See 362: *Corpse and Vultures*

Luke 17:37b (§A165.2)
[37] And they said to him, "Where, Lord?" He said to them, *"Where the body is, there the eagles will be gathered together."*

199 PAROUSIA OF JESUS

Matt 24:29–31 (§A166.1)
[29] *"Immediately after the tribulation of those days the sun will be darkened, and the moon will not give its light, and the stars will fall from heaven, and the powers of the heavens will be shaken;* [30] *then will appear the sign of the Son of man in heaven, and then all the tribes of the earth will mourn, and they will see the Son of man coming on the clouds of heaven with power and great glory;* [31] *and he will send out his angels with a loud trumpet call, and they will gather his elect from the four winds, from one end of heaven to the other."*

Mark 13:24–27 (§A166.2)
[24] *"But in those days, after that tribulation, the sun will be darkened, and the moon will not give its light,* [25] *and the stars will be falling from heaven, and the powers in the heavens will be shaken.* [26] *And then they will see the Son of man coming in clouds with great power and glory.* [27] *And then he will send out the angels, and gather his elect from the four winds, from the ends of the earth to the ends of heaven."*

Luke 21:25–28 (§A166.3)
[25] *"And there will be signs in sun and moon and stars, and upon the earth distress of nations in perplexity at the roaring of the sea and the waves,* [26] *men fainting with fear and with foreboding of what is coming on the world; for the powers of the heavens will be shaken.* [27] *And then they will see the Son of man coming in a cloud with power and great glory.* [28] *Now when these things begin to take place, look up and raise your heads, because your redemption is drawing near."*

Did 16:6–8 (§A166.4)
[6] *And "then shall appear the signs" of the truth. First, the sign spread out in Heaven, then the sign of the sound of the trumpet, and thirdly the resurrection of the dead:* [7] *but not of all the dead, but as it was said, "The Lord shall come and all his saints with him."* [8] *Then shall the world "see the Lord coming on the clouds of Heaven."*

200 FIG TREE'S LESSON

Matt 24:32–34 (§A167.1)
[32] *"From the fig tree learn its lesson: as soon as its branch becomes tender and puts forth its leaves, you know that summer is near.* [33] *So also, when you see all these things, you know that he is near, at the very gates.* [34] *Truly, I say to you, this generation will not pass away till all these things take place."*

Mark 13:28–30 (§A167.2)
[28] *"From the fig tree learn its lesson: as soon as its branch becomes tender and puts forth its leaves, you know that summer is near.* [29] *So also, when you see these things taking place, you know that he is near, at the very gates.* [30] *Truly, I say to you, this generation will not pass away before all these things take place."*

Luke 21:29b–32 (§A167.3)
[29] And he told them a parable: *"Look at the fig tree, and all the trees;* [30] *as soon as they come out in leaf, you see for yourselves and know that the summer is already near.* [31] *So also, when you see these things taking place, you know that the kingdom of God is near.* [32] *Truly, I say to you, this generation will not pass away till all has taken place."*

201 MY WORDS ETERNAL

Matt 24:35 (§A168.1)
35 "Heaven and earth will pass away, but my words will not pass away."

Mark 13:31 (§A168.2)
31 "Heaven and earth will pass away, but my words will not pass away."

Luke 21:33 (§A168.3)
33 "Heaven and earth will pass away, but my words will not pass away."

202 ONLY THE FATHER

Matt 24:36 (§A169.1)
36 "But of that day and hour no one knows, not even the angels of heaven, nor the Son, but the Father only."

Mark 13:32 (§A169.2)
32 "But of that day or that hour no one knows, not even the angels in heaven, nor the Son, but only the Father."

203 AS WITH NOAH

Matt 24:37–39 (§A170.1)
37 "As were the days of Noah, so will be the coming of the Son of man. 38 For as in those days before the flood they were eating and drinking, marrying and giving in marriage, until the day when Noah entered the ark, 39 and they did not know until the flood came and swept them all away, so will be the coming of the Son of man."

Luke 17:26–27 (§A170.2)
26 "As it was in the days of Noah, so will it be in the days of the Son of man. 27 They ate, they drank, they married, they were given in marriage, until the day when Noah entered the ark, and the flood came and destroyed them all."

204 TAKEN OR LEFT

Matt 24:40–41 (§A171.1)
40 "Then two men will be in the field; one is taken and one is left. 41 Two women will be grinding at the mill; one is taken and one is left."

Luke 17:34–35 (§A171.2)
34 "I tell you, in that night there will be two in one bed; one will be taken and the other left. 35 There will be two women grinding together; one will be taken and the other left."

GThom 61:1 (§A171.3)
(61) *1 Jesus said, "Two will rest on a bed: the one will die, the other will live."*
2 Salome said, "Who are You, man, that You, as though from the One, (or: as <whose son>, that You) have come up on my couch and eaten from my table?"
3 Jesus said to her, "I am He who exists from the Undivided. I was given some of the things of My father."
4 <Salome said,> "I am Your disciple."
5 <Jesus said to her,> "Therefore I say, if he is <undivided>, he will be filled with light, but if he is divided, he will be filled with darkness."

Matt 24:42 (§A172.1)

42 *"Watch therefore, for you do not know on what day your Lord is coming."*

Matt 25:13 (§A172.2)

1 "Then the kingdom of heaven shall be compared to ten maidens who took their lamps and went to meet the bridegroom. 2 Five of them were foolish, and five were wise. 3 For when the foolish took their lamps, they took no oil with them; 4 but the wise took flasks of oil with their lamps. 5 As the bridegroom was delayed, they all slumbered and slept. 6 But at midnight there was a cry, 'Behold, the bridegroom! Come out to meet him.' 7 Then all those maidens rose and trimmed their lamps. 8 And the foolish said to the wise, 'Give us some of your oil, for our lamps are going out.' 9 But the wise replied, 'Perhaps there will not be enough for us and for you; go rather to the dealers and buy for yourselves.' 10 And while they went to buy, the bridegroom came, and those who were ready went in with him to the marriage feast; and the door was shut. 11 Afterward the other maidens came also, saying, 'Lord, lord, open to us.' 12 But he replied, 'Truly, I say to you, I do not know you.' 13 *Watch therefore, for you know neither the day nor the hour."*

Mark 13:33 (§A172.3)

33 *"Take heed, watch; for you do not know when the time will come.* 34 It is like a man going on a journey, when he leaves home and puts his servants in charge, each with his work, and commands the doorkeeper to be on watch. 35 Watch therefore—for you do not know when the master of the house will come, in the evening, or at midnight, or at cockcrow, or in the morning— 36 lest he come suddenly and find you asleep. 37 And what I say to you I say to all: Watch."

Luke 12:40 (§A172.4)

35 "Let your loins be girded and your lamps burning, 36 and be like men who are waiting for their master to come home from the marriage feast, so that they may open to him at once when he comes and knocks. 37 Blessed are those servants whom the master finds awake when he comes; truly, I say to you, he will gird himself and have them sit at table, and he will come and serve them. 38 If he comes in the second watch, or in the third, and finds them so, blessed are those servants! 39 But know this, that if the householder had known at what hour the thief was coming, he would not have left his house to be broken into. 40 *You also must be ready; for the Son of man is coming at an unexpected hour."*

Luke 21:36 (§A172.5)

34 "But take heed to yourselves lest your hearts be weighed down with dissipation and drunkenness and cares of this life, and that day come upon you suddenly like a snare; 35 for it will come upon all who dwell upon the face of the whole earth. 36 *But watch at all times, praying that you may have strength to escape all these things that will take place, and to stand before the Son of man."*

Did 16:1 (§A172.6)

1 *"Watch" over your life: "let your lamps" be not quenched "and your loins" be not ungirded, but be "ready," for ye know not "the hour in which our Lord cometh."* 2 But be frequently gathered together seeking the things which are profitable for your souls, for the whole time of your faith shall not profit you except ye be found perfect at the last time.

Matt 24:43 (§A173.1)

[43] *"But know this, that if the householder had known in what part of the night the thief was coming, he would have watched and would not have let his house be broken into.* [44] Therefore you also must be ready; for the Son of man is coming at an hour you do not expect."

Luke 12:39 (§A173.2)

[39] *"But know this, that if the householder had known at what hour the thief was coming, he would not have left his house to be broken into.* [40] You also must be ready; for the Son of man is coming at an unexpected hour."

1 Thess 5:2,4b (§A173.3)

[1] But as to the times and the seasons, brethren, you have no need to have anything written to you. [2] *For you yourselves know well that the day of the Lord will come like a thief in the night.* [3] When people say, "There is peace and security," then sudden destruction will come upon them as travail comes upon a woman with child, and there will be no escape. [4] But you are not in darkness, brethren, *for that day to surprise you like a thief.* [5] For you are all sons of light and sons of the day; we are not of the night or of darkness. [6] So then let us not sleep, as others do, but let us keep awake and be sober. [7] For those who sleep sleep at night, and those who get drunk are drunk at night. [8] But, since we belong to the day, let us be sober, and put on the breastplate of faith and love, and for a helmet the hope of salvation. [9] For God has not destined us for wrath, but to obtain salvation through our Lord Jesus Christ, [10] who died for us so that whether we wake or sleep we might live with him. [11] Therefore encourage one another and build one another up, just as you are doing.

2 Pet 3:10a (§A173.4)

[8] But do not ignore this one fact, beloved, that with the Lord one day is as a thousand years, and a thousand years as one day. [9] The Lord is not slow about his promise as some count slowness, but is forbearing toward you, not wishing that any should perish, but that all should reach repentance. [10] But *the day of the Lord will come like a thief,* and then the heavens will pass away with a loud noise, and the elements will be dissolved with fire, and the earth and the works that are upon it will be burned up.

Rev 3:3b (§A173.5)

[1] "And to the angel of the church in Sardis write: 'The words of him who has the seven spirits of God and the seven stars.

"'I know your works; you have the name of being alive, and you are dead. [2] Awake, and strengthen what remains and is on the point of death, for I have not found your works perfect in the sight of my God. [3] Remember then what you received and heard; keep that, and repent. *If you will not awake, I will come like a thief, and you will not know at what hour I will come upon you.'"*

Rev 16:15a (§A173.6)

[12] The sixth angel poured his bowl on the great river Euphrates, and its water was dried up, to prepare the way for the kings from the east. [13] And I saw, issuing from the mouth of the dragon and from the mouth of the beast and from the mouth of the false prophet, three foul spirits like frogs; [14] for they are demonic spirits, performing signs, who go abroad to the kings of the whole world, to assemble them for battle on the great day of God the Almighty. [15] (*"Lo, I am coming like a thief!* Blessed is he who is awake, keeping his garments that he may not go naked and be seen exposed!") [16] And they assembled them at the place which is called in Hebrew Armageddon.

GThom 21:3 (§A173.7)

(21) [1] Mary said to Jesus, "Whom are Your disciples like?"

[2] He said, "They are like children who have settled in a field which is not theirs. When the owners of the field come, they will say, 'Let us have back our field.' They (will) undress in their presence in order to let them have back their field and to give it back to them. [3] *Therefore I say to you, if the owner of a house knows that the thief is coming, he will begin his vigil before he comes and will not let him dig through into his house of his domain to carry away his goods. You, then, be on your guard against the world. Arm yourselves with great strength lest the robbers find a way to come to you, for the difficulty which you expect will (surely) materialize.* [4] Let there be among you a man of understanding. When the grain ripened, he came quickly with his sickle in his hand and reaped it. [5] Whoever has ears to hear, let him hear."

GThom 103 (§A173.8)

(103) Jesus said, *"Fortunate is the man who knows where the brigands will enter, so that he may get up, muster his domain, and arm himself before they invade."*

207   MASTER AND STEWARD*

Matt 24:45–51a (§A174.1)
[45] *"Who then is the faithful and wise servant, whom his master has set over his household, to give them their food at the proper time? [46] Blessed is that servant whom his master when he comes will find so doing. [47] Truly, I say to you, he will set him over all his possessions. [48] But if that wicked servant says to himself, 'My master is delayed,' [49] and begins to beat his fellow servants, and eats and drinks with the drunken, [50] the master of that servant will come on a day when he does not expect him and at an hour he does not know, [51] and will punish him, and put him with the hypocrites;* there men will weep and gnash their teeth."

Luke 12:42–46 (§A174.2)
[41] Peter said, "Lord, are you telling this parable for us or for all?" [42] And the Lord said, *"Who then is the faithful and wise steward, whom his master will set over his household, to give them their portion of food at the proper time? [43] Blessed is that servant whom his master when he comes will find so doing. [44] Truly, I say to you, he will set him over all his possessions. [45] But if that servant says to himself, 'My master is delayed in coming,' and begins to beat the menservants and the maidservants, and to eat and drink and get drunk, [46] the master of that servant will come on a day when he does not expect him and at an hour he does not know, and will punish* him, and put him with the unfaithful. [47] And that servant who knew his master's will, but did not make ready or act according to his will, shall receive a severe beating. [48] But he who did not know, and did what deserved a beating, shall receive a light beating. Every one to whom much is given, of him will much be required; and of him to whom men commit much they will demand the more."

* See 244: *Blessed for Doing*
* See 263: *Master and Steward*

208   THE CLOSED DOOR*

Matt 25:11–12 (§A175.1)
[1] "Then the kingdom of heaven shall be compared to ten maidens who took their lamps and went to meet the bridegroom. [2] Five of them were foolish, and five were wise. [3] For when the foolish took their lamps, they took no oil with them; [4] but the wise took flasks of oil with their lamps. [5] As the bridegroom was delayed, they all slumbered and slept. [6] But at midnight there was a cry, 'Behold, the bridegroom! Come out to meet him.' [7] Then all those maidens rose and trimmed their lamps. [8] And the foolish said to the wise, 'Give us some of your oil, for our lamps are going out.' [9] But the wise replied, 'Perhaps there will not be enough for us and for you; go rather to the dealers and buy for yourselves.' [10] And while they went to buy, the bridegroom came, and those who were ready went in with him to the marriage feast; and the door was shut. [11] *Afterward the other maidens came also, saying, 'Lord, lord, open to us.' [12] But he replied, 'Truly, I say to you, I do not know you.'* [13] Watch therefore, for you know neither the day nor the hour."

Luke 13:25 (§A175.2)
[25] *"When once the householder has risen up and shut the door, you will begin to stand outside and to knock at the door, saying, 'Lord, open to us.' He will answer you, 'I do not know where you come from.'"*

* See 13: *The Closed Door*

Matt 25:31–46 (§A176)

[31] *"When the Son of man comes in his glory, and all the angels with him, then he will sit on his glorious throne.* [32] *Before him will be gathered all the nations, and he will separate them one from another as a shepherd separates the sheep from the goats,* [33] *and he will place the sheep at his right hand, but the goats at the left.* [34] *Then the King will say to those at his right hand, 'Come, O blessed of my Father, inherit the kingdom prepared for you from the foundation of the world;* [35] *for I was hungry and you gave me food, I was thirsty and you gave me drink, I was a stranger and you welcomed me,* [36] *I was naked and you clothed me, I was sick and you visited me, I was in prison and you came to me.'* [37] *Then the righteous will answer him, 'Lord, when did we see thee hungry and feed thee, or thirsty and give thee drink?* [38] *And when did we see thee a stranger and welcome thee, or naked and clothe thee?* [39] *And when did we see thee sick or in prison and visit thee?'* [40] *And the King will answer them, 'Truly, I say to you, as you did it to one of the least of these my brethren, you did it to me.'* [41] *Then he will say to those at his left hand, 'Depart from me, you cursed, into the eternal fire prepared for the devil and his angels;* [42] *for I was hungry and you gave me no food, I was thirsty and you gave me no drink,* [43] *I was a stranger and you did not welcome me, naked and you did not clothe me, sick and in prison and you did not visit me.'* [44] *Then they also will answer, 'Lord, when did we see thee hungry or thirsty or a stranger or naked or sick or in prison, and did not minister to thee?'* [45] *Then he will answer them, 'Truly, I say to you, as you did it not to one of the least of these, you did it not to me.'* [46] *And they will go away into eternal punishment, but the righteous into eternal life."*

Matt 26:24b (§A177.1)

[21] and as they were eating, he said, "Truly, I say to you, one of you will betray me." [22] And they were very sorrowful, and began to say to him one after another, "Is it I, Lord?" [23] He answered, "He who has dipped his hand in the dish with me, will betray me. [24] The Son of man goes as it is written of him, but *woe to that man by whom the Son of man is betrayed! It would have been better for that man if he had not been born."* [25] Judas, who betrayed him, said, "Is it I, Master?" He said to him, "You have said so."

Mark 14:21b (§A177.2)

[18] And as they were at table eating, Jesus said, "Truly, I say to you, one of you will betray me, one who is eating with me." [19] They began to be sorrowful, and to say to him one after another, "Is it I?" [20] He said to them, "It is one of the twelve, one who is dipping bread into the dish with me. [21] For the Son of man goes as it is written of him, but *woe to that man by whom the Son of man is betrayed! It would have been better for that man if he had not been born."*

Luke 22:22b (§A177.3)

[14] And when the hour came, he sat at table, and the apostles with him. [15] And he said to them, "I have earnestly desired to eat this passover with you before I suffer; [16] for I tell you I shall not eat it until it is fulfilled in the kingdom of God." [17] And he took a cup, and when he had given thanks he said, "Take this, and divide it among yourselves; [18] for I tell you that from now on I shall not drink of the fruit of the vine until the kingdom of God comes." [19] And he took bread, and when he had given thanks he broke it and gave it to them, saying, "This is my body which is given for you. Do this in remembrance of me." [20] And likewise the cup after supper, saying, "This cup which is poured out for you is the new covenant in my blood. [21] But behold the hand of him who betrays me is with me on the table. [22] For the Son of man goes as it has been determined; but *woe to that man by whom he is betrayed!"* [23] And they began to question one another, which of them it was that would do this.

* See 461: *Better Not Born*

1 Clem 46:8a (§A177.4)

[7] Why do we divide and tear asunder the members of Christ, and raise up strife against our own body, and reach such a pitch of madness as to forget that we are members one of another? Remember the words of the Lord Jesus; [8] for he said, *"Woe unto that man: it were good for him if he had not been born, than that he should offend one of my elect;* it were better for him that a millstone be hung on him, and he be cast into the sea, than that he should turn aside one of my elect." [9] Your schism has turned aside many, has cast many into discouragement, many to doubt, all of us to grief; and your sedition continues.

Herm Vis 4.2:6b (§A177.5)

[6] "Believe on the Lord, you who are double-minded, that he can do all things, and turns his wrath away from you, and sends scourges on you who are double-minded. *Woe to those who hear these words and disobey; it were better for them not to have been born."*

Matt 26:61b (§A178.1)

⁵⁹ Now the chief priests and the whole council sought false testimony against Jesus that they might put him to death, ⁶⁰ but they found none, though many false witnesses came forward. At last two came forward ⁶¹ and said, "This fellow said, *'I am able to destroy the temple of God, and to build it in three days.'"* ⁶² And the high priest stood up and said, "Have you no answer to make? What is it that these men testify against you?" ⁶³ But Jesus was silent. And the high priest said to him, "I adjure you by the living God, tell us if you are the Christ, the Son of God."

Matt 27:40a (§A178.2)

³⁸ Then two robbers were crucified with him, one on the right and one on the left. ³⁹ And those who passed by derided him, wagging their heads ⁴⁰ and saying, *"You who would destroy the temple and build it in three days, save yourself!* If you are the Son of God, come down from the cross."

Mark 14:58b (§A178.3)

⁵⁵ Now the chief priests and the whole council sought testimony against Jesus to put him to death; but they found none. ⁵⁶ For many bore false witness against him, and their witness did not agree. ⁵⁷ And some stood up and bore false witness against him, saying, ⁵⁸ "We heard him say, *'I will destroy this temple that is made with hands, and in three days I will build another, not made with hands.'"* ⁵⁹ Yet not even so did their testimony agree. ⁶⁰ And the high priest stood up in the midst, and asked Jesus, "Have you no answer to make? What is it that these men testify against you?" ⁶¹ But he was silent and made no answer. Again the high priest asked him, "Are you the Christ, the Son of the Blessed?"

Mark 15:29b (§A178.4)

²⁷ And with him they crucified two robbers, one on his right and one one his left. ²⁹ And those who passed by derided him, wagging their heads, and saying, *"Aha! You who would destroy the temple and build it in three days,* ³⁰ save yourself, and come down from the cross!"

John 2:19 (§A178.5)

¹³ The Passover of the Jews was at hand, and Jesus went up to Jerusalem. ¹⁴ In the temple he found those who were selling oxen and sheep and pigeons, and the money-changers at their business. ¹⁵ And making a whip of cords, he drove them all, with the sheep and oxen, out of the temple; and he poured out the coins of the money-changers and overturned their tables. ¹⁶ And he told those who sold the pigeons, "Take these things away; you shall not make my Father's house a house of trade." ¹⁷ His disciples remembered that it was written, "Zeal for thy house will consume me." ¹⁸ The Jews then said to him, "What sign have you to show us for doing this?" ¹⁹ Jesus answered them, *"Destroy this temple, and in three days I will raise it up."* ²⁰ The Jews then said, "It has taken forty-six years to build this temple, and will you raise it up in three days?" ²¹ But he spoke of the temple of his body. ²² When therefore he was raised from the dead, his disciples remembered that he had said this; and they believed the scripture and the word which Jesus had spoken.

Acts 6:14a (§A178.6)

⁸ And Stephen, full of grace and power, did great wonders and signs among the people. ⁹ Then some of those who belonged to the synagogue of the Freedman (as it was called), and of the Cyrenians, and of the Alexandrians, and of those from Cilicia and Asia, arose and disputed with Stephen. ¹⁰ But they could not withstand the wisdom and the Spirit with which he spoke. ¹¹ Then they secretly instigated men, who said, "We have heard him speak blasphemous words against Moses and God." ¹² And they stirred up the people and the elders and the scribes, and they came upon him and seized him and brought him before the council, ¹³ and set up false witnesses who said, "This man never ceases to speak words against this holy place and the law; ¹⁴ for we have heard him say that this *Jesus of Nazareth will destroy this place,* and will change the customs which Moses delivered to us."

GThom 71 (§A178.7)

(71) Jesus said, *"I shall destroy [this] house, and no one will be able to rebuild it."*

★ See 466: *Temple and Jesus*

★ See 466: *Temple and Jesus*

212

SALTED WITH FIRE

Mark 9:49 (§A179)

⁴⁹ *"For every one will be salted with fire.* ⁵⁰ Salt is good; but if the salt has lost its saltness, how will you season it? Have salt in yourselves, and be at peace with one another."

213 SALT AND PEACE

Mark 9:50b (§A180)

[49] "For every one will be salted with fire. [50] Salt is good; but if the salt has lost its saltness, how will you season it? *Have salt in yourselves, and be at peace with one another.*"

214 PHYSICIAN, HEAL YOURSELF*

Luke 4:23 (§A181)

[16] And he came to Nazareth, where he had been brought up; and he went to the synagogue, as his custom was, on the sabbath day. And he stood up to read; [17] and there was given to him the book of the prophet Isaiah. He opened the book and found the place where it was written,

[18] "The Spirit of the Lord is upon me,
because he has anointed me to preach
good news to the poor.
He has sent me to proclaim release to the
captives
and recovering of sight to the blind,
to set at liberty those who are oppressed,
[19] to proclaim the acceptable year of the
Lord."

[20] And he closed the book, and gave it back to the attendant, and sat down; and the eyes of all in the synagogue were fixed on him. [21] And he began to say to them, "Today this scripture has been fulfilled in your hearing." [22] And all spoke well of him, and wondered at the gracious words which proceeded out of his mouth; and they said, "Is not this Joseph's son?" [23] And he said to them, *"Doubtless you will quote to me this proverb, 'Physician, heal yourself;' what we have heard you did at Capernaum, do here also in your own country.'"*

* See 146 & 436: *Prophet's Own Country*
* See 476: *Jesus at Nazareth*

215 GENTILES PREFERRED*

Luke 4:25–27 (§A182)

[24] And he said, "Truly, I say to you, no prophet is acceptable in his own country. [25] *But in truth, I tell you, there were many widows in Israel in the days of Elijah, when the heaven was shut up three years and six months, when there came a great famine over all the land;* [26] *and Elijah was sent to none of them but only to Zarephath, in the land of Sidon, to a woman who was a widow.* [27] *And there were many lepers in Israel in the time of the prophet Elisha; and none of them was cleansed, but only Naaman the Syrian."* [28] When they heard this, all in the synagogue were filled with wrath. [29] And they rose up and put him out of the city, and led him to the brow of the hill on which their city was built, that they might throw him down headlong. [30] But passing through the midst of them he went away.

* See 476: *Jesus at Nazareth*

216 DRINKING OLD WINE

Luke 5:39 (§A183.1)
³⁶ He told them a parable also: "No one tears a piece from a new garment and puts it upon an old garment; if he does, he will tear the new, and the piece from the new will not match the old. ³⁷ And no one puts new wine into old wineskins; if he does, the new wine will burst the skins and it will be spilled, and the skins will be destroyed. ³⁸ But new wine must be put into fresh wineskins. ³⁹ *And no one after drinking old wine desires new; for he says, 'The old is good.'"*

GThom 47:2 (§A183.2)
(47) ¹ Jesus said, "It is impossible for a man to mount two horses or to stretch two bows. ² And it is impossible for a servant to serve two masters; otherwise, he will honor the one and treat the other contemptuously. ³ *No man drinks old wine and immediately desires to drink new wine.* ⁴ And new wine is not put into old wineskins, lest they burst; nor is old wine put into a new wineskin, lest it spoil it. An old patch is not sewn onto a new garment, because a tear would result."

217 WOE AGAINST RICHES

Luke 6:24 (§A184)
²⁴ *"But woe to you that are rich, for you have received your consolation."*

218 WOE AGAINST SATIETY

Luke 6:25a (§A185)
²⁵ *"Woe to you that are full now, for you shall hunger."*

219 WOE AGAINST LAUGHTER

Luke 6:25b (§A186)
²⁵ *". . . Woe to you that laugh now, for you shall mourn and weep."*

220 WOE AGAINST PRAISE

Luke 6:26 (§A187)
²⁶ *"Woe to you, when all men speak well of you, for so their fathers did to the false prophets."*

221 GIFT FOR GIFT

Luke 6:38ab (§A188.1)
[37] "Judge not, and you will not be judged; condemn not, and you will not be condemned; forgive, and you will be forgiven; [38] *give, and it will be given to you; good measure, pressed down, shaken together, running over, will be put into your lap.* For the measure you give will be the measure you get back."

1 Clem 13:2d (§A188.2)
[2]For he spoke thus: "Be merciful, that ye may obtain mercy. Forgive, that ye may be forgiven. As ye do, so shall it be done unto you. *As ye give, so shall it be given unto you.* As ye judge, so shall ye be judged. As ye are kind, so shall kindness be shewn you. With what measure ye mete, it shall be measured to you."

222 CONDEMNATION FOR CONDEMNATION

Luke 6:37b (§A189)
[37] "Judge not, and you will not be judged; *condemn not, and you will not be condemned*; forgive, and you will be forgiven; [38] give, and it will be given to you; good measure, pressed down, shaken together, running over, will be put into your lap. For the measure you give will be the measure you get back."

223 FRIEND AT MIDNIGHT

Luke 11:5–8 (§A190)
[5] And he said to them, *"Which of you who has a friend will go to him at midnight and say to him, 'Friend, lend me three loaves;* [6] *for a friend of mine has arrived on a journey, and I have nothing to set before him';* [7] *and he will answer from within, 'Do not bother me; the door is now shut, and my children are with me in bed; I cannot get up and give you anything'?* [8] *I tell you, though he will not get up and give him anything because he is his friend, yet because of his importunity he will rise and give him whatever he needs."*

224 LITTLE FLOCK

Luke 12:32 (§A191)
[32] *"Fear not, little flock, for it is your Father's good pleasure to give you the kingdom."*

225 MUCH AND MORE

Luke 12:48b (§A192)

[41] Peter said, "Lord, are you telling this parable for us or for all?" [42] And the Lord said, "Who then is the faithful and wise steward, whom his master will set over his household, to give them their portion of food at the proper time? [43] Blessed is that servant whom his master when he comes will find so doing. [44] Truly, I say to you, he will set him over all his possessions. [45] But if that servant says to himself, 'My master is delayed in coming,' and begins to beat the menservants and the maidservants, and to eat and drink and get drunk, [46] the master of that servant will come on a day when he does not expect him and at an hour he does not know, and will punish him, and put him with the unfaithful. [47] And that servant who knew his master's will, but did not make ready or act according to his will, shall receive a severe beating. [48] But he who did not know, and did what deserved a beating, shall receive a light beating. *Every one to whom much is given, of him will much be required; and of him to whom men commit much they will demand the more.*"

226 FIRE ON EARTH

Luke 12:49 (§A193.1)

[49] *"I came to cast fire upon the earth; and would that it were already kindled!"*

GThom 10 (§A193.2)

(10) Jesus said, *"I have cast fire upon the world, and see, I am guarding it until it blazes."*

227 PLACES AT TABLE

Luke 14:8–10 (§A194)

[7] Now he told a parable to those who were invited, when he marked how they chose the places of honor, saying to them, [8] *"When you are invited by any one to a marriage feast, do not sit down in a place of honor, lest a more eminent man than you be invited by him; [9] and he who invited you both will come and say to you, 'Give place to this man,' and then you will begin with shame to take the lowest place. [10] But when you are invited, go and sit in the lowest place, so that when your host comes he may say to you, 'Friend, go up higher'; then you will be honored in the presence of all who sit at table with you."*

228 INVITING THE OUTCASTS

Luke 14:12b–14 (§A195)

[12] He said also to the man who had invited him, *"When you give a dinner or a banquet, do not invite your friends or your brothers or your kinsmen or rich neighbors, lest they also invite you in return, and you be repaid. [13] But when you give a feast, invite the poor, the maimed, the lame, the blind, [14] and you will be blessed, because they cannot repay you. You will be repaid at the resurrection of the just."*

229 RENOUNCING ALL

Luke 14:33 (§A196)

25 Now great multitudes accompanied him; and he turned and said to them, 26 "If any one comes to me and does not hate his own father and mother and wife and children and brothers and sisters, yes, and even his own life, he cannot be my disciple. 27 Whoever does not bear his own cross and come after me, cannot be my disciple. 28 For which of you, desiring to build a tower, does not first sit down and count the cost, whether he has enough to complete it? 29 Otherwise, when he has laid a foundation, and is not able to finish, all who see it begin to mock him, 30 saying, 'This man began to build, and was not able to finish.' 31 Or what king, going to encounter another king in war, will not sit down first and take counsel whether he is able with ten thousand to meet him who comes against him with twenty thousand? 32 And if not, while the other is yet a great way off, he sends an embassy and asks terms of peace. 33 *So therefore, whoever of you does not renounce all that he has cannot be my disciple."*

230 UNRIGHTEOUS MAMMON

Luke 16:9 (§A197)

1 He also said to the disciples, "There was a rich man who had a steward, and charges were brought to him that this man was wasting his goods. 2 And he called him and said to him, 'What is this that I hear about you? Turn in the account of your stewardship, for you can no longer be steward.' 3 And the steward said to himself, 'What shall I do, since my master is taking the stewardship away from me? I am not strong enough to dig, and I am ashamed to beg. 4 I have decided what to do, so that people may receive me into their houses when I am put out of the stewardship.' 5 So, summoning his master's debtors one by one, he said to the first, 'How much do you owe my master?' 6 He said, 'A hundred measures of oil.' And he said to him, 'Take your bill, and sit down quickly and write fifty.' 7 Then he said to another, 'And how much do you owe?' He said, 'A hundred measures of wheat.' He said to him, 'Take your bill, and write eighty.' 8 The master commended the dishonest steward for his shrewdness; for the sons of this world are more shrewd in dealing with their own generation than the sons of light. 9 *And I tell you, make friends for yourselves by means of unrighteous mammon, so that when it fails they may receive you into the eternal habitations."*

231 FAITHFUL AND UNFAITHFUL

Luke 16:10–12 (§A198.1)

10 *"He who is faithful in a very little is faithful also in much; and he who is dishonest in a very little is dishonest also in much. 11 If then you have not been faithful in the unrighteous mammon, who will entrust to you the true riches? 12 And if you have not been faithful in that which is another's, who will give you that which is your own?"*

2 Clem 8:5 (§A198.2)

5 For the Lord says in the Gospel, *"If ye did not guard that which is small, who shall give you that which is great? For I tell you that he who is faithful in that which is least, is faithful also in that which is much."* 6 He means, then, this:— Keep the flesh pure, and the seal of baptism undefiled, that we may obtain eternal life.

232 THE SERVANT'S DUTY

Luke 17:7–10 (§A199)

7 *"Will any one of you, who has a servant plowing or keeping sheep, say to him when he has come in from the field, 'Come at once and sit down at table'?* 8 *Will he not rather say to him, 'Prepare supper for me, and gird youseslf and serve me, till I eat and* drink; *and afterward you shall eat and drink'?* 9 *Does he thank the servant because he did what was commanded?* 10 *So you also, when you have done all that is commanded you, say, 'We are unworthy servants; we have only done what was our duty.'"*

233 DAYS ARE COMING

Luke 17:22 (§A200)

22 And he said to the disciples, *"The days are coming when you will desire to see one of the days of the Son of man, and you will not see it.* 23 And they will say to you, 'Lo, there!' or 'Lo, here!' Do not go, do not follow them. 24 For as lightning flashes and lights up the sky from one side to the other, so will the Son of man be in his day. 25 But first he must suffer many things and be rejected by this generation."

234 AS WITH LOT

Luke 17:28–30 (§A201)

28 *"Likewise as it was in the days of Lot— they ate, they drank, they bought, they sold, they planted, they built,* 29 *but on the day when Lot went out from Sodom fire and sulphur rained from heaven and destroyed them all—* 30 *so will it be on the day when the Son of man is revealed."*

235 LIKE A SNARE

Luke 21:34–35 (§A202)

34 *"But take heed to yourselves lest your hearts be weighed down with dissipation and drunkenness and cares of this life, and that day come upon you suddenly like a snare;* 35 *for it will come upon all who dwell upon the face of the whole earth.* 36 But watch at all times, praying that you may have strength to escape all these things that will take place, and to stand before the Son of man."

236 JERUSALEM MOURNED*

Luke 23:29 (§A203.1)

²⁶ And as they led him away, they seized one Simon of Cyrene, who was coming in from the country, and laid on him the cross, to carry it behind Jesus. ²⁷ And there followed him a great multitude of the people, and of women who bewailed and lamented him. ²⁸ But Jesus turning to them said, "Daughters of Jerusalem, do not weep for me, but weep for yourselves and for your children. ²⁹ *For behold, the days are coming when they will say, 'Blessed are the barren, and the wombs that never bore, and the breasts that never gave suck!'* ³⁰ Then they will begin to say to the mountains, 'Fall on us'; and to the hills, 'Cover us.' ³¹ For if they do this when the wood is green, what will happen when it is dry?"

* See 490: *Jerusalem Mourned*

GThom 79:3 (§A203.2)

(79) ¹ A woman from the crowd said to Him, "Blessed are the womb which bore You and the breasts which nourished You."

² He said to her, "Blessed are those who have heard the word of the Father and have truly kept it. ³ *For there will be days when you will say, 'Blessed are the womb which has not conceived and the breasts which have not given milk.'*"

---

237 FAITH AGAINST SIGHT*

Luke 24:36–43 (§A204.1)

³⁶ As they were saying this, Jesus himself stood among them. ³⁷ But they were startled and frightened, and supposed that they saw a spirit. ³⁸ And he said to them, "Why are you troubled, and why do questionings rise in your hearts? ³⁹ See my hands and my feet, that it is I myself; handle me, and see; for a spirit has not flesh and bones as you see that I have." ⁴¹ And while they still disbelieved for joy, and wondered, he said to them, "Have you anything here to eat?" ⁴² They gave him a piece of broiled fish, ⁴³ and he took it and ate before them.

John 20:29b (§A204.2)

²⁴ Now Thomas, one of the twelve, called the Twin, was not with them when Jesus came. ²⁵ So the other disciples told him, "We have seen the Lord." But he said to them, "Unless I see in his hands the print of the nails, and place my finger in the mark of the nails, and place my hand in his side, I will not believe."

* See 493: *Faith Against Sight*

²⁶ Eight days later, his disciples were again in the house, and Thomas was with them. The doors were shut, but Jesus came and stood among them, and said, "Peace be with you." ²⁷ Then he said to Thomas, "Put your finger here, and see my hands; and put out your hand, and place it in my side; do not be faithless, but believing." ²⁸ Thomas answered him, "My Lord and my God!" ²⁹ Jesus said to him, "Have you believed because you have seen me? *Blessed are those who have not seen and yet believe.*"

ApJas 3:5 (§A204.3)

³ And now, waking or sleeping remember that you have seen the Son of Man, and with him you have spoken, and to him you have listened. ⁴ Woe to those who have seen the Son [of] Man! ⁵ *Blessed are those (or: you [pl.]) who have not seen the Man, and who have not consorted with him, and who have not spoken with him, and who have not listened to anything from him. Yours is life!* ⁶ Know, therefore, that he healed you when you were ill, in order that you might reign. ⁷ Woe to those who have rested from their illness, because they will relapse again into illness! ⁸ Blessed are those (or: you [pl.]) who have not been ill, and have known rest before they (or: you) became ill. Yours is the Kingdom of God!

ApJas 8:3c (§A204.4)

³ "As long as I am with you (pl.), give heed to me and obey me. But when I am to depart from you, remember me. And remember me because I was with you without your knowing me. Blessed are those who have known me. Woe to those who have heard and have not believed! *Blessed are those who have not seen [but] have [had faith].*"

Ign Smyr 3:1–3 (§A204.5)

¹ For I know and believe that he was in the flesh even after the Resurrection. ² And when he came to those with Peter he said to them: "Take, handle me and see that I am not a phantom without a body." And they immediately touched him and believed, being mingled both with his flesh and spirit. Therefore they despised even death, and were proved to be above death. ³ And after his Resurrection he ate and drank with them as a being of flesh, although he was united in spirit to the Father.

John 3:8 (§A205.1)

[1] Now there was a man of the Pharisees, named Nicodemus, a ruler of the Jews. [2] This man came to Jesus by night and said to him, "Rabbi, we know that you are a teacher come from God; for no one can do these signs that you do, unless God is with him." [3] Jesus answered him, "Truly, truly, I say to you, unless one is born anew, he cannot see the kingdom of God." [4] Nicodemus said to him, "How can a man be born when he is old? Can he enter a second time into his mother's womb and be born?" [5] Jesus answered, "Truly, truly, I say to you,

unless one is born of water and the Spirit, he cannot enter the kingdom of God. [6] That which is born of the flesh is flesh, and that which is born of the Spirit is spirit. [7] Do not marvel that I said to you, 'You must be born anew.' [8] *The wind blows where it wills, and you hear the sound of it, but you do not know whence it comes or whither it goes; so it is with every one who is born of the Spirit."* [9] Nicodemus said to him, "How can this be?" [10] Jesus answered him, "Are you a teacher of Israel, and yet you do not understand this?"

DialSav 35 (§A205.2)

(35) "If [one] does not [understand how] fire came into existence, he will burn in it, because he does not know the root of it. If one does not first understand water, he knows nothing. For what use is there for him to be baptized in it? *If one does not understand how blowing wind came into existence, he will blow away with it.* If one does not understand how body, which he bears, came into existence, he will [perish] with it. And how will someone who does [not] know [the Son] know the [Father]? And to someone who will not know the [root] of all things, they remain hidden. Someone who will not know the root of wickedness is no stranger to it. Whoever will not understand how he came will not understand how he will go, and he is no [stranger] to this cosmos which [will . . .], which will be humiliated."

239

LIVING WATER*

John 4:14 (§A206.1)

[1] Now when the Lord knew that the Pharisees had heard that Jesus was making and baptizing more disciples than John [2] (although Jesus himself did not baptize, but only his disciples), [3] he left Judea and departed again to Galilee. [4] He had to pass through Samaria. [5] So he came to a city of Samaria, called Sychar, near the field that Jacob gave to his son Joseph. [6] Jacob's well was there, and so Jesus, wearied as he was with his journey, sat down beside the well. It was about the sixth hour.

[7] There came a woman of Samaria to draw water. Jesus said to her, "Give me a drink." [8] For his disciples had gone away into the city to buy food. [9] The Samaritan woman said to him, "How is it that you, a Jew, ask a drink of me, a woman of Samaria?" For Jews have no dealings with Samaritans. [10] Jesus answered her, "If you knew the gift of God, and who it is that is saying to you, 'Give me a drink,' you would have asked him, and he would have given you living water." [11] The woman said to him, "Sir, you have nothing to draw with, and the well is deep; where do you get that living water? [12] Are you greater than our father Jacob, who gave us the well, and drank from it himself, and his sons, and his

cattle?" [13] Jesus said to her, "Every one who drinks of this water will thirst again, [14] *but whoever drinks of the water that I shall give him will never thirst; the water that I shall give him will become in him a spring of water welling up to eternal life."* [15] The woman said to him, "Sir, give me this water, that I may not thirst, nor come here to draw."

POxy840 (§A206.2)

(1) First before he does wrong (?) he thinks out everything that is crafty. But be ye on your guard that the same thing may not happen to you as does to them. For not only among the living do evil doers among men receive retribution, but they must also suffer punishment and great torment.

(2) And he took them (the disciples) with him into the place of purification itself and walked about in the Temple court. And a Pharisaic chief priest, Levi (?) by name, fell in with them and s[aid] to the Savior: Who gave thee leave to [trea]d this place of purification and to look upon [the]se holy utensils without having bathed thyself and even without thy disciples having [wa]shed their f[eet]? On the contrary, being de-fi[led], thou hast trodden the Temple court, this clean p[lace], although no [one who]

has [not] first bathed himself or [chang]ed his clot[hes] may tread it and [venture] to vi[ew these] holy utensils! Forthwith [the Savior] s[tood] still with h[is] disciples and [answered]: How stands it (then) with thee, thou art forsooth (also) here in the Temple court. Art thou then clean? He said to him: I am clean. For I have bathed myself in the pool of David and have gone down by the one stair and come up by the other and have put on white and clean clothes, and (only) then have I come hither and have viewed these holy utensils. Then said the Savior to him: Woe unto you blind that see not! Thou hast bathed thyself in water that is poured out, in which dogs and swine lie night and day and thou hast washed thyself and hast chafed thine outer skin, which prostitutes also and flute-girls anoint, bathe, chafe and rouge, in order to arouse desire in men, but within they are full of scorpions and of [bad]ness [of every kind]. *But I and [my disciples], of whom thou sayest that we have not im[mersed] our-selves, [have been im]mersed in the liv[ing . . .] water which comes down from [. . . B]ut woe unto them that . . .*

* See 496: *Living Water*

240 SCRIPTURES AND JESUS*

John 5:39–47 (§A207.1)
[39] *"You search the scriptures, because you think that in them you have eternal life; and it is they that bear witness to me;* [40] *yet you refuse to come to me that you may have life.* [41] I do not receive glory from men. [42] But I know that you have not the love of God within you. [43] I have come in my Father's name, and you do not receive me; if another comes in his own name, him you will receive. [44] How can you believe, who receive glory from one another and do not seek the glory that comes from the only God? [45] *Do not think that I shall accuse you to the Father; it is Moses who accuses you, on whom you set your hope.* [46] If you believed Moses, you would believe me, for he wrote of me. [47] But if you do not believe his writings, how will you believe my words?"

GThom 52 (§A207.2)
(52) [1] His disciples said to Him, "Twenty-four prophets spoke in Israel, and all of them spoke in You."
[2] He said to them, "You have omitted the one living in your presence and have spoken (only) of the dead."

PEger2 1 (§A207.3)
(1) . . . to the lawyer[s: " . . . e]very one who act[s contrary to the l]aw, but not me! . . . what he does, as he does it." [And] having turn[ed] to [the] rulers of the people he [sp]oke the following saying: *"(Ye) search the scriptures in which ye think that ye have life; these are they which bear witness of me. Do not think that I came to accuse [you] to my Father! There is one [that ac]cuses [you], even Moses, on whom ye have set your hope."* And when they

sa[id]: "We know that God [hath] spok[en] to Moses, but as for thee, we know not [whence thou art]," Jesus answered and said unto them: "Now (already) accusation is raised against [your] unbelief. [No one o]therwise . . ." (Fragment 1, verso [lines 1–20])
. . . [to gather] stones together to stone him. And the [rul]ers laid their hands on him that they might arrest him and [deliver] him to the multitude. But they w[ere not able] to arrest him because the hour of his betrayal [was] not yet c[ome]. But he himself, the Lord, escaped out of [their han]ds and turned away from them. (Fragment 1, recto [lines 22–41])

* See 367: *Scriptures and Jesus*

241 SEEKING TOO LATE

John 7:34a,36a (§A208.1)
[32] The Pharisees heard the crowd thus muttering about him, and the chief priests and Pharisees sent officers to arrest him. [33] Jesus then said, "I shall be with you a little longer, and then I go to him who sent me; [34] *you will seek me and you will not find me;* where I am you cannot come."

[35] The Jews said to one another, "Where does this man intend to go that we shall not find him? Does he intend to go to the Dispersion among the Greeks and teach the Greeks? [36] What does he mean by saying, *'You will seek me and you will not find me,'* and, 'Where I am you cannot come'?"

GThom 38:2 (§A208.2)
(38) [1] Jesus said, "Many times have you desired to hear these words which I am saying to you, and you have no one else to hear them from. [2] *There will be days when you will look for Me and will not find Me."*

242 NOT TASTE DEATH

John 8:51,52b (§A209.1)
[48] The Jews answered him, "Are we not right in saying that you are a Samaritan and have a demon?" [49] Jesus answered, "I have not a demon; but I honor my Father, and you dishonor me. [50] Yet I do not seek my own glory; there is One who seeks it and he will be the judge. [51] *Truly, truly, I say to you, if any one keeps my word, he will never see death."* [52] The Jews said to him, "Now we know that you have a demon. Abraham died, as did the prophets; and you say, *'If any one keeps my word, he will never taste death.'* [53] Are you greater than our father Abraham, who died? And the prophets died! Who do you claim to be?"

[54] Jesus answered, "If I glorify myself, my glory is nothing; it is my Father who glorifies me, of whom you say that he is your God. [55] But you have not known him; I know him. If I said, I do not know him, I should be a liar like you; but I do know him and I keep his word. [56] Your father Abraham rejoiced that he was to see my day; he saw it and was glad." [57] The Jews then said to him, "You are not yet fifty years old, and have you seen Abraham?" [58] Jesus said to them, "Truly, truly, I say to you, before Abraham was, I am." [59] So they took up stones to throw at him; but Jesus hid himself, and went out of the temple.

POxy654 1 (§A209.2)
(1) And he said, *"[Whoever finds the interpretation] of these sayings will not experience [death]."*

GThom 1 (§A209.3)
(1) And he said, *"Whoever finds the interpretation of these sayings will not experience death."*

243   LIFE FOR OTHERS

John 10:11b, 15b eb (§A210.1)

[11] "I am the good shepherd. *The good shepherd lays down his life for the sheep.* [12] He who is a hireling and not a shepherd, whose own the sheep are not, sees the wolf coming and leaves the sheep and flees; and the wolf snatches them and scatters them. [13] He flees because he is a hireling and cares nothing for the sheep. [14] I am the good shepherd; I know my own and my own know me, [15] as the Father knows me and I know the Father; and *I lay down my life for the sheep.* [16] And I have other sheep, that are not of this fold; I must bring them also, and they will heed my voice. So there shall be one flock, one shepherd. [17] For this reason the Father loves me, because I lay down my life, that I may take it again. [18] No one takes it from me, but I lay it down of my own accord. I have power to lay it down, and I have power to take it again; this charge I have received from my Father."

John 15:13 (§A210.2)

[12] "This is my commandment, that you love one another as I have loved you. [13] *Greater love has no man than this, that a man lay down his life for his friends.*"

1 John 3:16 (§A210.2)

[16] *By this we know love, that he laid down his life for us; and we ought to lay down our lives for the brethren.*

244   BLESSED FOR DOING*

John 13:17 (§A211.1)

[12] When he had washed their feet, and taken his garments, and resumed his place, he said to them, "Do you know what I have done to you? [13] You call me Teacher and Lord; and you are right, for so I am. [14] If I then, your Lord and Teacher, have washed your feet, you also ought to wash one another's feet. [15] For I have given you an example, that you also should do as I have done to you. [16] Truly, truly, I say to you, a servant is not greater than his master; nor is he who is sent greater than he who sent him. [17] *If you know these things, blessed are you if you do them.*"

Jas 1:25b (§A211.2)

[22] But be doers of the word, and not hearers only, deceiving yourselves. [23] For if any one is a hearer of the word and not a doer, he is like a man who observes his natural face in a mirror; [24] for he observes himself and goes away and at once forgets what he was like. [25] But he who looks into the perfect law, the law of liberty, and perseveres, *being no hearer that forgets but a doer that acts, he shall be blessed in his doing.*

* See 481: *Blessed the Womb*
* See 207 & 363: *Master and Steward*

245 GIVING AND RECEIVING

Acts 20:35b (§A212.1)

[32] "And now I commend you to God and to the word of his grace, which is able to build you up and to give you the inheritance among all those who are sanctified. [33] I coveted no one's silver or gold or apparel. [34] You yourselves know that these hands ministered to my necessities, and to those who were with me. [35] In all things I have shown you that by so toiling one must help the weak, remembering the words of the Lord Jesus, how he said, *'It is more blessed to give than to receive.'*"

Did 1:5 (§A212.2)

[5] Give to everyone that asks thee, and do not refuse, for the Father's will is that we give to all from the gifts we have received. *Blessed is he that gives according to the mandate;* for he is innocent. Woe to him who receives; for if any man receive alms under pressure of need he is innocent; but he who receives it without need shall be tried as to why he took and for what, and being in prison he shall be examined as to his deeds, and "he shall not come out thence until he pay the last farthing."

1 Clem 2:1 (§A212.3)

[1] And you were all humble-minded and in no wise arrogant, yielding subjection rather than demanding it, *"giving more gladly than receiving,"* satisfied with the provision of Christ, and paying attention to his words you stored them up carefully in your hearts, and kept his sufferings before your eyes.

Herm Man 2:4b (§A212.4)

[4] And put on reverence, in which is no evil stumbling-block, but all is smooth and joyful. Do good, and of all your toil which God gives you, give in simplicity to all who need, not doubting to whom you shall give and to whom not: *give to all, for to all God wishes gifts to be made of his own bounties.* [5] Those then who receive shall render an account to God why they received it and for what. For those who accepted through distress shall not be punished, but those who accepted in hyprocrisy shall pay the penalty. [6] He therefore who gives is innocent; for as he received from the Lord the fulfilment of this ministry, he fulfilled it in simplicity, not doubting to whom he should give or not give. Therefore this ministry fulfilled in simplicity was honourable before God. He therefore who serves in simplicity shall live to God.

246 EYE, EAR, MIND

1 Cor 2:9a (§A213.1)

[6] Yet among the mature we do impart wisdom, although it is not a wisdom of this age or of the rulers of this age, who are doomed to pass away. [7] But we impart a secret and hidden wisdom of God, which God decreed before the ages for our glorification. [8] None of the rulers of this age understood this; for if they had, they would not have crucified the Lord of glory. [9] But, as it is written,

"What no eye has seen, nor ear heard, nor the heart of man conceived,
what God has prepared for those who love him,"
[10] God has revealed to us through the Spirit. For the Spirit searches everything, even the depths of God. [11] For what person knows a man's thoughts except the spirit of the man which is in him? So also no one comprehends the thoughts of God except the Spirit of God.

GThom 17 (§A213.2)

(17) Jesus said, *"I shall give you what no eye has seen and what no ear has heard and what no hand has touched and what has never occurred to the human mind."*

DialSav 57a (§A213.3)

(57) The [Lord] said, "[You (masc. sing.) have] asked me about a saying [. . .] *which eye has not seen, [nor] have I heard it* except from you. But I say to you that when what invigorates a man is removed, he will be called 'dead.' And when what is alive leaves what is dead, what is alive will be called upon."

247 THE GREAT TORMENT

POxy840 1 (§A214)

(1) "First before he does wrong (?) he thinks out everything that is crafty. But be ye on your guard that the same thing may not happen to you as does to them. *For not only among the living do evil doers among men receive retribution, but they must also suffer punishment and great torment."*

POxy1224 2 (§A215)

(2) And pray for your enemies. For he who is not [against you] is for you. *[He who today] is far-off—tomorrow will be [near to you]....*

GPet 13:56b (§A216.1)

⁵⁰ Early in the morning of the Lord's day Mary Magdalene, a woman disciple of the Lord— for fear of the Jews, since (they) were inflamed with wrath, she had not done at the sepulchre of the Lord what women are wont to do for those beloved of them who die—took ⁵¹ with her her women friends and came to the sepulchre where he was laid. ⁵² And they feared lest the Jews should see them, and said, "Although we could not weep and lament on that day when he was crucified, yet let us now do so at his sepulchre. ⁵³ But who will roll away for us the stone also that is set on the entrance to the sepulchre, that we may go in and sit beside him and do what is due?— ⁵⁴ For the stone was great,— and we fear lest any one see us. And if we cannot do so, let us at least put down at the entrance what we bring for a memorial of him and let us weep and lament until we have again gone home." 13 ⁵⁵ So they went and found the sepulchre opened. And they came near, stooped down and saw there a young man sitting in the midst of the sepulchre, comely and clothed with a brightly shining robe, who said to them, ⁵⁶ "Wherefore are ye come? Whom seek ye? Not him that was crucified? He is risen and gone. But if ye believe not, stoop this way and see the place where he lay, for he is not here. *For he is risen and is gone thither whence he was sent."* ⁵⁷ Then the women fled affrighted.

ApJas 2:2a (§A216.2)

¹ Now the twelve disciples [were] sitting all together at [the same time], and, remembering what the Savior had said to each one of them, whether secretly or openly, they were setting it down in books. [And] I was writing what was in [my book]—lo, the Savior appeared, [after] he had departed from [us while we] gazed at him. And five hundred and fifty days after he arose from the dead, we said to him: "Have you gone and departed from us?"

² *And Jesus said: "No, but I shall go to the place from which I have come.* If you (pl.) desire to come with me, come."

ApJas 9:5b (§A216.3)

⁵ "These things I shall say to you (pl.) for the present. *But now I shall ascend to the place from which I have come.* ⁶ But you, when I was eager to go, have driven me out, and, instead of your accompanying me, you have pursued me. ⁷ But give heed to the glory which awaits me, and, having opened your heart(s), listen to the hymns which await me up in heaven. For today I am obliged to take (my place) at the right hand of my Father. ⁸ Now I have said (my) last word to you. I shall part from you. For a chariot of wind has taken me up, and from now on I shall strip myself in order that I may clothe myself. ⁹ But give heed: blessed are those who have preached the Son before he descended, in order that, when I have come, I (or: <they>) may ascend. Thrice blessed are those who [were] proclaimed by the Son before they came into being, in order that you may have a portion with them."

* See 499: *Place From Which*

ApJas 3:9 (§A217)

⁹ *"Therefore I say to you, become full and leave no place within you empty, since the Coming One is able to mock you."*

¹⁰ Then Peter answered: "<Lord>, three times you have said to us, '[Become full,' but] we are full."

¹¹ The [Lord answered and] said: "[Therefore I say] to you (pl.), [become full], in order that [you] may not [be diminished. Those who are diminished], however, will not [be saved]. ¹² For fullness is good [and diminution] is bad. ¹³ Therefore, just as it is good for you (sing.) to be diminished and, on the other hand, bad for you to be filled, so also the one who is full is diminished; and the one who is diminished is not filled as the one who is diminished is filled, and the one who is full, for his part, brings his sufficiency to completion. ¹⁴ Therefore, it is fitting to be diminished while you (pl.) can (still) be filled, and to be filled while it is (still) possible to be diminished, in order that you can [fill] yourselves the more. ¹⁵ Therefore, [become] full of the spirit but be diminished of reason. For reason is (of) the soul; and it is soul."

* See 369: *Become Full*

251 KINGDOM AND CROSS*

ApJas 4:9 (§A218)
[9]*"Scorn death, therefore, and take concern for life. Remember my cross and my death and you will live."*

5 [1]And I answered and said to him: "Lord, do not mention to us the cross and the death, for they are far from you."

[2]The Lord answered and said: "Truly I say to you (pl.), none will be saved unless they believe in my cross. [But] those who have believed in my cross, theirs is the Kingdom of God. [3]Therefore, become seekers for death, just as the dead who seek for life, for that for which they seek is revealed to them. And what is there to concern them? When you turn yourselves towards death, it will make known to you election. [4]In truth I say to you, none of those who are afraid of death will be saved. For the Kingdom of <God> belongs to those who have put themselves to death. [5]Become better than I; make yourselves like the son of the Holy Spirit."

* See 370: *Kingdom and Cross*

252 SECRETLY AND OPENLY

ApJas 6:5 (§A219)
[5]*"I first spoke with you in parables, and you did not understand. Now, in turn, I speak with you openly, and you do not perceive. But it is you who were to me a parable in parables and what is apparent in what are open."*

253 GO BEFORE ME

ApJas 6:6 (§A220)
[6]*"Be zealous to be saved without being urged. Rather, be ready on your (pl.) own and, if possible, go before me. For thus the Father will love you."*

254 HATE HYPOCRISY

ApJas 6:7 (§A221.1)
[7]*"Become haters of hypocrisy and evil thought. For it is thought which gives birth to hypocrisy, but hypocrisy is far from the truth."*

Did 4:12 (§A221.2)
[12]*Thou shall hate all hypocrisy, and everything that is not pleasing to the Lord.*

255 ASCENSION AND PARABLES

ApJas 6:9–10 (§A222)

⁹"<Since> *I have been glorified in this manner before this time, why do you (pl.) restrain me when I am eager to go? For after my [suffering] you have constrained me to remain with you eighteen more days (or: <months>) for the sake of the parables.* ¹⁰*It sufficed for some persons <to> pay attention to the teaching and to understand 'The Shepherds' and 'The Seed' and 'The Building' and 'The Lamps of the Virgins' and 'The Wage of the Workers' and 'The Double Drachma' and 'The Woman.'"*

256 SON NEEDS FATHER

ApJas 6:15b (§A223)

¹²"Therefore I say to you (pl.), be sober. Do not go astray. And many times I have said to you all together—and also to you (sing.) alone, James, I have said—be saved. And I have commanded you (sing.) to follow me, and I have taught you the response in the presence of the Rulers. ¹³Observe that I have descended, and I have spoken, and <I> have troubled myself, and I have received my crown, when I saved you (pl.). ¹⁴For I have descended to dwell with you in order that <you> also may dwell with me. And when I found that your houses had no ceilings over them, I dwelt in houses which would be able to receive me when I descended.

¹⁵"Therefore, obey me, my brothers. Understand what the great light is. The Father does not need me. *For a father does not need a son, but it is the son who needs the father.* To him I am going, for the Father of the Son is not in need of you (pl.)."

257 ON PERSECUTING ONESELF

ApJas 6:16 (§A224)

¹⁶"*Pay attention to the Word. Understand knowledge. Love life. And no one will persecute you (pl.), nor will any one oppress you, other than you yourselves.*"

258 IT IS EASIER

ApJas 6:17 (§A225)

¹⁷"O you (pl.) wretched! O you unfortunates! O you dissemblers of the truth! O you falsifiers of knowledge! O you sinners against the spirit! Do you even now dare to listen, when it behooved you to speak from the beginning? Do you even now dare to sleep, when it behooved you to be awake from the beginning, in order that the Kingdom of Heaven might receive you? *In truth I say to you, it is easier for a holy one to sink into defilement, and for a man of light to sink into darkness, than for you to reign—or (even) not to (reign)!*"

259 GRIEF AND SORROW

ApJas 6:18 (§A226)
[18] *"I have remembered your (pl.) tears and your grief and your sorrow. They are far from us. Now, then, you who are outside the inheritance of the Father, weep where it behooves (you) and grieve and proclaim that which is good, since the Son is ascending appropriately."*

260 HAD IT BEEN

ApJas 6:19 (§A227)
[19] *"In truth I say to you, had it been to those who would listen to me that I was sent, and had it been with them that I was to speak, I would have never descended upon the earth. And now, then, be ashamed on account of them."*

261 JESUS AS INTERCESSOR

ApJas 6:22b (§A228)
[20] "Behold, I shall depart from you (pl.). I am going and I do not desire to remain with you any longer—just as you yourselves have not desired. Now, then, follow me quickly. [21] Therefore I say to you, for your sake I have descended. You are the beloved; you are those who will become a cause of life for many. Beseech the Father. Implore God often, and he will give to you. [22] Blessed is the one who has seen you with him when he is proclaimed among the angels and glorified among the saints. Yours is life! Rejoice and be glad as children of God. Keep [his] will in order that you may be saved. Take reproof from me and save yourselves. *I intercede on your behalf with the Father, and he will forgive you much."*

262 INTERCESSOR NOT NEEDED

ApJas 7:2b (§A229)
[1] And when we heard these things, we became elated, for <we> had been depressed on account of what we had said earlier. [2] Now when he saw our rejoicing, he said: *"Woe to you (pl.) who are in want of an advocate! Woe to you who are in need of grace! Blessed are those who have spoken freely and have produced grace for themselves."*

263 BE LIKE STRANGERS

ApJas 7:3a (§A230)
[3] *"Make yourselves like strangers*; of what sort are they in the estimation of your city? Why are you troubled when you oust yourselves of your own accord and depart from your city? Why do you abandon your dwelling place of your own accord, readying it for those who desire to dwell in it? O you exiles and fugitives! Woe to you, because you will be caught! [4] Or perhaps you imagine that the Father is a lover of humanity? Or that he is persuaded by prayers? Or that he is gracious to one on behalf of another? Or that he bears with one who seeks?"

264 SOUL AND FLESH

ApJas 7:7 (§A231)
[5] "For he knows the desire and also that which the flesh needs. Because it is not it (i.e., the flesh) which yearns for the soul. [6] For without the soul the body does not sin, just as the soul is not saved without (the) spirit. But if the soul is saved (when it is) without evil, and if the spirit also is saved, (then) the body becomes sinless. For it is the spirit which <animates> the soul, but it is the body which kills it—that is, it is it (i.e., the soul) which kills itself. [7] *Truly I say to you (pl.), he (i.e., the Father) will not forgive the sin of the soul at all, nor the guilt of the flesh. For none of those who have worn the flesh will be saved."*

265 FEW IN HEAVEN

ApJas 7:8 (§A232)
[8] *"For do you imagine that many have found the Kingdom of Heaven? Blessed is the one who has seen himself as a fourth one in heaven."*

266 HOUSE FOR SHELTER

ApJas 8:4b (§A233)
[4] "And once again I [persuade] you (pl.). *For I am revealed to you building a house which is very valuable to you, since you take shelter under it; in the same way it will be able to support the house of your neighbors when (theirs) is in danger [of] falling."*

267 TO THE FATHER

ApJas 8:5 (§A234)
[5] *"In truth I say to you, woe to those on behalf of whom I was sent down to this place! Blessed are those who are to ascend to the Father."*

268 WHO ARE NOT

ApJas 8:6 (§A335)
[6] *"Again I reprove you. You who are, make yourselves like those who are not, in order that you may come to be with those who are not."*

269 KINGDOM BECOMES DESERT

ApJas 8:7a (§A236)
[7] *"Let not the Kingdom of Heaven become desolate among you (pl.)."*

270 BEING LIKE JESUS

ApJas 8:7b (§A237)
[7] *". . . Do not become arrogant on account of the light which illumines. Rather, become to yourselves in this manner, as I (am) to you. For you I have placed myself under the curse, in order that you may be saved."*

ApJas 9:9 (§A238)

⁵ "These things I shall say to you (pl.) for the present. But now I shall ascend to the place from which I have come. ⁶ But you, when I was eager to go, have driven me out, and, instead of your accompanying me, you have pursued me. ⁷ But give heed to the glory which awaits me, and, having opened your heart(s), listen to the hymns which await me up in heaven. For today I am obliged to take (my place) at the right hand of my Father. ⁸ Now I have said (my) last word to you. I shall part from you. For a chariot of wind has taken me up, and from now on I shall strip myself in order that I may clothe myself. ⁹ But give heed: *blessed are those who have preached the Son before he descended, in order that, when I have come, I (or: <they>) may ascend. Thrice blessed are those who [were] proclaimed by the Son before they came into being, in order that you may have a portion with them."*

POxy654 3:2 (§A239.1)

(3) ¹ Jesus said, "[If] those who lead you [say to you, 'See], the kingdom is in the sky,' then the birds of the sky [will precede you. If they say that] it is under the earth, then the fish of the sea [will enter it, preceding] you. And, the [kingdom of God] is inside of you, [and it is outside of you. ² Whoever] *knows [himself] will discover this. [And when you] come to know yourselves, [you will realize that] you are [sons] of the [living] father. [But if you] will [not] know yourselves, [you dwell] in [poverty] and it is you who are that poverty."*

GThom 3:2 (§A239.2)

(3) ¹ Jesus said, "If those who lead you say to you, 'See, the Kingdom is in the sky,' then the birds of the sky will precede you. If they say to you, 'It is in the sea,' then the fish will precede you. Rather, the Kingdom is inside of you, and it is outside of you. ² *When you come to know yourselves, then you will become known, and you will realize that it is you who are the sons of the living Father. But if you will not know yourselves, you dwell in poverty and it is you who are that poverty."*

DialSav 30 (§A239.3)

(30) The Lord [said], *"[Everyone] who has known himself has seen [it . . .] everything given to him to do [. . .] . . .and has come to [. . .] it in his [goodness]."*

POxy654 4:1 (§A240.1)

(4) ¹ [Jesus said], *"The [man old in days] will not hesitate to ask [a small child seven days old] about the place [of life, and] he will [live].* ² For many who are [first] will become [last, and] the last will be first, and [they will become one and the same]."

GThom 4:1 (§A240.2)

(4) ¹ Jesus said, *"The man old in days will not hesitate to ask a small child seven days old about the place of life, and he will live.* ² For many who are first will become last, and they will become one and the same."

274 IN YOUR SIGHT

POxy654 5:1 (§A241.1)
(5) [1] Jesus said, *"[Recognize what is in] your (sg.) sight, and [that which is hidden] from you (sg.) will become plain [to you (sg.).* [2] For there is nothing] hidden which [will] not [become] manifest, [3] nor buried that [will not be raised]."

GThom 5:1 (§A241.2)
(5) [1] Jesus said, *"Recognize what is in your sight, and that which is hidden from you will become plain to you.* [2] For there is nothing hidden which will not become manifest."

275 BURIED AND RESURRECTED

POxy654 5:3 (§A242.1)
(5) [1] Jesus said, "[Recognize what is in] your (sg.) sight, and [that which is hidden] from you (sg.) will become plain [to you (sg.). [2] For there is nothing] hidden which [will] not [become] manifest, [3] *nor buried that [will not be raised]."*

Oxyrhynchus Shroud (§A242.2)
"Jesus says, *'Nothing has been buried that will not be raised.'"* (Hennecke 1:300)

276 ON TELLING LIES

POxy654 6:2–3 (§A243.1)
(6) [1] [His disciples] questioned him [and said], "How [shall we] fast? [How shall we pray]? How [shall we give alms]? What [diet] shall [we] observe?"
[2] Jesus said, *"[Do not tell lies, [3] and]* do not do what you [hate, *for all things are plain in the sight] of truth.* [4] [For nothing] hidden [will not become manifest]."

GThom 6:2–3 (§A243.2)
(6) [1] His disciples questioned Him and said to Him, "Do You want us to fast? How shall we pray? Shall we give alms? What diet shall we observe?"
[2] Jesus said, *"Do not tell lies, [3] and* do not do what you hate, *for all things are plain in the sight of Heaven.* [4] For nothing hidden will not become manifest, and nothing covered will remain without being uncovered."

277 MAN AND LION

POxy654 7 (§A244.1)
(7) *[. . .] Blessed is [the lion] which becomes [man when consumed by man; and cursed is the man] whom [the lion consumes . . .]*

GThom 7 (§A244.2)
(7) Jesus said, *"Blessed is the lion which becomes man when consumed by man; and cursed is the man whom the lion consumes, and the lion becomes man."*

278   LIFE AND DEATH

GThom 11:1–2a (§A245.1)

(11) [1] Jesus said, *"This heaven will pass away, and the one above it will pass away. The dead are not alive, and the living will not die. In the days when you consumed what is dead, you made it what is alive. [2] When you come to dwell in the light, what will you do?* On the day when you were one you became two. But when you become two, what will you do?"

GThom 111:1 (§A245.2)

(111) [1] Jesus said, *"The heavens and the earth will be rolled up in your presence. And the one who lives from the Living One will not see death."* [2] Does not Jesus say, "Whoever finds himself is superior to the world?"

DialSav 56–57 (§A245.3)

(56) [Matthew] said, *"Tell me, Lord, how the dead die [and] how the living live."*

(57) *The [Lord] said, "[You (masc. sing.) have] asked me about a saying [. . .] which eye has not seen, [nor] have I heard it except from you. But I say to you that when what invigorates a man is removed, he will be called 'dead.' And when what is alive leaves what is dead, what is alive will be called upon."*

279   TWO AND ONE

GThom 11:2b (§A246)

(11) [1] Jesus said, "This heaven will pass away, and the one above it will pass away. The dead are not alive, and the living will not die. In the days when you consumed what is dead, you made it what is alive. [2] When you come to dwell in the light, what will you do? *On the day when you were one you became two. But when you become two, what will you do?"*

280   FASTING, PRAYING, ALMSGIVING★

GThom 14:1 (§A247)

(14) [1] Jesus said to them, *"If you fast, you will give rise to sin for yourselves; and if you pray, you will be condemned; and if you give alms, you will do harm to your spirits.* [2] When you go into any land and walk about in the districts, if they receive you, eat what they will set before you, and heal the sick among them. [3] For what goes into your mouth will not defile you, but that which issues from your mouth—it is that which will defile you."

★ See 373: *Fasting, Praying, Almsgiving*

281   YOUR FATHER

GThom 15 (§A248)

(15) Jesus said, *"When you see one who was not born of woman, prostrate yourselves on your faces and worship him. That one is your Father."*

282 BEGINNING AND END*

GThom 18:3b (§A249)

(18) [1] The disciples said to Jesus, "Tell us how our end will be."

[2] Jesus said, "Have you discovered, then, the beginning, that you look for the end? [3] For where the beginning is, there will the end be. *Blessed is he who will take his place in the beginning; he will know the end and will not experience death.*"

* See 376: *Beginning and End*

283 BEFORE ONE'S CREATION

GThom 19:1 (§A250)

(19) [1] Jesus said, *"Blessed is he who came into being before he came into being.* [2] If you become My disciples and listen to My words, these stones will minister to you. For there are five trees for you in Paradise which remain undisturbed summer and winter and whose leaves do not fall. Whoever becomes acquainted with them will not experience death."

284 STONES AND TREES

GThom 19:2 (§A251)

(19) [1] Jesus said, "Blessed is he who came into being before he came into being. [2] *If you become My disciples and listen to My words, these stones will minister to you. For there are five trees for you in Paradise which remain undisturbed summer and winter and whose leaves do not fall. Whoever becomes acquainted with them will not experience death.*"

285 THE CHOSEN FEW

GThom 23 (§A252)

(23) Jesus said, *"I shall choose you, one out of a thousand, and two out of ten thousand, and they shall stand as a single one."*

286 LOVE YOUR BROTHER

GThom 25 (§A253)

(25) Jesus said, *"Love your brother like your soul, guard him like the pupil of your eye."*

287 FASTING AND SABBATH

POxy1 27 (§A254.1)

(27) Jesus said, *"If you do not fast as regards the world, you will not find the kingdom of God. If you do not observe the Sabbath as a Sabbath, you will not see the father."*

GThom 27 (§A254.2)

(27) <Jesus said,> *"If you do not fast as regards the world, you will not find the Kingdom. If you do not observe the Sabbath as a Sabbath, you will not see the Father."*

288 DRUNK, BLIND, EMPTY

GThom 28 (§A255)

(28) Jesus said, *"I took My place in the midst of the world, and I appeared to them in flesh. I found all of them intoxicated; I found none of them thirsty. And My soul became afflicted for the sons of men, because they are blind in their hearts and do not have sight; for empty they came into the world, and empty too they seek to leave the world. But for the moment they are intoxicated. When they shake off their wine, then they will repent."*

289 FLESH AS POVERTY

GThom 29 (§A256)

(29) Jesus said, *"If the flesh came into being because of spirit, it is a wonder. But if spirit came into being because of the body, it is a wonder of wonders. Indeed, I am amazed at how this great wealth has made its home in this poverty."*

290 DESIRE TO HEAR

POxy655 38:1 (§A257.1)
(38) [1] [Jesus] said, *"[Many times have you desired to hear these words of mine], and [you have no one else to hear (them) from.* [2] There will be]* days [when you will look for me and will not find me]."

GThom 38:1 (§A257.2)
(38) [1] Jesus said, *"Many times have you desired to hear these words which I am saying to you, and you have no one else to hear them from.* [2] There will be* days when you will look for Me and will not find Me."

291 BECOME PASSERS-BY

GThom 42 (§A258)
(42) Jesus said, *"Become passers-by."*

292 HORSES AND BOWS

GThom 47:1 (§A259)
(47) [1] Jesus said, *"It is impossible for a man to mount two horses or to stretch two bows.* [2] And it is impossible for a servant to serve two masters; otherwise, he will honor the one and treat the other contemptuously. [3] No man drinks old wine and immediately desires to drink new wine. [4] And new wine is not put into old wineskins, lest they burst; nor is old wine put into a new wineskin, lest it spoil it. An old patch is not sewn onto a new garment, because a tear would result."

293 UNITY AND MOUNTAIN*

GThom 48 (§A260.1)
(48) Jesus said, *"If two make peace with each other in this one house, they will say to the mountain, 'Move away,' and it will move away."*

* See 345: *Faith's Power*

GThom 106 (§A260.2)
(106) Jesus said, *"When you make the two one, you will become the sons of man, and when you say, 'Mountain, move away,' it will move away."*

* See 452: *Faith and Mountain*

294 SOLITARY AND ELECT

GThom 49 (§A261)
(49) Jesus said, *"Blessed are the solitary and elect, for you will find the Kingdom. For you are from it, and to it you will return."*

295 IF THEY ASK

GThom 50 (§A262)
(50) Jesus said, *"If they say to you, 'Where did you come from?', say to them, 'We came from the light, the place where the light came into being on its own accord and established [itself] and became manifest through their image.' If they say to you, 'Is it you?', say, 'We are its children, and we are the elect of the Living Father.' If they ask you, 'What is the sign of your Father in you?', say to them, 'It is movement and repose.'"*

296 SUPERIOR TO WORLD

GThom 56 (§A263.1)
(56) Jesus said, *"Whoever has come to understand the world has found (only) a corpse, and whoever has found a corpse is superior to the world."*

GThom 80 (§A263.2)
(80) Jesus said, *"He who has recognized the world has found the body, but he who has found the body is superior to the world."*

297 BLESSED THE SUFFERER

GThom 58 (§A264)
(58) Jesus said, *"Blessed is the man who has suffered and found life."*

298 TAKE HEED NOW

GThom 59 (§A265)
(59) Jesus said, *"Take heed of the Living One while you are alive, lest you die and seek to see Him and be unable to do so."*

299 KNOWING THE ALL

GThom 67 (§A266)
(67) Jesus said, *"Whoever believes that the All itself is deficient is (himself) completely deficient."*

300 FROM WITHIN YOURSELVES

GThom 70 (§A267)
(70) Jesus said, *"That which you have will save you if you bring it forth from yourselves. That which you do not have within you will kill you if you do not have it within you."*

301 THE CISTERN

GThom 74 (§A268)
(74) He said, *"O Lord, there are many around the drinking trough, but there is nothing in the cistern."*

302 THE BRIDAL CHAMBER*

GThom 75 (§A269.1)

(75) Jesus said, *"Many are standing at the door, but it is the solitary who will enter the bridal chamber."*

* See 382: *The Bridal Chamber*

DialSav 50b (§A269.2)

(49) Judas said, "Behold! The governors dwell above us, so it is they who will rule over us!"

(50) The Lord said, "It is you who will rule over them! *But when you rid yourselves of jealousy, then you will clothe yourselves in light and enter the bridal chamber."*

303 LIGHT AND ALL

GThom 77:1 (§A270)

(77) [1] Jesus said, *"It is I who am the light which is above them all. It is I who am the All. From Me did the All come forth, and unto Me did the All extend.* [2] Split a piece of wood, and I am there. Lift up the stone, and you will find Me there."

304 STONE AND WOOD

POxy1 77:2 (§A271.1)

(30) [Jesus said], "Where there are [three], they are without God, and where there is but [a single one], I say that I am with [him]. (77) [2] *Lift up the stone, and you will find me there. Split the piece of wood, and I am there."*

GThom 77:2 (§A271.2)

(77) [1] Jesus said, "It is I who am the light which is above them all. It is I who am the All. From Me did the All come forth, and unto Me did the All extend. [2] *Split a piece of wood, and I am there. Lift up the stone, and you will find Me there."*

305 RICHES AND POWER

GThom 81 (§A272)

(81) Jesus said, *"Let him who has grown rich be king, and let him who possesses power renounce it."*

306 NEAR THE FIRE

GThom 82 (§A273)

(82) Jesus said, *"He who is near Me is near the fire, and he who is far from Me is far from the Kingdom."*

307 THE FATHER'S LIGHT

GThom 83 (§A274)

(83) Jesus said, *"The images are manifest to man, but the light in them remains concealed in the image of the light of the Father. He will become manifest, but his image will remain concealed by his light."*

308 THE PRIMORDIAL IMAGES

GThom 84 (§A275)

(84) Jesus said, *"When you see your likeness, you rejoice. But when you see your images which came into being before you, and which neither die nor become manifest, how much you will have to bear!"*

309 ADAM'S DEATH

GThom 85 (§A276)

(85) Jesus said, *"Adam came into being from a great power and a great wealth, but he did not become worthy of you. For had he been worthy, [he would] not [have experienced] death."*

310 BODY AND SOUL

GThom 87 (§A277)
(87) Jesus said, *"Wretched is the body that is dependent upon a body, and wretched is the soul that is dependent on these two."*

311 ANGELS AND PROPHETS

GThom 88 (§A278)
(88) Jesus said, *"The angels and the prophets will come to you and give to you those things you (already) have. And you too, give them those things which you have, and say to yourselves, 'When will they come and take what is theirs?'"*

312 THEN AND NOW

GThom 92:2 (§A279)
(92) [1] Jesus said, "Seek and you will find. [2] *Yet, what you asked Me about in former times and which I did not tell you then, now I do desire to tell, but you do not inquire after it."*

313 A HARLOT'S SON

GThom 105 (§A280)
(105) Jesus said, *"He who knows the father and the mother will be called the son of a harlot."*

314 FROM MY MOUTH

GThom 108 (§A281)
(108) Jesus said, *"He who will drink from My mouth will become like Me. I myself shall become he, and the things that are hidden will be revealed to him."*

315 FINDING THE WORLD

GThom 110 (§A282)
(110) Jesus said, *"Whoever finds the world and becomes rich, let him renounce the world."*

316 FINDING ONESELF

GThom 111:2 (§A283)
(111) [1] Jesus said, "The heavens and the earth will be rolled up in your presence. And the one who lives from the Living One will not see death." [2] Does not Jesus say, *"Whoever finds himself is superior to the world"?*

317 FLESH AND SOUL

GThom 112 (§A284)
(112) Jesus said, *"Woe to the flesh that depends on the soul; woe to the soul that depends on the flesh."*

318 ACTION FOR ACTION

1 Clem 13:2c (§A285)

[1]Let us, therefore, be humble-minded, brethren, putting aside all arrogance and conceit and foolishness and wrath, and let us do that which is written (for the Holy Spirit says, "Let not the wise man boast himself in his wisdom, nor the strong man in his strength, nor the rich man in his riches, but he that boasteth let him boast in the Lord, to seek him out and to do judgment and righteousness"), especially remembering the words of the Lord Jesus which he spoke when he was teaching gentleness and longsuffering. [2]For he spoke thus: "Be merciful, that ye may obtain mercy. Forgive, that ye may be forgiven. *As ye do, so shall it be done unto you.* As ye give, so shall it be given unto you. As ye judge, so shall ye be udged. As ye are kind, so shall kindness be shewn you. With what measure ye mete, it shall be measured to you."

319 KINDNESS FOR KINDNESS

1 Clem 13:2f (§A286)

[2]For he spoke thus: "Be merciful, that ye may obtain mercy. Forgive, that ye may be forgiven. As ye do, so shall it be done unto you. As ye give, so shall it be given unto you. As ye judge, so shall ye be judged. *As ye are kind, so shall kindness be shewn you.* With what measure ye mete, it shall be measured to you."

320 ONLY THROUGH SUFFERING

Barn 7:11b (§A287)

[6]Note what was commanded: "Take two goats, goodly and alike, and offer them, and let the priest take the one as a burnt offering for sins." [7]But what are they to do with the other? "The other," he says, "is accursed." Notice how the type of Jesus is manifested: [8]"And do ye all spit on it, and goad it, and bind the scarlet wool about its head, and so let it be cast into the desert." And when it is so done, he who takes the goat into the wilderness drives it forth, and takes away the wool, and puts it upon a shrub which is called Rachel, of which we are accustomed to eat the shoots when we find them in the country: thus of Rachel alone is the fruit sweet. [9]What does this mean? Listen: "the first goat is for the altar, but the other is accursed," and note that the one that is accursed is crowned, because then "they will see him" on that day with the long scarlet robe "down to the feet" on his body, and they will say, "Is not this he whom we once crucified and rejected and pierced and spat upon? Of a truth it was he who then said that he was the Son of God." [10]But how is he like to the goat? For this reason: "the goats shall be alike, beautiful, and a pair," in order that when they see him come at that time they may be astonished at the likeness of the goat. See then the type of Jesus destined to suffer. [11]But why is it that they put the wool in the middle of the thorns? It is a type of Jesus placed in the Church, because whoever wishes to take away the scarlet wool must suffer much because the thorns are terrible and he can gain it only through pain. Thus he says, *"those who will see me, and attain to my kingdom must lay hold of me through pain and suffering."*

321 THE MOST WORTHY

GNaz 23 (§A288)

(23) He (Christ) himself taught the reason for the separations of souls that take place in houses, as we have found somewhere in the Gospel that is spread abroad among the Jews in the Hebrew tongue, in which it is said:

I choose for myself the most worthy: the most worthy are those whom my Father in heaven has given me. (Eusebius, *Theophania* 4:12 [on Matthew 10:34–36])

322 AGAINST SACRIFICES

GEbi 6 (§A289)

(6) They say that he (Christ) was not begotten of God the Father, but created as one of the archangels. . . . that he rules over the angels and all the creatures of the Almighty, and that he came and declared, as their Gospel, which is called (according to Matthew? according to the Hebrews?), reports:

I am come to do away with sacrifices, and if ye cease not from sacrificing, the wrath of God will not cease from you. (Epiphanius, *Haer.* 30.16.4f.)

323 SPIRIT AS MOTHER

GHeb 3 (§A290)

(3) And if any accept the Gospel of the Hebrews—here the Savior says:

Even so did my mother, the Holy Spirit, take me by one of my hairs and carry me away on to the great mountain Tabor. (Origen, *Commentary on John* 2.12.87 [on John 1:3])

324 JOY IN LOVE

GHeb 5 (§A291)

(5) As we have read in the Hebrew Gospel, the Lord says to his disciples:

And never be ye joyful, save when ye behold your brother with love. (Jerome, *Commentary on Ephesians* [on Ephesians 5:4])

IHCOYC

DIALOGUES

Matt 5:14a (§D1.1)

[14] "You are the light of the world."

John 8:12–16 (§D1.2)

[12] Again Jesus spoke to them, saying, "I am the light of the world; he who follows me will not walk in darkness, but will have the light of life." [13] The Pharisees then said to him, "You are bearing witness to yourself; your testimony is not true." [14] Jesus answered, "Even if I do bear witness to myself, my testimony is true, for I know whence I have come and whither I am going, but you do not know whence I come or whither I am going. [15] You judge according to the flesh, I judge no one. [16] Yet even if I do judge, my judgment is true, for it is not I alone that judge, but I and he who sent me."

John 9:1–7 (§D1.3)

[1] As he passed by, he saw a man blind from his birth. [2] And his disciples asked him, "Rabbi, who sinned, this man or his parents, that he was born blind?" [3] Jesus answered, "It was not that this man sinned, or his parents, but that the works of God might be made manifest in him. [4] We must work the works of him who sent me, while it is day; night comes, when no one can work. [5] As long as I am in the world, I am the light of the world." [6] As he said this, he spat on the ground and made clay of the spittle and anointed the man's eyes with the clay, [7] saying to him, "Go, wash in the pool of Siloam" (which means Sent). So he went and washed and came back seeing.

John 11:5–16 (§D1.4)

[5] Now Jesus loved Martha and her sister and Lazarus. [6] So when he heard that he was ill, he stayed two days longer in the place where he was. [7] Then after this he said to the disciples, "Let us go into Judea again." [8] The disciples said to him, "Rabbi, the Jews were but now seeking to stone you, and are you going there again?" [9] Jesus answered, "Are there not twelve hours in the day? If any one walks in the day, he does not stumble, because he sees the light of this world. [10] But if any one walks in the night, he stumbles, because the light is not in him." [11] Thus he spoke, and then he said to them, "Our friend Lazarus has fallen asleep, but I go to awake him out of sleep." [12] The disciples said to him, "Lord, if he has fallen asleep, he will recover." [13] Now Jesus had spoken of his death, but they thought that he meant taking rest in sleep. [14] Then Jesus told them plainly, "Lazarus is dead; [15] and for your sake I am glad that I was not there, so that you may believe. But let us go to him." [16] Thomas, called the Twin, said to his fellow disciples, "Let us also go, that we may die with him."

John 12:27–36 (§D1.5)

[27] "Now is my soul troubled. And what shall I say? 'Father, save me from this hour'? No, for this purpose I have come to this hour. [28] Father, glorify thy name." Then a voice came from heaven, "I have glorified it, and I will glorify it again." [29] The crowd standing by heard it and said that it had thundered. Others said, "An angel has spoken to him." [30] Jesus answered, "This voice has come for your sake, not for mine. [31] Now is the judgment of this world, now shall the ruler of this world be cast out; [32] and I, when I am lifted up from the earth, will draw all men to myself." [33] He said this to show by what death he was to die. [34] The crowd answered him, "We have heard from the law that the Christ remains for ever. How can you say that the Son of man must be lifted up? Who is this Son of man?" [35] Jesus said to them, "The light is with you for a little longer. Walk while you have the light, lest the darkness overtake you; he who walks in the darkness does not know where he goes. [36] While you have the light, believe in the light, that you may become sons of light."

When Jesus had said this, he departed and hid himself from them.

POxy655 24 (§D1.6)

(24) [3] [. . . There is light within a man] of light, [and he (or: it) lights up the whole] world. [If he (or: it) does not shine, he (or: it)] is [darkness].

GThom 24 (§D1.7)

(24) [1] His disciples said to Him, "Show us the place where You are, since it is necessary for us to seek it."

[2] He said to them, "Whoever has ears, let him hear. [3] There is light within a man of light, and he (or: it) lights up the whole world. If he (or: it) does not shine, he (or: it) is darkness."

DialSav 14 (§D1.8)

(14) The Lord said, "[. . .] weep on account of its works [. . .] remain and the mind laughs [. . .]. . .[. . .] [. . .]. . . spirit. If one does not [. . .] darkness, he will be able to see [. . .]. So I tell you [. . .] light is the darkness [. . .]. . . stand in [. . .] not see the light [. . .] the lie [. . .]. . . they brought them from [. . .]. . .[. . .]. . . . You will give [. . .]. . . and [. . . exist] forever. [. . .]. . . [. . .]. . . [. . .] ever. Then [all] the powers which are above as well as those [below] will [. . .] you. In that place [there will] be weeping and [gnashing] of teeth over the end of [all] these things."

DialSav 34 (§D1.9)

(34) He [said] to them, "That which supports [the earth] is that which supports the heaven. When a Word comes forth from the Greatness, it will come on what supports the heaven and the earth. For the earth does not move. Were it to move, it would fall, though in order that the First Word might not fail. For it was that which established the cosmos and inhabited it and inhaled fragrance from it. For, . . .[. . .]. . . which do not move I [. . .]. . . you, all the sons of [men. For] you are from [that] place. [In] the hearts of those who speak out of [joy] and truth you exist. Even if it comes forth in [the body] of the Father among men and is not received, still it [does] return to its place. Whoever [does not] know [the work] of perfection [knows] nothing. If one does not stand in the darkness, he will not be able to see the light."

* See 45 & 414: *The World's Light*

Matt 5:31–32 (§D2.1)

[31] "It was also said, 'Whoever divorces his wife, let him give her a certificate of divorce.' [32] But I say to you that every one who divorces his wife, except on the ground of unchastity, makes her an adulteress; and whoever marries a divorced woman commits adultery."

Matt 19:9 (§D2.2)

[9] "And I say to you: whoever divorces his wife, except for unchastity, and marries another, commits adultery."

Mark 10:10–12 (§D2.3)

[10] And in the house the disciples asked him again about this matter. [11] And he said to them, "Whoever divorces his wife and marries another, commits adultery against her; [12] and if she divorces her husband and marries another, she commits adultery."

Luke 16:14–18 (§D2.4)

[14] The Pharisees, who were lovers of money, heard all this, and they scoffed at him. [15] But he said to them, "You are those who justify yourselves before men, but God knows your hearts; for what is exalted among men is an abomination in the sight of God.

[16] "The law and the prophets were until John; since then the good news of the kingdom of God is preached, and every one enters it violently. [17] But it is easier for heaven and earth to pass away, than for one dot of the law to become void.

[18] "Every one who divorces his wife and marries another commits adultery, and he who marries a woman divorced from her husband commits adultery."

1 Cor 7:1–11 (§D2.5)

[1] Now concerning the matters about which you wrote. It is well for a man not to touch a woman. [2] But because of the temptation to immorality, each man should have his own wife and each woman her own husband. [3] The husband should give to his wife her conjugal rights, and likewise the wife to her husband. [4] For the wife does not rule over her own body, but the husband does; likewise the husband does not rule over his own body, but the wife does. [5] Do not refuse one another except perhaps by agreement for a season, that you may devote yourselves to prayer; but then come together again, lest Satan tempt you through lack of self-control. [6] I say this by way of concession, not of command. [7] I wish that all were as I myself am. But each has his own special gift from God, one of one kind and one of another.

[8] To the unmarried and the widows I say that it is well for them to remain single as I do. [9] But if they cannot exercise self-control, they should marry. For it is better to marry than to be aflame with passion.

[10] To the married I give charge, not I but the Lord, that the wife should not separate from her husband [11] (but if she does, let her remain single or else be reconciled to her husband)—and that the husband should not divorce his wife.

Herm Man 4.1:4–11 (§D2.6)

[4] I said to him, "Sir, allow me to ask you a few questions." "Say on," said he. "Sir," said I, "if a man have a wife faithful in the Lord, and he finds her out in some adultery, does the husband sin if he lives with her?" [5] "So long as he is ignorant," said he, "he does not sin, but if the husband knows her sin, and the wife does not repent, but remains in her fornication, and the husband go on living with her, he becomes a partaker of her sin, and shares in her adultery." [6] "What then," said I, "sir, shall the husband do if the wife remain in this disposition?" "Let him put her away," he said, "and let the husband remain by himself. But 'if he put his wife away and marry another he also commits adultery himself.'" [7] "If then," said I, "Sir, after the wife be put away she repent, and wish to return to her own husband, shall she not be received?" [8] "Yes," said he; "if the husband do not receive her he sins and covers himself with a great sin; but it is necessary to receive the sinner who repents, but not often, for the servants of God have but one repentance. Therefore, for the sake of repentance the husband ought not to marry. This is the course of action for wife and husband. [9] Not only," said he, "is it adultery if a man defile his flesh, but whosoever acts as do the heathen is also guilty of adultery, so that if anyone continue in such practices, and repent not, depart from him and do not live with him, otherwise you are also a sharer in his sin. [10] For this reason it was enjoined on you to live by yourselves, whether husband or wife, for in such cases repentance is possible. [11] I, therefore," said he, "am not giving an opportunity to laxity that this business be thus concluded, but in order that he who has sinned sin no more, and for his former sin there is one who can give healing, for he it is who has the power over all."

* See 58: *Against Divorce*

Matt 6:13 (§D3.1)

¹³ "And lead us not into temptation,
But deliver us from evil."

Luke 11:4 (§D3.2)

⁴ "and forgive us our sins, for we ourselves forgive every one who is indebted to us; and lead us not into temptation."

ApJas 4:1–8 (§D3.3)

¹ And I answered and said to him: "Lord, we can obey you if you wish. For we have forsaken our fathers and our mothers and our villages and have followed you. Grant us, [therefore], not to be tempted by the wicked devil."

² The Lord answered and said: "What is your (pl.) merit when you do the will of the Father as if it had not been given to you by him as a gift, while you are tempted by Satan? ³ But if you are oppressed by Satan and are persecuted and you do his (i.e., the Father's) will, I [say] that he will love you and will make you equal with me and will consider that you have become [beloved] through his providence according to your free choice. ⁴ Will you not cease, then, being lovers of the flesh and being afraid of sufferings? ⁵ Or do you not know that you have not yet been mistreated and have not yet been accused unjustly, nor have you yet been shut up in prison, nor have you yet been condemned lawlessly, nor have you yet been crucified <without> reason, nor have you yet been buried <shamefully>, as (was) I myself, by the evil one? ⁶ Do you dare to spare the flesh, you for whom the spirit is an encircling wall? ⁷ If you contemplate the world, how long it is <before> you and also how long it is after you, you will find that your life is one single day and your sufferings, one single hour. ⁸ For the good (pl.) will not enter the world."

Did 8:2 (§D3.4)

² And do not pray as the hypocrites, but as the Lord commanded in his Gospel, pray thus: "Our Father, who are in Heaven, hallowed by thy Name, thy Kingdon come, thy will be done, as in Heaven so also upon earth; give us to-day our daily bread, and forgive us our debt as we forgive our debtors, and lead us not into trial, but deliver us from the Evil One, for thine is the power and the glory for ever."

★ See 71: *Temptation and Persecution*

Matt 7:7–8 (§D4.1)

[7] "Ask, and it will be given you; seek, and you will find; knock, and it will be opened to you. [8] For every one who asks receives, and he who seeks finds, and to him who knocks it will be opened."

Matt 21:20–22 (§D4.2)

[20] When the disciples saw it they marveled, saying, "How did the fig tree wither at once?" [21] And Jesus answered them, "Truly, I say to you, if you have faith and never doubt, you will not only do what has been done to the fig tree, but even if you say to this mountain, 'Be taken up and cast into the sea,' it will be done. [22] And whatever you ask in prayer, you will receive, if you have faith."

Mark 11:20–25 (§D4.3)

[20] As they passed by in the morning, they saw the fig tree withered away to its roots. [21] And Peter remembered and said to him, "Master, look! The fig tree which you cursed has withered." [22] And Jesus answered them, "Have faith in God. [23] Truly, I say to you, whoever says to this mountain, 'Be taken up and cast into the sea,' and does not doubt in his heart, but believes that what he says will come to pass, it will be done for him. [24] Therefore I tell you, whatever you ask in prayer, believe that you have received it, and it will be yours. [25] And whenever you stand praying, forgive, if you have anything against any one; so that your Father also who is in heaven may forgive you your trespasses."

Luke 11:9–10 (§D4.4)

[9] "And I tell you, Ask, and it will be given you; seek, and you will find; knock, and it will be opened to you. [10] For every one who asks receives, and he who seeks finds, and to him who knocks it will be opened."

* See 85: *Ask, Seek, Knock*

John 14:12–14 (§D4.5)

[12] "Truly, truly, I say to you, he who believes in me will also do the works that I do; and greater works than these will he do, because I go to the Father. [13] Whatever you ask in my name, I will do it, that the Father may be glorified in the Son; [14] if you ask anything in my name, I will do it."

John 15:1–7 (§D4.6)

[1] "I am the true vine, and my Father is the vinedresser. [2] Every branch of mine that bears no fruit, he takes away, and every branch that does bear fruit he prunes, that it may bear more fruit. [3] You are already made clean by the word which I have spoken to you. [4] Abide in me, and I in you. As the branch cannot bear fruit by itself, unless it abides in the vine, neither can you, unless you abide in me. [5] I am the vine, you are the branches. He who abides in me, and I in him, he it is that bears much fruit, for apart from me you can do nothing. [6] If a man does not abide in me, he is cast forth as a branch and withers; and the branches are gathered, thrown into the fire and burned. [7] If you abide in me, and my words abide in you, ask whatever you will, and it shall be done for you."

John 15:12–17 (§D4.7)

[12] "This is my commandment, that you love one another as I have loved you. [13] Greater love has no man than this, that a man lay down his life for his friends. [14] You are my friends if you do what I command you. [15] No longer do I call you servants, for the servant does not know what his master is doing; but I have called you friends, for all that I have heard from my Father I have made known to you. [16] You did not choose me, but I chose you and appointed you that you should go and bear fruit and that your fruit should abide; so that whatever you ask the Father in my name, he may give it to you. [17] This I command you, to love one another."

John 16:20–28 (§D4.8)

20 "Truly, truly, I say to you, you will weep and lament, but the world will rejoice; you will be sorrowful, but your sorrow will turn into joy. 21 When a woman is in travail she has sorrow, because her hour has come; but when she is delivered of the child, she no longer remembers the anguish, for joy that a child is born into the world. 22 So you have sorrow now, but I will see you again and your hearts will rejoice, and no one will take your joy from you. 23 In that day you will ask nothing of me. Truly, truly, I say to you, if you ask anything of the Father, he will give it to you in my name. 24 Hitherto you have asked nothing in my name; ask, and you will receive, that your joy may be full.

25 "I have said this to you in figures; the hour is coming when I shall no longer speak to you in figures but tell you plainly of the Father. 26 In that day you will ask in my name; and I do not say to you that I shall pray the Father for you; 27 for the Father himself loves you, because you have loved me and have believed that I came from the Father. 28 I came from the Father and have come into the world; again, I am leaving the world and going to the Father."

POxy654 2 (§D4.9)

(2) [Jesus said], "Let him who seeks continue [seeking until] he finds. When he finds, [he will be amazed. And] when he becomes [amazed], he will rule. And [once he has ruled], he will [attain rest]."

GThom 2 (§D4.10)

(2) Jesus said, "Let him who seeks continue seeking until he finds. When he finds, he will become troubled. When he becomes troubled, he will be astonished, and he will rule over the All."

GThom 92 (§D4.11)

(92) [1] Jesus said, "Seek and you will find. [2] Yet, what you asked Me about in former times and which I did not tell you then, now I do desire to tell, but you do not inquire after it."

GThom 94 (§D4.12)

(94) Jesus [said], "He who seeks will find, and [he who knocks] will be let in."

DialSav 9–12 (§D4.13)

(9) His [disciples said, "Lord], who is it who seeks, and [. . .] reveals?"

(10) [The Lord said . . .], "He who seeks [. . .] reveals . . .[. . .]."

(11) [Matthew said, "Lord, when] I [. . .] and [when] I speak, who is it who . . .[. . .] . . . who listens?"

(12) [The Lord] said, "it is the one who speaks who also [listens], and it is the one who can see who also reveals."

DialSav 19–20 (§D4.14)

(19) And Matthew [asked him] "[. . .]. . . took . . . [. . .]. . . it is he who . . . [. . .]."

(20) The Lord [said], "[. . . stronger] than . . . [. . .]. . . you . . . [. . .]. . .[. . .]. . . to follow [you] and all the works [. . .] your hearts. For just as your hearts [. . .], so [. . .] the means to overcome the powers [above] as well as those below [. . .]. I say to you, let him [who possesses] power renounce [it and repent]. And [let] him who [. . .] seek and find and [rejoice]."

GHeb 4a (§D4.15)

(4a) As also it stands written in the Gospel of the Hebrews:

He that marvels shall reign, and he that has reigned shall rest. (Clement, *Stromateis* 2.9.45.5)

GHeb 4b (§D4.16)

(4b) To those words (from Plato, *Timaeus* 90) this is equivalent:

He that seeks will not rest until he finds; and he that has found shall marvel; and he that has marvelled shall reign; and he that has reigned shall rest. (Clement, *Stromateis* 5.14.96.3)

Matt 8:5–13 (§D5.1)

[5] As he entered Capernaum, a centurion came forward to him, beseeching him [6] and saying, "Lord, my servant is lying paralyzed at home, in terrible distress." [7] And he said to him, "I will come and heal him." [8] But the centurion answered him, "Lord, I am not worthy to have you come under my roof; but only say the word, and my servant will be healed. [9] For I am a man under authority, with soldiers under me; and I say to one, 'Go,' and he goes, and to another, 'Come,' and he comes, and to my slave, 'Do this,' and he does it." [10] When Jesus heard him, he marveled, and said to those who followed him, "Truly, I say to you, not even in Israel have I found such faith. [11] I tell you, many will come from east and west and sit at table with Abraham, Isaac, and Jacob in the kingdom of heaven, [12] while the sons of the kingdom will be thrown into the outer darkness; there men will weep and gnash their teeth." [13] And to the centurion Jesus said, "Go; be it done for you as you have believed." And the servant was healed at that very moment.

Matt 13:36–43 (§D5.2)

[36] Then he left the crowds and went into the house. And his disciples came to him, saying, "Explain to us the parable of the weeds of the field." [37] He answered, "He who sows the good seed is the Son of man; [38] the field is the world, and the good seed means the sons of the kingdom; the weeds are the sons of the evil one, [39] and the enemy who sowed them is the devil; the harvest is the close of the age, and the reapers are angels. [40] Just as the weeds are gathered and burned with fire, so will it be at the close of the age. [41] The Son of man will send his angels, and they will gather out of his kingdom all causes of sin and all evildoers, [42] and throw them into the furnace of fire; there men will weep and gnash their teeth. [43] Then the righteous will shine like the sun in the kingdom of their Father. He who has ears, let him hear."

Matt 13:47–50 (§D5.3)

[47] "Again, the kingdom of heaven is like a net which was thrown into the sea and gathered fish of every kind; [48] when it was full, men drew it ashore and sat down and sorted the good into vessels but threw away the bad. [49] So it will be at the close of the age. The angels will come out and separate the evil from the righteous, [50] and throw them into the furnace of fire; there men will weep and gnash their teeth."

Matt 22:1–14 (§D5.4)

[1] And again Jesus spoke to them in parables, saying, [2] "The kingdom of heaven may be compared to a king who gave a marriage feast for his son, [3] and sent his servants to call those who were invited to the marriage feast; but they would not come. [4] Again he sent other servants, saying, 'Tell those who are invited, Behold, I have made ready my dinner, my oxen and my fat calves are killed, and everything is ready; come to the marriage feast.' [5] But they made light of it and went off, one to his farm, another to his business, [6] while the rest seized his servants, treated them shamefully, and killed them. [7] The king was angry, and he sent his troops and destroyed those murderers and burned their city. [8] Then he said to his servants, 'The wedding is ready, but those invited were not worthy. [9] Go therefore to the thoroughfares, and invite to the marriage feast as many as you find.' [10] And those servants went out into the streets and gathered all whom they found, both bad and good; so the wedding hall was filled with guests.
[11] "But when the king came in to look at the guests, he saw there a man who had no wedding garment; [12] and he said to him, 'Friend, how did you get in here without a wedding garment?' And he was speechless. [13] Then the king said to the attendants, 'Bind him hand and foot, and cast him into the outer darkness; there men will weep and gnash their teeth.' [14] For many are called, but few are chosen."

Matt 24:45–51 (§D56.5)

[45] "Who then is the faithful and wise servant, whom his master has set over his household, to give them their food at the proper time? [46] Blessed is that servant whom his master when he comes will find so doing. [47] Truly, I say to you, he will set him over all his possessions. [48] But if that wicked servant says to himself, 'My master is delayed,' [49] and begins to beat his fellow servants, and eats and drinks with the drunken, [50] the master of that servant will come on a day when he does not expect him and at an hour he does not know, [51] and will punish him, and put him with the hypocrites; there men will weep and gnash their teeth."

Matt 25:14–30 (§D5.6)

[14] "For it will be as when a man going on a journey called his servants and entrusted to them his property; [15] to one he gave five talents, to another two, to another one, to each according to his ability. Then he went away. [16] He who had received the five talents went at once and traded with them; and he made five talents more. [17] So also, he who had the two talents made two talents more. [18] But he who had received the one talent went and dug in the ground and hid his master's money. [19] Now after a long time the master of those servants came and settled accounts with them. [20] And he who had received the five talents came forward, bringing five talents more, saying, 'Master, you delivered to me five talents; here I have made five talents more.' [21] His master said to him, 'Well done, good and faithful servant; you have been faithful over a little, I will set you over much; enter into the joy of your master.' [22] And he also who had the two talents came forward, saying, 'Master, you delivered to me two talents; here I have made two talents more.' [23] His master said to him, 'Well done, good and faithful servant; you have been faithful over a little, I will set you over much; enter into the joy of your master.' [24] He also who had received the one talent came forward, saying, 'Master, I knew you to be a hard man, reaping where you did not sow, and gathering where you did not winnow; [25] so I was afraid, and I went and hid your talent in the ground. Here you have what is yours.' [26] But his master answered him, 'You wicked and slothful servant! You knew that I reap where I have not sowed, and gather where I have not winnowed? [27] Then you ought to have invested my money with the bankers, and at my coming I should have received what was my own with interest. [28] So take the talent from him, and give it to him who has the ten talents. [29] For to every one who has will more be given, and he will have abundance; but from him who has not, even what he has will be taken away. [30] And cast the worthless servant into the outer darkness; there men will weep and gnash their teeth.'"

Luke 13:22–30 (§D5.7)

[22] He went on his way through towns and villages, teaching, and journeying toward Jerusalem. [23] And some one said to him, "Lord, will those who are saved be few?" And he said to them, [24] "Strive to enter by the narrow door; for many, I tell you, will seek to enter and will not be able. [25] When once the householder has risen up and shut the door, you will begin to stand outside and to knock at the door, saying, 'Lord, open to us.' He will answer you, 'I do not know where you come from.' [26] Then you will begin to say, 'We ate and drank in your presence, and you taught in our streets.' [27] But he will say, 'I tell you, I do not know where you come from; depart from me, all you workers of iniquity!' [28] There you will weep and gnash your teeth, when you see Abraham and Isaac and Jacob and all the prophets in the kingdom of God and you yourselves thrust out. [29] And men will come from east and west, and from north and south, and sit at table in the kingdom of God. [30] And behold, some are last who will be first, and some are first who will be last."

DialSav 13–14 (§D5.8)

(13) [Mary] said, "Lord, behold! Whence [. . .]. . . the body [while I] weep, and whence while I [. . .]?"

(14) The Lord said, "[. . .] weep on account of its works [. . .] remain and the mind laughs [. . .]. . .[. . .] [. . .]. . . spirit. If one does not [. . .] darkness, he will be able to see [. . .]. So I tell you [. . .] light is the darkness [. . .]. . . stand in [. . .] not see the light [. . .] the lie [. . .]. . . they brought them from [. . .]. . .[. . .]. . . . You will give [. . .]. . . and [. . . exist] forever. [. . .]. . . [. . .]. . . [. . .] ever. Then [all] the powers which are above as well as those [below] will [. . .] you. In that place [there will] be weeping and [gnashing] of teeth over the end of [all] these things."

★ See 95: *Gnashing of Teeth*

330   LEAVE THE DEAD

Matt 8:21–22 (§D6.1)

²¹ Another of the disciples said to him, "Lord, let me first go and bury my father." ²² But Jesus said to him, "Follow me, and leave the dead to bury their own dead."

Luke 9:59–60 (§D6.2)

⁵⁹ To another he said, "Follow me." But he said, "Lord, let me first go and bury my father." ⁶⁰ But he said to him, "Leave the dead to bury their own dead; but as for you, go and proclaim the kingdom of God."

331   FASTING AND WEDDING

Matt 9:14–15 (§D7.1)

¹⁴ Then the disciples of John came to him, saying, "Why do we and the Pharisees fast, but your disciples do not fast?" ¹⁵ And Jesus said to them, "Can the wedding guests mourn as long as the bridegroom is with them? The days will come, when the bridegroom is taken away from them, and then they will fast."

Mark 2:18–20 (§D7.2)

¹⁸ Now John's disciples and the Pharisees were fasting; and people came and said to him, "Why do John's disciples and the disciples of the Pharisees fast, but your disciples do not fast?" ¹⁹ And Jesus said to them, "Can the wedding guests fast while the bridegroom is with them? As long as they have the bridegroom with them, they cannot fast. ²⁰ The days will come, when the bridegroom is taken away from them, and then they will fast in that day."

Luke 5:33–35 (§D7.3)

³³ And they said to him, "The disciples of John fast often and offer prayers, and so do the disciples of the Pharisees, but yours eat and drink." ³⁴ And Jesus said to them, "Can you make wedding guests fast while the bridegroom is with them? ³⁵ The days will come, when the bridegroom is taken away from them, and then they will fast in those days."

John 3:25–30 (§D7.4)

²⁵ Now a discussion arose between John's disciples and a Jew over purifying. ²⁶ And they came to John, and said to him, "Rabbi, he who was with you beyond the Jordan, to whom you bore witness, here he is, baptizing, and all are going to him." ²⁷ John answered, "No one can receive anything except what is given him from heaven. ²⁸ You yourselves bear me witness, that I said, I am not the Christ, but I have been sent before him. ²⁹ He who has the bride is the bridegroom; the friend of the bridegroom, who stands and hears him, rejoices greatly at the bridegroom's voice; therefore this joy of mine is now full. ³⁰ He must increase, but I must decrease."

GThom 104 (§D7.5)

(104) ¹ They said [to Jesus], "Come, let us pray today and let us fast."

² Jesus said, "What is the sin that I have committed, or wherein have I been defeated? But when the bridegroom leaves the bridal chamber, then let them fast and pray."

332

AT THE TOWN*

Matt 10:14–15 (§D8.1)
14 "And if any one will not receive you or listen to your words, shake off the dust from your feet as you leave that house or town. 15 Truly, I say to you, it shall be more tolerable on the day of judgment for the land of Sodom and Gomorrah than for that town."

Mark 6:11 (§D8.2)
11 "And if any place will not receive you and they refuse to hear you, when you leave, shake off the dust that is on your feet for a testimony against them."

Luke 9:5 (§D8.3)
5 "And wherever they do not receive you, when you leave that town shake off the dust from your feet as a testimony against them."

Luke 10:8–12 (§D8.4)
8 "Whenever you enter a town and they receive you, eat what is set before you; 9 heal the sick in it and say to them, 'The kingdom of God has come near to you.' 10 But whenever you enter a town and they do not receive you, go into its streets and say, 11 'Even the dust of your town that clings to our feet, we wipe off against you; nevertheless know this, that the kingdom of God has come near.' 12 I tell you, it shall be more tolerable on that day for Sodom than for that town."

1 Cor 10:27 (§D8.5)
27 If one of the unbelievers invites you to dinner and you are disposed to go, eat whatever is set before you without raising any question on the ground of conscience.

* See 106: *At the Town*

GThom 6:1,14 (§D8.6)
(6) 1 His disciples questioned Him and said to Him, "Do You want us to fast? How shall we pray? Shall we give alms? What diet shall we observe?"
2 Jesus said, "Do not tell lies, 3 and do not do what you hate, for all things are plain in the sight of Heaven. 4 For nothing hidden will not become manifest, and nothing covered will remain without being uncovered."
(14) 1 Jesus said to them, "If you fast, you will give rise to sin for yourselves; and if you pray, you will be condemned; and if you give alms, you will do harm to your spirits. 2 When you go into any land and walk about in the districts, if they receive you, eat what they will set before you, and heal the sick among them. 3 For what goes into your mouth will not defile you, but that which issues from your mouth—it is that which will defile you."

333

WHOM TO FEAR*

Matt 10:28 (§D9.1)
28 "And do not fear those who kill the body but cannot kill the soul; rather fear him who can destroy both soul and body in hell."

* See 117: *Whom To Fear*

Luke 12:4–5 (§D9.2)
4 "I tell you, my friends, do not fear those who kill the body, and after that have no more that they can do. 5 But I will warn you whom to fear: fear him who, after he has killed, has power to cast into hell; yes, I tell you, fear him!"

2 Clem 5:1–4 (§D9.3)
1 Wherefore, brethren, let us forsake our sojourning in this world, and do the will of him who called us, and let us not fear to go forth from this world, 2 for the Lord said, "Ye shall be as lambs in the midst of wolves," 3 and Peter answered and said to him, "If then the wolves tear the lambs?" 4 Jesus said to Peter, "Let the lambs have no fear of the wolves after their death; and do ye have no fear of those that slay you, and can do nothing more to you, but fear him who after your death hath power over body and soul, to cast them into the flames of hell."

334

YOKE AND BURDEN*

Matt 11:28–30 (§D10.1)
28 "Come to me, all who labor and are heavy laden, and I will give you rest. 29 Take my yoke upon you, and learn from me; for I am gentle and lowly in heart, and you will find rest for your souls. 30 For my yoke is easy, and my burden is light."

GThom 90 (§D10.2)
(90) Jesus said, "Come unto Me, for My yoke is easy and My lordship is mild, and you will find repose for yourselves."

* See 134: *Yoke and Burden*

DialSav 65–68 (§D10.3)
(65) Matthew said, "[Why] do we not rest [at once]?"
(66) The Lord said, "When you lay down these burdens!"
(67) Matthew said, "How does the small join itself to the big?"
(68) The Lord said, "When you abandon the works which will not be able to follow you, then you will rest."

335 REQUEST FOR SIGN

Matt 12:38–40 (§D11.1)

³⁸ Then some of the scribes and Pharisees said to him, "Teacher, we wish to see a sign from you." ³⁹ But he answered them, "An evil and adulterous generation seeks for a sign; but no sign shall be given to it except the sign of the prophet Jonah. ⁴⁰ For as Jonah was three days and three nights in the belly of the whale, so will the Son of man be three days and three nights in the heart of the earth."

Matt 16:1–4 (§D11.2)

¹ And the Pharisees and Sadducees came, and to test him they asked him to show them a sign from heaven. ² He answered them, "When it is evening, you say, 'It will be fair weather; for the sky is red.' ³ And in the morning, 'It will be stormy today, for the sky is red and threatening.' You know how to interpret the appearance of the sky, but you cannot interpret the signs of the times. ⁴ An evil and adulterous generation seeks for a sign, but no sign shall be given to it except the sign of Jonah." So he left them and departed.

Mark 8:11–12 (§D11.3)

¹¹ The Pharisees came and began to argue with him, seeking from him a sign from heaven, to test him. ¹² And he sighed deeply in his spirit, and said, "Why does this generation seek a sign? Truly, I say to you, no sign shall be given to this generation."

Luke 11:14–16,29–30 (§D11.4)

¹⁴ Now he was casting out a demon that was dumb; when the demon had gone out, the dumb man spoke, and the people marveled. ¹⁵ But some of them said, "He casts out demons by Beelzebul, the prince of demons"; ¹⁶ while others, to test him, sought from him a sign from heaven.

²⁹ When the crowds were increasing, he began to say, "This generation is an evil generation; it seeks a sign, but no sign shall be given to it except the sign of Jonah. ³⁰ For as Jonah became a sign to the men of Nineveh, so will the Son of man be to this generation."

GNaz 11 (§D11.5)

(11) The Jewish Gospel does not have: three d(ays and nights). (Variant to Matthew 12:40 in the "Zion Gospel" Edition)

336 KNOWING THE MYSTERY⋆

Matt 13:10–11 (§D12.1)

¹⁰ Then the disciples came and said to him, "Why do you speak to them in parables?" ¹¹ And he answered them, "To you it has been given to know the secrets of the kingdom of heaven, but to them it has not been given."

Mark 4:10–11 (§D12.2)

¹⁰ And when he was alone, those who were about him with the twelve asked him concerning the parables. ¹¹ And he said to them, "To you has been given the secret of the kingdom of God, but for those outside everything is in parables."

Luke 8:9–10 (§D12.3)

⁹ And when his disciples asked him what this parable meant, ¹⁰ he said, "To you it has been given to know the secrets of the kingdom of God; but for others they are in parables, so that seeing they may not see, and hearing they may not understand."

GThom 62:1 (§D12.4)

(62) ¹ Jesus said, "It is to those [who are worthy of My] mysteries that I tell My mysteries."

⋆ See 143: *Knowing the Mystery*

THE MUSTARD SEED★

Matt 13:31–32 (§D13.1)

[31] Another parable he put before them, saying, "The kingdom of heaven is like a grain of mustard seed which a man took and sowed in his field; [32] it is the smallest of all seeds, but when it has grown it is the greatest of shrubs and becomes a tree, so that the birds of the air come and make nests in its branches."

Mark 4:30–32 (§D13.2)

[30] And he said, "With what can we compare the kingdom of God, or what parable shall we use for it? [31] It is like a grain of mustard seed, which, when sown upon the ground, is the smallest of all the seeds on earth; [32] yet when it is sown it grows up and becomes the greatest of all shrubs, and puts forth large branches, so that the birds of the air can make nests in its shade."

Luke 13:18–19 (§D13.3)

[18] He said therefore, "What is the kingdom of God like? And to what shall I compare it? [19] It is like a grain of mustard seed which a man took and sowed in his garden; and it grew and became a tree, and the birds of the air made nests in its branches."

GThom 20 (§D13.4)

(20) [1] The disciples said to Jesus, "Tell us what the Kingdom of Heaven is like."

[2] He said to them, "It is like a mustard seed, the smallest of all seeds. But when it falls on tilled soil, it produces a great plant and becomes a shelter for birds of the sky."

★ See 3: *The Mustard Seed*

THE KINGDOM'S SCRIBE

Matt 13:51–52 (§D14)

[51] "Have you understood all this?" They said to him, "Yes." [52] And he said to them, "Therefore every scribe who has been trained for the kingdom of heaven is like a householder who brings out of his treasure what is new and what is old."

Matt 15:10–11 (§D15.1)

¹⁰ And he called the people to him and said to them, "Hear and understand: ¹¹ not what goes into the mouth defiles a man, but what comes out of the mouth, this defiles a man."

Mark 7:14–15 (§D15.2)

¹⁴ And he called the people to him again, and said to them, "Hear me, all of you, and understand: ¹⁵ there is nothing outside a man which by going into him can defile him; but the things which come out of a man are what defile him."

Acts 10:9–16 (§D15.3)

⁹ The next day, as they were on their journey and coming near the city, Peter went up on the housetop to pray, about the sixth hour. ¹⁰ And he became hungry and desired something to eat; but while they were preparing it, he fell into a trance ¹¹ and saw the heaven opened, and something descending, like a great sheet, let down by four corners upon the earth. ¹² In it were all kinds of animals and reptiles and birds of the air. ¹³ And there came a voice to him, "Rise, Peter; kill and eat." ¹⁴ But Peter said,

"No, Lord; for I have never eaten anything that is common or unclean." ¹⁵ And the voice came to him again a second time, "What God has cleansed, you must not call common." ¹⁶ This happened three times, and the thing was taken up at once to heaven.

Acts 11:1–10 (§D15.4)

¹ Now the apostles and the brethren who were in Judea heard that the Gentiles also had received the word of God. ² So when Peter went up to Jerusalem, the circumcision party criticized him, ³ saying, "Why did you go to uncircumcised men and eat with them?" ⁴ But Peter began and explained to them in order: ⁵ "I was in the city of Joppa praying; and in a trance I saw a vision, something descending, like a great sheet, let down from heaven by four corners; and it came down to me. ⁶ Looking at it closely I observed animals and beasts of prey and reptiles and birds of the air. ⁷ And I heard a voice saying to me, 'Rise, Peter; kill and eat.' ⁸ But I said, 'No, Lord; for nothing common or unclean has ever entered my mouth.' ⁹ But the voice answered a second time from heaven, 'What God has cleansed

you must not call common.' ¹⁰ This happened three times, and all was drawn up again into heaven."

GThom 6:1, 14 (§D15.5)

(6) ¹ His disciples questioned Him and said to Him, "Do You want us to fast? How shall we pray? Shall we give alms? What diet shall we observe?"

² Jesus said, "Do not tell lies, ³ and do not do what you hate, for all things are plain in the sight of Heaven. ⁴ For nothing hidden will not become manifest, and nothing covered will remain without being uncovered."

(14) ¹ Jesus said to them, "If you fast, you will give rise to sin for yourselves; and if you pray, you will be condemned; and if you give alms, you will do harm to your spirits. ² When you go into any land and walk about in the districts, if they receive you, eat what they will set before you, and heal the sick among them. ³ For what goes into your mouth will not defile you, but that which issues from your mouth—it is that which will defile you."

★ See 147 & 438: *What Goes In*

Matt 15:12–14 (§D16.1)

¹² Then the disciples came and said to him, "Do you know that the Pharisees were offended when they heard this saying?" ¹³ He answered, "Every plant which my heavenly Father has not planted will be rooted up. ¹⁴ Let them alone; they are blind guides. And if a blind man leads a blind man, both will fall into a pit."

GThom 40 (§D16.2)

(40) Jesus said, "A grapevine has been planted outside of the Father, but being unsound, it will be pulled up by its roots and destroyed."

★ See 148: *Plant Rooted Up*

Ign Tral 11:1–2 (§D16.3)

¹ Fly from these wicked offshoots, which bear deadly fruit, which if a man eat he presently dies. For these are not the planting of the Father. ² For if they were they would appear as branches of the Cross (and their fruit would be incorruptible) by which through his Passion he calls you who are his members. The head therefore cannot be borne without limbs, since God promises union, that is himself.

Ign Phld 3:1 (§D16.4)

¹ Abstain from evil growths, which Jesus Christ does not tend, because they are not the planting of the Father. Not that I have found division among you but 'filtering.'

341

PHARISEES AS BLIND*

Matt 15:10–14 (§D17.1)

[10] And he called the people to him and said to them, "Hear and understand: [11] not what goes into the mouth defiles a man, but what comes out of the mouth, this defiles a man." [12] Then the disciples came and said to him, "Do you know that the Pharisees were offended when they heard this saying?" [13] He answered, "Every plant which my heavenly Father has not planted will be rooted up. [14] Let them alone; they are blind guides. And if a blind man leads a blind man, both will fall into a pit."

Matt 23:16–26 (§D17.2)

[16] "Woe to you, blind guides, who say, 'If any one swears by the temple, it is nothing; but if any one swears by the gold of the temple, he is bound by his oath.' [17] You blind fools! For which is greater, the gold or the temple that has made the gold sacred? [18] And you say, 'If any one swears by the altar, it is nothing; but if any one swears by the gift that is on the altar, he is bound by his oath.' [19] You blind men! For which is greater, the gift or the altar that makes the gift sacred? [20] So he who swears by the altar, swears by it and by everything on it; [21] and he who swears by the temple, swears by it and by him who dwells in it; [22] and he who swears by heaven, swears by the throne of God and by him who sits upon it.

[23] "Woe to you, scribes and Pharisees, hypocrites! for you tithe mint and dill and cummin, and have neglected the weightier matters of the law, justice and mercy and faith; these you ought to have done, without neglecting the others. [24] You blind guides, straining out a gnat and swallowing a camel!

[25] "Woe to you, scribes and Pharisees, hypocrites! for you cleanse the outside of the cup and of the plate, but inside they are full of extortion and rapacity. [26] You blind Pharisee! first cleanse the inside of the cup and of the plate, that the outside also may be clean."

John 9:39–41 (§D17.3)

[39] Jesus said, "For judgment I came into this world, that those who do not see may see, and that those who see may become blind." [40] Some of the Pharisees near him heard this, and they said to him, "Are we also blind?" [41] Jesus said to them, "If you were blind, you would have no guilt; but now that you say, 'We see,' your guilt remains."

POxy840 (§D17.4)

(1) First before he does wrong (?) he thinks out everything that is crafty. But be ye on your guard that the same thing may not happen to you as does to them. For not only among the living do evil doers among men receive retribution, but they must also suffer punishment and great torment.

(2) And he took them (the disciples) with him into the place of purification itself and walked about in the Temple court. And a Pharisaic chief priest, Levi (?) by name, fell in with them and s[aid] to the Savior: Who gave thee leave to [trea]d this place of purification and to look upon [the]se holy utensils without having bathed thyself and even without thy disciples having [wa]shed their f[eet]? On the contrary, being defi[led], thou hast trodden the Temple court, this clean p[lace], although no [one who] has [not] first bathed himself or [chang]ed his clot[hes] may tread it and [venture] to vi[ew these] holy utensils! Forthwith [the Savior] s[tood] still with h[is] disciples and [answered]: How stands it (then) with thee, thou art forsooth (also) here in the Temple court. Art thou then clean? He said to him: I am clean. For I have bathed myself in the pool of David and have gone down by the one stair and come up by the other and have put on white and clean clothes, and (only) then have I come hither and have viewed these holy utensils. Then said the Savior to him: Woe unto you blind that see not! Thou hast bathed thyself in water that is poured out, in which dogs and swine lie night and day and thou hast washed thyself and hast chafed thine outer skin, which prostitutes also and flute-girls anoint, bathe, chafe and rouge, in order to arouse desire in men, but within they are full of scorpions and of [bad]ness [of every kind]. But I and [my disciples], of whom thou sayest that we have not im[mersed] ourselves, [have been im]mersed in the liv[ing ...] water which comes down from [... B]ut woe unto them that ...

* See 149: *Pharisees as Blind*

342

KNOWING THE TIMES*

Matt 16:1–4 (§D18.1)

[1] And the Pharisees and Sadducees came, and to test him they asked him to show them a sign from heaven. [2] He answered them, "When it is evening, you say, 'It will be fair weather; for the sky is red.' [3] And in the morning, 'It will be stormy today, for the sky is red and threatening.' You know how to interpret the appearance of the sky, but you cannot interpret the signs of the times. [4] An evil and adulterous generation seeks for a sign, but no sign shall be given to it except the sign of Jonah." So he left them and departed.

Luke 12:54–56 (§D18.2)

[54] He also said to the multitudes, "When you see a cloud rising in the west, you say at once, 'A shower is coming'; and so it happens. [55] And when you see the south wind blowing, you say, 'There will be scorching heat'; and it happens. [56] You hypocrites! You know how to interpret the appearance of the earth and sky; but why do you not know how to interpret the present time?"

* See 151: *Knowing the Times*

GThom 91 (§D18.3)

(91) [1] They said to Him, "Tell us who You are so that we may believe in You."

[2] He said to them, "You read the face of the sky and of the earth, but you have not recognized the one who (or: that which) is before you, and you do not know how to read this moment."

343 WHO IS JESUS?*

Matt 16:13–20 (§D19.1)

[13] Now when Jesus came into the district of Caesarea Philippi, he asked his disciples, "Who do men say that the Son of man is?" [14] And they said, "Some say John the Baptist, others say Elijah, and others Jeremiah or one of the prophets." [15] He said to them, "But who do you say that I am?" [16] Simon Peter replied, "You are the Christ, the Son of the living God." [17] And Jesus answered him, "Blessed are you, Simon Bar-Jona! For flesh and blood has not revealed this to you, but my Father who is in heaven. [18] And I tell you, you are Peter, and on this rock I will build my church, and the powers of death shall not prevail against it. [19] I will give you the keys of the kingdom of heaven, and whatever you bind on earth shall be bound in heaven, and whatever you loose on earth shall be loosed in heaven." [20] Then he strictly charged the disciples to tell no one that he was the Christ.

Mark 8:27–30 (§D19.2)

[27] And Jesus went on with his disciples, to the villages of Caesarea Philippi; and on the way he asked his disciples, "Who do men say that I am?" [28] And they told him, "John the Baptist; and others say, Elijah; and others one of the prophets." [29] And he asked them, "But who do you say that I am?" Peter answered him, "You are the Christ." [30] And he charged them to tell no one about him.

Luke 9:18–21a (§D19.3)

[18] Now it happened that as he was praying alone the disciples were with him; and he asked them, "Who do the people say that I am?" [19] And they answered, "John the Baptist; but others say, Elijah; and others, that one of the old prophets has risen." [20] And he said to them, "But who do you say that I am?" And Peter answered, "The Christ of God." [21] But he charged and commanded them to tell this to no one . . .

John 1:35–42 (§D19.4)

[35] The next day again John was standing with two of his disciples; [36] and he looked at Jesus as he walked, and said, "Behold, the Lamb of God!" [37] The two disciples heard him say this, and they followed Jesus. [38] Jesus turned, and saw them following, and said to them, "What do you seek?" And they said to him, "Rabbi" (which means Teacher), "where are you staying?" [39] He said to them, "Come and see." They came and saw where he was staying; and they stayed with him that day, for it was about the tenth hour. [40] One of the two who heard John speak, and followed him, was Andrew, Simon Peter's brother. [41] He first found his brother Simon, and said to him, "We have found the Messiah" (which means Christ). [42] He brought him to Jesus. Jesus looked at him, and said, "So you are Simon the son of John? You shall be called Cephas" (which means Peter).

* See 442: *Who is Jesus?*

John 6:66–69 (§D19.5)

[66] After this many of his disciples drew back and no longer went about with him. [67] Jesus said to the twelve, "Do you also wish to go away?" [68] Simon Peter answered him, "Lord, to whom shall we go? You have the words of eternal life; [69] and we have believed, and have come to know, that you are the Holy One of God."

GThom 13 (§D19.6)

(13) [1] Jesus said to His disciples, "Compare me to someone and tell Me whom I am like."

[2] Simon Peter said to Him, "You are like a righteous angel."

[3] Matthew said to Him, "You are like a wise philosopher."

[4] Thomas said to Him, "Master, my mouth is wholly incapable of saying whom You are like."

[5] Jesus said, "I am not your master. Because you have drunk, you have become intoxicated from the bubbling spring which I have measured out."

[6] And He took him and withdrew and told him three things. [7] When Thomas returned to his companions, they asked him, "What did Jesus say to you?"

[8] Thomas said to them, "If I tell you one of the things which he told me, you will pick up stones and throw them at me; a fire will come out of the stones and burn you up."

GNaz 14 (§D19.7)

(14) The Jewish Gospel: son of John.
(Variant to Matthew 16:17 in the "Zion Gospel" Edition)

344 ELIJAH HAS COME

Matt 17:10–13 (§D20.1)

[10] And the disciples asked him, "Then why do the scribes say that first Elijah must come?" [11] He replied, "Elijah does come, and he is to restore all things; [12] but I tell you that Elijah has already come, and they did not know him, but did to him whatever they pleased. So also the Son of man will suffer at their hands." [13] Then the disciples understood that he was speaking to them of John the Baptist.

Mark 9:11–13 (§D20.2)

[11] And they asked him, "Why do the scribes say that first Elijah must come?" [12] And he said to them, "Elijah does come first to restore all things; and how is it written of the Son of man, that he should suffer many things and be treated with contempt? [13] But I tell you that Elijah has come, and they did to him whatever they pleased, as it is written of him."

345 FAITH'S POWER★

Matt 17:14–21 (§D21.1)

¹⁴And when they came to the crowd, a man came up to him and kneeling before him said, ¹⁵"Lord, have mercy on my son, for he is an epileptic and he suffers terribly; for often he falls into the fire, and often into the water. ¹⁶And I brought him to your disciples, and they could not heal him." ¹⁷And Jesus answered, "O faithless and perverse generation, how long am I to be with you? How long am I to bear with you? Bring him here to me." ¹⁸And Jesus rebuked him, and the demon came out of him, and the boy was cured instantly. ¹⁹Then the disciples came to Jesus privately and said, "Why could we not cast it out?" ²⁰He said to them, "Because of your little faith. For truly I say to you, if you have faith as a grain of mustard seed, you will say to this mountain, 'Move from here to there,' and it will move; and nothing will be impossible to you."

Luke 17:5–6 (§D21.2)

⁵The apostles said to the Lord, "Increase our faith!" ⁶And the Lord said, "If you had faith as a grain of mustard seed, you could say to this sycamine tree, 'Be rooted up, and be planted in the sea,' and it would obey you."

★ See 293: *Unity and Mountain*
★ See 452: *Faith and Mountain*

346 UNLIMITED FORGIVENESS★

Matt 18:21–22 (§D22.1)

²¹Then Peter came up and said to him, "Lord, how often shall my brother sin against me, and I forgive him? As many as seven times?" ²²Jesus said to him, "I do not say to you seven times, but seventy times seven."

Luke 17:3–4 (§D22.2)

³"Take heed to yourselves; if your brother sins, rebuke him, and if he repents, forgive him; ⁴and if he sins against you seven times in the day, and turns to you seven times, and says, 'I repent,' you must forgive him."

GNaz 15a (§D22.3)

(15a) He (Jesus) said: If thy brother has sinned with a word and has made thee reparation, receive him seven times in a day. Simon his disciple said to him: Seven times in a day? The Lord answered and said to him: Yea, I say unto thee, until seventy times seven times. For in the prophets also after they were anointed with the Holy Spirit, the word of sin (sinful discourse?) was found. (Jerome, *Adversus Pelagianos* 3.2)

GNaz 15b (§D22.4)

(15b) The Jewish Gospel has after "seventy times seven times": For in the prophets also, after they were anointed with the Holy Spirit, the word of sin (sinful discourse?) was found. (Variant to Matthew 18:22 in the "Zion Gospel" Edition)

★ See 167: *Unlimited Forgiveness*

347 MOSES AND DIVORCE

Matt 19:3–8 (§D23.1)

³And Pharisees came up to him and tested him by asking, "Is it lawful to divorce one's wife for any cause?" ⁴He answered, "Have you not read that he who made them from the beginning made them male and female, ⁵and said, 'For this reason a man shall leave his father and mother and be joined to his wife, and the two shall become one flesh'? ⁶So they are no longer two but one flesh. What therefore God has joined together, let not man put asunder." ⁷They said to him, "Why then did Moses command one to give a certificate of divorce, and to put her away?" ⁸He said to them, "For your hardness of heart Moses allowed you to divorce your wives, but from the beginning it was not so."

Mark 10:2–9 (§D23.2)

²And Pharisees came up and in order to test him asked, "Is it lawful for a man to divorce his wife?" ³He answered them, "What did Moses command you?" ⁴They said, "Moses allowed a man to write a certificate of divorce, and to put her away." ⁵But Jesus said to them, "For your hardness of heart he wrote you this commandment. ⁶But from the beginning of creation, 'God made them male and female.' ⁷'For this reason a man shall leave his father and mother and be joined to his wife, ⁸and the two shall become one flesh.' So they are no longer two but one flesh. ⁹What therefore God has joined together, let not man put asunder."

Matt 19:10–12a (§D24)

[10] The disciples said to him, "If such is the case of a man with his wife, it is not expedient to marry." [11] But he said to them, "Not all men can receive this saying, but only those to whom it is given. [12] For there are eunuchs who have been so from birth, and there are eunuchs who have been made eunuchs by men, and there are eunuchs who have made themselves eunuchs for the sake of the kingdom of heaven."

349   THE RICH MAN

Matt 19:16–22 (§D25.1)

[16] And behold, one came up to him, saying, "Teacher, what good deed must I do, to have eternal life?" [17] And he said to him, "Why do you ask me about what is good? One there is who is good. If you would enter life, keep the commandments." [18] He said to him, "Which?" And Jesus said, "You shall not kill, You shall not commit adultery, You shall not steal, You shall not bear false witness, [19] Honor your father and mother, and, You shall love your neighbor as yourself." [20] The young man said to him, "All these I have observed; what do I still lack?" [21] Jesus said to him, "If you would be perfect, go, sell what you possess and give to the poor, and you will have treasure in heaven; and come, follow me." [22] When the young man heard this he went away sorrowful; for he had great possessions.

Mark 10:17–22 (§D25.2)

[17] And as he was setting out on his journey, a man ran up and knelt before him, and asked him, "Good Teacher, what must I do to inherit eternal life?" [18] And Jesus said to him, "Why do you call me good? No one is good but God alone. [19] You know the commandments: 'Do not kill, Do not commit adultery, Do not steal, Do not bear false witness, Do not defraud, Honor your father and mother.'" [20] And he said to him, "Teacher, all these I have observed from my youth." [21] And Jesus looking upon him loved him, and said to him, "You lack one thing; go, sell what you have, and give to the poor, and you will have treasure in heaven; and come, follow me." [22] At that saying his countenance fell, and he went away sorrowful; for he had great possessions.

Luke 18:18–23 (§D25.3)

[18] And a ruler asked him, "Good Teacher, what shall I do to inherit eternal life?" [19] And Jesus said to him, "Why do you call me good? No one is good but God alone. [20] You know the commandments: 'Do not commit adultery, Do not kill, Do not steal, Do not bear false witness, Honor your father and mother.'" [21] And he said, "All these I have observed from my youth." [22] And when Jesus heard it, he said to him, "One thing you still lack. Sell all that you have and distribute to the poor, and you will have treasure in heaven; and come, follow me." [23] But when he heard this he became sad, for he was very rich.

GNaz 16 (§D25.4)

(16) The other of the two rich men said to him: Master, what good thing must I do that I may live? He said to him: Man, fulfil the law and the prophets. He answered him: That have I done. He said to him: Go and sell all that thou possessest and distribute it among the poor, and then come and follow me. But the rich man then began to scratch his head and it (the saying) pleased him not. And the Lord said to him: How canst thou say, I have fulfilled the law and the prophets? For it stands written in the law: Love thy neighbour as thyself; and behold, many of thy brethren, sons of Abraham, are begrimed with dirt and die of hunger—and thy house is full of many good things and nothing at all comes forth from it to them! And he turned and said to Simon, his disciple, who was sitting by him: Simon, son of Jona, it is easier for a camel to go through the eye of a needle than for a rich man to enter into the kingdom of heaven. (Origen, *Commentary on Matthew* 15.14 [on Matthew 19:16–30])

Matt 19:23–26 (§D26.1)

²³ And Jesus said to his disciples, "Truly, I say to you, it will be hard for a rich man to enter the kingdom of heaven. ²⁴ Again I tell you, it is easier for a camel to go through the eye of a needle than for a rich man to enter the kingdom of God." ²⁵ When the disciples heard this they were greatly astonished, saying, "Who then can be saved?" ²⁶ But Jesus looked at them and said to them, "With men this is impossible, but with God all things are possible."

Mark 10:23–27 (§D26.2)

²³ And Jesus looked around and said to his disciples, "How hard it will be for those who have riches to enter the kingdom of God!" ²⁴ And the disciples were amazed at his words. But Jesus said to them again, "Children, how hard it is to enter the kingdom of God! ²⁵ It is easier for a camel to go through the eye of a needle than for a rich man to enter the kingdom of God." ²⁶ And they were exceedingly astonished, and said to him, "Then who can be saved?" ²⁷ Jesus looked at them and said, "With men it is impossible, but not with God; for all things are possible with God."

Luke 18:24–27 (§D26.3)

²⁴ Jesus looking at him said, "How hard it is for those who have riches to enter the kingdom of God! ²⁵ For it is easier for a camel to go through the eye of a needle than for a rich man to enter the kingdom of God." ²⁶ Those who heard it said, "Then who can be saved?" ²⁷ But he said, "What is impossible with men is possible with God."

GNaz 16 (§D26.4)

(16) The other of the two rich men said to him: Master, what good thing must I do that I may live? He said to him: Man, fulfil the law and the prophets. He answered him: That have I done. He said to him: Go and sell all that thou possessest and distribute it among the poor, and then come and follow me. But the rich man then began to scratch his head and it (the saying) pleased him not. And the Lord said to him: How canst thou say, I have fulfilled the law and the prophets? For it stands written in the law: Love thy neighbour as thyself; and behold, many of thy brethren, sons of Abraham, are begrimed with dirt and die of hunger—and thy house is full of many good things and nothing at all comes forth from it to them! And he turned and said to Simon, his disciple, who was sitting by him: Simon, son of Jona, it is easier for a camel to go through the eye of a needle than for a rich man to enter into the kingdom of heaven. (Origen, *Commentary on Matthew* 15.14 [on Matthew 19:16–30])

Herm Sim 9.20:1–4 (§D26.5)

¹"And from the third mountain, which has thorns and thistles, are such believers as these. Of them are those who are rich and are mixed up with many affairs of business, for the thistles are the rich, and the thorns are those who are mixed up with various affairs of business. ²These then who are engaged in many and various businesses do not cleave to the servants of God, but are choked by their work and go astray. And the rich cleave with difficulty to the servants of God, fearing that they will be asked for something by them. Such then 'will enter with difficulty into the kingdom of God.' ³For just as it is difficult to walk with naked feet among thistles, so it is also 'difficult' for such men 'to enter into the Kingdom of God.' ⁴But for all these there is repentance, but it must be speedy, that they may now retrace their days and the omissions of former years, and do some good. If then they repent and do some good they will live to God, but if they remain in their deeds they will be delivered to those women, and they will put them to death."

351   ON TWELVE THRONES*

Matt 19:27–28 (§D27.1)

²⁷ Then Peter said in reply, "Lo, we have left everything and followed you. What then shall we have?" ²⁸ Jesus said to them, "Truly, I say to you, in the new world, when the Son of man shall sit on his glorious throne, you who have followed me will also sit on twelve thrones, judging the twelve tribes of Israel."

* See 169: *On Twelve Thrones*

Luke 22:24–30 (§D27.2)

²⁴ A dispute also arose among them, which of them was to be regarded as the greatest. ²⁵ And he said to them, "The kings of the Gentiles exercise lordship over them; and those in authority over them are called benefactors. ²⁶ But not so with you; rather let the greatest among you become as the youngest, and the leader as one who serves. ²⁷ For which is the greater, one who sits at table, or one who serves? Is it not the one who sits at table? But I am among you as one who serves.

²⁸"You are those who have continued with me in my trials; ²⁹ and I assign to you, as my Father assigned to me, a kingdom, ³⁰ that you may eat and drink at my table in my kingdom, and sit on thrones judging the twelve tribes of Israel."

352 HUNDREDFOLD REWARD

Matt 19:27–29 (§D28.1)
[27] Then Peter said in reply, "Lo, we have left everything and followed you. What then shall we have?" [28] Jesus said to them, "Truly, I say to you, in the new world, when the Son of man shall sit on his glorious throne, you who have followed me will also sit on twelve thrones, judging the twelve tribes of Israel. [29] And every one who has left houses or brothers or sisters or father or mother or children or lands, for my name's sake, will receive a hundredfold, and inherit eternal life."

Mark 10:28–30 (§D28.2)
[28] Peter began to say to him, "Lo, we have left everything and followed you." [29] Jesus said, "Truly, I say to you, there is no one who has left house or brothers or sisters or mother or father or children or lands, for my sake and for the gospel, [30] who will not receive a hundredfold now in this time, houses and brothers and sisters and mothers and children and lands, with persecutions, and in the age to come eternal life."

Luke 18:28–30 (§D28.3)
[28] And Peter said, "Lo, we have left our homes and followed you." [29] And he said to them, "Truly, I say to you, there is no man who has left house or wife or brothers or parents or children, for the sake of the kingdom of God, [30] who will not receive manifold more in this time, and in the age to come eternal life."

ApJas 4:1–9 (§D28.4)
[1] And I answered and said to him: "Lord, we can obey you if you wish. For we have forsaken our fathers and our mothers and our villages and have followed you. Grant us, [therefore], not to be tempted by the wicked devil."
[2] The Lord answered and said: "What is your (pl.) merit when you do the will of the Father as if it had not been given to you by him as a gift, while you are tempted by Satan? [3] But if you are oppressed by Satan and are persecuted and you do his (i.e., the Father's) will, I [say] that he will love you and will make you equal with me and will consider that you have become [beloved] through his providence according to your free choice. [4] Will you not cease, then, being lovers of the flesh and being afraid of sufferings? [5] Or do you not know that you have not yet been mistreated and have not yet been accused unjustly, nor have you yet been shut up in prison, nor have you yet been condemned lawlessly, nor have you yet been crucified <without> reason, nor have you yet been buried <shamefully>, as (was) I myself, by the evil one? [6] Do you dare to spare the flesh, you for whom the spirit is an encircling wall? [7] If you contemplate the world, how long it is <before> you and also how long it is after you, you will find that your life is one single day and your sufferings, one single hour. [8] For the good (pl.) will not enter the world. [9] Scorn death, therefore, and take concern for life. Remember my cross and my death and you will live."

353 REQUEST FOR PRECEDENCE*

Matt 20:20–23 (§D29.1)
[20] Then the mother of the sons of Zebedee came up to him, with her sons, and kneeling before him she asked him for something. [21] And he said to her, "What do you want?" She said to him, "Command that these two sons of mine may sit, one at your right hand and one at your left, in your kingdom." [22] But Jesus answered, "You do not know what you are asking. Are you able to drink the cup that I am to drink?" They said to him, "We are able." [23] He said to them, "You will drink my cup, but to sit at my right hand and at my left is not mine to grant, but it is for those for whom it has been prepared by my Father."

* See 171: *Jesus' Baptism*

Mark 10:35–40 (§D29.2)
[35] And James and John, the sons of Zebedee, came forward to him, and said to him, "Teacher, we want you to do for us whatever we ask of you." [36] And he said to them, "What do you want me to do for you?" [37] And they said to him, "Grant us to sit, one at your right hand and one at your left, in your glory." [38] But Jesus said to them, "You do not know what you are asking. Are you able to drink the cup that I drink, or to be baptized with the baptism with which I am baptized?" [39] And they said to him, "We are able." And Jesus said to them, "The cup that I drink you will drink; and with the baptism with which I am baptized, you will be baptized; [40] but to sit at my right hand or at my left is not mine to grant, but it is for those for whom it has been prepared."

354

THE TWO SONS

Matt 21:28–32 (§D30)

[28] "What do you think? A man had two sons; and he went to the first and said, 'Son, go and work in the vineyard today.' [29] And he answered, 'I will not'; but afterward he repented and went. [30] And he went to the second and said the same; and he answered, 'I go, sir,' but did not go. [31] Which of the two did the will of his father?" They said, "The first." Jesus said to them, "Truly, I say to you, the tax collectors and the harlots go into the kingdom of God before you. [32] For John came to you in the way of righteousness, and you did not believe him, but the tax collectors and the harlots believed him; and even when you saw it, you did not afterward repent and believe him."

355

THE TENANTS*

Matt 21:33–43 (§D31.1)

[33] "Hear another parable. There was a householder who planted a vineyard, and set a hedge around it, and dug a wine press in it, and built a tower, and let it out to tenants, and went into another country. [34] When the season of fruit drew near, he sent his servants to the tenants, to get his fruit; [35] and the tenants took his servants and beat one, killed another, and stoned another. [36] Again he sent other servants, more than the first; and they did the same to them. [37] Afterward he sent his son to them, saying 'They will respect my son.' [38] But when the tenants saw the son, they said to themselves, 'This is the heir; come, let us kill him and have his inheritance.' [39] And they took him and cast him out of the vineyard, and killed him. [40] When therefore the owner of the vineyard comes, what will he do to those tenants?" [41] They said to him, "He will put those wretches to a miserable death, and let out the vineyard to other tenants who will give him the fruits in their seasons."

[42] Jesus said to them, "Have you never read in the scriptures:

'The very stone which the builders rejected
has become the head of the corner;
this was the Lord's doing,
and it is marvelous in our eyes'?

[43] Therefore I tell you, the kingdom of God will be taken away from you and given to a nation producing the fruits of it."

Mark 12:1–11 (§D31.2)

[1] And he began to speak to them in parables. "A man planted a vineyard, and set a hedge around it, and dug a pit for the wine press, and built a tower, and let it out to ten- ants, and went into another country. [2] When the time came, he sent a servant to the tenants, to get from them some of the fruit of the vineyard. [3] And they took him and beat him, and sent him away empty- handed. [4] Again he sent to them another servant, and they wounded him in the head, and treated him shamefully. [5] And he sent another, and him they killed; and so with many others, some they beat and some they killed. [6] He had still one other, a beloved son; finally he sent him to them, saying, 'They will respect my son.' [7] But those tenants said to one another, 'This is the heir; come, let us kill him, and the inheritance will be ours.' [8] And they took him and killed him, and cast him out of the vineyard. [9] What will the owner of the vineyard do? He will come and destroy the tenants, and give the vineyard to others. [10] Have you not read this scripture:

'The very stone which the builders rejected
has become the head of the corner;
[11] this was the Lord's doing,
and it is marvelous in our eyes'?"

Luke 20:9–18 (§D31.3)

[9] And he began to tell the people this parable: "A man planted a vineyard, and let it out to tenants, and went into another country for a long while. [10] When the time came, he sent a servant to the tenants, that they should give him some of the fruit of the vineyard; but the tenants beat him, and sent him away empty-handed. [11] And he sent another servant; him also they beat and treated shamefully, and sent him away empty-handed. [12] And he sent yet a third; this one they wounded and cast out. [13] Then the owner of the vineyard said, 'What shall I do? I will send my beloved son; it may be they will respect him.' [14] But when the tenants saw him, they said to themselves, 'This is the heir; let us kill him, that the inheritance may be ours.' [15] And they cast him out of the vineyard and killed him. What then will the owner of the vineyard do to them? [16] He will come and destroy those tenants, and give the vineyard to others." When they heard this, they said, "God forbid!" [17] But he looked at them and said, "What then is this that is written:

'The very stone which the builders rejected
has become the head of the corner'?
[18] Every one who falls on that stone will be broken to pieces; but when it falls on any one it will crush him."

GThom 65–66 (§D31.4)

(65) [1] He said, "There was a good man who owned a vineyard. He leased it to tenant farmers so that they might work it and he might collect the produce from them. He sent his servant so that the tenants might give him the produce of the vineyard. They seized his servant and beat him, all but killing him. The servant went back and told his master. The master said, 'Perhaps <they> did not recognize <him>.' He sent another servant. The tenants beat this one as well. Then the owner sent his son and said, 'Perhaps they will show respect to my son.' Because the tenants knew that it was he who was the heir to the vineyard, they seized him and killed him. [2] Let him who has ears hear."

(66) Jesus said, "Show me the stone which the builders have rejected. That one is the cornerstone."

* See 11: *The Tenants*

Matt 22:1–13 (§D32.1)

[1] And again Jesus spoke to them in parables, saying, [2] "The kingdom of heaven may be compared to a king who gave a marriage feast for his son, [3] and sent his servants to call those who were invited to the marriage feast; but they would not come. [4] Again he sent other servants, saying, 'Tell those who are invited, Behold, I have made ready my dinner, my oxen and my fat calves are killed, and everything is ready; come to the marriage feast.' [5] But they made light of it and went off, one to his farm, another to his business, [6] while the rest seized his servants, treated them shamefully, and killed them. [7] The king was angry, and he sent his troops and destroyed those murderers and burned their city. [8] Then he said to his servants, 'The wedding is ready, but those invited were not worthy. [9] Go therefore to the thoroughfares, and invite to the marriage feast as many as you find.' [10] And those servants went out into the streets and gathered all whom they found, both bad and good; so the wedding hall was filled with guests.

[11] "But when the king came in to look at the guests, he saw there a man who had no wedding garment; [12] and he said to him, 'Friend, how did you get in here without a wedding garment?' And he was speechless. [13] Then the king said to the attendants, 'Bind him hand and foot, and cast him into the outer darkness; there men will weep and gnash their teeth.'"

Luke 14:15–24 (§D32.2)

[15] When one of those who sat at table with him heard this, he said to him, "Blessed is he who shall eat bread in the kingdom of God!" [16] But he said to him "A man once gave a great banquet, and invited many; [17] and at the time for the banquet he sent his servant to say to those who had been invited, 'Come; for all is now ready.' [18] But they all alike began to make excuses. The first said to him, 'I have bought a field, and I must go out and see it; I pray you, have me excused.' [19] And another said, 'I have bought five yoke of oxen, and I go to examine them; I pray you, have me excused.' [20] And another said, 'I have married a wife, and therefore I cannot come.' [21] So the servant came and reported this to his master. Then the householder in anger said to his servant, 'Go out quickly to the streets and lanes of the city, and bring in the poor and maimed and blind and lame.' [22] And the servant said, 'Sir, what you commanded has been done, and still there is room.' [23] And the master said to the servant, 'Go out to the highways and hedges, and compel people to come in, that my house may be filled. [24] For I tell you, none of those men who were invited shall taste my banquet.'"

* See 12: *The Feast*

GThom 64 (§D32.3)

(64) [1] Jesus said, "A man had received visitors. And when he had prepared the dinner, he sent his servant to invite the guests. He went to the first one and said to him, 'My master invites you.' He said, 'I have claims against some merchants. They are coming to me this evening. I must go and give them my orders. I ask to be excused from the dinner.' He went to another and said to him, 'My master has invited you.' He said to him, 'I have just bought a house and am required for the day. I shall not have any spare time.' He went to another and said to him, 'My master invites you.' He said to him, 'My friend is going to get married, and I am to prepare the banquet. I shall not be able to come. I ask to be excused from the dinner.' He went to another and said to him, 'My master invites you.' He said to him, 'I have just bought a farm, and I am on my way to collect the rent. I shall not be able to come. I ask to be excused.' The servant returned and said to his master, 'Those whom you invited to the dinner have asked to be excused.' The master said to his servant, 'Go outside to the streets and bring back those whom you happen to meet, so that they may dine.' [2] Businessmen and merchants will not enter the Places of My Father."

Matt 22:23–32 (§D33.1)

²³ The same day Sadducees came to him, who say that there is no resurrection; and they asked him a question, ²⁴ saying, "Teacher, Moses said, 'If a man dies, having no children, his brother must marry the widow, and raise up children for his brother.' ²⁵ Now there were seven brothers among us; the first married, and died, and having no children left his wife to his brother. ²⁶ So too the second and third, down to the seventh. ²⁷ After them all, the woman died. ²⁸ In the resurrection, therefore, to which of the seven will she be wife? For they all had her."

²⁹ But Jesus answered them, "You are wrong, because you know neither the scriptures nor the power of God. ³⁰ For in the resurrection they neither marry nor are given in marriage, but are like angels in heaven. ³¹ And as for the resurrection of the dead, have you not read what was said to you by God, ³² 'I am the God of Abraham, and the God of Isaac, and the God of Jacob'? He is not God of the dead, but of the living."

Mark 12:18–27 (§D33.2)

¹⁸ And Sadducees came to him, who say that there is no resurrection; and they asked him a question, saying, ¹⁹ "Teacher, Moses wrote for us that if a man's brother dies and leaves a wife, but leaves no child, the man must take the wife, and raise up children for his brother. ²⁰ There were seven brothers; the first took a wife, and when he died left no children; ²¹ and the second took her, and died, leaving no children; and the third likewise; ²² and the seven left no children. Last of all the woman also died. ²³ In the resurrection whose wife will she be? For the seven had her as wife."

²⁴ Jesus said to them, "Is not this why you are wrong, that you know neither the scriptures nor the power of God? ²⁵ For when they rise from the dead, they neither marry nor are given in marriage, but are like angels in heaven. ²⁶ And as for the dead being raised, have you not read in the book of Moses, in the passage about the bush, how God said to him, 'I am the God of Abraham, and the God of Isaac, and the God of Jacob?' ²⁷ He is not God of the dead, but of the living; you are quite wrong."

Luke 20:27–39 (§D33.3)

²⁷ There came to him some Sadducees, those who say that there is no resurrection, ²⁸ and they asked him a question, saying, "Teacher, Moses wrote for us that if a man's brother dies, having a wife but no children, the man must take the wife and raise up children for his brother. ²⁹ Now there were seven brothers; the first took a wife, and died without children; ³⁰ and the second ³¹ and the third took her, and likewise all seven left no children and died. ³² Afterward the woman also died. ³³ In the resurrection, therefore, whose wife will the woman be? For the seven had her as wife."

³⁴ And Jesus said to them, "The sons of this age marry and are given in marriage; ³⁵ but those who are accounted worthy to attain to that age and to the resurrection from the dead neither marry nor are given in marriage, ³⁶ for they cannot die any more, because they are equal to angels and are sons of God, being sons of the resurrection. ³⁷ But that the dead are raised, even Moses showed, in the passage about the bush, where he calls the Lord the God of Abraham and the God of Isaac and the God of Jacob. ³⁸ Now he is not God of the dead, but of the living; for all live to him." ³⁹ And some of the scribes answered, "Teacher, you have spoken well."

Matt 22:34–40 (§D34.1)

[34] But when the Pharisees heard that he had silenced the Sadducees, they came together. [35] And one of them, a lawyer, asked him a question, to test him. [36] "Teacher, which is the great commandment in the law?" [37] And he said to him, "You shall love the Lord your God with all your heart, and with all your soul, and with all your mind. [38] This is the great and first commandment. [39] And a second is like it, You shall love your neighbor as yourself. [40] On these two commandments depend all the law and the prophets."

* See 13: *The Good Samaritan*

Mark 12:28–34 (§D34.2)

[28] And one of the scribes came up and heard them disputing with one another, and seeing that he answered them well, asked him, "Which commandment is the first of all?" [29] Jesus answered, "The first is, 'Hear, O Israel: The Lord our God, the Lord is one; [30] and you shall love the Lord your God with all your heart, and with all your soul, and with all your mind, and with all your strength.' [31] The second is this, 'You shall love your neighbor as yourself.' There is no other commandment greater than these." [32] And the scribe said to him, "You are right, Teacher; you have truly said that he is one, and there is no other but he; [33] and to love him with all the heart, and with all the understanding, and with all the strength, and to love one's neighbor as oneself, is much more than all whole burnt offerings and sacrifices." [34] And when Jesus saw that he answered wisely, he said to him, "You are not far from the kingdom of God." And after that no one dared to ask him any question.

Luke 10:25–37 (§D34.3)

[25] And behold, a lawyer stood up to put him to the test, saying, "Teacher, what shall I do to inherit eternal life?" [26] He said to him, "What is written in the law? How do you read?" [27] And he answered, "You shall love the Lord your God with all your heart, and with all your soul, and with all your strength, and with all your mind; and your neighbor as yourself." [28] And he said to him, "You have answered right; do this, and you will live."

[29] But he, desiring to justify himself, said to Jesus, "And who is my neighbor?" [30] Jesus replied, "A man was going down from Jerusalem to Jericho, and he fell among robbers, who stripped him and beat him, and departed, leaving him half dead. [31] Now by chance a priest was going down that road; and when he saw him he passed by on the other side. [32] So likewise a Levite, when he came to the place and saw him, passed by on the other side. [33] But a Samaritan, as he journeyed, came to where he was; and when he saw him, he had compassion, [34] and went to him and bound up his wounds, pouring on oil and wine; then he set him on his own beast and brought him to an inn, and took care of him. [35] And the next day he took out two denarii and gave them to the innkeeper, saying, 'Take care of him; and whatever more you spend, I will repay you when I come back.' [36] Which of these three, do you think, proved neighbor to the man who fell among the robbers?" [37] He said, "The one who showed mercy on him." And Jesus said to him "Go and do likewise."

359

SON OF DAVID★

Matt 22:41–46 (§D35.1)
[41] Now while the Pharisees were gathered together, Jesus asked them a question, [42] saying, "What do you think of the Christ? Whose son is he?" They said to him, "The son of David." [43] He said to them, "How is it then that David, inspired by the Spirit, calls him Lord, saying,
[44] 'The Lord said to my Lord,
Sit at my right hand,
till I put thy enemies under thy feet'?
[45] If David thus calls him Lord, how is he his son?" [46] And no one was able to answer him a word, nor from that day did any one dare to ask him any more questions.

Mark 12:35–37 (§D35.2)
[35] And as Jesus taught in the temple, he said, "How can the scribes say that the Christ is the son of David? [36] David himself, inspired by the Holy Spirit, declared,
'The Lord said to my Lord,
Sit at my right hand,
till I put thy enemies under thy feet.'
[37] David himself calls him Lord; so how is he his son?" And the great throng heard him gladly.

Luke 20:41–44 (§D35.3)
[41] But he said to them, "How can they say that the Christ is David's son? [42] For David himself says in the Book of Psalms,
'The Lord said to my Lord,
Sit at my right hand,
[43] till I make thy enemies a stool for thy feet.'
[44] David thus calls him Lord; so how is he his son?"

Barn 12:10–11 (§D35.4)
[10] See again Jesus, not as son of man, but as Son of God, but manifested in a type in the flesh. Since therefore they are going to say that the Christ is David's son, David himself prophesies, fearing and understanding the error of the sinners, "The Lord said to my Lord sit thou on my right hand until I make thy enemies thy footstool." [11] And again Isaiah speaks thus, "The Lord said to Christ my Lord, whose right hand I held, that the nations should obey before him, and I will shatter the strength of Kings." See how "David calls him Lord" and does not say Son.

★ See 175: *Son of David*

360

HELPING WITH BURDENS★

Matt 23:1–4 (§D36.1)
[1] Then said Jesus to the crowds and to his disciples, [2] "The scribes and the Pharisees sit on Moses' seat; [3] so practice and observe whatever they tell you, but not what they do; for they preach, but do not practice. [4] They bind heavy burdens, hard to bear, and lay them on men's shoulders; but they themselves will not move them with their finger."

★ See 177: *Helping with Burdens*

Luke 11:45–46 (§D36.2)
[45] One of the lawyers answered him, "Teacher, in saying this you reproach us also." [46] And he said, "Woe to you lawyers also! for you load men with burdens hard to bear, and you yourselves do not touch the burdens with one of your fingers."

361

Matt 24:11–12 (§D37.1)
[11] "And many false prophets will arise and lead many astray. [12] And because wickedness is multiplied, most men's love will grow cold."

Matt 24:23–26 (§D37.2)
[23] "Then if any one says to you, 'Lo, here is the Christ!' or 'There he is!' do not believe it. [24] For false Christs and false prophets will arise and show great signs and wonders, so as to lead astray, if possible, even the elect. [25] Lo, I have told you beforehand. [26] So, if they say to you, 'Lo, he is in the wilderness,' do not go out; if they say, 'Lo, he is in the inner rooms' do not believe it."

Mark 13:21–23 (§D37.3)
[21] "And then if any one says to you, 'Look, here is the Christ!' or 'Look, there he is!' do not believe it. [22] False Christs and false prophets will arise and show signs and wonders, to lead astray, if possible, the elect. [23] But take heed; I have told you all things beforehand."

* See 196: *When and Where*

Luke 17:20–23 (§D37.4)
[20] Being asked by the Pharisees when the kingdom of God was coming, he answered them, "The kingdom of God is not coming with signs to be observed; [21] nor will they say, 'Lo, here it is!' or 'There!' for behold, the kingdom of God is in the midst of you."
[22] And he said to the disciples, "The days are coming when you will desire to see one of the days of the Son of man, and you will not see it. [23] And they will say to you, 'Lo, there!' or 'Lo, here!' Do not go, do not follow them."

POxy654 3:1 (§D37.5)
(3) [1] Jesus said, "[If] those who lead you [say to you, 'See], the kingdom is in the sky,' then the birds of the sky [will precede you. If they say that] it is under the earth, then the fish of the sea [will enter it, preceding] you. And, the [kingdom of God] is inside of you, [and it is outside of you."

GThom 3:1 (§D37.6)
(3) [1] Jesus said, "If those who lead you say to you, 'See, the Kingdom is in the sky,' then the birds of the sky will precede you. If they say to you, 'It is in the sea,' then the fish will precede you. Rather, the Kingdom is inside of you, and it is outside of you."

GThom 51 (§D37.7)
(51) [1] His disciples said to Him, "When will the repose of the dead come about, and when will the new world come?"
[2] He said to them, "What you look forward to has already come, but you do not recognize it."

GThom 113 (§D37.8)
(113) [1] His disciples said to Him, "When will the Kingdom come?"
[2] <Jesus said,> "It will not come by waiting for it. It will not be a matter of saying 'Here it is' or 'There it is.' Rather, the Kingdom of the Father is spread out upon the earth, and men do not see it."

DialSav 15–16 (§D37.9)
(15) Judas [said], "Tell [us, Lord], what was [. . .] before [the heaven and the] earth existed."
(16) The Lord said, "There was darkness and water and spirit upon [water]. And I say [to you, . . .] what you seek and inquire after, [behold it is] within you . . .[. . .] . . . the power and the [mystery . . .] spirit, for from . . .[. . .] wickedness [. . .] come . . .[. . .] mind . . .[. . .] behold . . .[. . .] . . .[. . .]."

362

Matt 24:28 (§D38.1)
[28] "Wherever the body is, there the eagles will be gathered together."

* See 198: *Corpse and Vultures*

Luke 17:37 (§D38.2)
[37] And they said to him, "Where, Lord?" He said to them, "Where the body is, there the eagles will be gathered together."

363 MASTER AND STEWARD*

Matt 24:45–51 (§D39.1)

[45] "Who then is the faithful and wise servant, whom his master has set over his household, to give them their food at the proper time? [46] Blessed is that servant whom his master when he comes will find so doing. [47] Truly, I say to you, he will set him over all his possessions. [48] But if that wicked servant says to himself, 'My master is delayed,' [49] and begins to beat his fellow servants, and eats and drinks with the drunken, [50] the master of that servant will come on a day when he does not expect him and at an hour he does not know, [51] and will punish him, and put him with the hypocrites; there men will weep and gnash their teeth."

* See 207: *Master and Steward*
* See 244: *Blessed for Doing*

Luke 12:41–48a (§D39.2)

[41] Peter said, "Lord, are you telling this parable for us or for all?" [42] And the Lord said, "Who then is the faithful and wise steward, whom his master will set over his household, to give them their portion of food at the proper time? [43] Blessed is that servant whom his master when he comes will find so doing. [44] Truly, I say to you, he will set him over all his possessions. [45] But if that servant says to himself, 'My master is delayed in coming,' and begins to beat the menservants and the maidservants, and to eat and drink and get drunk, [46] the master of that servant will come on a day when he does not expect him and at an hour he does not know, and will punish him, and put him with the unfaithful. [47] And that servant who knew his master's will, but did not make ready or act according to his will, shall receive a severe beating. [48] But he who did not know, and did what deserved a beating, shall receive a light beating."

364 LOOKING BACKWARDS

Luke 9:61–62 (§D40)

[61] Another said, "I will follow you, Lord; but let me first say farewell to those at my home." [62] Jesus said to him, "No one who puts his hand to the plow and looks back is fit for the kingdom of God."

365 REPENT OR PERISH

Luke 13:1–5 (§D41)

[1] There were some present at that very time who told him of the Galileans whose blood Pilate had mingled with their sacrifices. [2] And he answered them, "Do you think that these Galileans were worse sinners than all the other Galileans, because they suffered thus? [3] I tell you, No; but unless you repent you will all likewise perish. [4] Or those eighteen upon whom the tower in Siloam fell and killed them, do you think that they were worse offenders than all the others who dwelt in Jerusalem? [5] I tell you, No; but unless you repent you will all likewise perish."

366

TWO SWORDS ENOUGH

Luke 22:35–38 (§D42)

[35] And he said to them, "When I sent you out with no purse or bag or sandals, did you lack anything?" They said, "Nothing." [36] He said to them, "But now, let him who has a purse take it, and likewise a bag. And let him who has no sword sell his mantle and buy one. [37] For I tell you that this scripture must be fulfilled in me, 'And he was reckoned with transgressors'; for what is written about me has its fulfilment." [38] And they said, "Look, Lord, here are two swords." And he said to them, "It is enough."

367

SCRIPTURES AND JESUS*

John 5:39–47 (§D43.1)

[39] "You search the scriptures, because you think that in them you have eternal life; and it is they that bear witness to me; [40] yet you refuse to come to me that you may have life. [41] I do not receive glory from men. [42] But I know that you have not the love of God within you. [43] I have come in my Father's name, and you do not receive me; if another comes in his own name, him you will receive. [44] How can you believe, who receive glory from one another and do not seek the glory that comes from the only God? [45] Do not think that I shall accuse you to the Father; it is Moses who accuses you, on whom you set your hope. [46] If you believed Moses, you would believe me, for he wrote of me. [47] But if you do not believe his writings, how will you believe my words?"

* See 240: *Scriptures and Jesus*

PEger2 1 (§D43.2)

(1) . . . to the lawyer[s: " . . . e]very one who act[s contrary to the l]aw, but not me! . . . what he does, as he does it." [And] having turn[ed] to [the] rulers of the people he [sp]oke the following saying: "(Ye) search the scriptures in which ye think that ye have life; these are they which bear witness of me. Do not think that I came to accuse [you] to my Father! There is one [that ac]cuses [you], even Moses, on whom ye have set your hope." And when they sa[id]: "We know that God [hath] spok[en] to Moses, but as for thee, we know not [whence thou art]," Jesus answered and said unto them: "Now (already) accusation is raised against [your] unbelief. [No one o]therwise . . ." (Fragment 1, verso [lines 1–20])

. . . [to gather] stones together to stone him. And the [rul]ers laid their hands on him that they might arrest him and [deliver] him to the multitude. But they w[ere not able] to arrest him because the hour of his betrayal [was] not yet c[ome]. But he himself, the Lord, escaped out of [their han]ds and turned away from them. (Fragment 1, recto [lines 22–41])

GThom 52 (§D43.3)

(52) [1] His disciples said to Him, "Twenty-four prophets spoke in Israel, and all of them spoke in You."

[2] He said to them, "You have omitted the one living in your presence and have spoken (only) of the dead."

368 PLACE OF LIFE

John 14:2–12 (§D44.1)

2 "In my Father's house are many rooms; if it were not so, would I have told you that I go to prepare a place for you? 3 And when I go and prepare a place for you, I will come again and will take you to myself, that where I am you may be also. 4 And you know the way where I am going." 5 Thomas said to him, "Lord, we do not know where you are going; how can we know the way?" 6 Jesus said to him, "I am the way, and the truth, and the life; no one comes to the Father, but by me. 7 If you had known me, you would have known my Father also; henceforth you know him and have seen him."

8 Philip said to him, "Lord, show us the Father, and we shall be satisfied." 9 Jesus said to him, "Have I been with you so long, and yet you do not know me, Philip? He who has seen me has seen the Father; how can you say, 'Show us the Father'? 10 Do you not believe that I am in the Father and the Father in me? The words that I say to you I do not speak on my own authority; but the Father who dwells in me does his works. 11 Believe me that I am in the Father and the Father in me; or else believe me for the sake of the works themselves.

12 "Truly, truly, I say to you, he who believes in me will also do the works that I do; and greater works than these will he do, because I go to the Father."

DialSav 27–30 (§D44.2)

(27) [Matthew] said, "Lord, I want [to see] that place of life [. . .] where there is no wickedness, [but rather] there is pure [light]!"

(28) The Lord [said], "Brother [Matthew], you will not be able to see it [as long as you are] carrying flesh around."

(29) [Matthew] said, "Lord, [even if I will] not [be able] to see it, let me [know it]!"

(30) The Lord [said], "[Everyone] who has known himself has seen [it . . .] everything given to him to do [. . .] . . .and has come to [. . .] it in his [goodness]."

369 BECOME FULL*

ApJas 3:9–15 (§D45)

9 "Therefore I say to you, become full and leave no place within you empty, since the Coming One is able to mock you."

10 Then Peter answered: "<Lord>, three times you have said to us, '[Become full,' but] we are full."

11 The [Lord answered and] said: "[Therefore I say] to you (pl.), [become full], in order that [you] may not [be diminished. Those who are diminished], however, will not [be saved]. 12 For fullness is good [and diminution] is bad. 13 Therefore, just as it is good for you (sing.) to be dimin-ished and, on the other hand, bad for you to be filled, so also the one who is full is diminished; and the one who is diminished is not filled as the one who is diminished is filled, and the one who is full, for his part, brings his sufficiency to completion. 14 Therefore, it is fitting to be diminished while you (pl.) can (still) be filled, and to be filled while it is (still) possible to be diminished, in order that you can [fill] yourselves the more. 15 Therefore, [become] full of the spirit but be diminished of reason. For reason is (of) the soul; and it is soul."

* See 250: *Become Full*

370 KINGDOM AND CROSS*

ApJas 4:9—5:5 (§D46)

9 "Scorn death, therefore, and take concern for life. Remember my cross and my death and you will live."

5 1 And I answered and said to him: "Lord, do not mention to us the cross and the death, for they are far from you."

2 The Lord answered and said: "Truly I say to you (pl.), none will be saved unless they believe in my cross. [But] those who have believed in my cross, theirs is the Kingdom of God. 3 Therefore, become seekers for death, just as the dead who seek for life, for that for which they seek is revealed to them. And what is there to concern them? When you turn yourselves towards death, it will make known to you election. 4 In truth I say to you, none of those who are afraid of death will be saved. For the Kingdom of <God> belongs to those who have put themselves to death. 5 Become better than I; make yourselves like the son of the Holy Spirit."

* See 251: *Kingdom and Cross*

371 HEAD OF PROPHECY

ApJas 6:1–4 (§D47)

[1] Then I questioned him: "Lord, how may we prophesy to those who ask us to prophesy to them? For there are many who ask us and who look to us to hear an oracle from us."

[2] The Lord answered and said: "Do you (pl.) not know that the head of prophecy was cut off with John?"

[3] And I said: "Lord, it is not possible to remove the head of prophecy, is it?"

[4] The Lord said to me: "When you (pl.) come to know what 'head' is, and that prophecy issues from the head, (then) understand what is (the meaning of) 'Its head was removed.'"

372 KINGDOM AND LIFE

ApJas 9:1–4 (§D48)

[1] And Peter answered to this and said: "Sometimes you urge us on to the Kingdom of Heaven, and other times you turn us away, Lord. Sometimes you persuade (us) and impel us to faith and promise us life, and other times you expel us from the Kingdom of Heaven."

[2] And the Lord answered and said to us: "I have given you (pl). faith many times. Moreover, I have revealed myself to you (sing.), James, and you (pl.) have not known me. [3] Again, now I see you rejoicing many times. And when you are elated over [the] promise of life, are you nevertheless glum? And are you distressed when you are taught about the Kingdom? But you through faith [and] knowledge have received life. Therefore, scorn rejection when you hear it, but, when you hear the promise, be the more glad. [4] In truth I say to you, the one who will receive life and believe in the Kingdom will never leave it—not even if the Father desires to banish him!"

373 FASTING, PRAYING, ALMSGIVING*

GThom 6, 14 (§D49)

(6) [1] His disciples questioned Him and said to Him, "Do You want us to fast? How shall we pray? Shall we give alms? What diet shall we observe?"

[2] Jesus said, "Do not tell lies, [3] and do not do what you hate, for all things are plain in the sight of Heaven. [4] For nothing hidden will not become manifest, and nothing covered will remain without being uncovered."

(14) [1] Jesus said to them, "If you fast, you will give rise to sin for yourselves; and if you pray, you will be condemned; and if you give alms, you will do harm to your spirits. [2] When you go into any land and walk about in the districts, if they receive you, eat what they will set before you, and heal the sick among them. [3] For what goes into your mouth will not defile you, but that which issues from your mouth—it is that which will defile you."

* See 280: *Fasting, Praying, Almsgiving*

374   JAMES AS LEADER

GThom 12 (§D50)

(12) [1] The disciples said to Jesus, "We know that You will depart from us. Who is to be our leader?"

[2] Jesus said to them, "Wherever you are, you are to go to James the righteous, for whose sake heaven and earth came into being."

375   BEGINNING AND END★

GThom 18 (§D51)

(18) [1] The disciples said to Jesus, "Tell us how our end will be."

[2] Jesus said, "Have you discovered, then, the beginning, that you look for the end? [3] For where the beginning is, there will the end be. Blessed is he who will take his place in the beginning; he will know the end and will not experience death."

★ See 282: *Beginning and End*

376   CHILDREN IN FIELD★

GThom 21:1–2 (§D52)

(21) [1] Mary said to Jesus, "Whom are Your disciples like?"

[2] He said, "They are like children who have settled in a field which is not theirs. When the owners of the field come, they will say, 'Let us have back our field.' They (will) undress in their presence in order to let them have back their field and to give it back to them."

★ See 31: *Children in Field*

GThom 22 (§D53.1)

(22) [1] Jesus saw infants being suckled. [2] He said to His disciples, "These infants being suckled are like those who enter the Kingdom."

[3] They said to Him, "Shall we then, as children, enter the Kingdom?"

[4] Jesus said to them, "When you make the two one, and when you make the inside like the outside and the outside like the inside, and the above like the below, and when you make the male and the female one and the same, so that the male not be male nor the female female; and when you fashion eyes in place of an eye, and a hand in place of a hand, and a foot in place of a foot, and a likeness in place of a likeness; then will you enter [the Kingdom]."

GEgy 5 (§D53.2)

(5) Contending further for the impious doctrine he (Julius Cassianus) adds: "And how could a charge not be rightly brought against the Savior, if he has transformed us and freed us from error, and delivered us from sexual intercourse?" In this matter his teaching is similar to that of Tatian. But he emerged from the school of Valentinus. Therefore Cassianus now says, When Salome asked when what she had inquired about would be known, the Lord said, "When you have trampled on the garment of shame and when the two become one and the male with the female (is) neither male nor female." Now in the first place we have not this word in the four Gospels that have been handed down to us, but in the Gospel of the Egyptians. Further he seems to me to fail to recognize that by the male impulse is meant wrath and by the female lust. (Clement, *Stromateis* 3.13.92.1–93.1)

2 Clem 12:1–6 (§D53.3)

[1] Let us then wait for the kingdom of God, from hour to hour, in love and righteousness, seeing that we know not the day of the appearing of God. [2] For when the Lord himself was asked by someone when his kingdom would come, he said: "When the two shall be one, and the outside as the inside, and the male with the female neither male nor female." [3] Now "the two are one" when we speak with one another in truth, and there is but one soul in two bodies without dissimulation. [4] And by "the outside as the inside" he means this, that the inside is the soul, and the outside is the body. Therefore, just as your body is visible, so let your soul be apparent in your good works. [5] And by "the male with the female neither male nor female" he means this, that when a brother sees a sister he should have no thought of her as female, nor she of him as male. [6] When you do this, he says, the kingdom of my Father will come.

POxy655 37 (§D54.1)

(37) [1] His disciples said to him, "When will you become revealed to us and when shall we see you?"

[2] He said, "When you disrobe and are not ashamed [. . . afraid]."

GThom 37 (§D54.2)

(37) [1] His disciples said, "When will You become revealed to us and when shall we see You?"

[2] Jesus said, "When you disrobe without being ashamed and take up your garments and place them under your feet like little children and tread on them, then [will you see] the Son of the Living One, and you will not be afraid."

DialSav 49–52 (§D54.3)

(49) Judas said, "Behold! The governors dwell above us, so it is they who will rule over us!"

(50) The Lord said, "It is you who will rule over them! But when you rid yourselves of jealousy, then you will clothe yourselves in light and enter the bridal chamber."

(51) Judas said, "How will [our] garments be brought to us?"

(52) The Lord said, "There are some who will provide for you, and there are others who will receive [. . .]. For [it is] they [who will give you] your garments. [For] who [will] be able to reach that place [which] is [the] reward? But the garments of life were given to man because he knows the path by which he will leave. And it is difficult even for me to reach it!"

DialSav 84–85 (§D54.4)

(84) Judas said to Matthew, "We [want] to understand the sort of garments we are to be [clothed] with [when] we depart the decay of the [flesh]."

(85) The Lord said, "The governors [and] the administrators possess garments granted [only for a time], which do not last. [But] you, as children of truth, not with these transitory garments are you to clothe yourselves. Rather, I say [to] you that you will become [blessed] when you strip [yourselves]! For it is no great thing . . .[. . .] outside."

GEgy 5 (§D54.5)

(5) Contending further for the impious doctrine he (Julius Cassianus) adds: "And how could a charge not be rightly brought against the Savior, if he has transformed us and freed us from error, and delivered us from sexual intercourse?" In this matter his teaching is similar to that of Tatian. But he emerged from the school of Valentinus. Therefore Cassianus now says, When Salome asked when what she had inquired about would be known, the Lord said, "When you have trampled on the garment of shame and when the two become one and the male with the female (is) neither male nor female." Now in the first place we have not this word in the four Gospels that have been handed down to us, but in the Gospel of the Egyptians. Further he seems to me to fail to recognize that by the male impulse is meant wrath and by the female lust. (Clement, *Stromateis* 3.13.92.1–93.1)

379 FROM MY WORDS

GThom 43 (§D55)

(43) [1] His disciples said to him, "Who are You, that You should say these things to us?"

[2] <Jesus said to them,> "You do not realize who I am from what I say to you, but you have become like the Jews, [3] for they (either) love the tree and hate its fruit (or) love the fruit and hate the tree."

380 THE TRUE CIRCUMCISION

GThom 53 (§D56)

(53) [1] His disciples said to Him, "Is circumcision beneficial or not?"

[2] He said to them, "If it were beneficial, their father would beget them already circumcised from their mother. Rather, the true circumcision in spirit has become completely profitable."

381 JESUS AND SALOME★

GThom 61 (§D57)

(61) [1] Jesus said, "Two will rest on a bed: the one will die, the other will live."

[2] Salome said, "Who are You, man, that You, as though from the One, (or: as <whose son>, that You) have come up on my couch and eaten from my table?"

[3] Jesus said to her, "I am He who exists from the Undivided. I was given some of the things of My father."

[4] <Salome said,> "I am Your disciple."

[5] <Jesus said to her,> "Therefore I say, if he is <undivided>, he will be filled with light, but if he is divided, he will be filled with darkness."

★ See 76: *The Body's Light*
★ See 133: *Father and Son*

382 THE BRIDAL CHAMBER★

GThom 75 (§D58.1)

(75) Jesus said, "Many are standing at the door, but it is the solitary who will enter the bridal chamber."

★ See 302: *The Bridal Chamber*

DialSav 49–50 (§D58.2)

(49) Judas said, "Behold! The governors dwell above us, so it is they who will rule over us!"

(50) The Lord said, "It is you who will rule over them! But when you rid yourselves of jealousy, then you will clothe yourselves in light and enter the bridal chamber."

383 PETER AND MARY

GThom 114 (§D59)

(114) [1] Simon Peter said to them, "Let Mary leave us, for women are not worthy of Life."

[2] Jesus said, "I myself shall lead her in order to make her male, so that she too may become a living spirit resembling you males. For every woman who will make herself male will enter the Kingdom of Heaven."

384 WISE AND RIGHTEOUS

DialSav 4–7 (§D60)

(4) [Matthew] said, "[How . . .]?"

(5) The Savior said, "[. . .] . . . the things inside you [. . .] . . . will remain, you [. . .]."

(6) Judas [said], "Lord, [. . .] . . . the works [. . . these] souls, these [. . .] these little ones, when [. . .] where will they be? [. . .] . . . [. . .] . . . the spirit [. . .]."

(7) The Lord [said], "[. . .] . . . [. . . receive] them. These do not die, [. . .] . . . they are not destroyed, for they have known [. . .] consort and him who would [receive them]. For the truth seeks [out the] wise and the righteous."

385 RENOUNCING POWER

DialSav 19–20 (§D61)

(19) And Matthew [asked him] "[. . .] . . . took . . . [. . .] . . . it is he who . . . [. . .]."

(20) The Lord [said], "[. . . stronger] than . . . [. . .] . . . you . . . [. . .] . . . [. . .] . . . to follow [you] and all the works [. . .] your hearts.

For just as your hearts [. . .], so [. . .] the means to overcome the powers [above] as well as those below [. . .]. I say to you, let him [who possesses] power renounce [it and repent]. And [let] him who [. . .] seek and find and [rejoice]."

386 THIS IMPOVERISHED COSMOS

DialSav 25–26 (§D62)

(25) [Mary] hailed her brethren [. . .] . . . you ask the son . . . [. . .] . . . them, where are you going to put them?"

(26) [The Lord said] to her, "Sister, [. . .] will be able to inquire about these things . . . [. . .] . . . he has somewhere to put them in his [heart . . .] . . . to come [forth . . .] and enter . . . [. . .] . . . [. . .] so that they might not hold back . . . [. . .] this impoverished cosmos."

387 VISION OF GOD

DialSav 41–46 (§D63)

(41) Mary [said, "..] see [evil ...]... them from the first [...] each other."

(42) The [Lord] said, "[...]... when you see them ...[...] become huge, they will ...[...].... But when you see the Eternal Existent, that is the great vision."

(43) Then they all said to him, "Tell us about it!"

(44) He said to them, "How do you wish to see it? [By means of a] transient vision or an eternal [vision]?" He went on and said, "[Strive] to save that [which] can follow [...], and to seek it out, and to speak from within it, so that, as you seek it out, [everything] might be in harmony with you! For I [say] to you, truly, the living God [...]... in you ...[...]... in him."

(45) [Judas said, "Truly], I want [...]."

(46) The [Lord said] to him, "[...] living [...] dwells [...]... entire ... the [deficiency...]."

388 THE TRUE RULE

DialSav 47–50 (§D64)

(47) [Judas said], "Who ...[...]?"

(48) The Lord said, "[...] all [the] works which ...[...] the remainder, it is they [which you ...]...[...]...."

(49) Judas said, "Behold! The governors dwell above us, so it is they who will rule over us!"

(50) The Lord said, "It is you who will rule over them! But when you rid yourselves of jealousy, then you will clothe yourselves in light and enter the bridal chamber."

389 FULLNESS AND DEFICIENCY

DialSav 54–55 (§D65)

(54) The disciples said to him, "What is the fullness and what is the deficiency?"

(55) He said to them, "You are from the fullness and you dwell in the place where the deficiency is. And lo! His light has poured [down] upon me!"

390 LIVING AND DEAD

DialSav 56–57 (§D66)

(56) [Matthew] said, "Tell me, Lord, how the dead die [and] how the living live."

(57) The [Lord] said, "[You (masc. sing.) have] asked me about a saying [...] which eye has not seen, [nor] have I heard it except from you. But I say to you that when what invigorates a man is removed, he will be called 'dead.' And when what is alive leaves what is dead, what is alive will be called upon."

391 WOMAN AND BIRTH

DialSav 58–59 (§D67.1)

(58) Judas said, "Why else, for the sake of truth, do they kill and live?"

(59) The Lord said, "Whatever is born of truth does not die. Whatever is born of woman dies."

DialSav 90–95 (§D67.2)

(90) Judas said, "You have told us this out of the mind of truth. When we pray, how should we pray?"

(91) The Lord said, "Pray in the place where there is no woman."

(92) Matthew said, "'Pray in the place where is [no woman],' he tells us, meaning, 'Destroy the works of womanhood,' not because there is any other [manner of birth], but because they will cease [giving birth]."

(93) Mary said, "They will never be obliterated."

(94) The Lord said, "[Who] knows that they will [not] dissolve and . . .[. . .]. . . [. . .]. . .[. . .]. . .?"

(95) Judas said [to Matthew], "[They] will dissolve [. . . works] of [. . .]. . .[. . .] the governors [. . .] will . . .[. . .]. . .. Thus will we [become] prepared [for] them."

GEgy 1–4,6 (§D67.3)

(1) When Salome asked, "How long will death have power?" the Lord answered, "So long as you women bear children"—not as if life was something bad and creation evil, but as teaching the sequence of nature. (Clement, *Stromateis* 3.6.45.3)

(2) Those who are opposed to God's creation because of continence, which has a fair-sounding name, also quote the words addressed to Salome which I mentioned earlier. They are handed down, as I believe, in the Gospel of the Egyptians. For, they say: the Savior himself said, "I am come to undo the works of the female," by the female meaning lust, and by the works birth and decay. (Clement, *Stromateis* 3.9.63.1–2)

(3) Since then the Word has alluded to the consummation, Salome saith rightly, "Until when shall men die?" Now Scripture uses the term 'man' in the two senses, of the visible outward form and of the soul, and again of the redeemed man and of him who is not redeemed. And sin is called the death of the soul. Wherefore the Lord answers advisedly, "So long as women bear children," i.e., so long as lusts are powerful. (Clement, *Stromateis* 3.9.64.1)

(4) Why do they not also adduce what follows the words spoken to Salome, these people who do anything but walk by the gospel rule according to truth? For when she said, "I have then done well in not bearing children," as if it were improper to engage in procreation, then the Lord answered and said, "Eat every plant, but that which has bitterness eat not." (Clement, *Stromateis* 3.9.66.1–2)

(6) And when the Savior says to Salome that death will reign as long as women bear children, he does not thereby slander procreation, for that indeed is necessary for the redemption of believers. (Clement, *Excerpta ex Theodoto* 67.2)

392 PLACE OF ABSENCE

DialSav 60–64 (§D68)

(60) Mary said, "Tell me, Lord, why I have come to this place to profit or to forfeit."

(61) The Lord said, "You make clear the abundance of the revealer!"

(62) Mary said to him, "Lord, is there then a place which is . . ., or lacking truth?"

(63) The Lord said, "The place where I am not!"

(64) Mary said, "Lord, you are fearful and [wonderful], and . . .[. . . turn]. . . away from those who do not know [you]."

393 LOVE AND GOODNESS

DialSav 73–74 (§D69)

(73) [Judas] said, "Tell me, Lord, what the beginning of the path is."

(74) He said, "Love and goodness. For if one of these existed among the governors, wickedness would never have come into existence."

394 TREASURES OF COSMOS

DialSav 69-70 (§D70)

(69) Mary said, "I want to understand all things, [just as] they are."

(70) The [Lord] said, "He who will seek out life! For [this] is their wealth. For the . . .[. . .]. . . of this cosmos is [. . .], and its gold and its silver are [misleading]."

395 THE PERFECT VICTORY

DialSav 71-72 (§D71)

(71) His [disciples] said to him, "What should we do to ensure that our work will be perfect?"

(72) The Lord [said] to them, "Be [prepared] in face of everything. [Blessed] is the man who has found . . .[. . .]. . . the contest . . . his eyes. [Neither] did he kill, nor was [he] killed, but he came forth victorious."

396 LOVE AND GOODNESS

DialSav 73-74 (§D72)

(73) [Judas] said, "Tell me, Lord, what the beginning of the path is."

(74) He said, "Love and goodness. For if one of these existed among the governors, wickedness would never have come into existence."

397 FAITH AND KNOWLEDGE

DialSav 75-76 (§D73)

(75) Matthew said, "Lord, you have spoken about the end of everything without concern."

(76) The Lord said, "You have understood all the things I have said to you and you have accepted them on faith. If you have known them, then they are [yours]. If not, then they are not yours."

398 REACHING THE PLACE

DialSav 77–78 (§D74)

(77) They said to him, "What is the place to which we are going?"

(78) The [Lord] said, "The place you can reach . . .[. . .], stand there!"

399 UNDERSTANDING EVERYTHING

DialSav 81–82 (§D75)

(81) His [disciples], numbering twelve, asked him, "Teacher, [. . .] [. . . serenity . . .] teach us . . .[. . .]."

(82) The Lord said, ". . .[. . .]. . . everything which I have . . .[. . .] you will . . . . . .[. . .]. . . you [. . .]. . . everything."

400 YOUR FATHER

DialSav 86–87 (§D76)

(86) [. . . said ". . .]. . . speak, I . . .[. . .]. . .."

(87) The Lord said ". . .[. . .]. . . your Father . . .[. . .]. . .."

401 MUCH LEFT OVER

DialSav 88–89 (§D77)

(88) [Mary said, "Of what] sort is that [mustard seed]? Is it something from heaven or is it something from earth?"

(89) The Lord said, "When the Father established the cosmos for himself, he left much over from the Mother of the All. Therefore, he speaks and he acts."

402 THE DISSOLVED WORKS

DialSav 97–98 (§D78)
(97) [Mary] said [to the Lord], "When the works [. . .]. . . . . .[. . . which] dissolves a . . .[. . .]."
(98) [The Lord said, "Right. For] you know [. . .]. . . if I dissolve [. . .]. . . will go to his [place]."

403 SPIRIT AND LIGHT

DialSav 99–102 (§D79)
(99) Judas said, "How is the [spirit] apparent?"
(100) The Lord said, "How [is] the sword [apparent]?"
(101) [Judas] said, "How is the [light] apparent?"
(102) The Lord said, ". . .[. . .] in it forever."

404 UNDERSTANDING THE WORKS

DialSav 103–104 (§D80)
(103) [Judas] said, "Who forgives the [works] of whom? [The works] which . . .[. . .] the cosmos [. . .]. . .[. . . who] forgives the [works]."
(104) The Lord [said], "[Who . . .]. . .? It behooves whomever has understood [the works] to do the [will] of the Father. And as for [you, strive] to rid [yourselves] of [anger] and [jealousy], and [to strip] yourselves of your [. . .]. . .s, and not to . . .[. . .] [. . .]. . . [. . .]. . . [. . .]. . . [. . .]. . . [. . .]. . . [. . .]. . . reproach [. . .]. For I say . . . [. . .]. . . you take . . . [. . .]. . . you . . . [. . .] who has sought, having [. . .]. . . this, will . . .[. . .] he will live [forever. And] I say to [you . . .]. . . so that you will not lead [your] spirits and your souls into error."

405 WHY BE BAPTIZED?

GNaz 2 (§D81)
(2) Behold, the mother of the Lord and his brethren said to him: John the Baptist baptizes unto the remission of sins, let us go and be baptized by him. But he said to them: Wherein have I sinned that I should go and be baptized by him? Unless what I have said is ignorance (a sin of ignorance). (Jerome, *Adversus Pelagianos* 3.2)

Ἰησοῦς

STORIES

406 KINGDOM AND REPENTANCE*

Matt 3:1–6 (§S1.1)

[1] In those days came John the Baptist, preaching in the wilderness of Judea, [2] "Repent, for the kingdom of heaven is at hand." [3] For this is he who was spoken of by the prophet Isaiah when he said,

"The voice of one crying in the wilderness:
Prepare the way of the Lord,
make his paths straight."

[4] Now John wore a garment of camel's hair, and a leather girdle around his waist; and his food was locusts and wild honey. [5] Then went out to him Jerusalem and all Judea and all the region about the Jordan, [6] and they were baptized by him in the river Jordan, confessing their sins.

* See 34: *Kingdom and Repentance*

Matt 4:12–17 (§S1.2)

[12] Now when he heard that John had been arrested, he withdrew into Galilee; [13] and leaving Nazareth he went and dwelt in Capernaum by the sea, in the territory of Zebulun and Naphtali, [14] that what was spoken by the prophet Isaiah might be fulfilled:

[15] "The land of Zebulun and the land of Naphtali,
toward the sea, across the Jordan,
Galilee of the Gentiles—
[16] the people who sat in darkness
have seen a great light,
and for those who sat in the region and shadow of death
light has dawned."

[17] From that time Jesus began to preach, saying, "Repent, for the kingdom of heaven is at hand."

Mark 1:14–15 (§S1.3)

[14] Now after John was arrested Jesus came into Galilee, preaching the gospel of God, [15] and saying, "The time is fulfilled, and the kingdom of God is at hand; repent, and believe in the gospel."

407 TREE CUT DOWN*

Matt 3:7–10 (§S2.1)

[7] But when he saw many of the Pharisees and Sadducees coming for baptism, he said to them, "You brood of vipers! Who warned you to flee from the wrath to come? [8] Bear fruit that befits repentance, [9] and do not presume to say to yourselves, 'We have Abraham as our father'; for I tell you, God is able from these stones to raise up children to Abraham. [10] Even now the axe is laid to the root of the trees; every tree therefore that does not bear good fruit is cut down and thrown into the fire."

Matt 7:15–20 (§S2.2)

[15] "Beware of false prophets, who come to you in sheep's clothing but inwardly are ravenous wolves. [16] You will know them by their fruits. Are grapes gathered from thorns, or figs from thistles? [17] So, every sound tree bears good fruit, but the bad tree bears evil fruit. [18] A sound tree cannot bear evil fruit, nor can a bad tree bear good fruit. [19] Every tree that does not bear good fruit is cut down and thrown into the fire. [20] Thus you will know them by their fruits."

* See 35: *Tree Cut Down*

Luke 3:7–9 (§S2.3)

[7] He said therefore to the multitudes that came out to be baptized by him, "You brood of vipers! Who warned you to flee from the wrath to come? [8] Bear fruits that befit repentance, and do not begin to say to yourselves, 'We have Abraham as our father'; for I tell you, God is able from these stones to raise up children to Abraham. [9] Even now the axe is laid to the root of the trees; every tree therefore that does not bear good fruit is cut down and thrown into the fire."

Matt 3:13–17 (§S3.1)

[13] Then Jesus came from Galilee to the Jordan to John, to be baptized by him. [14] John would have prevented him, saying, "I need to be baptized by you, and do you come to me?" [15] But Jesus answered him, "Let it be so now; for thus it is fitting for us to fulfil all righteousness." Then he consented. [16] And when Jesus was baptized, he went up immediately from the water, and behold, the heavens were opened and he saw the Spirit of God descending like a dove, and alighting on him; [17] and lo, a voice from heaven, saying, "This is my beloved Son, with whom I am well pleased."

Ign Smyr 1:1–2 (§S3.2)

[1] I give glory to Jesus Christ, the God who has thus given you wisdom; for I have observed that you are established in immoveable faith, as if nailed to the cross of the Lord Jesus Christ, both in flesh and spirit, and confirmed in love by the blood of Christ, being fully persuaded as touching our Lord, that he is in truth of the family of David according to the flesh, God's son by the will and power of God, truly born of a Virgin, baptised by John that "all righteousness might be fulfilled by him," [2] truly nailed to a tree in the flesh for our sakes under Pontius Pilate and Herod the Tetrarch, (and of its fruit are we from his divinely blessed Passion) that "he might set up an ensign" for all ages through his Resurrection, for his saints and believers, whether among the Jews, or among the heathen, in one body of his Church.

GEbi 4 (§S3.3)

(4) And after much has been recorded it proceeds:

When the people were baptized, Jesus also came and was baptized by John. And as he came up from the water, the heavens were opened and he saw the Holy Spirit in the form of a dove that descended and entered into him. And a voice (sounded) from heaven that said: Thou art my beloved Son, in thee I am well pleased. And again: I have this day begotten thee. And immediately a great light shone round about the place. When John saw this, it saith, he saith unto him: Who art thou, Lord? And again a voice from heaven (rang out) to him: This is my beloved Son in whom I am well pleased. And then, it saith, John fell down before him and said: I beseech thee, Lord, baptize thou me. But he prevented him and said: Suffer it; for thus it is fitting that everything should be fulfilled. (Epiphanius, *Haer.* 30.13.7f.)

Matt 4:1–4 (§S4.1)

[1] Then Jesus was led up by the Spirit into the wilderness to be tempted by the devil. [2] And he fasted forty days and forty nights, and afterward he was hungry. [3] And the tempter came and said to him, "If you are the Son of God, command these stones to become loaves of bread." [4] But he answered, "It is written,

'Man shall not live by bread alone,
but by every word that proceeds from the mouth of God.'"

Mark 1:12–13 (§S4.2)

[12] The Spirit immediately drove him out into the wilderness. [13] And he was in the wilderness forty days, tempted by Satan; and he was with the wild beasts; and the angels ministered to him.

Luke 4:1–4 (§S4.3)

[1] And Jesus, full of the Holy Spirit, returned from the Jordan, and was led by the Spirit [2] for forty days in the wilderness, tempted by the devil. And he ate nothing in those days; and when they were ended, he was hungry. [3] The devil said to him, "If you are the Son of God, command this stone to become bread." [4] And Jesus answered him, "It is written, 'Man shall not live by bread alone.'"

410 FROM THE PINNACLE

Matt 4:5–7 (§S5.1)

⁵ Then the devil took him to the holy city, and set him on the pinnacle of the temple, ⁶ and said to him, "If you are the Son of God, throw yourself down; for it is written,

 'He will give his angels charge of you,'
and
 'On their hands they will bear you up,
 lest you strike your foot against a stone.'"
⁷ Jesus said to him, "Again it is written, 'You shall not tempt the Lord your God.'"

Luke 4:9–13 (§S5.2)

⁹ And he took him to Jerusalem, and set him on the pinnacle of the temple, and said to him, "If you are the Son of God, throw yourself down from here; ¹⁰ for it is written,

 'He will give his angels charge of you, to
 guard you,'
¹¹ and
 'On their hands they will bear you up,
 lest you strike your foot against a stone.'"
¹² And Jesus answered him, "It is said, 'You shall not tempt the Lord your God.'" ¹³ And when the devil had ended every temptation, he departed from him until an opportune time.

GNaz 3 (§S5.3)

(3) The Jewish Gospel has not "into the holy city" but "to Jerusalem." (Variant to Matthew 4:5 in the "Zion Gospel" Edition)

411 ALL THE KINGDOMS

Matt 4:8–11 (§S6.1)

⁸ Again, the devil took him to a very high mountain, and showed him all the kingdoms of the world and the glory of them; ⁹ and he said to him, "All these I will give you, if you will fall down and worship me." ¹⁰ Then Jesus said to him, "Begone, Satan! for it is written,

 'You shall worship the Lord your God
 and him only shall you serve.'"
¹¹ Then the devil left him, and behold, angels came and ministered to him.

Luke 4:5–7 (§S6.2)

⁵ And the devil took him up, and showed him all the kingdoms of the world in a moment of time, ⁶ and said to him, "To you I will give all this authority and their glory; for it has been delivered to me, and I give it to whom I will. ⁷ If you, then, will worship me, it shall all be yours."

Matt 4:18–22 (§S7.1)

[18] As he walked by the Sea of Galilee, he saw two brothers, Simon who is called Peter and Andrew his brother, casting a net into the sea; for they were fishermen. [19] And he said to them, "Follow me, and I will make you fishers of men." [20] Immediately they left their nets and followed him. [21] And going on from there he saw two other brothers, James the son of Zebedee and John his brother, in the boat with Zebedee their father, mending their nets, and he called them. [22] Immediately they left the boat and their father, and followed him.

Mark 1:16–20 (§S7.2)

[16] And passing along by the Sea of Galilee, he saw Simon and Andrew the brother of Simon casting a net in the sea; for they were fishermen. [17] And Jesus said to them, "Follow me and I will make you become fishers of men." [18] And immediately they left their nets and followed him. [19] And going on a little farther, he saw James the son of Zebedee and John his brother, who were in their boat mending the nets. [20] And immediately he called them; and they left their father Zebedee in the boat with the hired servants, and followed him.

Luke 5:1–11 (§S7.3)

[1] While the people pressed upon him to hear the word of God, he was standing by the lake of Gennesaret. [2] And he saw two boats by the lake; but the fishermen had gone out of them and were washing their nets. [3] Getting into one of the boats, which was Simon's, he asked him to put out a little from the land. And he sat down and taught the people from the boat. [4] And when he had ceased speaking, he said to Simon, "Put out into the deep and let down your nets for a catch." [5] And Simon answered, "Master, we toiled all night and took nothing! But at your word I will let down the nets." [6] And when they had done this, they enclosed a great shoal of fish; and as their nets were breaking, [7] they beckoned to their partners in the other boat to come and help them. And they came and filled both the boats, so that they began to sink. [8] But when Simon Peter saw it, he fell down at Jesus' knees, saying, "Depart from me, for I am a sinful man, O Lord." [9] For he was astonished, and all that were with him, at the catch of fish which they had taken; [10] and so also were James and John, sons of Zebedee, who were partners with Simon. And Jesus said to Simon, "Do not be afraid; henceforth you will be catching men." [11] And when they had brought their boats to land, they left everything and followed him.

John 21:1–14 (§S7.4)

[1] After this Jesus revealed himself again to the disciples by the Sea of Tiberias; and he revealed himself in this way. [2] Simon Peter, Thomas called the Twin, Nathanael of Cana in Galilee, the sons of Zebedee, and two others of his disciples were together. [3] Simon Peter said to them, "I am going fishing." They said to him, "We will go with you." They went out and got into the boat; but that night they caught nothing.

[4] Just as day was breaking, Jesus stood on the beach; yet the disciples did not know that it was Jesus. [5] Jesus said to them, "Children have you any fish?" They answered him, "No." [6] He said to them, "Cast the net on the right side of the boat, and you will find some." So they cast it, and now they were not able to haul it in, for the quantity of fish. [7] That disciple whom Jesus loved said to Peter, "It is the Lord!" When Simon Peter heard that it was the Lord, he put on his clothes, for he was stripped for work, and sprang into the sea. [8] But the other disciples came in the boat, dragging the net full of fish, for they were not far from the land, but about a hundred yards off.

[9] When they got out on land, they saw a charcoal fire there, with fish lying on it, and bread. [10] Jesus said to them, "Bring some of the fish that you have just caught." [11] So Simon Peter went aboard and hauled the net ashore, full of large fish, a hundred and fifty-three of them; and although there were so many, the net was not torn. [12] Jesus said to them, "Come and have breakfast." Now none of the disciples dared ask him, "Who are you?" They knew it was the Lord. [13] Jesus came and took the bread and gave it to them, and so with the fish. [14] This was now the third time that Jesus was revealed to the disciples after he was raised from the dead.

GEbi 1 (§S7.5)

(1) In the Gospel that is in general use amongst them, which is called according to Matthew, which however is not whole (and) complete but forged and mutilated— they call it the Hebrew Gospel—it is reported:

There appeared a certain man named Jesus of about thirty years of age, who chose us. And when he came to Capernaum, he entered into the house of Simon whose surname was Peter, and opened his mouth and said: As I passed along the Lake of Tiberias, I chose John and James the sons of Zebedee, and Simon and Andrew and Thaddaeus and Simon the Zealot and Judas Iscariot, and thee, Matthew, I called as thou didst sit at the receipt of custom, and thou didst follow me. You therefore I will to be twelve apostles for a testimony unto Israel. (Epiphanius, *Haer.* 30.13.2f.)

Matt 4:23 (§S8.1)

[23] And he went about all Galilee teaching in their synagogues and preaching the gospel of the kingdom and healing every disease and every infirmity among the people.

Matt 9:35 (§S8.2)

[35] And Jesus went about all the cities and villages, teaching in their synagogues and preaching the gospel of the kingdom, and healing every disease and every infirmity.

Mark 1:35–39 (§S8.3)

[35] And in the morning, a great while before day, he rose and went out to a lonely place, and there he prayed. [36] And Simon and those who were with him pursued him, [37] and they found him and said to him, "Every one is searching for you." [38] And he said to them, "Let us go on to the next towns, that I may preach there also; for that is why I came out." [39] And he went throughout all Galilee, preaching in their synagogues and casting out demons.

Luke 4:42–44 (§S8.4)

[42] And when it was day he departed and went into a lonely place. And the people sought him and came to him, and would have kept him from leaving them; [43] but he said to them, "I must preach the good news of the kingdom of God to the other cities also; for I was sent for this purpose." [44] And he was preaching in the synagogues of Judea.

Matt 5:14a (§S9.1)

14 "You are the light of the world."

John 8:12–16 (§S9.2)

12 Again Jesus spoke to them, saying, "I am the light of the world; he who follows me will not walk in darkness, but will have the light of life." 13 The Pharisees then said to him, "You are bearing witness to yourself; your testimony is not true." 14 Jesus answered, "Even if I do bear witness to myself, my testimony is true, for I know whence I have come and whither I am going, but you do not know whence I come or whither I am going. 15 You judge according to the flesh, I judge no one. 16 Yet even if I do judge, my judgment is true, for it is not I alone that judge, but I and he who sent me."

John 11:5–16 (§S9.4)

5 Now Jesus loved Martha and her sister and Lazarus. 6 So when he heard that he was ill, he stayed two days longer in the place where he was. 7 Then after this he said to the disciples, "Let us go into Judea again." 8 The disciples said to him, "Rabbi, the Jews were but now seeking to stone you, and are you going there again?" 9 Jesus answered, "Are there not twelve hours in the day? If any one walks in the day, he does not stumble, because he sees the light of this world. 10 But if any one walks in the night, he stumbles, because the light is not in him." 11 Thus he spoke, and then he said to them, "Our friend Lazarus has fallen asleep, but I go to awake him out of sleep." 12 The disciples said to him, "Lord, if he has fallen asleep, he will recover." 13 Now Jesus had spoken of his death, but they thought that he meant taking rest in sleep. 14 Then Jesus told them plainly, "Lazarus is dead; 15 and for your sake I am glad that I was not there, so that you may believe. But let us go to him." 16 Thomas, called the Twin, said to his fellow disciples, "Let us also go, that we may die with him."

John 12:27–36 (§S9.5)

27 "Now is my soul troubled. And what shall I say? 'Father, save me from this hour'? No, for this purpose I have come to this hour. 28 Father, glorify thy name." Then a voice came from heaven, "I have glorified it, and I will glorify it again." 29 The crowd standing by heard it and said that it had thundered. Others said, "An angel has spoken to him." 30 Jesus answered, "This voice has come for your sake, not for mine. 31 Now is the judgment of this world, now shall the ruler of this world be cast out; 32 and I, when I am lifted up from the earth, will draw all men to myself." 33 He said this to show by what death he was to die. 34 The crowd answered him, "We have heard from the law that the Christ remains for ever. How can you say that the Son of man must be lifted up? Who is this Son of man?" 35 Jesus said to them, "The light is with you for a little longer. Walk while you have the light, lest the darkness overtake you; he who walks in the darkness does not know where he goes. 36 While you have the light, believe in the light, that you may become sons of light."

When Jesus had said this, he departed and hid himself from them.

POxy655 24 (§S9.6)

(24) 3 [. . . There is light within a man] of light, [and he (or: it) lights up the whole] world. [If he (or: it) does not shine, he (or: it)] is [darkness].

GThom 24 (§S9.7)

(24) 1 His disciples said to Him, "Show us the place where You are, since it is necessary for us to seek it."

2 He said to them, "Whoever has ears, let him hear." 3 There is light within a man of light, and he (or: it) lights up the whole world. If he (or: it) does not shine, he (or: it) is darkness."

DialSav 14 (§S9.8)

(14) The Lord said, "[. . .] weep on account of its works [. . .] remain and the mind laughs [. . .]. . .[. . .] [. . .]. . . spirit. If one does not [. . .] darkness, he will be able to see [. . .]. So I tell you [. . .] light is the darkness [. . .]. . . stand in [. . .] not see the light [. . .] the lie [. . .]. . . they brought them from [. . .]. . .[. . .]. . . . You will give [. . .]. . . and [. . . exist] forever. [. . .]. . . [. . .]. . . [. . .] ever. Then [all] the powers which are above as well as those [below] will [. . .] you. In that place [there will] be weeping and [gnashing] of teeth over the end of [all] these things."

DialSav 34 (§S9.9)

(34) He [said] to them, "That which supports [the earth] is that which supports the heaven. When a Word comes forth from the Greatness, it will come on what supports the heaven and the earth. For the earth does not move. Were it to move, it would fall, though in order that the First Word might not fail. For it was that which established the cosmos and inhabited it and inhaled fragrance from it. For, . . .[. . .]. . . which do not move I [. . .]. . . you, all the sons of [men. For] you are from [that] place. [In] the hearts of those who speak out of [joy] and truth you exist. Even if it comes forth in [the body] of the Father among men and is not received, still it [does] return to its place. Whoever [does not] know [the work] of perfection [knows] nothing. If one does not stand in the darkness, he will not be able to see the light."

★ See 45 & 325: *The World's Light*

415

THE LORD'S PRAYER*

Matt 6:9–13 (§S10.1)
[9] Pray then like this:
Our Father who art in heaven,
Hallowed be thy name.
[10] Thy kingdom come,
Thy will be done,
On earth as it is in heaven.
[11] Give us this day our daily bread;
[12] And forgive us our debts,
As we also have forgiven our debtors;
[13] And lead us not into temptation,
But deliver us from evil.

Luke 11:1–4 (§S10.2)
[1] He was praying in a certain place, and when he ceased, one of his disciples said to him, "Lord teach us to pray, as John taught his disciples." [2] And he said to them, "When you pray, say:
"Father, hallowed be thy name. Thy kingdom come. [3] Give us each day our daily bread; [4] and forgive us our sins, for we ourselves forgive every one who is indebted to us; and lead us not into temptation."

* See 70: *The Lord's Prayer*

Did 8:2–3 (§S10.3)
[2] And do not pray as the hypocrites, but as the Lord commanded in his Gospel, pray thus: "Our Father, who are in Heaven, hallowed by thy Name, thy Kingdon come, thy will be done, as in Heaven so also upon earth; give us to-day our daily bread, and forgive us our debt as we forgive our debtors, and lead us not into trial, but deliver us from the Evil One, for thine is the power and the glory for ever." [3] Pray thus three times a day.

GNaz 5 (§S10.4)
(5) In the so-called Gospel according to the Hebrews instead of "essential to existence" I found *"maḥar,"* which means "of tomorrow," so that the sense is:
Our bread of tomorrow—that is, of the future—give us this day. (Jerome, *Commentary on Matthew* 1 [on Matthew 6:11])

416

THE NARROW DOOR*

Matt 7:13–14 (§S11.1)
[13] "Enter by the narrow gate; for the gate is wide and the way is easy, that leads to destruction, and those who enter by it are many. [14] For the gate is narrow and the way is hard, that leads to life, and those who find it are few."

* See 88: *The Narrow Door*

Luke 13:22–24 (§S11.2)
[22] He went on his way through towns and villages, teaching, and journeying toward Jerusalem. [23] And some one said to him, "Lord, will those who are saved be few?" And he said to them, [24] "Strive to enter by the narrow door; for many, I tell you, will seek to enter and will not be able."

417

Matt 7:21 (§S12.1)

[21] "Not every one who says to me, 'Lord, Lord,' shall enter the kingdom of heaven, but he who does the will of my Father who is in heaven."

Luke 6:46 (§S12.2)

[46] "Why do you call me 'Lord, Lord,' and not do what I tell you?"

PEger2 3 (§S12.3)

(3) . . . [ca]me to him to put him to the pro[of] and to tempt him, whilst [they said]: "Master Jesus, we know that thou art come [from God], for what thou doest bears a tes-t[imony] (to thee which goes) beyond (that) of all the prophets. [Wherefore tell] us: is it admissible [to p]ay to the kings the (charges) appertaining to their rule? [Should we] pay [th]em or not?" But Jesus saw through their [in]tention, became [angry] and said to them: "Why call ye me

with yo[ur mou]th Master and yet [do] not what I say? Well has Is[aiah] prophesied [concerning y]ou saying: This [people honours] me with the[ir li]ps but their heart is far from me; [their worship is] vain. [They teach] precepts [of men]." (Fragment 2, recto [lines 43–59])

2 Clem 3:1–5 (§S12.4)

[1] Seeing, then, that he has shewn such mercy towards us, first that we who are living do not sacrifice to the dead gods, and do not worship them, but through him know the father of truth, what is the true knowledge concerning him except that we should not deny him through whom we knew him? [2] And he himself also says, "Whosoever confessed me before men, I will confess him before my Father"; [3] this then is our reward, if we confess him through whom we were saved. [4] But how do we confess him? By doing what he says, and

not disregarding his commandments, and honouring him not only with our lips, but "with all our heart and all our mind." [5] And he says also in Isaiah, "This people honoureth me with their lips, but their heart is far from me."

2 Clem 4:1–3 (§S12.5)

[1] Let us, then, not merely call him Lord, for this will not save us. [2] For he says, "Not everyone that saith to me Lord, Lord, shall be saved, but he that doeth righteousness." [3] So then, brethren, let us confess him in our deeds, by loving one another, by not committing adultery, nor speaking one against another, nor being jealous, but by being self-controlled, merciful, good; and we ought to sympathise with each other, and not to be lovers of money. By these deeds we confess him, and not by the opposite kind.

* See 91: *Invocation Without Obedience*

418

THE CENTURION'S FAITH

Matt 8:5–13 (§S13.1)

[5] As he entered Capernaum, a centurion came forward to him, beseeching him [6] and saying, "Lord, my servant is lying paralyzed at home, in terrible distress." [7] And he said to him, "I will come and heal him." [8] But the centurion answered him, "Lord, I am not worthy to have you come under my roof; but only say the word, and my servant will be healed. [9] For I am a man under authority, with soldiers under me; and I say to one, 'Go,' and he goes, and to another, 'Come,' and he comes, and to my slave, 'Do this,' and he does it." [10] When Jesus heard him, he marveled, and said to those who followed him, "Truly, I say to you, not even in Israel have I found such faith. [11] I tell you, many will come from east and west and sit at table with Abraham, Isaac, and Jacob in the kingdom of heaven, [12] while the sons of the kingdom will be thrown into the outer darkness; there men will weep and gnash their teeth."
[13] And to the centurion Jesus said, "Go; be it done for you as you have believed." And the servant was healed at that very moment.

Luke 7:1–10 (§S13.2)

[1] After he had ended all his sayings in the hearing of the people he entered Capernaum. [2] Now a centurion had a slave who was dear to him, who was sick and at the point of death. [3] When he heard of Jesus, he sent to him elders of the Jews, asking him to come and heal his slave. [4] And when they came to Jesus, they besought him earnestly, saying, "He is worthy to have you do this for him, [5] for he loves our nation, and he built us our synagogue." [6] And Jesus went with them. When he was not far from the house, the centurion sent friends to him, saying to him, "Lord, do not trouble yourself, for I am not worthy to have you come under my roof; [7] therefore I did not presume to come to you. But say the word, and let my servant be healed. [8] For I am a man set under authority, with soldiers under me: and I say to one, 'Go,' and he goes; and to another, 'Come,' and he comes; and to my slave, 'Do this,' and he does it." [9] When Jesus heard this he marveled at him, and turned and said to the multitude that followed him, "I tell you, not even in Israel have I found such faith." [10] And when those who had been sent returned to the house, they found the slave well.

John 4:46–53 (§S13.3)

[46] So he came again to Cana in Galilee, where he had made the water wine. And at Capernaum there was an official whose son was ill. [47] When he heard that Jesus had come from Judea to Galilee, he went and begged him to come down and heal his son, for he was at the point of death. [48] Jesus therefore said to him, "Unless you see signs and wonders you will not believe." [49] The official said to him, "Sir, come down before my child dies." [50] Jesus said to him, "Go; your son will live." The man believed the word that Jesus spoke to him and went his way. [51] As he was going down, his servants met him and told him that his son was living. [52] So he asked them the hour when he began to mend, and they said to him, "Yesterday at the seventh hour the fever left him." [53] The father knew that was the hour when Jesus had said to him, "Your son will live"; and he himself believed, and all his household.

Mark 8:5–13 (§S14.1)

⁵And he asked them, "How many loaves have you?" They said, "Seven." ⁶And he commanded the crowd to sit down on the ground; and he took the seven loaves, and having given thanks he broke them and gave them to his disciples to set before the people; and they set them before the crowd. ⁷And they had a few small fish; and having blessed them, he commanded that these also should be set before them. ⁸And they ate, and were satisfied; and they took up the broken pieces left over, seven baskets full. ⁹And there were about four thousand people. ¹⁰And he sent them away and immediately he got into the boat with his disciples, and went to the district of Dalmanutha.

¹¹The Pharisees came and began to argue with him, seeking from him a sign from heaven, to test him. ¹²And he sighed deeply in his spirit, and said, "Why does this generation seek a sign? Truly, I say to you, no sign shall be given to this generation." ¹³And he left them, and getting into the boat again he departed to the other side.

Luke 13:22–29 (§S14.2)

²²He went on his way through towns and villages, teaching, and journeying toward Jerusalem. ²³And some one said to him, "Lord, will those who are saved be few?" And he said to them, ²⁴"Strive to enter by the narrow door; for many, I tell you, will seek to enter and will not be able. ²⁵When once the householder has risen up and shut the door, you will begin to stand outside and to knock at the door, saying, 'Lord, open to us.' He will answer you, 'I do not know where you come from.' ²⁶Then you will begin to say, 'We ate and drank in your presence, and you taught in our streets.' ²⁷But he will say, 'I tell you, I do not know where you come from; depart from me, all you workers of iniquity!' ²⁸There you will weep and gnash your teeth, when you see Abraham and Isaac and Jacob and all the prophets in the kingdom of God and you yourselves thrust out. ²⁹And men will come from east and west, and from north and south, and sit at table in the kingdom of God."

2 Esdr 1:28–40 (§S14.3)

²⁸"Thus says the Lord Almighty: Have I not entreated you as a father entreats his sons or a mother her daughters or a nurse her children, ²⁹that you should be my people and I should be your God, and that you should be my sons and I should be your father? ³⁰I gathered you as a hen gathers her brood under her wings. But now, what shall I do to you? I will cast you out from my presence. ³¹When you offer oblations to me, I will turn my face from you; for I have rejected your feast days, and new moons, and circumcisions of the flesh. ³²I sent to you my servants the prophets, but you have taken and slain them and torn their bodies in pieces; their blood I will require of you, says the Lord.

³³"Thus says the Lord Almighty: Your house is desolate; I will drive you out as the wind drives straw; ³⁴and your sons will have no children, because with you they have neglected my commandment and have done what is evil in my sight. ³⁵I will give your houses to a people that will come, who without having heard me will believe. Those to whom I have shown no signs will do what I have commanded. ³⁶They have seen no prophets, yet will recall their former state. ³⁷I call to witness the gratitude of the people that is to come, whose children rejoice with gladness; though they do not see me with bodily eyes, yet with the spirit they will believe the things I have said.

³⁸"And now, father, look with pride and see the people coming from the east; ³⁹to them I will give as leaders Abraham, Isaac, and Jacob and Hose'a and Amos and Micah and Jo'el and Obadi'ah and Jonah ⁴⁰and Nahum and Habak'kuk, Zephani'ah, Haggai, Zechari'ah and Mal'achi, who is also called the Messenger of the Lord."

* See 94: *Patriarchs and Gentiles*

Matt 8:18–20 (§S15.1)

¹⁸Now when Jesus saw great crowds around him, he gave orders to go over to the other side. ¹⁹And a scribe came up and said to him, "Teacher, I will follow you wherever you go." ²⁰And Jesus said to him, "Foxes have holes, and birds of the air have nests; but the Son of man has nowhere to lay his head."

Luke 9:57–58 (§S15.2)

⁵⁷As they were going along the road, a man said to him, "I will follow you wherever you go." ⁵⁸And Jesus said to him, "Foxes have holes, and birds of the air have nests; but the Son of man has nowhere to lay his head."

GThom 86 (§S15.3)

(86) Jesus said, "[The foxes have their holes] and the birds have [their] nests, but the Son of Man has no place to lay his head and rest."

* See 96: *Foxes Have Holes*

Matt 9:1–8 (§S16.1)

[1] And getting into a boat he crossed over and came to his own city. [2] And behold, they brought to him a paralytic, lying on his bed; and when Jesus saw their faith he said to the paralytic, "Take heart, my son; your sins are forgiven." [3] And behold, some of the scribes said to themselves, "This man is blaspheming." [4] But Jesus, knowing their thoughts, said, "Why do you think evil in your hearts? [5] For which is easier, to say, 'Your sins are forgiven,' or to say, 'Rise and walk'? [6] But that you may know that the Son of man has authority on earth to forgive sins"—he then said to the paralytic— "Rise, take up your bed and go home." [7] And he rose and went home. [8] When the crowds saw it, they were afraid, and they glorified God, who had given such authority to men.

Mark 2:1–12 (§S16.2)

[1] And when he returned to Capernaum after some days, it was reported that he was at home. [2] And many were gathered together, so that there was no longer room for them, not even about the door; and he was preaching the word to them. [3] And they came, bringing to him a paralytic carried by four men. [4] And when they could not get near him because of the crowd, they removed the roof above him; and when they had made an opening, they let down the pallet on which the paralytic lay. [5] And when Jesus saw their faith, he said to the paralytic, "My son, your sins are forgiven." [6] Now some of the scribes were sitting there, questioning in their hearts, [7] "Why does this man speak thus? It is blasphemy! Who can forgive sins but God alone?" [8] And immediately Jesus, perceiving in his spirit that they thus questioned within themselves, said to them, "Why do you question thus in your hearts? [9] Which is easier, to say to the paralytic, 'Your sins are forgiven,' or to say, 'Rise, take up your pallet and walk'? [10] But that you may know that the Son of man has authority on earth to forgive sins"—he said to the paralytic— [11] "I say to you, rise, take up your pallet and go home." [12] And he rose, and immediately took up the pallet and went out before them all; so that they were all amazed and glorified God, saying, "We never saw anything like this!"

Luke 5:17–26 (§S16.3)

[17] On one of those days, as he was teaching, there were Pharisees and teachers of the law sitting by, who had come from every village of Galilee and Judea and from Jerusalem; and the power of the Lord was with him to heal. [18] And behold, men were bringing on a bed a man who was paralyzed, and they sought to bring him in and lay him before Jesus; [19] but finding no way to bring him in, because of the crowd, they went up on the roof and let him down with his bed through the tiles into the midst before Jesus. [20] And when he saw their faith he said, "Man, your sins are forgiven you." [21] And the scribes and the Pharisees began to question, saying, "Who is this that speaks blasphemies? Who can forgive sins but God only?" [22] When Jesus perceived their questionings, he answered them, "Why do you question in your hearts? [23] Which is easier, to say, 'Your sins are forgiven you,' or to say, 'Rise and walk'? [24] But that you may know that the Son of man has authority on earth to forgive sins"—he said to the man who was paralyzed—"I say to you, rise, take up your bed and go home." [25] And immediately he rose before them, and took up that on which he lay, and went home, glorifying God. [26] And amazement seized them all, and they glorified God and were filled with awe, saying, "We have seen strange things today."

John 5:1–9 (§S16.4)

[1] After this there was a feast of the Jews, and Jesus went up to Jerusalem.

[2] Now there is in Jerusalem by the Sheep Gate a pool, in Hebrew called Bethzatha, which has five porticoes. [3] In these lay a multitude of invalids, blind, lame, paralyzed. [5] One man was there, who had been ill for thirty-eight years. [6] When Jesus saw him and knew that he had been lying there a long time, he said to him, "Do you want to be healed?" [7] The sick man answered him, "Sir, I have no man to put me into the pool when the water is troubled, and while I am going another steps down before me." [8] Jesus said to him, "Rise, take up your pallet, and walk." [9] And at once the man was healed, and he took up his pallet and walked.

Now that day was the sabbath.

422 TAX COLLECTOR CALLED

Matt 9:9 (§S17.1)

[9] As Jesus passed on from there, he saw a man called Matthew sitting at the tax office; and he said to him, "Follow me." And he rose and followed him.

Mark 2:13–14 (§S17.2)

[13] He went out again beside the sea; and all the crowd gathered about him, and he taught them. [14] And as he passed on, he saw Levi the son of Alphaeus sitting at the tax office, and he said to him, "Follow me." And he rose and followed him.

Luke 5:27–28 (§S17.3)

[27] After this he went out, and saw a tax collector, named Levi, sitting at the tax office; and he said to him, "Follow me." [28] And he left everything, and rose and followed him.

GEbi 1 (§S17.4)

(1) In the Gospel that is in general use amongst them, which is called according to Matthew, which however is not whole (and) complete but forged and mutilated—they call it the Hebrew Gospel—it is reported:

There appeared a certain man named Jesus of about thirty years of age, who chose us. And when he came to Capernaum, he entered into the house of Simon whose surname was Peter, and opened his mouth and said: As I passed along the Lake of Tiberias, I chose John and James the sons of Zebedee, and Simon and Andrew and Thaddaeus and Simon the Zealot and Judas Iscariot, and thee, Matthew, I called as thou didst sit at the receipt of custom, and thou didst follow me. You therefore I will to be twelve apostles for a testimony unto Israel. (Epiphanius, *Haer.* 30.13.2f.)

Matt 9:10–13 (§S18.1)

[10] And as he sat at table in the house, behold, many tax collectors and sinners came and sat down with Jesus and his disciples. [11] And when the Pharisees saw this, they said to his disciples, "Why does your teacher eat with tax collectors and sinners?" [12] But when he heard it, he said, "Those who are well have no need of a physician, but those who are sick. [13] Go and learn what this means, 'I desire mercy, and not sacrifice.' For I came not to call the righteous, but sinners."

Mark 2:15–17 (§S18.2)

[15] And as he sat at table in his house, many tax collectors and sinners were sitting with Jesus and his disciples; for there were many who followed him. [16] And the scribes of the Pharisees, when they saw that he was eating with sinners and tax collectors, said to his disciples, "Why does he eat with tax collectors and sinners?" [17] And when Jesus heard it, he said to them, "Those who are well have no need of a physician, but those who are sick; I came not to call the righteous, but sinners."

Luke 5:29–32 (§S18.3)

[29] And Levi made him a great feast in his house; and there was a large company of tax collectors and others sitting at table with them. [30] And the Pharisees and their scribes murmured against his disciples, saying, "Why do you eat and drink with tax collectors and sinners?" [31] And Jesus answered them, "Those who are well have no need of a physician, but those who are sick; [32] I have not come to call the righteous, but sinners to repentance."

Luke 19:1–10 (§S18.4)

[1] He entered Jericho and was passing through. [2] And there was a man named Zacchaeus; he was a chief tax collector, and rich. [3] And he sought to see who Jesus was, but could not, on account of the crowd, because he was small of stature. [4] So he ran on ahead and climbed up into a sycamore tree to see him, for he was to pass that way. [5] And when Jesus came to the place, he looked up and said to him, "Zacchaeus, make haste and come down; for I must stay at your house today." [6] So he made haste and came down, and received him joyfully. [7] And when they saw it they all murmured, "He has gone in to be the guest of a man who is a sinner." [8] And Zacchaeus stood and said to the Lord, "Behold, Lord, the half of my goods I give to the poor; and if I have defrauded any one of anything, I restore it fourfold." [9] And Jesus said to him, "Today salvation has come to this house, since he also is a son of Abraham. [10] For the Son of man came to seek and to save the lost."

1 Tim 1:12–17 (§S18.5)

[12] I thank him who has given me strength for this, Christ Jesus our Lord, because he judged me faithful by appointing me to his service, [13] though I formerly blasphemed and persecuted and insulted him; but I received mercy because I had acted ignorantly in unbelief, [14] and the grace of our Lord overflowed for me with the faith and love that are in Christ Jesus. [15] The saying is sure and worthy of full acceptance, that Christ Jesus came into the world to save sinners. And I am the foremost of sinners; [16] but I received mercy for this reason, that in me, as the foremost, Jesus Christ might display his perfect patience for an example to those who were to believe in him for eternal life. [17] To the King of ages, immortal, invisible, the only God, be honor and glory for ever and ever. Amen.

POxy1224 1 (§S18.6)

(1) And the scribes and [Pharisees] and priests, when they sa[w] him, were angry [that with sin] ners in the midst he [reclined] at table. But Jesus heard [it and said:] The he[althy need not the physician.] . . .

2 Clem 2:4–7 (§S18.7)

[4] And another Scripture also says, "I came not to call righteous, but sinners"; [5] He means that those who are perishing must be saved, [6] for it is great and wonderful to give strength, not to the things which are standing, but to those which are falling. [7] So Christ also willed to save the perishing, and he saved many, coming and calling us who were already perishing.

Barn 5:8–9 (§S18.8)

[8] Furthermore, while teaching Israel and doing such great signs and wonders he preached to them and loved them greatly; [9] but when he chose out his own Apostles who were to preach his Gospel, he chose those who were iniquitous above all sin to show that "he came not to call the righteous but sinners,"—then he manifested himself as God's Son.

* See 97: *Righteous and Sinners*

Matt 9:32–34 (§S19.1)

[32] As they were going away, behold, a dumb demoniac was brought to him. [33] And when the demon had been cast out, the dumb man spoke; and the crowds marveled, saying, "Never was anything like this seen in Israel." [34] But the Pharisees said, "He casts out demons by the prince of demons."

Matt 12:22–26 (§S19.2)

[22] Then a blind and dumb demoniac was brought to him, and he healed him, so that the dumb man spoke and saw. [23] And all the people were amazed, and said, "Can this be the Son of David?" [24] But when the Pharisees heard it they said, "It is only by Beelzebul, the prince of demons, that this man casts out demons." [25] Knowing their thoughts, he said to them, "Every kingdom divided against itself is laid waste, and no city or house divided against itself will stand; [26] and if Satan casts out Satan, he is divided against himself; how then will his kingdom stand?"

Mark 3:22–26 (§S19.3)

[22] And the scribes who came down from Jerusalem said, "He is possessed by Beelzebul, and by the prince of demons he casts out the demons." [23] And he called them to him, and said to them in parables, "How can Satan cast out Satan? [24] If a kingdom is divided against itself, that kingdom cannot stand. [25] And if a house is divided against itself, that house will not be able to stand. [26] And if Satan has risen up against himself and is divided, he cannot stand, but is coming to an end."

Luke 11:14–18 (§S19.4)

[14] Now he was casting out a demon that was dumb; when the demon had gone out, the dumb man spoke, and the people marveled. [15] But some of them said, "He casts out demons by Beelzebul, the prince of demons"; [16] while others, to test him, sought from him a sign from heaven. [17] But he, knowing their thoughts, said to them, "Every kingdom divided against itself is laid waste, and a divided household falls. [18] And if Satan also is divided against himself, how will his kingdom stand? For you say that I cast out demons by Beelzebul."

Matt 9:35–38 (§S20.1)

[35] And Jesus went about all the cities and villages, teaching in their synagogues and preaching the gospel of the kingdom, and healing every disease and every infirmity. [36] When he saw the crowds, he had compassion for them, because they were harassed and helpless, like sheep without a shepherd. [37] Then he said to his disciples, "The harvest is plentiful, but the laborers are few; [38] pray therefore the Lord of the harvest to send out laborers into his harvest."

★ See 99: *Harvest is Great*

Luke 10:1–2 (§S20.2)

[1] After this the Lord appointed seventy others, and sent them on ahead of him, two by two, into every town and place where he himself was about to come. [2] And he said to them, "The harvest is plentiful, but the laborers are few; pray therefore the Lord of the harvest to send out laborers into his harvest."

John 4:35–38 (§S20.3)

[35] "Do you not say, 'There are yet four months, then comes the harvest'? I tell you, lift up your eyes, and see how the fields are already white for harvest. [36] He who reaps receives wages, and gathers fruit for eternal life, so that sower and reaper may rejoice together. [37] For here the saying holds true, 'One sows and another reaps.' [38] I sent you to reap that for which you did not labor; others have labored, and you have entered into their labor."

GThom 73 (§S20.4)

(73) Jesus said, "The harvest is great but the laborers are few. Beseech the Lord, therefore, to send out laborers to the harvest."

Matt 10:1–6 (§S21.1)

[1] And he called to him his twelve disciples and gave them authority over unclean spirits, to cast them out, and to heal every disease and every infirmity. [2] The names of the twelve apostles are these: first, Simon, who is called Peter, and Andrew his brother; James the son of Zebedee, and John his brother; [3] Philip and Bartholomew; Thomas and Matthew the tax collector; James the son of Alphaeus, and Thaddaeus; [4] Simon the Cananaean, and Judas Iscariot, who betrayed him. [5] These twelve Jesus sent out, charging them, "Go nowhere among the Gentiles, and enter no town of the Samaritans, [6] but go rather to the lost sheep of the house of Israel."

Matt 15:21–28 (§S21.2)

[21] And Jesus went away from there and withdrew to the district of Tyre and Sidon. [22] And behold, a Canaanite woman from that region came out and cried, "Have mercy on me, O Lord, Son of David; my daughter is severely possessed by a demon." [23] But he did not answer her a word. And his disciples came and begged him, saying, "Send her away, for she is crying after us." [24] He answered, "I was sent only to the lost sheep of the house of Israel." [25] But she came and knelt before him, saying, "Lord, help me." [26] And he answered, "It is not fair to take the children's bread and throw it to the dogs." [27] She said, "Yes, Lord, yet even the dogs eat the crumbs that fall from their master's table." [28] Then Jesus answered her, "O woman, great is your faith! Be it done for you as you desire." And her daughter was healed instantly.

★ See 100: *Israel's Lost Sheep*

427 MISSION BY DISCIPLES*

Matt 10:7–8 (§S22.1)
[7] "And preach as you go, saying, 'The kingdom of heaven is at hand.' [8] Heal the sick, raise the dead, cleanse lepers, cast out demons. You received without paying, give without pay."

Mark 6:12–13 (§S22.2)
[12] So they went out and preached that men should repent. [13] And they cast out many demons, and anointed with oil many that were sick and healed them.

Luke 9:6 (§S22.3)
[6] And they departed and went through the villages, preaching the gospel and healing everywhere.

* See 101: *Mission by Disciples*
* See 102: *Give Without Pay*

428 HATING ONE'S FAMILY*

Matt 10:34–38 (§S23.1)
[34] "Do not think that I have come to bring peace on earth; I have not come to bring peace, but a sword. [35] For I have come to set a man against his father, and a daughter against her mother, and a daughter-in-law against her mother-in-law; [36] and a man's foes will be those of his own household. [37] He who loves father or mother more than me is not worthy of me; and he who loves son or daughter more than me is not worthy of me; [38] and he who does not take his cross and follow me is not worthy of me."

Luke 14:25–27 (§S23.2)
[25] Now great multitudes accompanied him; and he turned and said to them, [26] "If any one comes to me and does not hate his own father and mother and wife and children and brothers and sisters, yes, and even his own life, he cannot be my disciple. [27] Whoever does not bear his own cross and come after me, cannot be my disciple."

* See 121: *Hating One's Family*

GThom 55 (§S23.3)
(55) [1] Jesus said, "Whoever does not hate his father and his mother cannot become a disciple to Me. [2] And whoever does not hate his brothers and sisters and take up his cross in My way will not be worthy of Me."

GThom 101 (§S23.4)
(101) <Jesus said,> "Whoever does not hate his father and his mother as I do cannot become a disciple to Me. And whoever does [not] love his father and his mother as I do cannot become a [disciple] to Me. For My mother [gave me falsehood], but [My] true [Mother] gave me life."

429 CARRYING ONE'S CROSS*

Matt 10:38 (§S24.1)
[34] "Do not think that I have come to bring peace on earth; I have not come to bring peace, but a sword. [35] For I have come to set a man against his father, and a daughter against her mother, and a daughter-in-law against her mother-in-law; [36] and a man's foes will be those of his own household. [37] He who loves father or mother more than me is not worthy of me; and he who loves son or daughter more than me is not worthy of me; [38] and he who does not take his cross and follow me is not worthy of me."

* See 122: *Carrying One's Cross*

Matt 16:24 (§S24.2)
[24] Then Jesus told his disciples, "If any man would come after me, let him deny himself and take up his cross and follow me."

Mark 8:34 (§S24.3)
[34] And he called to him the multitude with his disciples, and said to them, "If any man would come after me, let him deny himself and take up his cross and follow me."

Luke 9:23 (§S24.4)
[23] And he said to all, "If any man would come after me, let him deny himself and take up his cross daily and follow me."

Luke 14:25–27 (§S24.5)
[25] Now great multitudes accompanied him; and he turned and said to them, [26] "If any one comes to me and does not hate his own father and mother and wife and children and brothers and sisters, yes, and even his own life, he cannot be my disciple. [27] Whoever does not bear his own cross and come after me, cannot be my disciple."

GThom 55 (§S24.6)
(55) [1] Jesus said, "Whoever does not hate his father and his mother cannot become a disciple to Me. [2] And whoever does not hate his brothers and sisters and take up his cross in My way will not be worthy of Me."

Matt 10:40 (§S25.1)

[40] "He who receives you receives me, and he who receives me receives him who sent me."

Matt 18:1–5 (§S25.2)

[1] At that time the disciples came to Jesus, saying, "Who is the greatest in the kingdom of heaven?" [2] And calling to him a child, he put him in the midst of them, [3] and said, "Truly, I say to you, unless you turn and become like children, you will never enter the kingdom of heaven. [4] Whoever humbles himself like this child, he is the greatest in the kingdom of heaven.
[5] "Whoever receives one such child in my name receives me."

Mark 9:33–37 (§S25.3)

[33] And they came to Capernaum; and when he was in the house he asked them, "What were you discussing on the way?" [34] But they were silent; for on the way they had discussed with one another who was the greatest. [35] And he sat down and called the twelve; and he said to them, "If any one would be first, he must be last of all and servant of all." [36] And he took a child, and put him in the midst of them; and taking him in his arms, he said to them, [37] "Whoever receives one such child in my name receives me; and whoever receives me, receives not me but him who sent me."

Luke 9:46–48 (§S25.4)

[46] And an argument arose among them as to which of them was the greatest. [47] But when Jesus perceived the thought of their hearts, he took a child and put him by his side, [48] and said to them, "Whoever receives this child in my name receives me, and whoever receives me receives him who sent me; for he who is least among you all is the one who is great."

Luke 10:16 (§S25.5)

[16] "He who hears you hears me, and he who rejects you rejects me, and he who rejects me rejects him who sent me."

John 5:19–24 (§S25.6)

[19] Jesus said to them, "Truly, truly, I say to you, the Son can do nothing of his own accord, but only what he sees the Father doing; for whatever he does, that the Son does likewise. [20] For the Father loves the Son, and shows him all that he himself is doing; and greater works than these will he show him, that you may marvel. [21] For as the Father raises the dead and gives them life, so also the Son gives life to whom he will. [22] The Father judges no one, but has given all judgment to the Son, [23] that all may honor the Son, even as they honor the Father. He who does not honor the Son does not honor the Father who sent him. [24] Truly, truly, I say to you, he who hears my word and believes him who sent me, has eternal life; he does not come into judgment, but has passed from death to life."

John 12:44–45 (§S25.7)

[44] And Jesus cried out and said, "He who believes in me, believes not in me but in him who sent me. [45] And he who sees me sees him who sent me."

John 13:20 (§S25.8)

[20] "Truly, truly, I say to you, he who receives any one whom I send receives me; and he who receives me receives him who sent me."

Ign Eph 6:1 (§S25.9)

[1] And the more anyone sees that the bishop is silent, the more let him fear him. For every one whom the master of the house sends to do his business ought we to receive as him who sent him. Therefore it is clear that we must regard the bishop as the Lord himself.

Did 11:3–4 (§S25.10)

[3] And concerning the Apostles and Prophets, act thus according to the ordinance of the Gospel. [4] Let every Apostle who comes to you be received as the Lord.

* See 124: *Receiving the Sender*

431   REPLY TO JOHN

Matt 11:2–6 (§S26.1)

[2] Now when John heard in prison about the deeds of the Christ, he sent word by his disciples [3] and said to him, "Are you he who is to come, or shall we look for another?" [4] And Jesus answered them, "Go and tell John what you hear and see: [5] the blind receive their sight and the lame walk, lepers are cleansed and the deaf hear, and the dead are raised up, and the poor have good news preached to them. [6] And blessed is he who takes no offense at me."

Luke 7:18–23 (§S26.2)

[18] The disciples of John told him of all these things. [19] And John, calling to him two of his disciples, sent them to the Lord, saying, "Are you he who is to come, or shall we look for another?" [20] And when the men had come to him, they said, "John the Baptist has sent us to you, saying, 'Are you he who is to come, or shall we look for another?'" [21] In that hour he cured many of diseases and plagues and evil spirits, and on many that were blind he bestowed sight. [22] And he answered them, "Go and tell John what you have seen and heard: the blind receive their sight, the lame walk, lepers are cleansed, and the deaf hear, the dead are raised up, the poor have good news preached to them. [23] And blessed is he who takes no offense at me."

432 INTO THE DESERT*

Matt 11:7–10 (§S27.1)

[7] As they went away, Jesus began to speak to the crowds concerning John: "What did you go out into the wilderness to behold? A reed shaken by the wind? [8] Why then did you go out? To see a man clothed in soft raiment? Behold, those who wear soft raiment are in kings' houses. [9] Why then did you go out? To see a prophet? Yes, I tell you, and more than a prophet. [10] This is he of whom it is written,

'Behold, I send my messenger before thy face,
who shall prepare thy way before thee.'"

* See 127: *Into the Desert*

Mark 1:1–5 (§S27.2)

[1] The beginning of the Gospel of Jesus Christ, the Son of God. [2] As it is written in Isaiah the prophet,

"Behold, I send my messenger before thy face,
who shall prepare thy way;
[3] the voice of one crying in the wilderness:
Prepare the way of the Lord,
make his paths straight—"

[4] John the baptizer appeared in the wilderness, preaching a baptism of repentance for the forgiveness of sins. [5] And there went out to him all the country of Judea, and all the people of Jerusalem; and they were baptized by him in the river Jordan, confessing their sins.

Luke 7:24–27 (§S27.3)

[24] When the messengers of John had gone, he began to speak to the crowds concerning John: "What did you go out into the wilderness to behold? A reed shaken by the wind? [25] What then did you go out to see? A man clothed in soft clothing? Behold, those who are gorgeously appareled and live in luxury are in kings' courts. [26] What then did you go out to see? A prophet? Yes, I tell you, and more than a prophet. [27] This is he of whom it is written,

'Behold, I send my messenger before thy face,
who shall prepare thy way before thee.'"

GThom 78 (§S27.4)

(78) Jesus said, "Why have you come out into the desert? To see a reed shaken by the wind? And to see a man clothed in fine garments like your kings and your great men? Upon them are the fine [garments], and they are unable to discern the truth."

433 GRAIN AND SABBATH

Matt 12:1–7 (§S28.1)

[1] At that time Jesus went through the grainfields on the sabbath; his disciples were hungry, and they began to pluck heads of grain and to eat. [2] But when the Pharisees saw it, they said to him, "Look, your disciples are doing what is not lawful to do on the sabbath." [3] He said to them, "Have you not read what David did, when he was hungry, and those who were with him: [4] how he entered the house of God and ate the bread of the Presence, which it was not lawful for him to eat nor for those who were with him, but only for the priests? [5] Or have you not read in the law how on the sabbath the priests in the temple profane the sabbath, and are guiltless? [6] I tell you, something greater than the temple is here. [7] And if you had known what this means, 'I desire mercy, and not sacrifice,' you would not have condemned the guiltless."

Mark 2:23–26 (§S28.2)

[23] One sabbath he was going through the grainfields; and as they made their way his disciples began to pluck heads of grain. [24] And the Pharisees said to him, "Look, why are they doing what is not lawful on the sabbath?" [25] And he said to them, "Have you never read what David did, when he was in need and was hungry, he and those who were with him: [26] how he entered the house of God, when Abiathar was high priest, and ate the bread of the Presence, which it is not lawful for any but the priests to eat, and also gave it to those who were with him?"

Luke 6:1–4 (§S28.3)

[1] On a sabbath, while he was going through the grainfields, his disciples plucked and ate some heads of grain, rubbing them in their hands. [2] But some of the Pharisees said, "Why are you doing what is not lawful to do on the sabbath?" [3] And Jesus answered, "Have you not read what David did when he was hungry, he and those who were with him: [4] how he entered the house of God, and took and ate the bread of the Presence, which it is not lawful for any but the priests to eat, and also gave it to those with him?"

Matt 12:9–14 (§S29.1)

[9] And he went on from there, and entered their synagogue. [10] And behold, there was a man with a withered hand. And they asked him, "Is it lawful to heal on the sabbath?" so that they might accuse him. [11] He said to them, "What man of you, if he has one sheep and it falls into a pit on the sabbath, will not lay hold of it and lift it out? [12] Of how much more value is a man than a sheep! So it is lawful to do good on the sabbath." [13] Then he said to the man, "Stretch out your hand." And the man stretched it out, and it was restored, whole like the other. [14] But the Pharisees went out and took counsel against him, how to destroy him.

Mark 3:1–6 (§S29.2)

[1] Again he entered the synagogue, and a man was there who had a withered hand. [2] And they watched him, to see whether he would heal him on the sabbath, so that they might accuse him. [3] And he said to the man who had the withered hand, "Come here." [4] And he said to them, "Is it lawful on the sabbath to do good or to do harm, to save life or to kill?" But they were silent. [5] And he looked around at them with anger, grieved at their hardness of heart, and said to the man, "Stretch out your hand." He stretched it out, and his hand was restored. [6] The Pharisees went out, and immediately held counsel with the Herodians against him, how to destroy him.

Luke 6:6–11 (§S29.3)

[6] On another sabbath, when he entered the synagogue and taught, a man was there whose right hand was withered. [7] And the scribes and the Pharisees watched him, to see whether he would heal on the sabbath, so that they might find an accusation against him. [8] But he knew their thoughts, and he said to the man who had the withered hand, "Come and stand here." And he rose and stood there. [9] And Jesus said to them, "I ask you, is it lawful on the sabbath to do good or to do harm, to save life or to destroy it?" [10] And he looked around on them all, and said to him, "Stretch out your hand." And he did so, and his hand was restored. [11] But they were filled with fury and discussed with one another what they might do to Jesus.

GNaz 10 (§S29.4)

(10) In the Gospel which the Nazarenes and the Ebionites use, which we have recently translated out of Hebrew into Greek, and which is called by most people the authentic (Gospel) of Matthew, the man who had the withered hand is described as a mason who pleaded for help in the following words:

I was a mason and earned (my) livelihood with (my) hands; I beseech thee, Jesus, to restore to me my health that I may not with ignominy have to beg for my bread. (Jerome, *Commentary on Matthew* 2 [on Matthew 12:13])

435

JESUS' TRUE FAMILY

Matt 12:46–50 (§S30.1)

[46] While he was still speaking to the people, behold, his mother and his brothers stood outside, asking to speak to him. [48] But he replied to the man who told him, "Who is my mother, and who are my brothers?" [49] And stretching out his hand toward his disciples, he said, "Here are my mother and my brothers! [50] For whoever does the will of my Father in heaven is my brother, and sister, and mother."

Mark 3:19b–21,31–35 (§S30.2)

[19] . . . Then he went home; [20] and the crowd came together again, so that they could not even eat. [21] And when his family heard it, they went out to seize him, for people were saying, "He is beside himself." [31] And his mother and his brothers came; and standing outside they sent to him and called him. [32] And a crowd was sitting about him; and they said to him, "Your mother and your brothers are outside, asking for you." [33] And he replied, "Who are my mother and my brothers?" [34] And looking around on those who sat about him, he said, "Here are my mother and my brothers! [35] Whoever does the will of God is my brother, and sister, and mother."

Luke 8:19–21 (§S30.3)

[19] Then his mother and his brothers came to him, but they could not reach him for the crowd. [20] And he was told, "Your mother and your brothers are standing outside, desiring to see you." [21] But he said to them, "My mother and my brothers are those who hear the word of God and do it."

GThom 99 (§S30.4)

(99) [1] The disciples said to him, "Your brothers and Your mother are standing outside."

[2] He said to them, "Those here who do the will of My Father are My brothers and My mother. It is they who will enter the Kingdom of My Father."

2 Clem 9:10–11 (§S30.5)

[10] Let us then give him praise, not only with our mouth, but also from our heart, that he may receive us as sons. [11] For the Lord said "My brethren are these who do the will of my Father."

GEbi 5 (§S30.6)

(5) Moreover they deny that he was a man, evidently on the ground of the word which the Saviour spoke when it was reported to him: "Behold, thy mother and thy brethren stand without," namely:

Who is my mother and who are my brethren? And he stretched forth his hand towards his disciples and said: These are my brethren and mother and sisters, who do the will of my Father. (Epiphanius, *Haer.* 30.14.5)

Matt 13:53–58 (§S31.1)

53 And when Jesus had finished these parables, he went away from there, 54 and coming to his own country he taught them in their synagogue, so that they were astonished, and said, "Where did this man get this wisdom and these mighty works? 55 Is not this the carpenter's son? Is not his mother called Mary? And are not his brothers James and Joseph and Simon and Judas? 56 And are not all his sisters with us? Where then did this man get all this?" 57 And they took offense at him. But Jesus said to them, "A prophet is not without honor except in his own country and in his own house." 58 And he did not do many mighty works there, because of their unbelief.

Mark 6:1–6 (§S31.2)

1 He went away from there and came to his own country; and his disciples followed him. 2 And on the sabbath he began to teach in the synagogue; and many who heard him were astonished, saying, "Where did this man get all this? What is the wisdom given to him? What mighty works are wrought by his hands! 3 Is not this the carpenter, the son of Mary and brother of James and Joses and Judas and Simon, and are not his sisters here with us?" And they took offense at him. 4 And Jesus said to them, "A prophet is not without honor, except in his own country, and among his own kin, and in his own house." 5 And he could do no mighty work there, except that he laid his hands upon a few sick people and healed them. 6 And he marveled because of their unbelief. And he went about among the villages teaching.

Luke 4:16–30 (§S31.3)

16 And he came to Nazareth, where he had been brought up; and he went to the synagogue, as his custom was, on the sabbath day. And he stood up to read; 17 and there was given to him the book of the prophet Isaiah. He opened the book and found the place where it was written,

18 "The Spirit of the Lord is upon me,
because he has anointed me to preach good news to the poor.
He has sent me to proclaim release to the captives
and recovering of sight to the blind,
to set at liberty those who are oppressed,
19 to proclaim the acceptable year of the Lord."

20 And he closed the book, and gave it back to the attendant, and sat down; and the eyes of all in the synagogue were fixed on him. 21 And he began to say to them, "Today this scripture has been fulfilled in your hearing." 22 And all spoke well of him, and wondered at the gracious words which proceeded out of his mouth; and they said, "Is not this Joseph's son?" 23 And he said to them, "Doubtless you will quote to me this proverb, 'Physician, heal yourself; what we have heard you did at Capernaum, do here also in your own country.'" 24 And he said, "Truly, I say to you, no prophet is acceptable in his own country. 25 But in truth, I tell you, there were many widows in Israel in the days of Elijah, when the heaven was shut up three years and six months, when there came a great famine over all the land; 26 and Elijah was sent to none of them but only to Zarephath, in the land of Sidon, to a woman who was a widow. 27 And there were many lepers in Israel in the time of the prophet Elisha; and none of them was cleansed, but only Naaman the Syrian." 28 When they heard this, all in the synagogue were filled with wrath. 29 And they rose up and put him out of the city, and led him to the brow of the hill on which their city was built, that they might throw him down headlong. 30 But passing through the midst of them he went away.

John 4:43–45 (§S31.4)

43 After the two days he departed to Galilee. 44 For Jesus himself testified that a prophet has no honor in his own country. 45 So when he came to Galilee, the Galileans welcomed him, having seen all that he had done in Jerusalem at the feast, for they too had gone to the feast.

POxy1 31 (§S31.5)

(31) Jesus said, "No prophet is accepted in his own country; no physician heals those who know him."

GThom 31 (§S31.6)

(31) Jesus said, "No prophet is accepted in his own village; no physician heals those who know him."

* See 214: *Physician, Heal Yourself*
* See 146: *Prophet's Own Country*

Matt 15:1-9 (§S32.1)

[1] Then Pharisees and scribes came to Jesus from Jerusalem and said, [2] "Why do your disciples transgress the tradition of the elders? For they do not wash their hands when they eat." [3] He answered them, "And why do you transgress the commandment of God for the sake of your tradition? [4] For God commanded 'Honor your father and your mother,' and, 'He who speaks evil of father or mother, let him surely die.' [5] But you say, 'If any one tells his father or his mother, What you would have gained from me is given to God, he need not honor his father.' [6] So, for the sake of your tradition, you have made void the word of God. [7] You hypocrites! Well did Isaiah prophesy of you, when he said:

[8] 'This people honors me with their lips,
but their heart is far from me;
[9] in vain do they worship me,
teaching as doctrines the precepts of men.'"

Mark 7:1-13 (§S32.2)

[1] Now when the Pharisees gathered together to him, with some of the scribes, who had come from Jerusalem, [2] they saw that some of his disciples ate with hands defiled, that is, unwashed. [3] (For the Pharisees, and all the Jews, do not eat unless they wash their hands, observing the tradition of the elders; [4] and when they come from the market place, they do not eat unless they purify themselves; and there are many other traditions which they observe, the washing of cups and pots and vessels of bronze.) [5] And the Pharisees and the scribes asked him, "Why do your disciples not live according to the tradition of the elders, but eat with hands defiled?" [6] And he said to them, "Well did Isaiah prophesy of you hypocrites, as it is written,

'This people honors me with their lips,
but their heart is far from me;
[7] in vain do they worship me,
teaching as doctrines the precepts of men.'
[8] You leave the commandment of God, and hold fast the tradition of men."

[9] And he said to them, "You have a fine way of rejecting the commandment of God, in order to keep your tradition! [10] For Moses said, 'Honor your father and your mother'; and, 'He who speaks evil of father or mother, let him surely die'; [11] but you say, 'If a man tells his father or his mother, What you would have gained from me is Corban' (that is, given to God)— [12] then you no longer permit him to do anything for his father or mother, [13] thus making void the word of God through your tradition which you hand on. And many such things you do."

PEger2 3 (§S32.3)

(3) . . . [ca]me to him to put him to the pro[of] and to tempt him, whilst [they said]: "Master Jesus, we know that thou art come [from God], for what thou doest bears a test[imony] (to thee which goes) beyond (that) of all the prophets. [Wherefore tell] us: is it admissible [to p]ay to the kings the (charges) appertaining to their rule? [Should we] pay [th]em or not?" But Jesus saw through their [in]tention, became [angry] and said to them: "Why call ye me with yo[ur mou]th Master and yet [do] not what I say? Well has Is[aiah] prophesied [concerning y]ou saying: This [people honours] me with the[ir li]ps but their heart is far from me; [their worship is] vain. [They teach] precepts [of men]." (Fragment 2, recto [lines 43–59])

GNaz 12 (§S32.4)

(12) The Jewish Gospel: corban is what you should obtain from us. (Variant to Matthew 15:5 in the "Zion Gospel" Edition)

Matt 15:10–11 (§S33.1)

¹⁰ And he called the people to him and said to them, "Hear and understand: ¹¹ not what goes into the mouth defiles a man, but what comes out of the mouth, this defiles a man."

Mark 7:14–15 (§S33.2)

¹⁴ And he called the people to him again, and said to them, "Hear me, all of you, and understand: ¹⁵ there is nothing outside a man which by going into him can defile him; but the things which come out of a man are what defile him."

Acts 10:9–16 (§S33.3)

⁹ The next day, as they were on their journey and coming near the city, Peter went up on the housetop to pray, about the sixth hour. ¹⁰ And he became hungry and desired something to eat; but while they were preparing it, he fell into a trance ¹¹ and saw the heaven opened, and something descending, like a great sheet, let down by four corners upon the earth. ¹² In it were all kinds of animals and reptiles and birds of the air. ¹³ And there came a voice to him, "Rise, Peter; kill and eat." ¹⁴ But Peter said,

"No, Lord; for I have never eaten anything that is common or unclean." ¹⁵ And the voice came to him again a second time, "What God has cleansed, you must not call common." ¹⁶ This happened three times, and the thing was taken up at once to heaven.

Acts 11:1–10 (§S33.4)

¹ Now the apostles and the brethren who were in Judea heard that the Gentiles also had received the word of God. ² So when Peter went up to Jerusalem, the circumcision party criticized him, ³ saying, "Why did you go to uncircumcised men and eat with them?" ⁴ But Peter began and explained to them in order: ⁵ "I was in the city of Joppa praying; and in a trance I saw a vision, something descending, like a great sheet, let down from heaven by four corners; and it came down to me. ⁶ Looking at it closely I observed animals and beasts of prey and reptiles and birds of the air. ⁷ And I heard a voice saying to me, 'Rise, Peter; kill and eat.' ⁸ But I said, 'No, Lord; for nothing common or unclean has ever entered my mouth.' ⁹ But the voice answered a second time from heaven, 'What God has cleansed

you must not call common.' ¹⁰ This happened three times, and all was drawn up again into heaven."

GThom 6, 14 (§S33.5)

(6) ¹ His disciples questioned Him and said to Him, "Do You want us to fast? How shall we pray? Shall we give alms? What diet shall we observe?"

² Jesus said, "Do not tell lies, ³ and do not do what you hate, for all things are plain in the sight of Heaven. ⁴ For nothing hidden will not become manifest, and nothing covered will remain without being uncovered."

(14) ¹ Jesus said to them, "If you fast, you will give rise to sin for yourselves; and if you pray, you will be condemned; and if you give alms, you will do harm to your spirits. ² When you go into any land and walk about in the districts, if they receive you, eat what they will set before you, and heal the sick among them. ³ For what goes into your mouth will not defile you, but that which issues from your mouth—it is that which will defile you."

* See 147 & 339: *What Goes In*

Matt 15:15–20 (§S34.1)

¹⁵ But Peter said to him, "Explain the parable to us." ¹⁶ And he said, "Are you also still without understanding? ¹⁷ Do you not see that whatever goes into the mouth passes into the stomach, and so passes on? ¹⁸ But what comes out of the mouth proceeds from the heart, and this defiles a man. ¹⁹ For out of the heart come evil thoughts, murder, adultery, fornication, theft, false witness, slander. ²⁰ These are what defile a man; but to eat with unwashed hands does not defile a man."

Mark 7:17–23 (§S34.2)

¹⁷ And when he had entered the house, and left the people, his disciples asked him about the parable. ¹⁸ And he said to them, "Then are you also without understanding? Do you not see that whatever goes into a man from outside cannot defile him, ¹⁹ since it enters, not his heart but his stomach, and so passes on?" (Thus he declared all foods clean.) ²⁰ And he said, "What comes out of a man is what defiles a man. ²¹ For from within, out of the heart of man, come evil thoughts, fornication, theft, murder, adultery, ²² coveting, wickedness, deceit, licentiousness, envy, slander, pride, foolishness. ²³ All these evil things come from within, and they defile a man."

440

Matt 15:21–28 (§S35.1)

²¹ And Jesus went away from there and withdrew to the district of Tyre and Sidon. ²² And behold, a Canaanite woman from that region came out and cried, "Have mercy on me, O Lord, Son of David; my daughter is severely possessed by a demon." ²³ But he did not answer her a word. And his disciples came and begged him, saying, "Send her away, for she is crying after us." ²⁴ He answered, "I was sent only to the lost sheep of the house of Israel." ²⁵ But she came and knelt before him, saying, "Lord, help me." ²⁶ And he answered, "It is not fair to take the children's bread and throw it to the dogs." ²⁷ She said, "Yes, Lord, yet even the dogs eat the crumbs that fall from their master's table." ²⁸ Then Jesus answered her, "O woman, great is your faith! Be it done for you as you desire." And her daughter was healed instantly.

Mark 7:24–30 (§S35.2)

²⁴ And from there he arose and went away to the region of Tyre and Sidon. And he entered a house, and would not have any one know it; yet he could not be hid. ²⁵ But immediately a woman, whose little daughter was possessed by an unclean spirit, heard of him, and came and fell down at his feet. ²⁶ Now the woman was a Greek, a Syrophoenician by birth. And she begged him to cast the demon out of her daughter. ²⁷ And he said to her, "Let the children first be fed, for it is not right to take the children's bread and throw it to the dogs." ²⁸ But she answered him, "Yes, Lord; yet even the dogs under the table eat the children's crumbs." ²⁹ And he said to her, "For this saying you may go your way; the demon has left your daughter." ³⁰ And she went home, and found the child lying in bed, and the demon gone.

441

LEAVEN OF PHARISEES★

Matt 16:5–12 (§S36.1)

⁵ When the disciples reached the other side, they had forgotten to bring any bread. ⁶ Jesus said to them, "Take heed and beware of the leaven of the Pharisees and Sadducees." ⁷ And they discussed it among themselves, saying, "We brought no bread." ⁸ But Jesus, aware of this, said, "O men of little faith, why do you discuss among yourselves the fact that you have no bread? ⁹ Do you not yet perceive? Do you not remember the five loaves of the five thousand, and how many baskets you gathered? ¹⁰ Or the seven loaves of the four thousand, and how many baskets you gathered? ¹¹ How is it that you fail to perceive that I did not speak about bread? Beware of the leaven of the Pharisees and Sadducees." ¹² Then they understood that he did not tell them to beware of the leaven of bread, but of the teaching of the Pharisees and Sadducees.

Mark 8:14–21 (§S36.2)

¹⁴ Now they had forgotten to bring bread; and they had only one loaf with them in the boat. ¹⁵ And he cautioned them, saying, "Take heed, beware of the leaven of the Pharisees and the leaven of Herod." ¹⁶ And they discussed it with one another, saying, "We have no bread." ¹⁷ And being aware of it, Jesus said to them, "Why do you discuss the fact that you have no bread? Do you not yet perceive or understand? Are your hearts hardened? ¹⁸ Having eyes do you not see, and having ears do you not hear? And do you not remember? ¹⁹ When I broke the five loaves for the five thousand, how many baskets full of broken pieces did you take up?" They said to him, "Twelve." ²⁰ "And the seven for the four thousand, how many baskets full of broken pieces did you take up?" And they said to him, "Seven." ²¹ And he said to them, "Do you not yet understand?"

Luke 12:1 (§S36.3)

¹ In the meantime, when so many thousands of the multitude had gathered together that they trod upon one another, he began to say to his disciples first, "Beware of the leaven of the Pharisees, which is hypocrisy."

★ See 152: *Leaven of Pharisees*

442   WHO IS JESUS?*

Matt 16:13–20 (§S37.1)

[13] Now when Jesus came into the district of Caesarea Philippi, he asked his disciples, "Who do men say that the Son of man is?" [14] And they said, "Some say John the Baptist, others say Elijah, and others Jeremiah or one of the prophets." [15] He said to them, "But who do you say that I am?" [16] Simon Peter replied, "You are the Christ, the Son of the living God." [17] And Jesus answered him, "Blessed are you, Simon Bar-Jona! For flesh and blood has not revealed this to you, but my Father who is in heaven. [18] And I tell you, you are Peter, and on this rock I will build my church, and the powers of death shall not prevail against it. [19] I will give you the keys of the kingdom of heaven, and whatever you bind on earth shall be bound in heaven, and whatever you loose on earth shall be loosed in heaven." [20] Then he strictly charged the disciples to tell no one that he was the Christ.

Mark 8:27–30 (§S37.2)

[27] And Jesus went on with his disciples, to the villages of Caesarea Philippi; and on the way he asked his disciples, "Who do men say that I am?" [28] And they told him, "John the Baptist; and others say, Elijah; and others one of the prophets." [29] And he asked them, "But who do you say that I am?" Peter answered him, "You are the Christ." [30] And he charged them to tell no one about him.

* See 343: *Who is Jesus?*

Luke 9:18–21 (§S37.3)

[18] Now it happened that as he was praying alone the disciples were with him; and he asked them, "Who do the people say that I am?" [19] And they answered, "John the Baptist; but others say, Elijah; and others, that one of the old prophets has risen." [20] And he said to them, "But who do you say that I am?" And Peter answered, "The Christ of God." [21] But he charged and commanded them to tell this to no one,

John 1:35–42 (§S37.4)

[35] The next day again John was standing with two of his disciples; [36] and he looked at Jesus as he walked, and said, "Behold, the Lamb of God!" [37] The two disciples heard him say this, and they followed Jesus. [38] Jesus turned, and saw them following, and said to them, "What do you seek?" And they said to him, "Rabbi" (which means Teacher), "where are you staying?" [39] He said to them, "Come and see." They came and saw where he was staying; and they stayed with him that day, for it was about the tenth hour. [40] One of the two who heard John speak, and followed him, was Andrew, Simon Peter's brother. [41] He first found his brother Simon, and said to him, "We have found the Messiah" (which means Christ). [42] He brought him to Jesus. Jesus looked at him, and said, "So you are Simon the son of John? You shall be called Cephas" (which means Peter).

John 6:66–69 (§S37.5)

[66] After this many of his disciples drew back and no longer went about with him. [67] Jesus said to the twelve, "Do you also wish to go away?" [68] Simon Peter answered him, "Lord, to whom shall we go? You have the words of eternal life; [69] and we have believed, and have come to know, that you are the Holy One of God."

GThom 13 (§S37.6)

(13) [1] Jesus said to His disciples, "Compare me to someone and tell Me whom I am like."

[2] Simon Peter said to Him, "You are like a righteous angel."

[3] Matthew said to Him, "You are like a wise philosopher."

[4] Thomas said to Him, "Master, my mouth is wholly incapable of saying whom You are like."

[5] Jesus said, "I am not your master. Because you have drunk, you have become intoxicated from the bubbling spring which I have measured out."

[6] And He took him and withdrew and told him three things. [7] When Thomas returned to his companions, they asked him, "What did Jesus say to you?"

[8] Thomas said to them, "If I tell you one of the things which he told me, you will pick up stones and throw them at me; a fire will come out of the stones and burn you up."

GNaz 14 (§S37.7)

(14) The Jewish Gospel: son of John. (Variant to Matthew 16:17 in the "Zion Gospel" Edition)

---

443   BINDING AND LOOSING*

Matt 16:17–19 (§S38.1)

[17] And Jesus answered him, "Blessed are you, Simon Bar-Jona! For flesh and blood has not revealed this to you, but my Father who is in heaven. [18] And I tell you, you are Peter, and on this rock I will build my church, and the powers of death shall not prevail against it. [19] I will give you the keys of the kingdom of heaven, and whatever you bind on earth shall be bound in heaven, and whatever you loose on earth shall be loosed in heaven."

* See 153: *Binding and Loosing*

Matt 18:15–18 (§S38.2)

[15] "If your brother sins against you, go and tell him his fault, between you and him alone. If he listens to you, you have gained your brother. [16] But if he does not listen, take one or two others along with you, that every word may be confirmed by the evidence of two or three witnesses. [17] If he refuses to listen to them, tell it to the church; and if he refuses to listen even to the church, let him be to you as a Gentile and a tax collector. [18] Truly, I say to you, whatever you bind on earth shall be bound in heaven, and whatever you loose on earth shall be loosed in heaven."

John 20:19–23 (§S38.3)

[19] On the evening of that day, the first day of the week, the doors being shut where the disciples were, for fear of the Jews, Jesus came and stood among them and said to them, "Peace be with you." [20] When he had said this, he showed them his hands and his side. Then the disciples were glad when they saw the Lord. [21] Jesus said to them again, "Peace be with you. As the Father has sent me, even so I send you." [22] And when he had said this, he breathed on them, and said to them, "Receive the Holy Spirit. [23] If you forgive the sins of any, they are forgiven; if you retain the sins of any, they are retained."

Matt 16:21–23 (§S39.1)

²¹ From that time Jesus began to show his disciples that he must go to Jerusalem and suffer many things from the elders and chief priests and scribes, and be killed, and on the third day be raised. ²² And Peter took him and began to rebuke him, saying, "God forbid, Lord! This shall never happen to you." ²³ But he turned and said to Peter, "Get behind me, Satan! You are a hindrance to me; for you are not on the side of God, but of men."

Matt 17:22–23 (§S39.2)

²² As they were gathering in Galilee, Jesus said to them, "The Son of man is to be delivered into the hands of men, ²³ and they will kill him, and he will be raised on the third day." And they were greatly distressed.

Matt 20:17–19 (§S39.3)

¹⁷ And as Jesus was going up to Jerusalem, he took the twelve disciples aside, and on the way he said to them, ¹⁸ "Behold, we are going up to Jerusalem; and the Son of man will be delivered to the chief priests and scribes, and they will condemn him to death, ¹⁹ and deliver him to the Gentiles to be mocked and scourged and crucified, and he will be raised on the third day."

Matt 26:2 (§S39.4)

² "You know that after two days the Passover is coming, and the Son of man will be delivered up to be crucified."

★ See 154: *Passion-Resurrection Prophecy*

Mark 8:31–33 (§S39.5)

³¹ And he began to teach them that the Son of man must suffer many things, and be rejected by the elders and the chief priests and the scribes, and be killed, and after three days rise again. ³² And he said this plainly. And Peter took him, and began to rebuke him. ³³ But turning and seeing his disciples, he rebuked Peter, and said, "Get behind me, Satan! For you are not on the side of God, but of men."

Mark 9:30–32 (§S39.6)

³⁰ They went on from there and passed through Galilee. And he would not have any one know it; ³¹ for he was teaching his disciples, saying to them, "The Son of man will be delivered into the hands of men, and they will kill him; and when he is killed, after three days he will rise." ³² But they did not understand the saying, and they were afraid to ask him.

Mark 10:32–34 (§S39.7)

³² And they were on the road, going up to Jerusalem, and Jesus was walking ahead of them; and they were amazed, and those who followed were afraid. And taking the twelve again, he began to tell them what was to happen to him, ³³ saying, "Behold, we are going up to Jerusalem; and the Son of man will be delivered to the chief priests and the scribes, and they will condemn him to death, and deliver him to the Gentiles; ³⁴ and they will mock him, and spit upon him, and scourge him, and kill him; and after three days he will rise."

Luke 9:22 (§S39.8)

²² saying, "The Son of man must suffer many things, and be rejected by the elders and chief priests and scribes, and be killed, and on the third day be raised."

Luke 9:43–45 (§S39.9)

⁴³ And all were astonished at the majesty of God.

But while they were all marveling at everything he did, he said to his disciples, ⁴⁴ "Let these words sink into your ears; for the Son of man is to be delivered into the hands of men." ⁴⁵ But they did not understand this saying, and it was concealed from them, that they should not perceive it; and they were afraid to ask him about this saying.

Luke 17:22–25 (§S39.10)

²² And he said to the disciples, "The days are coming when you will desire to see one of the days of the Son of man, and you will not see it. ²³ And they will say to you, 'Lo, there!' or 'Lo, here!' Do not go, do not follow them. ²⁴ For as lightning flashes and lights up the sky from one side to the other, so will the Son of man be in his day. ²⁵ But first he must suffer many things and be rejected by this generation."

Luke 18:31–34 (§S39.11)

³¹ And taking the twelve, he said to them, "Behold, we are going up to Jerusalem, and everything that is written of the Son of man by the prophets will be accomplished. ³² For he will be delivered to the Gentiles, and will be mocked and shamefully treated and spit upon; ³³ they will scourge him and kill him, and on the third day he will rise." ³⁴ But they understood none of these things; this saying was hid from them, and they did not grasp what was said.

445 THE TEMPLE TAX

Matt 17:24–27 (§S40)

24 When they came to Capernaum, the collectors of the half-shekel tax went up to Peter and said, "Does not your teacher pay the tax?" 25 He said "Yes." And when he came home, Jesus spoke to him first, saying, "What do you think, Simon? From whom do kings of the earth take toll or tribute? From their sons or from others?" 26 And when he said, "From others," Jesus said to him, "Then the sons are free. 27 However, not to give offense to them, go to the sea and cast a hook, and take the first fish that comes up, and when you open its mouth you will find a shekel; take that and give it to them for me and for yourself."

446 KINGDOM AND CHILDREN*

Matt 18:1–3 (§S41.1)

1 At that time the disciples came to Jesus, saying, "Who is the greatest in the kingdom of heaven?" 2 And calling to him a child, he put him in the midst of them, 3 and said, "Truly, I say to you, unless you turn and become like children, you will never enter the kingdom of heaven."

Matt 19:13–15 (§S41.2)

13 Then children were brought to him that he might lay his hands on them and pray. The disciples rebuked the people; 14 but Jesus said, "Let the children come to me, and do not hinder them; for to such belongs the kingdom of heaven." 15 And he laid his hands on them and went away.

Mark 10:13–16 (§S41.3)

13 And they were bringing children to him, that he might touch them; 13 and the disciples rebuked them. 14 But when Jesus saw it he was indignant, and said to them, "Let the children come to me, do not hinder them; for to such belongs the kingdom of God. 15 Truly, I say to you, whoever does not receive the kingdom of God like a child shall not enter it." 16 And he took them in his arms and blessed them, laying his hands upon them.

Luke 18:15–17 (§S41.4)

15 Now they were bringing even infants to him that he might touch them; and when the disciples saw it, they rebuked them. 16 But Jesus called them to him, saying, "Let the children come to me, and do not hinder them; for to such belongs the kingdom of God. 17 Truly, I say to you, whoever does not receive the kingdom of God like a child shall not enter it."

John 3:1–10 (§S41.5)

1 Now there was a man of the Pharisees, named Nicodemus, a ruler of the Jews. 2 This man came to Jesus by night and said to him, "Rabbi, we know that you are a teacher come from God; for no one can do these signs that you do, unless God is with him." 3 Jesus answered him, "Truly, truly, I say to you, unless one is born anew, he cannot see the kingdom of God." 4 Nicodemus said to him, "How can a man be born when he is old? Can he enter a second time into his mother's womb and be born?" 5 Jesus answered, "Truly, truly, I say to you, unless one is born of water and the Spirit, he cannot enter the kingdom of God. 6 That which is born of the flesh is flesh, and that which is born of the Spirit is spirit. 7 Do not marvel that I said to you, 'You must be born anew.' 8 The wind blows where it wills, and you hear the sound of it, but you do not know whence it comes or whither it goes; so it is with every one who is born of the Spirit." 9 Nicodemus said to him, "How can this be?" 10 Jesus answered him, "Are you a teacher of Israel, and yet you do not understand this?"

GThom 22 (§S41.6)

(22) 1 Jesus saw infants being suckled. 2 He said to His disciples, "These infants being suckled are like those who enter the Kingdom."

3 They said to Him, "Shall we then, as children, enter the Kingdom?"

4 Jesus said to them, "When you make the two one, and when you make the inside like the outside and the outside like the inside, and the above like the below, and when you make the male and the female one and the same, so that the male not be male nor the female female; and when you fashion eyes in place of an eye, and a hand in place of a hand, and a foot in place of a foot, and a likeness in place of a likeness; then will you enter [the Kingdom]."

* See 158: *Kingdom and Children*

447 LEADER AS SERVANT*

Matt 20:20–28 (§S42.1)

[20] Then the mother of the sons of Zebedee came up to him, with her sons, and kneeling before him she asked him for something. [21] And he said to her, "What do you want?" She said to him, "Command that these two sons of mine may sit, one at your right hand and one at your left, in your kingdom." [22] But Jesus answered, "You do not know what you are asking. Are you able to drink the cup that I am to drink?" They said to him, "We are able." [23] He said to them, "You will drink my cup, but to sit at my right hand and at my left is not mine to grant, but it is for those for whom it has been prepared by my Father." [24] And when the ten heard it, they were indignant at the two brothers. [25] But Jesus called them to him and said, "You know that the rulers of the Gentiles lord it over them, and their great men exercise authority over them. [26] It shall not be so among you; but whoever would be great among you must be your servant, [27] and whoever would be first among you must be your slave; [28] even as the Son of man came not to be served but to serve, and to give his life as a ransom for many."

Matt 23:8–11 (§S42.2)

[8] "But you are not to be called rabbi, for you have one teacher, and you are all brethren. [9] And call no man your father on earth, for you have one Father, who is in heaven. [10] Neither be called masters, for you have one master, the Christ. [11] He who is greatest among you shall be your servant."

Mark 9:33–37 (§S42.3)

[33] And they came to Capernaum; and when he was in the house he asked them, "What were you discussing on the way?" [34] But they were silent; for on the way they had discussed with one another who was the greatest. [35] And he sat down and called the twelve; and he said to them, "If any one would be first, he must be last of all and servant of all." [36] And he took a child, and put him in the midst of them; and taking him in his arms, he said to them, [37] "Whoever receives one such child in my name receives me; and whoever receives me, receives not me but him who sent me."

* See 172: *Leader as Servant*

Mark 10:35–45 (§S42.4)

[35] And James and John, the sons of Zebedee, came forward to him, and said to him, "Teacher, we want you to do for us whatever we ask of you." [36] And he said to them, "What do you want me to do for you?" [37] And they said to him, "Grant us to sit, one at your right hand and one at your left, in your glory." [38] But Jesus said to them, "You do not know what you are asking. Are you able to drink the cup that I drink, or to be baptized with the baptism with which I am baptized?" [39] And they said to him, "We are able." And Jesus said to them, "The cup that I drink you will drink; and with the baptism with which I am baptized, you will be baptized; [40] but to sit at my right hand or at my left is not mine to grant, but it is for those for whom it has been prepared." [41] And when the ten heard it, they began to be indignant at James and John. [42] And Jesus called them to him and said to them, "You know that those who are supposed to rule over the Gentiles lord it over them, and their great men exercise authority over them. [43] But it shall not be so among you; but whoever would be great among you must be your servant, [44] and whoever would be first among you must be slave of all. [45] For the Son of man also came not to be served but to serve, and to give his life as a ransom for many."

Luke 9:46–48 (§S42.5)

[46] And an argument arose among them as to which of them was the greatest. [47] But when Jesus perceived the thought of their hearts, he took a child and put him by his side, [48] and said to them, "Whoever receives this child in my name receives me, and whoever receives me receives him who sent me; for he who is least among you all is the one who is great."

Luke 22:24–27 (§S42.6)

[24] A dispute also arose among them, which of them was to be regarded as the greatest. [25] And he said to them, "The kings of the Gentiles exercise lordship over them; and those in authority over them are called benefactors. [26] But not so with you; rather let the greatest among you become as the youngest, and the leader as one who serves. [27] For which is the greater, one who sits at table, or one who serves? Is it not the one who sits at table? But I am among you as one who serves."

John 13:1–20 (§S42.7)

[1] Now before the feast of the Passover, when Jesus knew that his hour had come to depart out of this world to the Father, having loved his own who were in the world, he loved them to the end. [2] And during supper, when the devil had already put it into the heart of Judas Iscariot, Simon's son, to betray him, [3] Jesus, knowing that the Father had given all things into his hands, and that he had come from God and was going to God, [4] rose from supper, laid aside his garments, and girded himself with a towel. [5] Then he poured water into a basin, and began to wash the disciples' feet and to wipe them with the towel with which he was girded. [6] He came to Simon Peter; and Peter said to him, "Lord, do you wash my feet?" [7] Jesus answered him, "What I am doing you do not know now, but afterward you will understand." [8] Peter said to him, "You shall never wash my feet." Jesus answered him, "If I do not wash you, you have no part in me." [9] Simon Peter said to him, "Lord, not my feet only but also my hands and my head!" [10] Jesus said to him, "He who has bathed does not need to wash, except for his feet, but he is clean all over; and you are clean, but not every one of you." [11] For he knew who was to betray him; that was why he said, "You are not all clean."

[12] When he had washed their feet, and taken his garments, and resumed his place, he said to them, "Do you know what I have done to you? [13] You call me Teacher and Lord; and you are right, for so I am. [14] If I then, your Lord and Teacher, have washed your feet, you also ought to wash one another's feet. [15] For I have given you an example, that you also should do as I have done to you. [16] Truly, truly, I say to you, a servant is not greater than his master; nor is he who is sent greater than he who sent him. [17] If you know these things, blessed are you if you do them. [18] I am not speaking of you all; I know whom I have chosen; it is that the scripture may be fulfilled, 'He who ate my bread has lifted his heel against me.' [19] I tell you this now, before it takes place, that when it does take place you may believe that I am he. [20] Truly, truly, I say to you, he who receives any one whom I send receives me; and he who receives me receives him who sent me."

Matt 21:1–11 (§S43.1)

[1] And when they drew near to Jerusalem and came to Bethphage, to the Mount of Olives, then Jesus sent two disciples, [2] saying to them, "Go into the village opposite you, and immediately you will find an ass tied, and a colt with her; untie them and bring them to me. [3] If any one says anything to you, you shall say, 'The Lord has need of them,' and he will send them immediately." [4] This took place to fulfil what was spoken by the prophet, saying,

[5] "Tell the daughter of Zion,
Behold, your king is coming to you,
humble, and mounted on an ass,
and on a colt, the foal of an ass."

[6] The disciples went and did as Jesus had directed them; [7] they brought the ass and the colt, and put their garments on them, and he sat thereon. [8] Most of the crowd spread their garments on the road, and others cut branches from the trees and spread them on the road. [9] And the crowds that went before him and that followed him shouted, "Hosanna to the Son of David! Blessed is he who comes in the name of the Lord! Hosanna in the highest!" [10] And when he entered Jerusalem, all the city was stirred, saying, "Who is this?" [11] And the crowds said, "This is the prophet Jesus from Nazareth of Galilee."

Mark 11:1–11 (§S43.2)

[1] And when they drew near to Jerusalem, to Bethphage and Bethany, at the Mount of Olives, he sent two of his disciples, [2] and said to them, "Go into the village opposite you, and immediately as you enter it you will find a colt tied, on which no one has ever sat; untie it and bring it. [3] If any one says to you, 'Why are you doing this?' say, 'The Lord has need of it and will send it back here immediately.'" [4] And they went away, and found a colt tied at the door out in the open street; and they untied it. [5] And those who stood there said to them, "What are you doing, untying the colt?" [6] And they told them what Jesus had said; and they let them go. [7] And they brought the colt to Jesus, and threw their garments on it; and he sat upon it. [8] And many spread their garments on the road, and others spread leafy branches which they had cut from the fields. [9] And those who went before and those who followed cried out, "Hosanna! Blessed is he who comes in the name of the Lord! [10] Blessed is the kingdom of our father David that is coming! Hosanna in the highest!"

[11] And he entered Jerusalem, and went into the temple; and when he had looked round at everything, as it was already late, he went out to Bethany with the twelve.

Luke 19:28–40 (§S43.3)

[28] And when he had said this, he went on ahead, going up to Jerusalem. [29] When he drew near to Bethphage and Bethany, at the mount that is called Olivet, he sent two of the disciples, [30] saying, "Go into the village opposite, where on entering you will find a colt tied, on which no one has ever yet sat; untie it and bring it here. [31] If any one asks you, 'Why are you untying it?' you shall say this, 'The Lord has need of it.'" [32] So those who were sent went away and found it as he had told them. [33] And as they were untying the colt, its owners said to them, "Why are you untying the colt?" [34] And they said, "The Lord has need of it." [35] And they brought it to Jesus, and throwing their garments on the colt they set Jesus upon it. [36] And as he rode along, they spread their garments on the road. [37] As he was now drawing near, at the descent of the Mount of Olives, the whole multitude of the disciples began to rejoice and praise God with a loud voice for all the mighty works that they had seen, [38] saying, "Blessed is the King who comes in the name of the Lord! Peace in heaven and glory in the highest!" [39] And some of the Pharisees in the multitude said to him, "Teacher, rebuke your disciples." [40] He answered, "I tell you, if these were silent, the very stones would cry out."

449 TEMPLE'S SYMBOLIC DESTRUCTION

Matt 21:12–13 (§S44.1)

[12] And Jesus entered the temple of God and drove out all who sold and bought in the temple, and he overturned the tables of the money-changers and the seats of those who sold pigeons. [13] He said to them, "It is written, 'My house shall be called a house of prayer'; but you make it a den of robbers."

Mark 11:15–17 (§S44.2)

[15] And they came to Jerusalem. And he entered the temple and began to drive out those who sold and those who bought in the temple, and he overturned the tables of the money-changers and the seats of those who sold pigeons; [16] and he would not allow any one to carry anything through the temple. [17] And he taught, and said to them, "Is it not written, 'My house shall be called a house of prayer for all the nations'? But you have made it a den of robbers."

Luke 19:45–46 (§S44.3)

[45] And he entered the temple and began to drive out those who sold, [46] saying to them, "It is written, 'My house shall be a house of prayer'; but you have made it a den of robbers."

John 2:13–17 (§S44.4)

[13] The Passover of the Jews was at hand, and Jesus went up to Jerusalem. [14] In the temple he found those who were selling oxen and sheep and pigeons, and the money-changers at their business. [15] And making a whip of cords, he drove them all, with the sheep and oxen, out of the temple; and he poured out the coins of the money-changers and overturned their tables. [16] And he told those who sold the pigeons, "Take these things away; you shall not make my Father's house a house of trade." [17] His disciples remembered that it was written, "Zeal for thy house will consume me."

450 THE CHILDREN'S CONFESSION*

Matt 21:14–16 (§S45)
14 And the blind and the lame came to him in the temple, and he healed them. 15 But when the chief priests and the scribes saw the wonderful things that he did, and the children crying out in the temple, "Hosanna to the Son of David!" they were indignant; 16 and they said to him, "Do you hear what these are saying?" And Jesus said to them, "Yes, have you never read,

'Out of the mouth of babes and sucklings thou hast brought perfect praise'?"

* See 489: *The Disciples' Confession*

451 CURSED FIG TREE

Matt 21:18–19 (§S46.1)
18 In the morning, as he was returning to the city, he was hungry. 19 And seeing a fig tree by the wayside he went to it, and found nothing on it but leaves only. And he said to it, "May no fruit ever come from you again!" And the fig tree withered at once.

Mark 11:12–14,20–21 (§S46.2)
12 On the following day, when they came from Bethany, he was hungry. 13 And seeing in the distance a fig tree in leaf, he went to see if he could find anything on it. When he came to it, he found nothing but leaves, for it was not the season for figs. 14 And he said to it, "May no one ever eat fruit from you again." And his disciples heard it.

20 As they passed by in the morning, they saw the fig tree withered away to its roots. 21 And Peter remembered and said to him, "Master, look! The fig tree which you cursed has withered."

452 FAITH AND MOUNTAIN*

Matt 21:20–22 (§S47.1)
20 When the disciples saw it they marveled, saying, "How did the fig tree wither at once?" 21 And Jesus answered them, "Truly, I say to you, if you have faith and never doubt, you will not only do what has been done to the fig tree, but even if you say to this mountain, 'Be taken up and cast into the sea,' it will be done. 22 And whatever you ask in prayer, you will receive, if you have faith."

Mark 11:20–24 (§S47.2)
20 As they passed by in the morning, they saw the fig tree withered away to its roots. 21 And Peter remembered and said to him, "Master, look! The fig tree which you cursed has withered." 22 And Jesus answered them, "Have faith in God. 23 Truly, I say to you, whoever says to this mountain, 'Be taken up and cast into the sea,' and does not doubt in his heart, but believes that what he says will come to pass, it will be done for him. 24 Therefore I tell you, whatever you ask in prayer, believe that you have received it, and it will be yours."

1 Cor 13:2 (§S47.3)
2 And if I have prophetic powers, and understand all mysteries and all knowledge, and if I have all faith, so as to remove mountains, but have not love, I am nothing.

* See 293: *Unity and Mountain*
* See 345: *Faith's Power*

Matt 21:23-27 (§S48.1)

23 And when he entered the temple, the chief priests and the elders of the people came up to him as he was teaching, and said, "By what authority are you doing these things, and who gave you this authority?" 24 Jesus answered them, "I also will ask you a question; and if you tell me the answer, then I also will tell you by what authority I do these things. 25 The baptism of John, whence was it? From heaven or from men?" And they argued with one another, "If we say, 'From heaven,' he will say to us, 'Why then did you not believe him?' 26 But if we say, 'From men,' we are afraid of the multitude; for all hold that John was a prophet." 27 So they answered Jesus, "We do not know." And he said to them, "Neither will I tell you by what authority I do these things."

Mark 11:27-33 (§S48.2)

27 And they came again to Jerusalem. And as he was walking in the temple, the chief priests and the scribes and the elders came to him, 28 and they said to him, "By what authority are you doing these things, or who gave you this authority to do them?" 29 Jesus said to them, "I will ask you a question; answer me, and I will tell you by what authority I do these things. 30 Was the baptism of John from heaven or from men? Answer me." 31 And they argued with one another, "If we say, 'From heaven,' he will say, 'Why then did you not believe him?' 32 But shall we say, 'From men'?"—they were afraid of the people, for all held that John was a real prophet. 33 So they answered Jesus, "We do not know." And Jesus said to them, "Neither will I tell you by what authority I do these things."

Luke 20:1-8 (§S48.3)

1 One day, as he was teaching the people in the temple and preaching the gospel, the chief priests and the scribes with the elders came up 2 and said to him, "Tell us by what authority you do these things, or who it is that gave you this authority." 3 He answered them, "I also will ask you a question; now tell me, 4 Was the baptism of John from heaven or from men?" 5 And they discussed it with one another, saying, "If we say, 'From heaven,' he will say, 'Why did you not believe him?' 6 But if we say, 'From men,' all the people will stone us; for they are convinced that John was a prophet." 7 So they answered that they did not know whence it was. 8 And Jesus said to them, "Neither will I tell you by what authority I do these things."

Matt 22:15-22 (§S49.1)

15 Then the Pharisees went and took counsel how to entangle him in his talk. 16 And they sent their disciples to him, along with the Herodians, saying, "Teacher, we know that you are true, and teach the way of God truthfully, and care for no man; for you do not regard the position of men. 17 Tell us, then, what you think. Is it lawful to pay taxes to Caesar, or not?" 18 But Jesus, aware of their malice, said, "Why put me to the test, you hypocrites? 19 Show me the money for the tax." And they brought him a coin. 20 And Jesus said to them, "Whose likeness and inscription is this?" 21 They said, "Caesar's." Then he said to them, "Render therefore to Caesar the things that are Caesar's, and to God the things that are God's" 22 When they heard it, they marveled; and they left him and went away.

Mark 12:13-17 (§S49.2)

13 And they sent to him some of the Pharisees and some of the Herodians, to entrap him in his talk. 14 And they came and said to him, "Teacher, we know that you are true, and care for no man; for you do not regard the position of men; but truly teach the way of God. Is it lawful to pay taxes to Caesar, or not? 15 Should we pay them, or should we not?" But knowing their hypocrisy, he said to them, "Why put me to the test? Bring me a coin, and let me look at it." 16 And they brought one. And he said to them, "Whose likeness and inscription is this?" They said to him, "Caesar's." 17 Jesus said to them, "Render to Caesar the things that are Caesar's, and to God the things that are God's." And they were amazed at him.

Luke 20:20-26 (§S49.3)

20 So they watched him, and sent spies, who pretended to be sincere, that they might take hold of what he said, so as to deliver him up to the authority and jurisdiction of the governor. 21 They asked him, "Teacher, we know that you speak and teach rightly, and show no partiality, but truly teach the way of God. 22 Is it lawful for us to give tribute to Caesar, or not?" 23 But he perceived their craftiness, and said to them, 24 "Show me a coin. Whose likeness and inscription has it?" They said, "Caesar's." 25 He said to them, "Then render to Caesar the things that are Caesar's, and to God the things that are God's." 26 And they were not able in the presence of the people to catch him by what he said; but marveling at his answer they were silent.

PEger2 3 (§S49.4)

(3) . . . [ca]me to him to put him to the pro[of] and to tempt him, whilst [they said]: "Master·Jesus, we know that thou art come [from God], for what thou doest bears a test[imony] (to thee which goes) beyond (that) of all the prophets. [Wherefore tell] us: is it admissible [to p]ay to the kings the (charges) appertaining to their rule? [Should we] pay [th]em or not?" But Jesus saw through their [in]tention, became [angry] and said to them: "Why call ye me with yo[ur mou]th Master and yet [do] not what I say? Well has Is[aiah] prophesied [concerning y]ou saying: This [people honours] me with the[ir li]ps but their heart is far from me; [their worship is] vain. [They teach] precepts [of men] . . ." (Fragment 2, recto [lines 43–59])

GThom 100 (§S49.5)

(100) 1 They showed Jesus a gold coin and said to Him, "Caesar's men demand taxes from us."

2 He said to them, "Give Caesar what belongs to Caesar, give God what belongs to God, and give Me what is Mine."

455

INSIDE AND OUTSIDE*

Matt 23:25–26 (§S50.1)

²⁵ "Woe to you, scribes and Pharisees, hypocrites! for you cleanse the outside of the cup and of the plate, but inside they are full of extortion and rapacity. ²⁶ You blind Pharisee! first cleanse the inside of the cup and of the plate, that the outside also may be clean."

Luke 11:37–41 (§S50.2)

³⁷ While he was speaking, a Pharisee asked him to dine with him; so he went in and sat at table. ³⁸ The Pharisee was astonished to see that he did not first wash before dinner. ³⁹ And the Lord said to him, "Now you Pharisees cleanse the outside of the cup and of the dish, but inside you are full of extortion and wickedness. ⁴⁰ You fools! Did not he who made the outside make the inside also? ⁴¹ But give for alms those things which are within; and behold, everything is clean for you."

GThom 89 (§S50.3)

(89) Jesus said, "Why do you wash the outside of the cup? Do you not realize that he who made the inside is the same one who made the outside?"

* See 187: *Inside and Outside*

456

TEMPLE'S ACTUAL DESTRUCTION*

Matt 24:1–2 (§S51.1)

¹ Jesus left the temple and was going away, when his disciples came to point out to him the buildings of the temple. ² But he answered them, "You see all these, do you not? Truly, I say to you, there will not be left here one stone upon another, that will not be thrown down."

Mark 13:1–2 (§S51.2)

¹ And as he came out of the temple, one of his disciples said to him, "Look, Teacher, what wonderful stones and what wonderful buildings!" ² And Jesus said to him, "Do you see these great buildings? There will not be left here one stone upon another, that will not be thrown down."

Luke 19:41–44 (§S51.3)

⁴¹ And when he drew near and saw the city he wept over it, ⁴² saying, "Would that even today you knew the things that make for peace! But now they are hid from your eyes. ⁴³ For the days shall come upon you, when your enemies will cast up a bank about you and surround you, and hem you in on every side, ⁴⁴ and dash you to the ground, you and your children within you, and they will not leave one stone upon another in you; because you did not know the time of your visitation."

Luke 21:5–6 (§S51.4)

⁵ And as some spoke of the temple, how it was adorned with noble stones and offerings, he said, ⁶ "As for these things which you see, the days will come when there shall not be left here one stone upon another that will not be thrown down."

* See 192: *Temple's Actual Destruction*
* See 457: *Jerusalem Destroyed*

457 JERUSALEM DESTROYED*

Matt 24:1-2 (§S52.1)

[1] Jesus left the temple and was going away, when his disciples came to point out to him the buildings of the temple. [2] But he answered them, "You see all these, do you not? Truly, I say to you, there will not be left here one stone upon another, that will not be thrown down."

Mark 13:1-2 (§S52.2)

[1] And as he came out of the temple, one of his disciples said to him, "Look, Teacher, what wonderful stones and what wonderful buildings!" [2] And Jesus said to him, "Do you see these great buildings? There will not be left here one stone upon another, that will not be thrown down."

Luke 19:41-44 (§S52.3)

[41] And when he drew near and saw the city he wept over it, [42] saying, "Would that even today you knew the things that make for peace! But now they are hid from your eyes. [43] For the days shall come upon you, when your enemies will cast up a bank about you and surround you, and hem you in on every side, [44] and dash you to the ground, you and your children within you, and they will not leave one stone upon another in you; because you did not know the time of your visitation."

Luke 21:5-6 (§S52.4)

[5] And as some spoke of the temple, how it was adorned with noble stones and offerings, he said, [6] "As for these things which you see, the days will come when there shall not be left here one stone upon another that will not be thrown down."

* See 192 & 456: *Temple's Actual Destruction*

458 DECEPTION AND STRIFE*

Matt 24:3-8 (§S53.1)

[3] As he sat on the Mount of Olives, the disciples came to him privately, saying, "Tell us, when will this be, and what will be the sign of your coming and of the close of the age?" [4] And Jesus answered them, "Take heed that no one leads you astray. [5] For many will come in my name, saying, 'I am the Christ,' and they will lead many astray. [6] And you will hear of wars and rumors of wars; see that you are not alarmed; for this must take place, but the end is not yet. [7] For nation will rise against nation, and kingdom against kingdom, and there will be famines and earthquakes in various places: [8] all this is but the beginning of the birth-pangs."

* See 193: *Deception and Strife*

Mark 13:3-8 (§S53.2)

[3] And as he sat on the Mount of Olives opposite the temple, Peter and James and John and Andrew asked him privately, [4] "Tell us, when will this be, and what will be the sign when these things are all to be accomplished?" [5] And Jesus began to say to them, "Take heed that no one leads you astray. [6] Many will come in my name, saying, 'I am he!' and they will lead many astray. [7] And when you hear of wars and rumors of wars, do not be alarmed; this must take place, but the end is not yet. [8] For nation will rise against nation, and kingdom against kingdom; there will be earthquakes in various places, there will be famines; this is but the beginning of the birth-pangs."

Luke 21:7-11 (§S53.3)

[7] And they asked him, "Teacher, when will this be, and what will be the sign when this is about to take place?" [8] And he said, "Take heed that you are not led astray; for many will come in my name, saying, 'I am he!' and, 'The time is at hand!' Do not go after them. [9] And when you hear of wars and tumults, do not be terrified; for this must first take place, but the end will not be at once."

[10] Then he said to them, "Nation will rise against nation, and kingdom against kingdom; [11] there will be great earthquakes, and in various places famines and pestilences; and there will be terrors and great signs from heaven."

Did 16:3 (§S53.4)

[3] for in the last days the false prophets and the corrupters shall be multiplied, and the sheep shall be turned into wolves, and love shall change to hate . . .

Matt 26:6–13 (§S54.1)

⁶ Now when Jesus was at Bethany in the house of Simon the leper, ⁷ a woman came up to him with an alabaster flask of very expensive ointment, and she poured it on his head, as he sat at table. ⁸ But when the disciples saw it, they were indignant, saying, "Why this waste? ⁹ For this ointment might have been sold for a large sum, and given to the poor." ¹⁰ But Jesus, aware of this, said to them, "Why do you trouble the woman? For she has done a beautiful thing to me. ¹¹ For you always have the poor with you, but you will not always have me. ¹² In pouring this ointment on my body she has done it to prepare me for burial. ¹³ Truly, I say to you, wherever this gospel is preached in the whole world, what she has done will be told in memory of her."

Mark 14:3–9 (§S54.2)

³ And while he was at Bethany in the house of Simon the leper, as he sat at table, a woman came with an alabaster flask of ointment of pure nard, very costly, and she broke the flask and poured it over his head. ⁴ But there were some who said to themselves indignantly, "Why was the ointment thus wasted? ⁵ For this ointment might have been sold for more than three hundred denarii, and given to the poor." And they reproached her. ⁶ But Jesus said, "Let her alone; why do you trouble her? She has done a beautiful thing to me. ⁷ For you always have the poor with you, and whenever you will, you can do good to them; but you will not always have me. ⁸ She has done what she could; she has anointed my body beforehand for burying. ⁹ And truly, I say to you, wherever the gospel is preached in the whole world, what she has done will be told in memory of her."

Luke 7:36–50 (§S54.3)

³⁶ One of the Pharisees asked him to eat with him, and he went into the Pharisee's house, and took his place at table. ³⁷ And behold, a woman of the city, who was a sinner, when she learned that he was at table in the Pharisee's house, brought an alabaster flask of ointment, ³⁸ and standing behind him at his feet, weeping, she began to wet his feet with her tears, and wiped them with the hair of her head, and kissed his feet, and anointed them with the ointment. ³⁹ Now when the Pharisee who had invited him saw it, he said to himself, "If this man were a prophet, he would have known who and what sort of woman this is who is touching him, for she is a sinner." ⁴⁰ And Jesus answering said to him, "Simon, I have something to say to you." And he answered, "What is it, Teacher?" ⁴¹ "A certain creditor had two debtors; one owed five hundred denarii, and the other fifty. ⁴² When they could not pay, he forgave them both. Now which of them will love him more?" ⁴³ Simon answered, "The one, I suppose, to whom he forgave more." And he said to him "You have judged rightly." ⁴⁴ Then turning toward the woman he said to Simon, "Do you see this woman? I entered your house, you gave me no water for my feet, but she has wet my feet with her tears and wiped them with her hair. ⁴⁵ You gave me no kiss, but from the time I came in she has not ceased to kiss my feet. ⁴⁶ You did not anoint my head with oil, but she has anointed my feet with ointment. ⁴⁷ Therefore I tell you, her sins, which are many, are forgiven, for she loved much; but he who is forgiven little, loves little." ⁴⁸ And he said to her, "Your sins are forgiven." ⁴⁹ Then those who were at table with him began to say among themselves, "Who is this, who even forgives sins?" ⁵⁰ And he said to the woman, "Your faith has saved you; go in peace."

John 12:1–8 (§S54.4)

¹ Six days before the Passover, Jesus came to Bethany, where Lazarus was, whom Jesus had raised from the dead. ² There they made him a supper; Martha served, and Lazarus was one of those at table with him. ³ Mary took a pound of costly ointment of pure nard and anointed the feet of Jesus and wiped his feet with her hair; and the house was filled with the fragrance of the ointment. ⁴ But Judas Iscariot, one of his disciples (he who was to betray him), said, ⁵ "Why was this ointment not sold for three hundred denarii and given to the poor?" ⁶ This he said, not that he cared for the poor but because he was a thief, and as he had the money box he used to take what was put into it. ⁷ Jesus said, "Let her alone, let her keep it for the day of my burial. ⁸ The poor you always have with you, but you do not always have me."

Ign Eph. 17:1 (§S54.5)

¹ For this end did the Lord receive ointment on his head that he might breathe immortality on the Church. Be not anointed with the evil odour of the doctrine of the Prince of this world, lest he lead you away captive from the life which is set before you.

Matt 26:17–20 (§S55.1)

[17] Now on the first day of Unleavened Bread the disciples came to Jesus, saying, "Where will you have us prepare for you to eat the passover?" [18] He said, "Go into the city to a certain one, and say to him, 'The Teacher says, My time is at hand; I will keep the passover at your house with my disciples.'" [19] And the disciples did as Jesus had directed them, and they prepared the passover.

[20] When it was evening, he sat at table with the twelve disciples.

Mark 14:12–17 (§S55.2)

[12] And on the first day of Unleavened Bread, when they sacrificed the passover lamb, his disciples said to him, "Where will you have us go and prepare for you to eat the passover?" [13] And he sent two of his disciples, and said to them, "Go into the city, and a man carrying a jar of water will meet you; follow him, [14] and wherever he enters, say to the householder, 'The Teacher says, Where is my guest room, where I am to eat the passover with my disciples?' [15] And he will show you a large upper room furnished and ready; there prepare for us." [16] And the disciples set out and went to the city, and found it as he had told them; and they prepared the passover.

[17] And when it was evening he came with the twelve.

Luke 22:7–14 (§S55.3)

[7] Then came the day of Unleavened Bread, on which the passover lamb had to be sacrificed. [8] So Jesus sent Peter and John, saying, "Go and prepare the passover for us, that we may eat it." [9] They said to him, "Where will you have us prepare it?" [10] He said to them, "Behold, when you have entered the city, a man carrying a jar of water will meet you; follow him into the house which he enters, [11] and tell the householder, 'The Teacher says to you, Where is the guest room, where I am to eat the passover with my disciples?' [12] And he will show you a large upper room furnished; there make ready." [13] And they went, and found it as he had told them; and they prepared the passover.

[14] And when the hour came, he sat at table, and the apostles with him.

GEbi 7 (§S55.4)

(7) But they abandon the proper sequence of the words and pervert the saying, as is plain to all from the readings attached, and have let the disciples say:

Where wilt thou that we prepare for thee the passover? and him to answer to that:

Do I desire with desire at this Passover to eat flesh with you? (Epiphanius, *Haer.* 30.22.4)

Matt 26:21–25 (§S56.1)

²¹ and as they were eating, he said, "Truly, I say to you, one of you will betray me." ²² And they were very sorrowful, and began to say to him one after another, "Is it I, Lord?" ²³ He answered, "He who has dipped his hand in the dish with me, will betray me. ²⁴ The Son of man goes as it is written of him, but woe to that man by whom the Son of man is betrayed! It would have been better for that man if he had not been born." ²⁵ Judas, who betrayed him, said, "Is it I, Master?" He said to him, "You have said so."

Mark 14:18–21 (§S56.2)

¹⁸ And as they were at table eating, Jesus said, "Truly, I say to you, one of you will betray me, one who is eating with me." ¹⁹ They began to be sorrowful, and to say to him one after another, "Is it I?" ²⁰ He said to them, "It is one of the twelve, one who is dipping bread into the dish with me. ²¹ For the Son of man goes as it is written of him, but woe to that man by whom the Son of man is betrayed! It would have been better for that man if he had not been born."

Luke 22:14–23 (§S56.3)

¹⁴ And when the hour came, he sat at table, and the apostles with him. ¹⁵ And he said to them, "I have earnestly desired to eat this passover with you before I suffer; ¹⁶ for I tell you I shall not eat it until it is fulfilled in the kingdom of God." ¹⁷ And he took a cup, and when he had given thanks he said, "Take this, and divide it among yourselves; ¹⁸ for I tell you that from now on I shall not drink of the fruit of the vine until the kingdom of God comes." ¹⁹ And he took bread, and when he had given thanks he broke it and gave it to them, saying, "This is my body which is given for you. Do this in remembrance of me." ²⁰ And likewise the cup after supper, saying, "This cup which is poured out for you is the new covenant in my blood. ²¹ But behold the hand of him who betrays me is with me on the table. ²² For the Son of man goes as it has been determined; but woe to that man by whom he is betrayed!" ²³ And they began to question one another, which of them it was that would do this.

John 13:21–30 (§S56.4)

²¹ When Jesus had thus spoken, he was troubled in spirit, and testified, "Truly, truly, I say to you, one of you will betray me." ²² The disciples looked at one another, uncertain of whom he spoke. ²³ One of his disciples, whom Jesus loved, was lying close to the breast of Jesus; ²⁴ so Simon Peter beckoned to him and said, "Tell us who it is of whom he speaks." ²⁵ So lying thus, close to the breast of Jesus, he said to him, "Lord, who is it?" ²⁶ Jesus answered, "It is he to whom I shall give this morsel when I have dipped it." So when he had dipped the morsel, he gave it to Judas, the son of Simon Iscariot. ²⁷ Then after the morsel, Satan entered into him. Jesus said to him, "What you are going to do, do quickly." ²⁸ Now no one at the table knew why he said this to him. ²⁹ Some thought that, because Judas had the money box, Jesus was telling him, "Buy what we need for the feast"; or, that he should give something to the poor. ³⁰ So, after receiving the morsel, he immediately went out; and it was night.

1 Clem 46:5–9 (§S56.5)

⁵ Why are there strife and passion and divisions and schisms and war among you? ⁶ Or have we not one God, and one Christ, and one Spirit of grace poured out upon us? And is there not one calling in Christ? ⁷ Why do we divide and tear asunder the members of Christ, and raise up strife against our own body, and reach such a pitch of madness as to forget that we are members one of another? Remember the words of the Lord Jesus; ⁸ for he said, "Woe unto that man: it were good for him if he had not been born, than that he should offend one of my elect; it were better for him that a millstone be hung on him, and he be cast into the sea, than that he should turn aside one of my elect." ⁹ Your schism has turned aside many, has cast many into discouragement, many to doubt, all of us to grief; and your sedition continues.

Herm Vis 4.2:6 (§S56.6)

⁶ "Believe on the Lord, you who are double-minded, that he can do all things, and turns his wrath away from you, and sends scourges on you who are double-minded. Woe to those who hear these words and disobey; it were better for them not to have been born."

* See 210: *Better not Born*

462 SUPPER AND EUCHARIST

Matt 26:26–29 (§S57.1)

[26] Now as they were eating, Jesus took bread, and blessed, and broke it, and gave it to the disciples and said, "Take, eat; this is my body." [27] And he took a cup, and when he had given thanks he gave it to them, saying, "Drink of it, all of you; [28] for this is my blood of the covenant, which is poured out for many for the forgiveness of sins. [29] I tell you I shall not drink again of this fruit of the vine until that day when I drink it new with you in my Father's kingdom."

Mark 14:22–25 (§S57.2)

[22] And as they were eating, he took bread, and blessed, and broke it, and gave it to them, and said, "Take; this is my body." [23] And he took a cup, and when he had given thanks he gave it to them, and they all drank of it. [24] And he said to them, "This is my blood of the covenant, which is poured out for many. [25] Truly, I say to you, I shall not drink again of the fruit of the vine until that day when I drink it new in the kingdom of God."

Luke 22:15–20 (§S57.3)

[15] And he said to them, "I have earnestly desired to eat this passover with you before I suffer; [16] for I tell you I shall not eat it until it is fulfilled in the kingdom of God." [17] And he took a cup, and when he had given thanks he said, "Take this, and divide it among yourselves; [18] for I tell you that from now on I shall not drink of the fruit of the vine until the kingdom of God comes." [19] And he took bread, and when he had given thanks he broke it and gave it to them, saying, "This is my body which is given for you. Do this in remembrance of me." [20] And likewise the cup after supper, saying, "This cup which is poured out for you is the new covenant in my blood."

John 6:51–58 (§S57.4)

[51] "I am the living bread which came down from heaven; if any one eats of this bread, he will live for ever; and the bread which I shall give for the life of the world is my flesh." [52] The Jews then disputed among themselves, saying, "How can this man give us his flesh to eat?" [53] So Jesus said to them, "Truly, truly, I say to you, unless you eat the flesh of the Son of man and drink his blood, you have no life in you; [54] he who eats my flesh and drinks my blood has eternal life, and I will raise him up at the last day. [55] For my flesh is food indeed, and my blood is drink indeed. [56] He who eats my flesh and drinks my blood abides in me, and I in him. [57] As the living Father sent me, and I live because of the Father, so he who eats me will live because of me. [58] This is the bread which came down from heaven, not such as the fathers ate and died; he who eats this bread will live for ever."

1 Cor 11:23–25 (§S57.5)

[23] For I received from the Lord what I also delivered to you, that the Lord Jesus on the night when he was betrayed took bread, [24] and when he had given thanks, he broke it, and said, "This is my body which is for you. Do this in remembrance of me." [25] In the same way also the cup, after supper, saying, "This cup is the new covenant in my blood. Do this, as often as you drink it, in remembrance of me."

Did 9:1–4 (§S57.6)

[1] And concerning the Eucharist, hold Eucharist thus: [2] First concerning the Cup, "We give thanks to thee, our Father, for the Holy Vine of David thy child, which, thou didst make known to us through Jesus thy child; to thee be glory for ever." [3] And concerning the broken Bread: "We give thee thanks, our Father, for the life and knowledge which thou didst make known to us through Jesus thy child. To thee be glory for ever. [4] As this broken bread was scattered upon the mountains, but was brought together and became one, so let thy Church be gathered together from the ends of the earth into thy kingdom, for thine is the glory and the power through Jesus Christ for ever."

---

463 PETER'S BETRAYAL FORETOLD

Matt 26:30–35 (§S58.1)

[30] And when they had sung a hymn, they went out to the Mount of Olives. [31] Then Jesus said to them, "You will all fall away because of me this night; for it is written, 'I will strike the shepherd, and the sheep of the flock will be scattered.' [32] But after I am raised up, I will go before you to Galilee." [33] Peter declared to him, "Though they all fall away because of you, I will never fall away." [34] Jesus said to him, "Truly, I say to you, this very night, before the cock crows, you will deny me three times." [35] Peter said to him, "Even if I must die with you, I will not deny you." And so said all the disciples.

Mark 14:26–31 (§S58.2)

[26] And when they had sung a hymn, they went out to the Mount of Olives. [27] And Jesus said to them, "You will all fall away; for it is written, 'I will strike the shepherd, and the sheep will be scattered.' [28] But after I am raised up, I will go before you to Galilee." [29] Peter said to him, "Even though they all fall away, I will not." [30] And Jesus said to him, "Truly, I say to you, this very night, before the cock crows twice, you will deny me three times." [31] But he said vehemently, "If I must die with you, I will not deny you." And they all said the same.

Luke 22:31–34 (§S58.3)

[31] "Simon, Simon, behold, Satan demanded to have you, that he might sift you like wheat, [32] but I have prayed for you that your faith may not fail; and when you have turned again, strengthen your brethren." [33] And he said to him, "Lord, I am ready to go with you to prison and to death." [34] He said, "I tell you, Peter, the cock will not crow this day, until you three times deny that you know me."

John 13:36–38 (§S58.4)

[36] Simon Peter said to him, "Lord, where are you going?" Jesus answered, "Where I am going you cannot follow me now; but you shall follow afterward." [37] Peter said to him, "Lord, why cannot I follow you now? I will lay down my life for you." [38] Jesus answered, "Will you lay down your life for me? Truly, truly, I say to you, the cock will not crow, till you have denied me three times."

Fayyum Fragment (§S58.5)

. . . while he was going out, he said, "This night you will all fall away, as it is written, 'I will strike the shepherd, and the sheep will be scattered.'" When Peter said, "Even though all, not I," Jesus said, "Before the cock crows twice, you will this day deny me three times."

Matt 26:36–46 (§S59.1)

[36] Then Jesus went with them to a place called Gethsemane, and he said to his disciples, "Sit here, while I go yonder and pray." [37] And taking with him Peter and the two sons of Zebedee, he began to be sorrowful and troubled. [38] Then he said to them, "My soul is very sorrowful, even to death; remain here, and watch with me." [39] And going a little farther he fell on his face and prayed, "My father, if it be possible, let this cup pass from me; nevertheless, not as I will, but as thou wilt." [40] And he came to the disciples and found them sleeping; and he said to Peter, "So, could you not watch with me one hour? [41] Watch and pray that you may not enter into temptation; the spirit indeed is willing, but the flesh is weak." [42] Again, for the second time, he went away and prayed, "My Father, if this cannot pass unless I drink it, thy will be done." [43] And again he came and found them sleeping, for their eyes were heavy. [44] So, leaving them again, he went away and prayed for the third time, saying the same words. [45] Then he came to the disciples and said to them, "Are you still sleeping and taking your rest? Behold, the hour is at hand, and the Son of man is betrayed into the hands of sinners. [46] Rise, let us be going; see, my betrayer is at hand."

Mark 14:32–42 (§S59.2)

[32] And they went to a place which was called Gethsemane; and he said to his disciples, "Sit here, while I pray." [33] And he took with him Peter and James and John, and began to be greatly distressed and troubled. [34] And he said to them, "My soul is very sorrowful, even to death; remain here, and watch." [35] And going a little farther, he fell on the ground and prayed that, if it were possible, the hour might pass from him. [36] And he said, "Abba, Father, all things are possible to thee; remove this cup from me; yet not what I will, but what thou wilt." [37] And he came and found them sleeping, and he said to Peter, "Simon, are you asleep? Could you not watch one hour? [38] Watch and pray that you may not enter into temptation; the spirit indeed is willing, but the flesh is weak." [39] And again he went away and prayed, saying the same words. [40] And again he came and found them sleeping, for their eyes were very heavy; and they did not know what to answer him. [41] And he came the third time, and said to them, "Are you still sleeping and taking your rest? It is enough; the hour has come; the Son of man is betrayed into the hands of sinners. [42] Rise, let us be going; see, my betrayer is at hand."

Luke 22:39–46 (§S59.3)

[39] And he came out, and went, as was his custom, to the Mount of Olives; and the disciples followed him. [40] And when he came to the place he said to them, "Pray that you may not enter into temptation." [41] And he withdrew from them about a stone's throw, and knelt down and prayed, [42] "Father, if thou art willing, remove this cup from me; nevertheless not my will, but thine, be done." [45] And when he rose from prayer, he came to the disciples and found them sleeping for sorrow, [46] and he said to them, "Why do you sleep? Rise and pray that you may not enter into temptation."

John 12:27 (§S59.4)

[27] "Now is my soul troubled. And what shall I say? 'Father, save me from this hour'? No, for this purpose I have come to this hour."

Pol Phil 7:1–2 (§S59.5)

[1] "For everyone who does not confess that Jesus Christ has come in the flesh is an anti-Christ"; and whosoever does not confess the testimony of the Cross is of the devil: and whosoever perverts the oracles of the Lord for his own lusts, and says that there is neither resurrection nor judgment,—this man is the first-born of Satan. [2] Wherefore, leaving the foolishness of the crowd, and their false teaching, let us turn back to the word which was delivered to us in the beginning, "watching unto prayer" and persevering in fasting, beseeching the all-seeing God in our supplications "to lead us not into temptation," even as the Lord said, "The spirit is willing, but the flesh is weak."

465 JESUS ARRESTED

Matt 26:47–56 (§S60.1)

⁴⁷While he was still speaking, Judas came, one of the twelve, and with him a great crowd with swords and clubs, from the chief priests and the elders of the people. ⁴⁸Now the betrayer had given them a sign, saying, "The one I shall kiss is the man; seize him." ⁴⁹And he came up to Jesus at once and said, "Hail, Master!" And he kissed him. ⁵⁰Jesus said to him, "Friend, why are you here?" Then they came up and laid hands on Jesus and seized him. ⁵¹And behold, one of those who were with Jesus stretched out his hand and drew his sword, and struck the slave of the high priest, and cut off his ear. ⁵²Then Jesus said to him, "Put your sword back into its place; for all who take the sword will perish by the sword. ⁵³Do you think that I cannot appeal to my Father, and he will at once send me more than twelve legions of angels? ⁵⁴But how then should the scriptures be fulfilled, that it must be so?" ⁵⁵At that hour Jesus said to the crowds, "Have you come out as against a robber, with swords and clubs to capture me? Day after day I sat in the temple teaching, and you did not seize me. ⁵⁶But all this has taken place, that the scriptures of the prophets might be fulfilled." Then all the disciples forsook him and fled.

Mark 14:43–50 (§S60.2)

⁴³And immediately, while he was still speaking, Judas came, one of the twelve, and with him a crowd with swords and clubs, from the chief priests and the scribes and the elders. ⁴⁴Now the betrayer had given them a sign, saying, "The one I shall kiss is the man; seize him and lead him away under guard." ⁴⁵And when he came, he went up to him at once, and said,

"Master!" And he kissed him. ⁴⁶And they laid hands on him and seized him. ⁴⁷But one of those who stood by drew his sword, and struck the slave of the high priest and cut off his ear. ⁴⁸And Jesus said to them, "Have you come out as against a robber, with swords and clubs to capture me? ⁴⁹Day after day I was with you in the temple teaching, and you did not seize me. But let the scriptures be fulfilled." ⁵⁰And they all forsook him, and fled.

Luke 22:47–53 (§S60.3)

⁴⁷While he was still speaking, there came a crowd, and the man called Judas, one of the twelve, was leading them. He drew near to Jesus to kiss him; ⁴⁸but Jesus said to him, "Judas, would you betray the Son of man with a kiss?" ⁴⁹And when those who were about him saw what would follow, they said, "Lord, shall we strike with the sword?" ⁵⁰And one of them struck the slave of the high priest and cut off his right ear. ⁵¹But Jesus said, "No more of this!" And he touched his ear and healed him. ⁵²Then Jesus said to the chief priests and officers of the temple and elders, who had come out against him, "Have you come out as against a robber, with swords and clubs? ⁵³When I was with you day after day in the temple, you did not lay hands on me. But this is your hour, and the power of darkness."

John 18:2–12 (§S60.4)

²Now Judas, who betrayed him, also knew the place; for Jesus often met there with his disciples. ³So Judas, procuring a band of soldiers and some officers from the chief priests and the Pharisees, went there with lanterns and torches and weapons. ⁴Then

Jesus, knowing all that was to befall him, came forward and said to them, "Whom do you seek?" ⁵They answered him, "Jesus of Nazareth." Jesus said to them, "I am he." Judas, who betrayed him, was standing with them. ⁶When he said to them, "I am he," they drew back and fell to the ground. ⁷Again he asked them, "Whom do you seek?" And they said, "Jesus of Nazareth." ⁸Jesus answered, "I told you that I am he; so, if you seek me, let these men go." ⁹This was to fulfil the word which he had spoken, "Of those whom thou gavest me I lost not one." ¹⁰Then Simon Peter, having a sword, drew it and struck the high priest's slave and cut off his right ear. The slave's name was Malchus. ¹¹Jesus said to Peter, "Put your sword into its sheath; shall I not drink the cup which the Father has given me?"

¹²So the band of soldiers and their captain and the officers of the Jews seized Jesus and bound him.

John 18:19–23 (§S60.5)

¹⁹The high priest then questioned Jesus about his disciples and his teaching. ²⁰Jesus answered him, "I have spoken openly to the world; I have always taught in synagogues and in the temple, where all Jews come together; I have said nothing secretly. ²¹Why do you ask me? Ask those who have heard me, what I said to them; they know what I said." ²²When he had said this, one of the officers standing by struck Jesus with his hand, saying, "Is that how you answer the high priest?" ²³Jesus answered him, "If I have spoken wrongly, bear witness to the wrong; but if I have spoken rightly, why do you strike me?"

206

Matt 26:59–63a (§S61.1)

[59] Now the chief priests and the whole council sought false testimony against Jesus that they might put him to death, [60] but they found none, though many false witnesses came forward. At last two came forward [61] and said, "This fellow said, 'I am able to destroy the temple of God, and to build it in three days.'" [62] And the high priest stood up and said, "Have you no answer to make? What is it that these men testify against you?" [63] But Jesus was silent.

Matt 27:38–40 (§S61.2)

[38] Then two robbers were crucified with him, one on the right and one on the left. [39] And those who passed by derided him, wagging their heads [40] and saying, "You who would destroy the temple and build it in three days, save yourself! If you are the Son of God, come down from the cross."

Mark 14:55–61a (§S61.3)

[55] Now the chief priests and the whole council sought testimony against Jesus to put him to death; but they found none. [56] For many bore false witness against him, and their witness did not agree. [57] And some stood up and bore false witness against him, saying, [58] "We heard him say, 'I will destroy this temple that is made with hands, and in three days I will build another, not made with hands.'" [59] Yet not even so did their testimony agree. [60] And the high priest stood up in the midst, and

asked Jesus, "Have you no answer to make? What is it that these men testify against you?" [61] But he was silent and made no answer.

Mark 15:27–30 (§S61.4)

[27] And with him they crucified two robbers, one on his right and one one his left. [29] And those who passed by derided him, wagging their heads, and saying, "Aha! You who would destroy the temple and build it in three days, [30] save yourself, and come down from the cross!"

John 2:13–22 (§S61.5)

[13] The Passover of the Jews was at hand, and Jesus went up to Jerusalem. [14] In the temple he found those who were selling oxen and sheep and pigeons, and the money-changers at their business. [15] And making a whip of cords, he drove them all, with the sheep and oxen, out of the temple; and he poured out the coins of the money-changers and overturned their tables. [16] And he told those who sold the pigeons, "Take these things away; you shall not make my Father's house a house of trade." [17] His disciples remembered that it was written, "Zeal for thy house will consume me." [18] The Jews then said to him, "What sign have you to show us for doing this?" [19] Jesus answered them, "Destroy this temple, and in three days I will raise it up." [20] The Jews then said, "It has taken forty-six years to build this temple, and will you raise

it up in three days?" [21] But he spoke of the temple of his body. [22] When therefore he was raised from the dead, his disciples remembered that he had said this; and they believed the scripture and the word which Jesus had spoken.

Acts 6:8–14 (§S61.6)

[8] And Stephen, full of grace and power, did great wonders and signs among the people. [9] Then some of those who belonged to the synagogue of the Freedmen (as it was called), and of the Cyre'nians, and the Alexandrians, and of those from Cili'cia and Asia, arose and disputed with Stephen. [10] But they could not withstand the wisdom and the Spirit with which he spoke. [11] Then they secretly instigated men, who said, "We have heard him speak blasphemous words against Moses and God." [12] And they stirred up the people and the elders and the scribes, and they came upon him before the council, [13] and set up false witnesses who said, "This man never ceases to speak words against this holy place and the law; [14] for we have heard him say that this Jesus of Nazareth will destroy this place, and will change the customs which Moses delivered to us."

GThom 71 (§S61.7)

(71) Jesus said, "I shall destroy [this] house, and no one will be able to rebuild it."

* See 211: *Temple and Jesus*

467

PRIEST'S QUESTION

Matt 26:63b–68 (§S62.1)

[63] . . . And the high priest said to him, "I adjure you by the living God, tell us if you are the Christ, the Son of God." [64] Jesus said to him, "You have said so. But I tell you, hereafter you will see the Son of man seated at the right hand of Power, and coming on the clouds of heaven." [65] Then the high priest tore his robes, and said, "He has uttered blasphemy. Why do we still need witnesses? You have now heard his blasphemy. [66] What is your judgment?" They answered, "He deserves death." [67] Then they spat in his face, and struck him; and some slapped him, [68] saying, "Prophesy to us, you Christ! Who is it that struck you?"

Mark 14:61b–65 (§S62.2)

[61] . . . Again the high priest asked him, "Are you the Christ, the Son of the Blessed?" [62] And Jesus said, "I am; and you will see the Son of man seated at the right hand of Power, and coming with the clouds of heaven." [63] And the high priest tore his garments, and said, "Why do we still need witnesses? [64] You have heard his blasphemy. What is your decision?" And they all condemned him as deserving death. [65] And some began to spit on him, and to cover his face, and to strike him, saying to him, "Prophesy!" And the guards received him with blows.

Luke 22:66–71 (§S62.3)

[66] When day came, the assembly of the elders of the people gathered together, both chief priests and scribes; and they led him away to their council, and they said, [67] "If you are the Christ, tell us." But he said to them, "If I tell you, you will not believe; [68] and if I ask you, you will not answer. [69] But from now on the Son of man shall be seated at the right hand of the power of God." [70] And they all said, "Are you the Son of God, then?" And he said to them, "You say that I am." [71] And they said, "What further testimony do we need? We have heard it ourselves from his own lips."

468 PILATE'S QUESTION

Matt 27:11 (§S63.1)

[11] Now Jesus stood before the governor; and the governor asked him, "Are you the King of the Jews?" Jesus said, "You have said so."

Mark 15:2 (§S63.2)

[2] And Pilate asked him, "Are you the King of the Jews?" And he answered him, "You have said so."

Luke 23:2–3 (§S63.3)

[2] And they began to accuse him, saying, "We found this man perverting our nation, and forbidding us to give tribute to Caesar, and saying that he himself is Christ a king." [3] And Pilate asked him, "Are you the King of the Jews?" And he answered him, "You have said so."

John 18:33–38a (§S63.4)

[33] Pilate entered the praetorium again and called Jesus, and said to him, "Are you the King of the Jews?" [34] Jesus answered, "Do you say this of your own accord, or did others say it to you about me?" [35] Pilate answered, "Am I a Jew? Your own nation and the chief priests have handed you over to me; what have you done?" [36] Jesus answered, "My kingship is not of this world; if my kingship were of this world, my servants would fight, that I might not be handed over to the Jews; but my kingship is not from the world." [37] Pilate said to him, "So you are a king?" Jesus answered, "You say that I am a king. For this I was born, and for this I have come into the world, to bear witness to the truth. Every one who is of the truth hears my voice." [38] Pilate said to him, "What is truth?"

469 THE TWO THIEVES

Matt 27:38–44 (§S64.1)

[38] Then two robbers were crucified with him, one on the right and one on the left. [39] And those who passed by derided him, wagging their heads [40] and saying, "You who would destroy the temple and build it in three days, save yourself! If you are the Son of God, come down from the cross." [41] So also the chief priests, with the scribes and elders, mocked him, saying, [42] "He saved others; he cannot save himself. He is the King of Israel; let him come down now from the cross, and we will believe in him. [43] He trusts in God; let God deliver him now, if he desires him; for he said, 'I am the Son of God.'" [44] And the robbers who were crucified with him also reviled him in the same way.

Mark 15:27–32 (§S64.2)

[27] And with him they crucified two robbers, one on his right and one one his left. [29] And those who passed by derided him, wagging their heads, and saying, "Aha! You who would destroy the temple and build it in three days, [30] save yourself, and come down from the cross!" [31] So also the chief priests mocked him to one another with the scribes, saying, "He saved others; he cannot save himself. [32] Let the Christ, the King of Israel, come down now from the cross, that we may see and believe." Those who were crucified with him also reviled him.

Luke 23:32–43 (§S64.3)

[32] Two others also, who were criminals, were led away to be put to death with him. [33] And when they came to the place which is called The Skull, there they crucified him, and the criminals, one on the right and one on the left. [34] And Jesus said, "Father, forgive them; for they know not what they do." And they cast lots to divide his garments. [35] And the people stood by, watching; but the rulers scoffed at him, saying, "He saved others; let him save himself, if he is the Christ of God, his Chosen One!" [36] The soldiers also mocked him, coming up and offering him vinegar, [37] and saying, "If you are the King of the Jews, save yourself!" [38] There was also an inscription over him, "This is the King of the Jews."

[39] One of the criminals who were hanged railed at him, saying, "Are you not the Christ? Save yourself and us!" [40] But the other rebuked him, saying, "Do you not fear God, since you are under the same sentence of condemnation? [41] And we indeed justly; for we are receiving the due reward of our deeds; but this man has done nothing wrong." [42] And he said, "Jesus, remember me when you come into your kingdom." [43] And he said to him, "Truly, I say to you, today you will be with me in Paradise."

GPet 4:10–14 (§S64.4)

[10] And they brought two malefactors and crucified the Lord in the midst between them. But he held his peace, as if he felt no pain. [11] And when they had set up the cross, they wrote upon it: this is the King of Israel. [12] And they laid down his garments before him and divided them among themselves and cast the lot upon them. [13] But one of the malefactors rebuked them, saying, "We have landed in suffering for the deeds of wickedness which we have committed, but this man, who has become the saviour of men, what wrong has he done you?" [14] And they were wroth with him and commanded that his legs should not be broken, so that he might die in torments.

Matt 27:45–50 (§S65.1)

⁴⁵ Now from the sixth hour there was darkness over all the land until the ninth hour. ⁴⁶ And about the ninth hour Jesus cried with a loud voice, "Eli, Eli, lama sabachthani?" that is, "My God, my God, why hast thou forsaken me?" ⁴⁷ And some of the bystanders hearing it said, "This man is calling Elijah." ⁴⁸ And one of them at once ran and took a sponge, filled it with vinegar, and put it on a reed, and gave it to him to drink. ⁴⁹ But the others said, "Wait, let us see whether Elijah will come to save him." ⁵⁰ And Jesus cried again with a loud voice and yielded up his spirit.

Mark 15:33–37 (§S65.2)

³³ And when the sixth hour had come, there was darkness over the whole land until the ninth hour. ³⁴ And at the ninth hour Jesus cried with a loud voice, "Eloi, Eloi, lama sabachthani?" which means, "My God, my God, why hast thou forsaken me?" ³⁵ And some of the bystanders hearing it said, "Behold, he is calling Elijah." ³⁶ And one ran and, filling a sponge full of vinegar, put it on a reed and gave it to him to drink, saying, "Wait, let us see whether Elijah will come to take him down." ³⁷ And Jesus uttered a loud cry, and breathed his last.

Luke 23:36,44–46 (§S65.3)

³⁶ The soldiers also mocked him, coming up and offering him vinegar,

⁴⁴ It was now about the sixth hour, and there was darkness over the whole land until the ninth hour, ⁴⁵ while the sun's light failed; and the curtain of the temple was torn in two. ⁴⁶ Then Jesus, crying with a loud voice, said, "Father, into thy hands I commit my spirit!" And having said this he breathed his last.

John 19:28–30 (§S65.4)

²⁸ After this Jesus, knowing that all was now finished, said (to fulfil the scripture), "I thirst." ²⁹ A bowl full of vinegar stood there; so they put a sponge full of the vinegar on hyssop and held it to his mouth. ³⁰ When Jesus had received the vinegar, he said, "It is finished"; and he bowed his head and gave up his spirit.

GPet 5:15–19 (§S65.5)

¹⁵ Now it was midday and a darkness covered all Judaea. And they became anxious and uneasy lest the sun had already set, since he was still alive. <For> it stands written for them: the sun should not set on one that has been put to death. ¹⁶ And one of them said, "Give him to drink gall with vinegar." And they mixed it and gave him to drink. ¹⁷ And they fulfilled all things and completed the measure of their sins on their head. ¹⁸ And many went about with lamps, <and> as they supposed that it was night, they went to bed (or: they stumbled). ¹⁹ And the Lord called out and cried, "My power, O power, thou hast forsaken me!" And having said this he was taken up.

Matt 28:1–10 (§S66.1)

¹ Now after the sabbath, toward the dawn of the first day of the week, Mary Magdalene and the other Mary went to see the sepulchre. ² And behold, there was a great earthquake; for an angel of the Lord descended from heaven and came and rolled back the stone, and sat upon it. ³ His appearance was like lightning, and his raiment white as snow. ⁴ And for fear of him the guards trembled and became like dead men. ⁵ But the angel said to the women, "Do not be afraid; for I know that you seek Jesus who was crucified. ⁶ He is not here; for he has risen, as he said. Come, see the place where he lay. ⁷ Then go quickly and tell his disciples that he has risen from the dead, and behold, he is going before you to Galilee; there you will see him. Lo, I have told you." ⁸ So they departed quickly from the tomb with fear and great joy, and ran to tell his disciples. ⁹ And behold, Jesus met them and said, "Hail!" And they came and took hold of his feet and worshiped him. ¹⁰ Then Jesus said to them, "Do not be afraid; go and tell my brethren to go to Galilee, and there they will see me."

Mark 16:1–8 (§S66.2)

¹ And when the sabbath was past, Mary Magdalene, and Mary the mother of James, and Salome, bought spices, so that they might go and anoint him. ² And very early on the first day of the week they went to the tomb when the sun had risen. ³ And they were saying to one another, "Who will roll away the stone for us from the door of the tomb?" ⁴ And looking up, they saw that the stone was rolled back—it was very large. ⁵ And entering the tomb, they saw a young man sitting on the right side, dressed in a white robe; and they were amazed. ⁶ And he said to them, "Do not be amazed; you seek Jesus of Nazareth, who was crucified. He has risen, he is not here; see the place where they laid him. ⁷ But go, tell his disciples and Peter that he is going before you to Galilee; there you will see him, as he told you." ⁸ And they went out and fled from the tomb; for trembling and astonishment had come upon them; and they said nothing to any one, for they were afraid.

Luke 24:1–11 (§S66.3)

¹ But on the first day of the week, at early dawn, they went to the tomb, taking the spices which they had prepared. ² And they found the stone rolled away from the tomb, ³ but when they went in they did not find the body. ⁴ While they were perplexed about this, behold, two men stood by them in dazzling apparel; ⁵ and as they were frightened and bowed their faces to the ground, the men said to them, "Why do you seek the living among the dead? ⁶ Remember how he told you, while he was still in Galilee, ⁷ that the Son of man must be delivered into the hands of sinful men, and be crucified, and on the third day rise." ⁸ And they remembered his words, ⁹ and returning from the tomb they told all this to the eleven and to all the rest. ¹⁰ Now it was Mary Magdalene and Joanna and Mary the mother of James and the other women with them who told this to the apostles; ¹¹ but these words seemed to them an idle tale, and they did not believe them.

472 TEACH AND BAPTIZE

Matt 28:16–20 (§S67)
[16] Now the eleven disciples went to Galilee, to the mountain to which Jesus had directed them. [17] And when they saw him they worshiped him; but some doubted. [18] And Jesus came and said to them, "All authority in heaven and on earth has been given to me. [19] Go therefore and make disciples of all nations, baptizing them in the name of the Father and of the Son and of the Holy Spirit, [20] teaching them to observe all that I have commanded you; and lo, I am with you always, to the close of the age."

473 STRANGER AS EXORCIST

Mark 9:38–40 (§S68.1)
[38] John said to him, "Teacher, we saw a man casting out demons in your name, and we forbade him, because he was not following us." [39] But Jesus said, "Do not forbid him; for no one who does a mighty work in my name will be able soon after to speak evil of me. [40] For he that is not against us is for us."

Luke 9:49–50 (§S68.2)
[49] John answered, "Master, we saw a man casting out demons in your name, and we forbade him, because he does not follow with us." [50] But Jesus said to him, "Do not forbid him; for he that is not against you is for you."

474 WIDOW'S MITE

Mark 12:41–44 (§S69.1)
[41] And he sat down opposite the treasury, and watched the multitude putting money into the treasury. Many rich people put in large sums. [42] And a poor widow came, and put in two copper coins, which make a penny. [43] And he called his disciples to him, and said to them, "Truly, I say to you, this poor widow has put in more than all those who are contributing to the treasury. [44] For they all contributed out of their abundance; but she out of her poverty has put in everything she had, her whole living."

Luke 21:1–4 (§S69.2)
[1] He looked up and saw the rich putting their gifts into the treasury; [2] and he saw a poor widow put in two copper coins. [3] And he said, "Truly I tell you, this poor widow has put in more than all of them; [4] for they all contributed out of their abundance, but she out of her poverty put in all the living that she had."

475 JESUS AT TWELVE

Luke 2:41–51 (§S70)

[41] Now his parents went to Jerusalem every year at the feast of the Passover. [42] And when he was twelve years old, they went up according to custom; [43] and when the feast was ended, as they were returning, the boy Jesus stayed behind in Jerusalem. His parents did not know it, [44] but supposing him to be in the company they went a day's journey, and they sought him among their kinsfolk and acquaintances; [45] and when they did not find him, they returned to Jerusalem, seeking him. [46] After three days they found him in the temple, sitting among the teachers, listening to them and asking them questions; [47] and all who heard him were amazed at his understanding and his answers. [48] And when they saw him they were astonished; and his mother said to him, "Son, why have you treated us so? Behold, your father and I have been looking for you anxiously." [49] And he said to them, "How is it that you sought me? Did you not know that I must be in my Father's house?" [50] And they did not understand the saying which he spoke to them. [51] And he went down with them and came to Nazareth, and was obedient to them; and his mother kept all these things in her heart.

476 JESUS AT NAZARETH★

Luke 4:16–22 (§S71)

[16] And he came to Nazareth, where he had been brought up; and he went to the synagogue, as his custom was, on the sabbath day. And he stood up to read; [17] and there was given to him the book of the prophet Isaiah. He opened the book and found the place where it was written,

[18] "The Spirit of the Lord is upon me,
because he has anointed me to preach good news to the poor.
He has sent me to proclaim release to the captives
and recovering of sight to the blind,
to set at liberty those who are oppressed,
[19] to proclaim the acceptable year of the Lord."

[20] And he closed the book, and gave it back to the attendant, and sat down; and the eyes of all in the synagogue were fixed on him. [21] And he began to say to them, "Today this scripture has been fulfilled in your hearing." [22] And all spoke well of him, and wondered at the gracious words which proceeded out of his mouth; and they said, "Is not this Joseph's son?"

★ See 214: *Physician, Heal Yourself*
★ See 215: *Gentiles Preferred*

477 ON SABBATH LABOR

Luke 6:1–10 (§S72)★

[1] On a sabbath, while he was going through the grainfields, his disciples plucked and ate some heads of grain, rubbing them in their hands. [2] But some of the Pharisees said, "Why are you doing what is not lawful to do on the sabbath?" [3] And Jesus answered, "Have you not read what David did when he was hungry, he and those who were with him: [4] how he entered the house of God, and took and ate the bread of the Presence, which it is not lawful for any but the priests to eat, and also gave it to those with him?"★ [5] And he said to them, "The Son of man is lord of the sabbath."

[6] On another sabbath, when he entered the synagogue and taught, a man was there whose right hand was withered. [7] And the scribes and the Pharisees watched him, to see whether he would heal on the sabbath, so that they might find an accusation against him. [8] But he knew their thoughts, and he said to the man who had the withered hand, "Come and stand here." And he rose and stood there. [9] And Jesus said to them, "I ask you, is it lawful on the sabbath to do good or to do harm, to save life or to destroy it?" [10] And he looked around on them all, and said to him, "Stretch out your hand." And he did so, and his hand was restored.

★ Codex Bezal (D) places 6:5 after 6:10 and replaces it with a new unit. The sequence is: (1) 6:1–4; (2) 477; (3) 6:6–10; (4) 6:5. The new unit is: On the same day he saw a man working on the sabbath and said to him "Man, if you know what you are doing, you are blessed; but if you do not know, you are accursed and a transgressor of the law."

478 INHOSPITABLE SAMARITANS

Luke 9:51–55 (§S73)

⁵¹ When the days drew near for him to be received up, he set his face to go to Jerusalem. ⁵² And he sent messengers ahead of him, who went and entered a village of the Samaritans, to make ready for him; ⁵³ but the people would not receive him, because his face was set toward Jerusalem. ⁵⁴ And when his disciples James and John saw it, they said, "Lord, do you want us to bid fire come down from heaven and consume them?" ⁵⁵ But he turned and rebuked them.

479 THE SEVENTY RETURN

Luke 10:17–20 (§S74)

¹⁷ The seventy returned with joy, saying, "Lord, even the demons are subject to us in your name!" ¹⁸ And he said to them, "I saw Satan fall like lightning from heaven. ¹⁹ Behold, I have given you authority to tread upon serpents and scorpions, and over all the power of the enemy; and nothing shall hurt you. ²⁰ Nevertheless do not rejoice in this, that the spirits are subject to you; but rejoice that your names are written in heaven."

480 MARTHA AND MARY

Luke 10:38–42 (§S75)

³⁸ Now as they went on their way, he entered a village; and a woman named Martha received him into her house. ³⁹ And she had a sister called Mary, who sat at the Lord's feet and listened to his teaching. ⁴⁰ But Martha was distracted with much serving; and she went to him and said, "Lord, do you not care that my sister has left me to serve alone? Tell her then to help me." ⁴¹ But the Lord answered her, "Martha, Martha, you are anxious and troubled about many things; ⁴² one thing is needful. Mary has chosen the good portion, which shall not be taken away from her."

481 BLESSED THE WOMB*

Luke 11:27–28 (§S76.1)

27 As he said this, a woman in the crowd raised her voice and said to him, "Blessed is the womb that bore you, and the breasts that you sucked!" 28 But he said, "Blessed rather are those who hear the word of God and keep it!"

* See 236 & 490: *Jerusalem Mourned*
* See 244: *Blessed for Doing*

John 13:17 (§S76.2)

17 "If you know these things, blessed are you if you do them."

Jas 1:25b (§S76.3)

25 But he who looks into the perfect law, the law of liberty, and perseveres, being no hearer that forgets but a doer that acts, he shall be blessed in his doing.

GThom 79 (§S76.4)

(79) 1 A woman from the crowd said to Him, "Blessed are the womb which bore You and the breasts which nourished You."

2 He said to her, "Blessed are those who have heard the word of the Father and have truly kept it. 3 For there will be days when you will say, 'Blessed are the womb which has not conceived and the breasts which have not given milk.'"

482 THE DISPUTED INHERITANCE

Luke 12:13–15 (§S77.1)

13 One of the multitude said to him, "Teacher, bid my brother divide the inheritance with me." 14 But he said to him, "Man, who made me a judge or divider over you?" 15 And he said to them, "Take heed, and beware of all covetousness; for a man's life does not consist in the abundance of his possessions."

GThom 72 (§S77.2)

(72) 1 [A man said] to Him, "Tell my brothers to divide my father's possessions with me."

2 He said to him, "O man, who has made Me a divider?"

3 He turned to His disciples and said to them, "I am not a divider, am I?"

483 CRIPPLE AND SABBATH

Luke 13:10–17 (§S78)

10 Now he was teaching in one of the synagogues on the sabbath. 11 And there was a woman who had had a spirit of infirmity for eighteen years; she was bent over and could not fully straighten herself. 12 And when Jesus saw her, he called her and said to her, "Woman, you are freed from your infirmity." 13 And he laid his hands upon her, and immediately she was made straight, and she praised God. 14 But the ruler of the synagogue, indignant because Jesus had healed on the sabbath, said to the people, "There are six days on which work ought to be done; come on those days and be healed, and not on the sabbath day." 15 Then the Lord answered him, "You hypocrites! Does not each of you on the sabbath untie his ox or his ass from the manger, and lead it away to water it? 16 And ought not this woman, a daughter of Abraham whom Satan bound for eighteen years, be loosed from this bond on the sabbath day?" 17 As he said this, all his adversaries were put to shame; and all the people rejoiced at all the glorious things that were done by him.

484 JESUS AND HEROD

Luke 13:31-33 (§S79)
[31] At that very hour some Pharisees came, and said to him, "Get away from here, for Herod wants to kill you." [32] And he said to them, "Go and tell that fox, 'Behold, I cast out demons and perform cures today and tomorrow, and the third day I finish my course. [33] Nevertheless I must go on my way today and tomorrow and the day following; for it cannot be that a prophet should perish away from Jerusalem.'"

485 DROPSY AND SABBATH

Luke 14:1-6 (§S80)
[1] One sabbath when he went to dine at the house of a ruler who belonged to the Pharisees, they were watching him. [2] And behold, there was a man before him who had dropsy. [3] And Jesus spoke to the lawyers and Pharisees, saying, "Is it lawful to heal on the sabbath, or not?" [4] But they were silent. Then he took him and healed him, and let him go. [5] And he said to them, "Which of you, having a son or an ox that has fallen into a well, will not immediately pull him out on a sabbath day?" [6] And they could not reply to this.

486 EXALTATION AND ABOMINATION

Luke 16:14-15 (§S81)
[14] The Pharisees, who were lovers of money, heard all this, and they scoffed at him. [15] But he said to them, "You are those who justify yourselves before men, but God knows your hearts; for what is exalted among men is an abomination in the sight of God."

487 THE TEN LEPERS

Luke 17:11-19 (§S82)
[11] On the way to Jerusalem he was passing along between Samaria and Galilee. [12] And as he entered a village, he was met by ten lepers, who stood at a distance [13] and lifted up their voices and said, "Jesus, Master, have mercy on us." [14] When he saw them he said to them, "Go and show yourselves to the priests." And as they went they were cleansed. [15] Then one of them, when he saw that he was healed, turned back, praising God with a loud voice; [16] and he fell on his face at Jesus' feet, giving him thanks. Now he was a Samaritan. [17] Then said Jesus, "Were not ten cleansed? Where are the nine? [18] Was no one found to return and give praise to God except this foreigner?" [19] And he said to him, "Rise and go your way; your faith has made you well."

488 SALVATION FOR ZACCHEUS

Luke 19:1–9 (§S83)

[1] He entered Jericho and was passing through. [2] And there was a man named Zacchaeus; he was a chief tax collector, and rich. [3] And he sought to see who Jesus was, but could not, on account of the crowd, because he was small of stature. [4] So he ran on ahead and climbed up into a sycamore tree to see him, for he was to pass that way. [5] And when Jesus came to the place, he looked up and said to him, "Zacchaeus, make haste and come down; for I must stay at your house today." [6] So he made haste and came down, and received him joyfully. [7] And when they saw it they all murmured, "He has gone in to be the guest of a man who is a sinner." [8] And Zacchaeus stood and said to the Lord, "Behold, Lord, the half of my goods I give to the poor; and if I have defrauded any one of anything, I restore it fourfold." [9] And Jesus said to him, "Today salvation has come to this house, since he also is a son of Abraham."

489 THE DISCIPLE'S CONFESSION*

Luke 19:28–40 (§S84)

[28] And when he had said this, he went on ahead, going up to Jerusalem. [29] When he drew near to Bethphage and Bethany, at the mount that is called Olivet, he sent two of the disciples, [30] saying, "Go into the village opposite, where on entering you will find a colt tied, on which no one has ever yet sat; untie it and bring it here. [31] If any one asks you, 'Why are you untying it?' you shall say this, 'The Lord has need of it.'" [32] So those who were sent went away and found it as he had told them. [33] And as they were untying the colt, its owners said to them, "Why are you untying the colt?" [34] And they said, "The Lord has need of it." [35] And they brought it to Jesus, and throwing their garments on the colt they set Jesus upon it. [36] And as he rode along, they spread their garments on the road. [37] As he was now drawing near, at the descent of the Mount of Olives, the whole multitude of the disciples began to rejoice and praise God with a loud voice for all the mighty works that they had seen, [38] saying, "Blessed is the King who comes in the name of the Lord! Peace in heaven and glory in the highest!" [39] And some of the Pharisees in the multitude said to him, "Teacher, rebuke your disciples." [40] He answered, "I tell you, if these were silent, the very stones would cry out."

* See 450: *The Children's Confession*

490 JERUSALEM MOURNED*

Luke 23:27–31 (§S85.1)

[27] And there followed him a great multitude of the people, and of women who bewailed and lamented him. [28] But Jesus turning to them said, "Daughters of Jerusalem, do not weep for me, but weep for yourselves and for your children. [29] For behold, the days are coming when they will say, 'Blessed are the barren, and the wombs that never bore, and the breasts that never gave suck!' [30] Then they will begin to say to the mountains, 'Fall on us'; and to the hills, 'Cover us.' [31] For if they do this when the wood is green, what will happen when it is dry?"

GThom 79 (§S85.2)

(79) [1] A woman from the crowd said to Him, "Blessed are the womb which bore You and the breasts which nourished You."

[2] He said to her, "Blessed are those who have heard the word of the Father and have truly kept it. [3] For there will be days when you will say, 'Blessed are the womb which has not conceived and the breasts which have not given milk.'"

* See 236: *Jerusalem Mourned*

FATHER, FORGIVE THEM

Luke 23:32–34 (§§S86.1)

³²Two others also, who were criminals, were led away to be put to death with him. ³³And when they came to the place which is called The Skull, there they crucified him, and the criminals, one on the right and one on the left. ³⁴And Jesus said, "Father, forgive them; for they know not what they do." And they cast lots to divide his garments.

Acts 7:54–60 (§§S86.2)

⁵⁴Now when they heard these things they were enraged, and they ground their teeth against him. ⁵⁵But he, full of the Holy Spirit, gazed into heaven and saw the glory of God, and Jesus standing at the right hand of God; ⁵⁶and he said, "Behold, I see the heavens opened, and the Son of man standing at the right hand of God." ⁵⁷But they cried out with a loud voice and stopped their ears and rushed together upon him. ⁵⁸Then they cast him out of the city and stoned him; and the witnesses laid down their garments at the feet of a young man named Saul. ⁵⁹And as they were stoning Stephen, he prayed, "Lord Jesus, receive my spirit." ⁶⁰And he knelt down and cried with a loud voice, "Lord, do not hold this sin against them." And when he had said this, he fell asleep.

JESUS AT EMMAUS

Luke 24:13–35 (§§S87)

¹³That very day two of them were going to a village named Emmaus, about seven miles from Jerusalem, ¹⁴and talking with each other about all these things that had happened. ¹⁵While they were talking and dicussing together, Jesus himself drew near and went with them. ¹⁶But their eyes were kept from recognizing him. ¹⁷And he said to them, "What is this conversation which you are holding with each other as you walk?" And they stood still, looking sad. ¹⁸Then one of them, named Cleopas, answered him, "Are you the only visitor to Jerusalem who does not know the things that have happened there in these days?" ¹⁹And he said to him, "What things?" And they said to him, "Concerning Jesus of Nazareth, who was a prophet mighty in deed and word before God and all the people, ²⁰and how our chief priests and rulers delivered him up to be condemned to death, and crucified him. ²¹But we had hoped that he was the one to redeem Israel. Yes, and besides all this, it is now the third day since this happened. ²²Moreover, some women of our company amazed us. They were at the tomb early in the morning ²³and did not find his body; and they came back saying that they had even seen a vision of angels, who said that he was alive. ²⁴Some of those who were with us went to the tomb, and found it just as the women had said; but him they did not see." ²⁵And he said to them, "O foolish men, and slow of heart to believe all that the prophets have spoken! ²⁶Was it not necessary that the Christ should suffer these things and enter into his glory?" ²⁷And beginning with Moses and all the prophets, he interpreted to them in all the scriptures the things concerning himself.

²⁸So they drew near to the village to which they were going. He appeared to be going further, ²⁹but they constrained him, saying, "Stay with us, for it is toward evening and the day is now far spent." So he went in to stay with them. ³⁰When he was at table with them, he took the bread and blessed, and broke it, and gave it to them. ³¹And their eyes were opened and they recognized him; and he vanished out of their sight. ³²They said to each other, "Did not our hearts burn within us while he talked to us on the road, while he opened to us the scriptures?" ³³And they rose that same hour and returned to Jerusalem; and they found the eleven gathered together and those who were with them, ³⁴who said, "The Lord has risen indeed, and has appeared to Simon!" ³⁵Then they told what had happened on the road, and how he was known to them in the breaking of the bread.

493 FAITH AGAINST SIGHT*

Luke 24:36-43 (§§88.1)

[36] As they were saying this, Jesus himself stood among them. [37] But they were startled and frightened, and supposed that they saw a spirit. [38] And he said to them, "Why are you troubled, and why do questionings rise in your hearts? [39] See my hands and my feet, that it is I myself; handle me, and see; for a spirit has not flesh and bones as you see that I have." [41] And while they still disbelieved for joy, and wondered, he said to them, "Have you anything here to eat?" [42] They gave him a piece of broiled fish, [43] and he took it and ate before them.

John 20:24-29 (§§88.2)

[24] Now Thomas, one of the twelve, called the Twin, was not with them when Jesus came. [25] So the other disciples told him, "We have seen the Lord." But he said to them, "Unless I see in his hands the print of the nails, and place my finger in the mark of the nails, and place my hand in his side, I will not believe."

[26] Eight days later, his disciples were again in the house, and Thomas was with them. The doors were shut, but Jesus came and stood among them, and said, "Peace be with you." [27] Then he said to Thomas, "Put your finger here, and see my hands; and put out your hand, and place it in my side; do not be faithless, but believing." [28] Thomas answered him, "My Lord and my God!" [29] Jesus said to him, "Have you believed because you have seen me? Blessed are those who have not seen and yet believe."

ApJas 3:3-8 (§§88.3)

[3] "And now, waking or sleeping remember that you have seen the Son of Man, and with him you have spoken, and to him you have listened. [4] Woe to those who have seen the Son [of] Man! [5] Blessed are those (or: you [pl.]) who have not seen the Man, and who have not consorted with him, and who have not spoken with him, and who have not listened to anything from him. Yours is life! [6] Know, therefore, that he healed you when you were ill, in order that you might reign. [7] Woe to those who have rested from their illness, because they will relapse again into illness! [8] Blessed are those (or: you [pl.]) who have not been ill, and have known rest before they (or: you) became ill. Yours is the Kingdom of God!"

ApJas 8:3 (§§88.4)

[3] "As long as I am with you (pl.), give heed to me and obey me. But when I am to depart from you, remember me. And remember me because I was with you without your knowing me. Blessed are those who have known me. Woe to those who have heard and have not believed! Blessed are those who have not seen [but] have [had] faith]."

Ign Smyr 3:1-3 (§§88.5)

[1] For I know and believe that he was in the flesh even after the Resurrection. [2] And when he came to those with Peter he said to them: "Take, handle me and see that I am not a phantom without a body." And they immediately touched him and believed, being mingled both with his flesh and spirit. Therefore they despised even death, and were proved to be above death. [3] And after his Resurrection he ate and drank with them as a being of flesh, although he was united in spirit to the Father.

* See 237: *Faith Against Sight*

494 THE PROMISED SPIRIT

Luke 24:44-52 (§§89.1)

[44] Then he said to them, "These are my words which I spoke to you, while I was still with you, that everything written about me in the law of Moses and the prophets and the psalms must be fulfilled." [45] Then he opened their minds to understand the scriptures, [46] and said to them, "Thus it is written, that the Christ should suffer and on the third day rise from the dead, [47] and that repentance and forgiveness of sins should be preached in his name to all nations, beginning from Jerusalem. [48] You are witnesses of these things. [49] And behold, I send the promise of my Father upon you; but stay in the city, until you are clothed with power from on high."

[50] Then he led them out as far as Bethany, and lifting up his hands he blessed them. [51] While he blessed them, he parted from them, and was carried up into heaven. [52] And they returned to Jerusalem with great joy,

Acts 1:1-11 (§§89.2)

[1] In the first book, O Theophilus, I have dealt with all that Jesus began to do and teach, [2] until the day when he was taken up, after he had given commandment through the Holy Spirit to the apostles whom he had chosen. [3] To them he presented himself alive after his passion by many proofs, appearing to them during forty days, and speaking of the kingdom of God. [4] And while staying with them he charged them not to depart from Jerusalem, but to wait for the promise of the Father, which, he said, "you heard from me, [5] for John baptized with water, but before many days you shall be baptized with the Holy Spirit."

[6] So when they had come together, they asked him, "Lord, will you at this time restore the kingdom to Israel?" [7] He said to them, "It is not for you to know times or seasons which the Father has fixed by his own authority. [8] But you shall receive power when the Holy Spirit has come upon you; and you shall be my witnesses in Jerusalem and in all Judea and Samaria and to the end of the earth." [9] And when he had said this, as they were looking on, he was lifted up, and a cloud took him out of their sight. [10] And while they were gazing into heaven as he went, behold, two men stood by them in white robes, [11] and said, "Men of Galilee, why do you stand looking into heaven? This Jesus, who was taken up from you into heaven, will come in the same way as you saw him go into heaven."

495   JESUS AND NATHANIEL

John 1:43–51 (§S90)

⁴³The next day Jesus decided to go to Galilee. And he found Philip and said to him, "Follow me." ⁴⁴Now Philip was from Bethsaida, the city of Andrew and Peter. ⁴⁵Philip found Nathanael, and said to him, "We have found him of whom Moses in the law and also the prophets wrote, Jesus of Nazareth, the son of Joseph." ⁴⁶Nathanael said to him, "Can anything good come out of Nazareth?" Philip said to him, "Come and see." ⁴⁷Jesus saw Nathanael coming to him, and said of him, "Behold, an Israelite indeed, in whom is no guile!" ⁴⁸Nathanael said to him, "How do you know me?" Jesus answered him, "Before Philip called you, when you were under the fig tree, I saw you." ⁴⁹Nathanael answered him, "Rabbi, you are the Son of God! You are the King of Israel!" ⁵⁰Jesus answered him, "Because I said to you, I saw you under the fig tree, do you believe? You shall see greater things than these." ⁵¹And he said to him, "Truly, truly, I say to you, you will see heaven opened, and the angels of God ascending and descending upon the Son of man."

496   LIVING WATER*

John 4:1–15 (§S91.1)

¹Now when the Lord knew that the Pharisees had heard that Jesus was making and baptizing more disciples than John ²(although Jesus himself did not baptize, but only his disciples), ³he left Judea and departed again to Galilee. ⁴He had to pass through Samaria. ⁵So he came to a city of Samaria, called Sychar, near the field that Jacob gave to his son Joseph. ⁶Jacob's well was there, and so Jesus, wearied as he was with his journey, sat down beside the well. It was about the sixth hour.

⁷There came a woman of Samaria to draw water. Jesus said to her, "Give me a drink." ⁸For his disciples had gone away into the city to buy food. ⁹The Samaritan woman said to him, "How is it that you, a Jew, ask a drink of me, a woman of Samaria?" For Jews have no dealings with Samaritans. ¹⁰Jesus answered her, "If you knew the gift of God, and who it is that is saying to you, 'Give me a drink,' you would have asked him, and he would have given you living water." ¹¹The woman said to him, "Sir, you have nothing to draw with, and the well is deep; where do you get that living water? ¹²Are you greater than our father Jacob, who gave us the well, and drank from it himself, and his sons, and his cattle?" ¹³Jesus said to her, "Every one who drinks of this water will thirst again, ¹⁴but whoever drinks of the water that I shall give him will never thirst; the water that I shall give him will become in him a spring of water welling up to eternal life." ¹⁵The woman said to him, "Sir, give me this water, that I may not thirst, nor come here to draw."

POxy840 (§S91.2)

(1) First before he does wrong (?) he thinks out everything that is crafty. But be ye on your guard that the same thing may not happen to you as does to them. For not only among the living do evil doers among men receive retribution, but they must also suffer punishment and great torment.

(2) And he took them (the disciples) with him into the place of purification itself and walked about in the Temple court. And a Pharisaic chief priest, Levi (?) by name, fell in with them and s[aid] to the Savior: Who gave thee leave to [trea]d this place of purification and to look upon [the]se holy utensils without having bathed thyself and even without thy disciples having [wa]shed their f[eet]? On the contrary, being defi[led], thou hast trodden the Temple court, this clean p[lace], although no [one who] has [not] first bathed himself or [chang]ed his clot[hes] may tread it and [venture] to vi[ew these] holy utensils! Forthwith [the Savior] s[tood] still with h[is] disciples and [answered]: How stands it (then) with thee, thou art forsooth (also) here in the Temple court. Art thou then clean? He said to him: I am clean. For I have bathed myself in the pool of David and have gone down by the one stair and come up by the other and have put on white and clean clothes, and (only) then have I come hither and have viewed these holy utensils. Then said the Savior to him: Woe unto you blind that see not! Thou hast bathed thyself in water that is poured out, in which dogs and swine lie night and day and thou hast washed thyself and hast chafed thine outer skin, which prostitutes also and flute-girls anoint, bathe, chafe and rouge, in order to arouse desire in men, but within they are full of scorpions and of [bad]ness [of every kind]. But I and [my disciples], of whom thou sayest that we have not im[mersed] ourselves, [have been im]mersed in the liv[ing . . .] water which comes down from [. . . B]ut woe unto them that . . .

*See 239: *Living Water*

497 ADULTEROUS WOMAN FORGIVEN

John 7:53–8:11 (§S92)

⁵³They went each to his own house, 8 ¹but Jesus went to the Mount of Olives. ²Early in the morning he came again to the temple; all the people came to him, and he sat down and taught them. ³The scribes and the Pharisees brought a woman who had been caught in adultery, and placing her in the midst ⁴they said to him, "Teacher, this woman has been caught in the act of adultery. ⁵Now in the law Moses commanded us to stone such. What do you say about her?" ⁶This they said to test him, that they might have some charge to bring against him. Jesus bent down and wrote with his finger on the ground. ⁷And as they continued to ask him, he stood up and said to them, "Let him who is without sin among you be the first to throw a stone at her." ⁸And once more he bent down and wrote with his finger on the ground. ⁹But when they heard it, they went away, one by one, beginning with the eldest, and Jesus was left alone with the woman standing before him. ¹⁰Jesus looked up and said to her, "Woman, where are they? Has no one condemned you?" ¹¹She said, "No one, Lord." And Jesus said, "Neither do I condemn you; go, and do not sin again."

498 PURIFICATION BY WATER?

POxy840 2 (§S93)

(2) And he took them (the disciples) with him into the place of purification itself and walked about in the Temple court. And a Pharisaic chief priest, Levi (?) by name, fell in with them and s[aid] to the Savior: Who gave thee leave to [trea]d this place of purification and to look upon [the]se holy utensils without having bathed thyself and even without thy disciples having [wa]shed their f[eet]? On the contrary, being defi[led], thou hast trodden the Temple court, this clean p[lace], although no [one who] has [not] first bathed himself or [chang]ed his clot[hes] may tread it and [venture] to vi[ew these] holy utensils! Forthwith [the Savior] s[tood] still with h[is] disciples and [answered]: How stands it (then) with thee, thou art forsooth (also) here in the Temple court. Art thou then clean? He said to him: I am clean. For I have bathed myself in the pool of David and have gone down by the one stair and come up by the other and have put on white and clean clothes, and (only) then have I come hither and have viewed these holy utensils. Then said the Savior to him: Woe unto you blind that see not! Thou hast bathed thyself in water that is poured out, in which dogs and swine lie night and day and thou hast washed thyself and hast chafed thine outer skin, which prostitutes also and flute-girls anoint, bathe, chafe and rouge, in order to arouse desire in men, but within they are full of scorpions and of [bad]ness [of every kind]. But I and [my disciples], of whom thou sayest that we have not im[mersed] ourselves, [have been im]mersed in the liv[ing . . .] water which comes down from [. . . B]ut woe unto them that . . .

PLACE FROM WHICH*

GPet 12:50–13:57 (§S94.1)

[50] Early in the morning of the Lord's day Mary Magdalene, a woman disciple of the Lord— for fear of the Jews, since (they) were inflamed with wrath, she had not done at the sepulchre of the Lord what women are wont to do for those beloved of them who die—took [51] with her her women friends and came to the sepulchre where he was laid. [52] And they feared lest the Jews should see them, and said, "Although we could not weep and lament on that day when he was crucified, yet let us now do so at his sepulchre. [53] But who will roll away for us the stone also that is set on the entrance to the sepulchre, that we may go in and sit beside him and do what is due?— [54] For the stone was great,— and we fear lest any one see us. And if we cannot do so, let us at least put down at the entrance what we bring for a memorial of him and let us weep and lament until we have again gone home." 13 [55] So they went and found the sepulchre opened. And they came near, stooped down and saw there a young man sitting in the midst of the sepulchre, comely and clothed with a brightly shining robe, who said to them, [56] "Wherefore are ye come? Whom seek ye? Not him that was crucified? He is risen and gone. But if ye believe not, stoop this way and see the place where he lay, for he is not here. For he is risen and is gone thither whence he was sent." [57] Then the women fled affrighted.

ApJas 2:1–2 (§S94.2)

[1] Now the twelve disciples [were] sitting all together at [the same time], and, remembering what the Savior had said to each one of them, whether secretly or openly, they were setting it down in books. [And] I was writing what was in [my book]—lo, the Savior appeared, [after] he had departed from [us while we] gazed at him. And five hundred and fifty days after he arose from the dead, we said to him: "Have you gone and departed from us?"

[2] And Jesus said: "No, but I shall go to the place from which I have come. If you (pl.) desire to come with me, come."

ApJas 9:5–9 (§S94.3)

[5] "These things I shall say to you (pl.) for the present. But now I shall ascend to the place from which I have come. [6] But you, when I was eager to go, have driven me out, and, instead of your accompanying me, you have pursued me. [7] But give heed to the glory which awaits me, and, having opened your heart(s), listen to the hymns which await me up in heaven. For today I am obliged to take (my place) at the right hand of my Father. [8] Now I have said (my) last word to you. I shall part from you. For a chariot of wind has taken me up, and from now on I shall strip myself in order that I may clothe myself. [9] But give heed: blessed are those who have preached the Son before he descended, in order that, when I have come, I (or: <they>) may ascend. Thrice blessed are those who [were] proclaimed by the Son before they came into being, in order that you may have a portion with them."

* See 249: *Place From Which*

KINGDOM AND FULLNESS

ApJas 2:1–4 (§S95)

[1] Now the twelve disciples [were] sitting all together at [the same time], and, remembering what the Savior had said to each one of them, whether secretly or openly, they were setting it down in books. [And] I was writing what was in [my book]—lo, the Savior appeared, [after] he had departed from [us while we] gazed at him. And five hundred and fifty days after he arose from the dead, we said to him: "Have you gone and departed from us?"

[2] And Jesus said: "No, but I shall go to the place from which I have come. If you (pl.) desire to come with me, come."

[3] They all answered and said: "If you bid us, we'll come."

[4] He said: "Truly I say to you (pl.), no one ever will enter the Kingdom of Heaven if I bid him, but rather because you yourselves are full. Let me have James and Peter, in order that I may fill them." And when he called these two, he took them aside, and commanded the rest to busy themselves with that with which they had been busy.

501 SAMARITAN AND LAMB

GThom 60 (§S96)

(60) [1] <They saw> a Samaritan carrying a lamb on his way to Judea. [2] He said to his disciples. "(Why does) that man (carry) the lamb around?"

[3] They said to Him, "So that he may kill it and eat it."

[4] He said to them, "While it is alive, he will not eat it, but only when he has killed it and it has become a corpse."

[5] They said to Him, "He cannot do so otherwise."

[6] He said to them, "You too, look for a place for yourselves within Repose, lest you become a corpse and be eaten."

502 STONE AND WORD

DialSav 31–34 (§S97)

(31) [Judas] responded, saying, "Tell me, Lord, [how it is that . . .] . . . which shakes the earth moves."

(32) The Lord picked up a [stone and] held it in his hand [say] [ing, "What] am I holding [in] my [hand]?"

(33) He said, "[It is] a stone."

(34) He [said] to them, "That which supports [the earth] is that which supports the heaven. When a Word comes forth from the Greatness, it will come on what supports the heaven and the earth. For the earth does not move. Were it to move, it would fall, though in order that the First Word might not fail. For it was that which established the cosmos and inhabited it and inhaled fragrance from it. For, . . .[. . .]. . . which do not move I [. . .]. . . you, all the sons of [men. For] you are from [that] place. [In] the hearts of those who speak out of [joy] and truth you exist. Even if it comes forth in [the body] of the Father among men and is not received, still it [does] return to its place. Whoever [does not] know [the work] of perfection [knows] nothing. If one does not stand in the darkness, he will not be able to see the light."

503 JESUS AND JAMES

GHeb 7 (§S98)

(7) The Gospel called according to the Hebrews which was recently translated by me into Greek and Latin, which Origen frequently uses, records after the resurrection of the Savior:

And when the Lord had given the linen cloth to the servant of the priest, he went to James and appeared to him. For James had sworn that he would not eat bread from that hour in which he had drunk the cup of the Lord until he should see him risen from among them that sleep. And shortly thereafter the Lord said: Bring a table and bread! And immediately it is added: he took the bread, blessed it and brake it and gave it to James the Just and said to him: My brother, eat thy bread, for the Son of man is risen from among them that sleep. (Jerome, *De viris inlustribus* 2)

Note: References are to inventory numbers, not to page numbers.

New Testament Writings

Index of Passages

Ign Tral
11:1–2 340
11:1b 148

Pol Phil
2:3b 36, 81
2:3c 43, 72
2:3e 82
6:2a 72
7:1–2 464
12:3 62

Did
1:2b 87
1:3ac 62
1:3b 63
1:4a 56
1:4b–5a 61
1:4b 60
1:5 245
1:5b 55
3:7 38
4:12 254
8:1 73
8:2–3 415
8:2 327, 71
8:2a 68
8:2b–3 70
9:1–4 462
9:5b 84
11:3–4 430
11:4 124
11:7b 139
13:1–2 104
14:2 54
16:1 205
16:1a 17
16:3 458
16:3a 193
16:4–5 111
16:6–8 199

Barn
4:14b 174
5:8–9 423
5:9b 97
6:4a 173
6:13a 170
7:11b 320
12:10–11 359
12:10b 175
12:11b 175

Herm Man
2:4b 245
4.1:4–11 326
4.1:6b 58
4.1:10 58

Herm Sim
9.20:1–4 350

Herm Vis
4.2:6 461
4.2:6b 210

Patristic Citations

GNaz
2 405
3 410
4 53
5 415, 70
6 92
7 108
8 129
9 133
10 434
11 335
12 437
13 151
14 343, 442
15a 167, 346
15b 167, 346
16 349, 350
17 190
18 15
23 321

GEbi
1 412, 422
4 408
5 435
6 322
7 460

GHeb
3 323
4a 328, 85
4b 328, 85
5 324
7 503

GEgy
1–4 391
5 377, 378
6 391
e 166

Old Testament Apocrypha

2 Esdr
1:28–40 419
1:30a 191
1:32 190
1:32a 191
1:33–39a 94
1:33a 191

233